Justice at Nuremberg

Leo Alexander and the Nazi Doctors' Trial

Ulf Schmidt

Senior Lecturer in Modern History,
University of Kent, Canterbury, UK

First published 2004
This edition published 2006 by
PALGRAVE MACMILLAN
Houndmills, Basingstoke, Hampshire RG21 6XS and
175 Fifth Avenue, New York, N.Y. 10010
Companies and representatives throughout the world

PALGRAVE MACMILLAN is the global academic imprint of the Palgrave Macmillan division of St. Martin's Press, LLC and of Palgrave Macmillan Ltd. Macmillan® is a registered trademark in the United States, United Kingdom and other countries. Palgrave is a registered trademark in the European Union and other countries.

ISBN 13: 978-0-333-92147-0   hardback
ISBN 10: 0-333-92147-X   hardback
ISBN 13: 978-0-230-00641-6   paperback
ISBN 10: 0-230-00641-8   paperback

This book is printed on paper suitable for recycling and made from fully managed and sustained forest sources.

A catalogue record for this book is available from the British Library.

The Library of Congress has catalogued the hardcover edition as follows:
Schmidt, Ulf.
    Justice at Nuremberg : Leo Alexander and the Nazi doctors' trial / Ulf Schmidt.
        p. cm. – (St. Antony's series)
    Includes bibliographical references and index.
    ISBN 0–333–92147–X (cloth)
    ISBN 0–230–00641–8 (pbk)
    1. Alexander, Leo, 1905. 2. Nuremberg Medical Trial, Nuremberg, Germany, 1946–1947. 3. Human experimentation in medicine–Moral and ethical aspects. 4. Human experimentation in medicine–Law and legislation. 5. Medical ethics–History–20th century. I. Title. II. Series.

R853.H8S345 2004
174.2'8–dc22

10 9 8 7 6
15 14 13 12 11

Printed and bound in
Antony Rowe Ltd, Ch

For Katia Mai

By the same author

MEDICAL FILMS, ETHICS AND EUTHANASIA IN NAZI GERMANY (2002)

Contents

Acknowledgements

Like humans, books have their own history. Indeed, this book has become part of my own history. I wanted to write this book and I wanted it to be published. For a long time, however, it was far from clear whether this would ever happen. The existence of the book itself, and the odd typographical error, which I am sure every author fears to find, will eventually convince me that the book is real. To thank those who made this happen goes far beyond acknowledging their contribution. Their unflinching support and encouragement have been absolutely essential. It is almost impossible to thank the many people who over the years provided me with insight into some of the issues discussed in the book and who willingly shared their ideas and documents. Others supported me at critical junctures or gave me shelter and help when I needed it. The book has truly brought out the very best in my friends and colleagues. I am forever grateful to them and hope that those whom I have not mentioned by name will forgive me.

There is one person to whom I owe the greatest thanks of all: Cecily Alexander-Grable, the daughter of Leo Alexander. When I first visited her in 1998 in Boston, Massachusetts, she readily gave me access to an unprecedented collection of private papers, letters and diaries. Cecily also gave me access to Alexander's extensive photographic collection, showed me his paintings and sculptures, and introduced me to her family. Her warm welcome and support throughout the years have been especially important to me. I believe that our conversations helped me to understand much more clearly Alexander's complex personality and the nature of the Nazi Doctors' Trial. Very special thanks also goes to Irene Hulst, Alexander's niece, who provided me with archival sources and photographs. I would also like to thank Brian Alexander, Alexander's nephew, for his help. I am truly indebted to all of them.

I am also grateful to the organisations that generously supported this work and continued to support it through difficult times. My thanks go first of all to the Wellcome Trust, which granted me a three-year postdoctoral fellowship that enabled me to carry out the research in archives in the United States, Germany, Austria and Great Britain. The project on which this book is largely based was originally sponsored by Paul J. Weindling, now at Oxford Brookes University, who has made major contributions in this subject area. As will be evident from what follows, our approaches began to diverge at a relatively early stage, and our interpretations of the

Nazi Doctors' Trial and Nuremberg Code now differ considerably. The Wellcome Unit for the History of Medicine at the University of Oxford provided me with an excellent academic environment for a significant part of the project. I am particularly grateful to Jane Lewis and Mary Dobson for all their assistance and support. For the last three years the School of History at the University of Kent has been my academic home and I cannot think of a better place for a young scholar. I am sincerely grateful to my colleagues for providing me with the necessary security and stability, which, I believe, all scholars need in order to flourish. Their encouragement and friendship were central in completing this book. I am particularly grateful to Philip Boobbyer, Mark Connelly, Antony Copley, Kenneth Fincham, Richard Eales, William Fortescue and Charlotte Sleigh. My Head of School, David Turley, was indispensable in steering the project away from unexpected cliffs. I am truly grateful to him (and I think I have learned a lot from him).

I am indebted to many archives and their staff who helped me find information about the history of the Nuremberg Doctors' Trial, only some of whom can be mentioned here. I am especially grateful to the staff of the American Heritage Center at the University of Wyoming; the Archive for the History of the Max Planck Society, Berlin; the Bodleian Library, Oxford; the Duke University Medical Center, Durham, especially to James F. Gifford and Charles Rutt; the Federal Archives in Berlin and Koblenz; the Francis A. Countway Library of Medicine, Boston; the Holocaust Memorial Museum, especially to Patrica Heberer; the Imperial War Museum, London; the International Physicians for the Prevention of Nuclear War; the Mugar Memorial Library, Boston; the National Archives and Record Administration, Washington DC; the National Library of Medicine, Bethesda; the Public Library, New York; the Public Record Office, London; the Rockefeller Archive Center, North Terrytown; the State Archive, Nuremberg, especially to Gunther Friedrich; the Supreme Court Historical Society, Tallahassee, especially to Nancy Dobson for her kind hospitality; and to the Center for Research into Anti-Semitism in Berlin. I am grateful to Davis House, Washington DC, for a pleasant stay during my numerous visits, to Michael Dolan for the many insightful discussions, to Alexa Potter for carrying out some last-minute research, and to Sandra Marlow for her warm hospitality and for information about long-forgotten archival collections.

Work on a book of this nature would not have been possible without the help of other scholars and experts from a variety of subject areas. I would like to thank George Annas, Robert Baker, Richard Bessel, Michael Clark, Sev Fluss, Benjamin Ferencz, Andreas Frewer, Andrew Markus, Francesco Masedu, Jonathan Moreno, Anthony Nicholls, Martin Pernick, Robert

Proctor, Alice Riccardi (von) Platen, Henry Ries, Eli M. Rosenbaum, Karl-Heinz Roth, Ben Shephard, Telford Taylor and Rolf Winau for valuable discussions about my work and for sharing previously unpublished sources. I am especially grateful to Michael Grodin for giving me access to a series of previously unpublished sources on the Nazi Doctors' Trial. I am also grateful to Jürgen Peiffer for supplying me with primary material about Alexander. I am grateful to Cecily Alexander-Grable, Ivan Brown, Adelheid Kleist, Nicholas Camera-Peon, Irene Hulst, H. L. (Tom) Sebring, Gitta Sereny and Eleonore Strümpel for their willingness to be interviewed on tape in order to supplement archival evidence with oral testimony. I also wish to thank Eugene Rogan, my commissioning editor at St Antony's College, Oxford, as well as Richard Clogg for their support. I am very much indebted to Alison Howson, my publisher at Palgrave, and to Guy Edwards, for their professionalism throughout the production process. Emma Mahoney and Kay Schiller helped me proofread the manuscript, and Jo North was indispensable in the editing of the book. Finally, I wish to thank Jo Fox, Regine Jaszinski, Gert Niedl, Margaret Pelling and David Welch for all they have done. The book would not exist without them. I hope I have shown myself worthy of their support and friendship.

Canterbury, Kent 2004

List of Tables and Illustrations

Abbreviations

AA, PA	Auswärtiges Amt, Politisches Archiv
ANA	American Neurological Association
AP	Alexander Papers, Boston (in possession of Cecily Alexander-Grable)
BA-BDC	Bundesarchiv, Abt.III, Außenstelle Zehlendorf
BAFA	Bundesarchiv-Filmarchiv, Berlin
BAK	Bundesarchiv, Koblenz
BAOR	British Army of the Rhine
CAD	Central Affairs Division
CIC	Counter Intelligence Corps
CIOS	Combined Intelligence Operative Sub-committee
CMB	China Medical Board
CROWCASS	Central Registry of War Criminals and Security Suspects
DFA	Deutsche Forschungsanstalt für Psychiatrie
DJAG	Deputy Judge Advocate General
DUMC	Duke University Archives, Depository for Medical Center Records, Durham, North Carolina
ECT	Electroconvulsive Therapy
ETO	European Theatre of Operation
FCLM	Francis A. Countway Library of Medicine, Boston, Mass.
FIAT	Field Information Agency, Technical
G-2	Army Intelligence Branch
GMA	German Medical Association
HBAB	Hauptarchiv der von Bodelschwinghschen Anstalten Bethel
HMG	Her Majesty's Government
ICT	Insulin Coma Treatment
IPPNW	International Physicians for the Prevention of Nuclear War, Nuremberg, Germany
ISC (WC)	International Scientific Commission (for the Investigation of War Crimes of a Medical Nature)
IWM	Imperial War Museum
JAG	Judge Advocate General
MPG	Archiv der Max-Planck-Gesellschaft, Berlin
NARA	National Archives and Record Administration, Washington DC
NCO	Non-Commissioned Officer

NDT	NDT-Records and NDT-Documents and Material, in: Dörner and Ebbinghaus 1999
NYPL	New York Public Library
NYU	New York University
OCCWC	Office of Chief of Counsel for War Crimes
OMGUS	Office of Military Governor of the United States
OSS	Office of Strategic Services
PoW	Prisoner of War
PUMC	Peking Union Medical College
RA	Ravensbrück Archive
RAC	Rockefeller Archive Center
RAFMC	Royal Air Force Medical Corps
RAMC	Royal Army Medical Corps
RF	Rockefeller Foundation
RFR	Reichsforschungsrat
SA	Sturmabteilung
SCHST	Supreme Court Historical Society Tallahassee, Florida
SHAEF	Supreme Headquarters Allied Expeditionary Forces
SPSL	Society for the Protection of Science and Learning, Bodlean Library, Oxford
SS	Schutzstaffel
StaNü	Staatsarchiv Nürnberg
StUF	Archivzentrum der Stadt- und Universitätsbibliothek Frankfurt am Main
UAV	University Archive Vienna
UNRRA	United Nations Relief and Rehabilitation Administration
UNWCC	United Nations War Crimes Commission
UWAHC	University of Wyoming, American Heritage Center
WMA	World Medical Association
ZfA	Zentrum für Antisemitismusforschung

1
Prologue

On or around 12 July 1947, at the height of the Nuremberg Doctors' Trial, shortly before the rendering of judgement, a mysterious stranger, barely visible, broke into the office in the Palace of Justice of Major Leo Alexander, Consultant to the Secretary of War of the United States and medical expert of the Chief of Counsel for War Crimes. The stranger left a series of notes that were invisible in ordinary daylight. Alexander's enquiry revealed that the stranger had been a gremlin who 'claimed to have had a fleeting acquaintance with Archie the Cockroach and Mehitabel the Cat, but did not otherwise wish to identify himself'.[1] After having studied and transcribed the notes 'in a setting of infra-red illumination provided by high hydro-carbon compound during the late hours of the night', Alexander decided that the nature of the document required it to be 'classified as secret'. Its distribution was to be strictly limited to 'those members of the inside circle of OCCWC [Office of Chief of Counsel for War Crimes] who have had direct dealings with the Medical Case'.[2] What had happened? Had the medical expert for the prosecution finally gone mad or was he suffering from some undiagnosed hallucinations? Why was this document in any way relevant, and why must it be sent to the 'inner circle' of the US prosecution team under the leadership of Brigadier General Telford Taylor? Surely, members of Taylor's staff must have had more on their minds than Archie the Cockroach. Perhaps it was one of those foolish office pranks to lighten the depressing atmosphere of the awfully long trial proceedings? It was certainly that. But it was more than that. It was a parody of the Doctors' Trial in the form of a theatre play called 'Saturnalia', a feast celebrated in the Roman period in honour of the God Saturn.

Alexander tells us the story of a newly established court in New York City in which the judges had been recruited from the planet 'Saturnus' to ensure the 'utmost in complete detachment and objectivity'.[3] The defendants, Bullet-Hole Pete, Frog-Face Joe and Scar-Face Tony, were charged with the robbery and murder of John Doe, a payroll clerk.[4] Although the prosecution, represented by James M. McHaney, Alexander G. Hardy and Arnost

Horlik-Hochwald – and these, their real names – had amassed an enormous wealth of incriminating evidence, they were constantly challenged by the defence, which succeeded in shifting the emphasis of the trial on to a question that had little to do with the murder of the payroll clerk. The judges, in their attempt to be absolutely impartial, did not realise that they were playing into the hands of the murderers. The cast in the play obviously resembles the major players in the Nuremberg Doctors' Trial, including Alexander, who plays himself as the medical expert of the prosecution. Alexander must have loathed the judges for their legalistic approach to the case. In fact, he did so to such an extent that he transformed them into inhuman, alien creatures from another planet who had no conception of life and death, right and wrong, justice and injustice. Like machines, emotionless and without any sense of morality, they followed the cold logic of the trial procedure and what they considered to be the law. This is not the story of some Kafkaesque moral maze in which the hero finds himself charged by his own paranoid feelings of guilt. It is rather the opposite. These defendants and their lawyers have no moral conscience, no sense of guilt and responsibility. They felt they had done nothing wrong, nothing other than obeying orders; they saw themselves as the victims of circumstance, of victors' justice. As in this piece of theatre, none of the defendants in the Nazi Doctors' Trial was willing to take individual responsibility for the crimes he had committed; each argued instead that he had acted under orders from a higher authority.

The judges in the play do not speak the language of the defendants. They are ignorant men. Like silent listeners they receive information only through the 'distilling mechanism of translation', cleansed from any unwanted social, emotional and cultural connotations that might taint their apparent judicial impartiality. What Alexander seems to be asking is whether the judges in the Doctors' Trial really understood what was being said in the courtroom. Were they aware of the enormous human and material resources that were sometimes used for matters profoundly irrelevant to the trial? Throughout the play the twisted legal logic of the Doctors' Trial is humorously called forth and criticised – to the point at which the victim becomes the guilty party, a reference to the recorded humiliation of some of the victims in war crimes trials after the war. In the end the victim's corpse is ruled 'immaterial to case' because it raises too many controversial issues and the prosecution is asked to remove the exhibit. Mr Hardy, dragging the corpse across the stage and stopping next to Dr Alexander's chair, says: 'Doctor, you sure let us down this time. You said this guy was dead.' Dr Alexander: 'But isn't he dead?' Mr Hardy: 'He sure is – but we couldn't prove it.'[5]

This unusual document reveals some of the contemporary inner thoughts and feelings of one of the chief medical experts at the Nuremberg Doctors' Trial – the focus of this book. Who was this man who not only parodied the Doctors' Trial, but who also challenged the judicial and moral belief system that made it so enormously difficult to prove the guilt of doctors who had immersed themselves so deeply in criminal behaviour? Alexander's biography allows us to look behind the curtain of Nuremberg and see the inherent problems of the trial, its artificiality and improvised construction. It was a unique event in modern legal history. Established by the American military authorities, the Nazi Doctors' Trial was the first of twelve Nuremberg war crimes trials that followed the trial of the major war criminals by the International Military Tribunal (IMT). Its official title was United States of America *versus* Karl Brandt et al. (Case I). Twenty doctors, including Hitler's personal escort physician Karl Brandt and three administrators, were charged with a common design or conspiracy, with war crimes, crimes against humanity and membership of an organisation declared criminal by the IMT.[6]

Yet, at the same time, the entire German medical profession was on trial – their moral integrity and scientific reputation. It was a scenario that had been totally unthinkable in pre-war Europe: German medical science had led the world, particularly in the fields of physiology, biochemistry, surgery and public health. The country's leading medical experts had been hailed for their innovative medical research and achievements for humanity. Now an 'odd' selection of this profession, as commentators noted, was on trial for murder and unspeakably cruel torture committed in the name of medicine and scientific progress. Contemporary observers noted that something must have gone badly wrong. But what it was and how exactly it had happened was a matter of enormous complexity, far too complicated for a trial in which the instrument of new and untested international law was being applied.[7]

Even more problematic was the task of developing a mechanism that would prevent doctors from committing such crimes ever again. Ultimately, the judges had to find a solution to resolve one of the most fundamental conflicts in human experimentation: to balance the need for advancements in medical science that benefit all human society with the right of the individual to personal inviolability, autonomy and self-determination. After 139 trial days, and after studying thousands of pages of evidence, the judges gave a tentative answer: a ten-point medical ethics code that laid down, for the first time, unmistakably and in writing, the human rights of patient-subjects and the responsibilities of physician-researchers conducting experiments on humans. Not all, but only 'certain types' of experiments on humans conformed to the ethics of the medical profession in the civilised world, the judges said. Human experimentation needed to remain within 'reasonably well-defined bounds'. Unless 'certain basic principles' were observed in order to 'satisfy moral, ethical and legal concepts', experiments on humans were not permissible. The medical ethics code became known as the Nuremberg Code.[8]

The Code established for the first time, and in written form, fundamental human rights in medicine, and placed the welfare of the patients in the foreground of medical practice. In the Nuremberg Code, as historian Michael Wunder has emphasised, neither medicine, nor science, nor society – nor any kind of collective or utilitarian ethics – has priority over the protection of the individual to remain physically and psychologically unharmed.[9] A person's right to self-determination and inviolability cannot be calculated against a more abstract need for medical progress, nor any other claim that society and science may or may not have towards its citizens. The principles of the Code demand it to be universally applicable so that 'experiments on humans do not violate moral, ethical and legal principles'.[10] Long before any kind of biomedical ethics movement was identifiable on the horizon, the Code stated, in lucid and unambiguous language, that the rights and integrity of the research subjects have to be preserved at all times.[11]

Of the ten principles, two (numbers one and nine)[12] specifically refer to the protection and rights of the experimental subject, and principle eight to their well-being. In the history of medical ethics, the importance of principle one has extended far beyond Nuremberg. The principle links the experiment to the *voluntary consent* of the experimental subject, meaning that the experiment can only be carried out after the 'voluntary, personal consent' has been obtained and after the subject has been clearly informed in the best possible manner.[13] The Code makes it unequivocally and categorically clear that the person involved in the experiment has to have the legal capacity to give a voluntary consent. Moreover, prior to obtaining consent, the exact nature, duration and objective of the experiment, the applied methods and means as well as all potential risks and all possible implications of the experiments for the health of the person have to be made clear. The research subject has to have sufficient knowledge and the capacity to comprehend the subject matter in order to make an enlightened and informed decision. This was meant to protect unconscious and mentally handicapped persons who, because of their specific illness, are unable to give voluntary consent. The Code made it clear that no experiments are legally and ethically permissible on the aforementioned patient groups. Since the late nineteenth century the status of the voluntary consent principle was greatly enhanced as a central element of medical research. For the first time, the Code transferred this principle as part of the Nuremberg judgement into international law.[14]

Likewise, principle nine deserves attention as another essential medical ethics law: the right of the medical subject to terminate the experiment at any time. The judges consciously formulated this principle as a right and not just a professional guideline. It constituted another legal precedent. These innovative patient rights were given further weight through the formulation of unequivocal responsibilities of the physicians to act responsibly towards the patient at all times. The rights of the patient *do not* replace the obligations of the physician as outlined in principles two to eight. A patient who has given his or her voluntary consent cannot be used for a random number of experiments; these experiments cannot violate professional medical ethics standards just because the patient has consented to the research. That is why, according to principle ten of the Code, it is the duty of the scientist in charge to terminate the experiment on his or her own initiative and at any stage if there is reason to believe that the continuation of the experiment would, in all probability, result in injury, disability or death of the experimental subject.

The Nuremberg Code therefore constitutes a particular, and in many ways unique combination of human rights which are part of international law *and* the Hippocratic medical ethic.[15] For the judges Hippocratic medical ethics were certainly an important precedent and although they offered much with regard to protecting the welfare and lives of patients, they were insufficient in protecting lives in human experimentation. They realised that research subjects needed to have quite specific rights if they were to be sufficiently protected from potential harm. That is why the Code defined the conditions under which informed voluntary consent could be obtained in a more comprehensive and legalistic fashion than any medical ethics code preceding it. The consent principle in the Code thus demands the status of an absolute, *a priori* principle. Moreover, the experimental subject is given the right to terminate the experiment at any time. The Nuremberg Code is therefore a legal code and, at the same time, a medical ethics code. This is the Code's particular strength. Yet it is also the profound weakness of many other ethics codes: they have no legal status whatsoever and are little more than 'guidelines' to be interpreted by respective experts.

The Code was partly instrumental in supporting the judgement, but it was also directed towards a future world in which men, women and children would be protected from any unwanted violation of their rights to the integrity of the human body. It was not unusual for American judges to go beyond the facts of the case in front of them, if they felt that it constituted a precedent. Their judgement reflected a new case law to address the legal issues that had arisen from the precedent. The judges believed in the creation of an international legal and professional framework that would empower those who had suffered harm to defend their rights against those who had violated them. The Nuremberg Code was in many ways a visionary and innovative medical ethics code and its principles were designed to apply to all research involving human subjects. Even today, the Nuremberg Code has a significant symbolic, and in many ways an influential role in the field of medical politics, ethics and law.[16] It also serves as a major point of reference to determine whether scientists who conducted experimental research on humans complied with, or violated, medical ethics standards during the Cold War period.[17]

One person who helped formulate the Code was Leo Alexander. This is the story of one footsoldier working behind the scenes who managed to make a lasting impact on major historical events. Alexander's life can tell us much about an important, and in many ways controversial chapter in the history of modern research ethics. Since the early 1990s, I have been interested in the history of medical ethics, particularly in social, political and cultural history. Work by Charles Webster and Margaret Pelling, to name but two, has made significant contributions to the social history of medicine, and I believe that there is a need for a distinctly social historical perspective on modern biomedical ethics. Moreover, those who have 'written' the history of bioethics thus far too often appear to have been coloured by their relationship to the institutionalisation and professionalisation of bioethics as a discipline. In some cases their historical narratives were meant to serve vested interests or to canonise a certain image of the field. Since 1997 I have been publishing short articles and editorial works aimed at drawing attention to the role of history in the field of medical ethics.[18]

In 2002, I completed a study on the history of medical films, ethics and 'euthanasia' in Nazi Germany.[19] A great deal of archival research in Germany and Austria, Israel and Poland, Great Britain and the United States was needed in order to piece together a previously neglected film genre. A key focus of the study was the film work undertaken at the University of Frankfurt am Main by the German psychiatrist Karl Kleist and his pupils in the late 1920s. Among them was Leo Alexander.[20] These researchers were interested in eugenics, the science of improving the hereditary make-up of a particular people. Research in the field of eugenics was later put in the service of Nazi racial policies. Medical films made by Kleist and others during the Third Reich affirmed theories of racial purity and sanctioned eugenic policies. Yet Alexander's name was absent from films produced after 1933. When the Nazis came to power in January 1933, he found himself stranded in China, where he was conducting research under the support of a Rockefeller fellowship. Unable to return to Germany because of his Jewish background and Austrian citizenship, he emigrated to the United States. Whilst undertaking research at the Imperial War Museum, London, and the National Archives, Washington DC, I repeatedly encountered Alexander's name, not as a film-maker, but as a high-profile US war crimes investigator and the author of a series of highly classified intelligence reports that he had written on behalf of the Supreme Headquarters Allied Expeditionary Forces (SHAEF). My curiosity became greater still when I came across a footnote about Alexander in a manuscript on German neuropathologists.[21] Apparently Alexander had kept a number of diaries during his war crimes investigations in 1945, and I was surprised that no one had ever edited or published excerpts from them. Was it that that had turned this young, successful Austrian physician into a major war crimes investigator and, as I soon realised, into the medical expert for the prosecution in the Doctors' Trial?

I became interested in the social history of the Nuremberg Doctors' Trial, this trial of trials that put the issue of human rights in relation to human experimentation so strongly on the map of international law and medical morality. Through a contact in Holland, I was able to get in touch with Alexander's daughter, Cecily Alexander-Grable, who lives in Boston. She readily opened up the family home that had housed her father's private papers for years. Other archives in Koblenz, Boston and New York supplemented Alexander's official and unofficial papers. In 1997/98 I also discovered one of Alexander's original diaries in the Depository for Medical Center Records in the Duke University Archives in Durham, North Carolina.[22] It soon became clear that Alexander was a man who had done much of the essential background work in the Doctors' Trial. He had interrogated the defendants, both before and during the trial, studied their mentalities and rationale for committing medical crimes, followed the witnesses who were prepared to testify in court, written dozens of memoranda in preparation for the prosecution's case, and published extensively on the possible psychological causes behind the perpetration of war crimes. Despite this, his contribution to the Nazi Doctors' Trial had received very little recognition.[23] The present study addresses some of the misconceptions about the trial, and it aims to pose new questions, particularly about the work which happened in the background, before, during and after the trial.

A book about a single individual in the context of the Doctors' Trial obviously involves a number of methodological and conceptual risks. There was, after all, no shortage of literature and published material on the trial. Alexander Mitscherlich and Fred Mielke's acclaimed edition *Das Diktat der Menschenverachtung* from 1947, published as *Wissenschaft ohne Menschlichkeit* in 1949 and as *Medizin ohne Menschlichkeit* in 1960, as well as Alice Platen-Hallermund's book *Die Tötung Geisteskranker in Deutschland* from 1948, were important milestones in the historiography about the trial.[24] All three authors had been members of the official doctors' commission (*Ärztekommission*) that was sent to Nuremberg by the German medical profession to report on the ongoing trial, work that was extensively examined by Jürgen Peter.[25] Most of this body of literature looked at the official side of the trial, presented evidence of grim experiments that had been introduced by the prosecution, and attempted to find an explanation – psychological or otherwise – as to why doctors had become murderers in the name of medical science. In 1950 the French naval psychologist Françoise Bayle published *Croix Gammée Contre Caducée*, a book that was largely based on handwriting samples and physical measurements of the defendants. Bayle's work stood in the tradition of nineteenth-century European racial anthropologists and psychologists such as

Paul Broca (1824–80) in France or Cesare Lombroso (1836–1909) in Italy, who wanted to establish a scientific link between physiognomy and criminality.[26] Likewise, the publication of the 'desk notebook' of the presiding judge in the Doctors' Trial, Walter B. Beals, offered little to improve our understanding of the history and long-term effects of the trial.[27] What all the work had in common was that it failed to examine the origins of the trial, and overlooked the Allies' alternative plans and controversies, as well as the role of the men and women involved in staging this international media and legal event at the dawn of the Cold War. It was not until the early 1990s, with the publication of George Annas and Michael Grodin's pioneering study, *The Nazi Doctors and the Nuremberg Code: Human Rights in Human Experimentation*, that the trial and its implications for the history of bioethics eventually received the scholarly attention it deserves.[28] In this volume, Grodin offered an excellent initial survey of the historical origins of the Nuremberg Code, one that addressed the role of the medical experts, including Leo Alexander and Andrew Ivy. Since then, the fiftieth anniversary of the Nuremberg Code gave historians of medicine, health professionals and legal experts an opportunity to address the far-reaching importance and shortcomings of the Code in protecting human rights in experimental medicine.[29]

The availability of secondary materials, and the publication of new primary sources, makes a comprehensive study, in this case through the medium of a biography, particularly appropriate. For example, the superb microfiche edition of the entire trial transcripts, edited by Klaus Dörner and Angelika Ebbinghaus in 1999, includes previously unpublished documents by the prosecution and the defence as well as material related to the background and consequences of the trial. It offers scholars an extensive body of new material that allows for an in-depth analysis of the evolution of one of the most significant events in modern legal history.[30] This book is an attempt to link the personal history of Alexander's life with the social and political history that shaped the responses to the legacy of the Third Reich in the mid-twentieth century. The implications of this history reach far into our present-day reality, where war crimes tribunals and truth commissions are being established to put criminals like Slobodan Milosevic on trial at The Hague, or offer spaces for collective catharsis and, perhaps, societal healing in places such as Chile and South Africa. The history of the Nuremberg Doctors' Trial and the Nuremberg Code also plays a central part in the debate about modern medical research ethics, particularly in relation to the extraordinary advances witnessed in modern biotechnology and genetics. These developments make us question the extent to which society can (or should) permit scientists to manipulate and control human life. They also raise the question as to whether the continuing modification of ethics codes and the establishment of ethics committees in places of medical learning provide sufficient safeguards to protect the rights and dignity of patient-subjects. Scholars of modern medical ethics need to examine the tradition in which the Nuremberg Code was formulated to determine whether previous ethics codes were merely token documents to protect medical professionals from legal liability and embarrassment or whether they constituted meaningful and effective tools to regulate contemporary research practices. Only then are we able to appreciate the historicity and universality of the Nuremberg Code.[31]

A biography naturally runs the risk of turning into a whiggish history of a 'famous great man', or one of many who have apparently determined the course of history. In the past, scholars have often written with hidden admiration, or in some instances with a revulsion for their subject that tends to cloud our understanding of the complexities that shape human societies and direct the course of history. Biography assumes a certain empathy on the part of the author for his subject, but not so much sympathy or uncritical admiration. A central concern of this book is the social, political and cultural realm in which the subject operates, sometimes actively, but more often passively and in response to developments that are largely beyond his sphere of influence. I am interested in how individuals, in this case the Jewish émigré scientist Alexander, attempt to remain in control of their lives, and how they regain control if they feel they are about to lose it. In other words, I am interested in how people devise survival strategies in the face of ever-changing political situations, or how they adapt and acculturate to new and foreign environments that demand different social and professional codes of conduct. How do people think and feel who live lives of permanent transience, uprooted in many ways, undoubtedly, but also strangely rooted by default, so to speak, in themselves and their moral belief system? This naturally involves conflicts with institutions and large administrations, with other individuals and ideas that challenge or appear to challenge their role in society.

A history of modern medical ethics must, I believe, be a social history of interest groups and organisations that attempt to succeed (sometimes through negotiation and compromise, at other times through power and command) by defining and codifying what is ethically right and good for a society. It should also be a history of individuals who, when confronted with particular circumstances, attempted to influence the debate, either directly or indirectly, and with varying degrees of success – as Alexander did in Nuremberg and thereafter. This being the case, the present study has two points of focus: it examines the key historical forces that shaped the creation and implementation of ethics guidelines before, during and after the Doctors' Trial, and at the same time, it concentrates on the life of Alexander, the man who was himself responsible for many of these developments. Alexander realised that any useful analysis of Nazi medicine and its ethical implications required a broad social and political perspective: 'I believe that we do not contribute to our understanding of historical events if we simply "question" whether these experiments had been carried out when they seem incredible to us. Instead we must face the facts, ascribing them to the power which social and political forces have upon the practical aspects of scientific and medical endeavour.'[32]

The trial stands at the crossroads of modern biomedical research ethics and highlights the importance of patients' rights and medical jurisprudence in medical science and practice. We need to acknowledge, however, that these issues are part of a long and complex history of medical professionalisation that saw doctors negotiating and renegotiating their position with respect to both society and the state. Historically, the trial is part of a series of failed attempts to introduce effective regulations in medical research involving human participants. To be clear, the Nuremberg Doctors' Trial is not a success story: it is quite the contrary. The tension between nineteenth-century medicine as a middle-class, bourgeois profession in which courts of honour functioned as self-disciplinary bodies that codified medical ethics, on the one hand, and the increasing political and state influence on medical practice, on the other, meant that the organisation of vested medical interests became a central objective of the profession. In general, medical practice and research continued to be governed by professional and social duties. It was a paternalistic system in which doctors decided what was best for patients on the basis of existing medical knowledge and codes of professional conduct.

Medical ethics codes were to guide the profession in its conduct and secure its social and professional standing, but were not to rule, govern or interfere with experimental medicine. In 1803, Thomas Percival commented that the principles of his ethics code were 'not laws to govern but principles to guide to correct conduct'.[33] But Percival also noted that investigators searching for new remedies had to be 'scrupulously and conscientiously governed by sound reason, just analogy, or well authenticated facts' and had to consult with their peers before departing into uncharted medical territory. One of America's oldest ethics codes, formulated by William Beaumont in 1833, already contained many of the principles (although most of them only by inference) that would later inform the judges at Nuremberg. According to Beaumont, researchers should conduct experimental work on humans only if the information could not be obtained by other means, for example through animal experimentation, and if the investigators were conscientious and responsible in their research. They had to abstain from random trials, obtain the voluntary consent from the patient-subject and had to be prepared to discontinue the experiment if it caused distress to the subject, a principle which the Nuremberg judges turned into a 'moral duty' of the physician/investigator.[34] The language in which most medical ethics codes were written, especially those within the Anglo-Saxon tradition, was often rather vague and subject to general interpretation in order to leave investigators with the freedom of discretion, as was the case with the Code of Ethics of the American Medical Association that was adopted in May 1847.[35] Claude Bernhard's personal code from 1865, which was based on Christian morals, is another case in point. He claimed that human experiments 'that can only do harm are forbidden, those that are harmless are permissible, and those that may do good are obligatory'. Yet Bernhard did not define the boundaries of what constituted permissible and non-permissible experiments on humans, nor did he make it clear whether experiments were permitted if they were random, badly organised or unnecessary, even if they were harmless.[36] Ironically, the country that began to develop the most stringent and clearly defined medical ethics regulations at the end of the nineteenth century was Germany.

As early as 1891 the Prussian Ministry of the Interior issued a regulation ensuring that tuberculin would 'in no case be used against the patients' will' for the treatment of tuberculosis. Three years later the German Supreme Court stressed that surgical and other potentially life-threatening treatments required the patients' consent. In 1900, the Albert Neisser case caused a public furore when it was discovered that Neisser had injected serum from patients suffering from syphilis into a group of eight patients, mostly prostitutes, who were suffering from other diseases. He had neither informed the women about the risks involved, nor had he obtained their consent. Legal experts pointed out that, according to criminal jurisprudence, Neisser had committed an act of physical injury by failing to obtain the women's consent, and one of them even noted that the 'respect for rights and morality has the same importance for the good of mankind as medical and scientific progress'.[37] Although the medical profession closed ranks to protect one of its peers, some doctors stressed the importance of the informed consent principle for upholding medical ethics standards.

Among these doctors was Albert Moll, a Berlin psychiatrist and advocate of Christian medical ethics. In 1902, Moll published *Ärztliche Ethik. Die Pflichten des Arztes*, a book that chronicled dozens of cases of unethical research on humans.[38] Moll had observed that the violation of medical ethics principles appeared to be the result of increasing specialisation of physician-researchers in modern medical practice. The over-emphasis on a particular field of expertise sometimes led to the narrowing of doctors' perspectives. It was not uncommon for experiments on humans to reveal a lack of protection for research subjects; they were often wholly unnecessary and badly organised, and showed a disrespect for the dignity of the subjects, both in the language used to describe the experiment and in its execution. Some scientists simply seemed to 'gamble' with human lives.[39] For Moll, issues of autonomy, beneficence and informed and voluntary consent were of fundamental importance in research involving human participants.[40] He also questioned the so-called voluntary nature of the consent that patient-subjects gave to their physician-researchers, suggesting that in many instances a certain degree of coercion was not uncommon. Moll seems to have been particularly concerned about the welfare and rights of vulnerable patient groups such as children, the handicapped and terminally ill patients, who were, and often still are, used for experimental research on a regular basis.[41]

In 1900, hospital and clinic directors had already been advised by the authorities that research on humans was prohibited 'if the human subject was a minor or not competent for other reasons', or had not given unambiguous and informed consent.[42] Nonetheless, the response to these new guidelines was mixed. Medical ethicists such as Moll realised that the new regulations were insufficient and probably would turn out to be ineffective in protecting patient-subjects from psychological and physical harm because they were too general in certain areas and too specific in others.[43] Moreover, it was not the case that the informed consent principle suddenly became a matter of great significance for the profession as a result of these changes in medical regulations. Likewise, informed consent did not figure prominently in the profession's disciplinary procedures. On the contrary, throughout the early part of the twentieth century the majority of doctors continued to engage in controversies about illegitimate competition through advertising, the poaching of patients, financial misconduct, slander and libel, lack of collegiality or alleged sexual offences: in short, about matters relating to professional status and reputation.[44] Medical ethics issues, in other words, continued to be largely concerned with (and defined by) the profession itself. This meant that the concerns of patients and their families would only receive sufficient attention when the reputation of the profession as a whole was at stake, as it was during the Nuremberg Doctors' Trial, or in a number of previous scandals that involved the use of human subjects. Since the turn of the century, a certain pattern had begun to emerge: whenever members of the medical profession were guilty of serious professional misconduct that aroused the public conscience, the authorities reacted by issuing modified or stricter ethics guidelines which, as soon as the public debate subsided, were mostly ignored or treated as a mere pro-forma measure by the profession.

For example, at the end of the 1920s, a series of unethical and in some cases fatal experiments on children prompted public debate about medical ethics standards and the reform of the German penal code.[45] In February 1931 the Reich Ministry of the Interior therefore issued the 'Regulations Concerning New Therapy and Human Experimentation'.[46] The directives were among the most comprehensive research rules by any contemporary standards and some elements were even more elaborate than the principles of the Nuremberg Code. Contentious issues such as individual autonomy, beneficence, informed voluntary consent or therapeutic and non-therapeutic research were addressed in order to protect the rights and dignity of patients. Thus, remarkably, Germany was one of the few countries which, by the 1930s, had introduced state directives for the protection of human subjects in clinical research. In particular, the guidelines aimed to protect the most vulnerable groups of society: the handicapped and children, for example. Significantly, they were also the first victims of the Nazi racial programme. These German ethics guidelines from the 1930s offer poignant proof that ethics codes and other professional regulations are insufficient in themselves to protect patients from serious bodily harm, disability and death.

In the frank discussions that preceded the promulgation of the regulations, Julius Moses, a social hygienist and member of the German parliament, criticised doctors for their lack of respect for patients, for their use of humans as research objects and for their general ignorance of medical ethics issues.[47] Many Weimar physicians, on the other hand, argued that unethical experiments on children were rare instances of professional malpractice that needed to be balanced against the importance of medical progress for society. Without such experiments, they proclaimed, the advancement of medical science would be prevented.[48] The representatives of the German medical profession were in agreement that a set of official ethics regulations for research on humans needed to be formulated. But they also realised that medical ethics codes (and legal regulations, more generally) would be of limited effectiveness unless the profession itself was fully committed to adhering to its own principles.

Central to the effectiveness of ethics regulations is an efficient dissemination and communication process. We know, for example, that the 1931 regulations were given to the Reich Justice Ministry and to the Reich Ministry of the Interior for comment, and that they were accepted in both cases.[49] As for original intentions, we know that all German doctors were to acknowledge the regulations in writing when entering into a new employment contract with hospitals and other health-care institutions. It is unclear, however, why the regulations failed to achieve wide circulation, and why their influence on the profession remained almost negligible. The incoming Nazi regime may well have blocked any further distribution, but there is also relatively little information showing that young doctors acknowledged the Reich regulations. The German medical profession does not seem to have been indifferent to the issue of medical ethics in human experimentation, but doctors appear to have been inadequately informed about their professional responsibilities and about legal limitations in experimental research. Without the commitment of the medical profession and the government to protect the health of human subjects – something that was in short supply during the Third Reich – the ethics regulations remained ineffective and were probably of little relevance.

The crimes under discussion at Nuremberg, especially the Nazi concentration camp experiments, represented a profound departure from previously accepted medical and human behaviour in Western societies. It was the 'low water mark in twentieth century moral culture', as Robert Proctor has written.[50] In February 1947, a trial commentator compared the fundamental shift in medical morality in Nazi Germany to a slow and invisible chemical reaction until a sudden change of colour (*Farbumschlag*) indicated that the reaction had already taken place.[51] Central to this 'change of colour' was a shift from ethical positions concerned with the well-being of the individual to biologistic ethics aimed at purifying the race, an uneven and twisted process that was rooted in nineteenth-century social Darwinism and the racial hygiene movement. This book attempts to understand those individuals whose lives were profoundly affected by these developments, and those who wanted to ensure that medicine would never again follow the path of racial and social engineering.

To reiterate, this book has a dual focus: it places a single individual within the context of major political developments that shaped the character of modern European history, and, at the time, it looks closely at the Nuremberg Doctors' Trial, examining its historical genesis and addressing its implications for modern biomedical research ethics. A central concern of the study is how at Nuremberg the United States and its allies put Nazi medical 'science' on trial through the commitment and visionary outlook of men like Alexander. This is therefore not a biography in the conventional sense, one in which the subject remains the focus of the narrative at all times, but rather one that allows itself to be guided by the richness and diversity of the source material, and by the multiplicity of factors that help to explain the nature and outcome of the trial. The first two chapters explore the historical forces that shaped Alexander's social background and intellectual mentality before the end of the Second World War. This analysis offers fundamental insight into the cultural, professional and religious beliefs that would eventually inform the positions and decisions he reached later, especially during his time in Europe. I will discuss his upbringing in Austria around the turn of the century and life among the Jewish medical élite. This includes his early experience of anti-Semitism and the process of assimilation in Austria in the 1910s and 1920s. Alexander's professional training in Weimar Germany, his experience of emigration after 1933, first to China and later to the United States, and his cultural and religious roots are key stages and recurring themes in his life necessary for understanding his responses and attitudes towards German medical war crimes. Their analysis helps to gain insight into Alexander's obsessive search for incriminating evidence and explains why he was most suited as an Allied war crimes investigator.

In Chapters 4 and 5 I turn to the period that first saw the discovery and then the investigation of medical war crimes, followed by largely improvised Allied preparations for a series of international war crimes trials. Alexander's relatively brief tour of duty through various occupied zones in the war's immediate aftermath is reconstructed in detail to allow for an understanding of the historical environment in which the Doctors' Trial occurred. Most of Alexander's investigative work was carried out in a climate that approximated a political, administrative and legal vacuum. It was an environment in which most of the future defendants were willing to co-operate and in which war crimes trials were not yet instituted. Particular attention is given to the planning and organisational stages of the trial in which different approaches to prosecuting war crimes were discussed and dismissed, modified and sometimes influenced by developments that were outside the control of those on the ground. More specifically, I examine the groups of experts who pushed the Nazi Doctors' Trial forward, to the point at which individual defendants were 'shared' between the Allies or 'moved' to different occupied zones in order to stage the American-led Doctors' Trial. In short, these chapters document the road that led to Nuremberg through the life and work of Leo Alexander, particularly the social and political forces that dictated the shape of the trial.

The construction of the trial and the origin of the Nuremberg Code form the basis of Chapters 6 and 7, where I examine the strategies employed – and failures experienced – by the team of prosecutors in mounting their case against the Nazi doctors. I explore Alexander's understanding of Thanatology, the science of producing death, an offshoot of Raphaël Lemkin's genocide concept, which had previously been applied with some success in the IMT. The genocide concept became the overarching conceptual framework for all subsequent Nuremberg trials. Here, some particular dramatic moments of the trial are discussed, for example when Alexander presented four of the Ravensbrück victims of medical experiments to a shocked international audience in the courtroom. In addition, the chapter will explore the response which Alexander's presentation generated from the defendants and their lawyers. His first-hand knowledge of some of the defendants and his in-depth understanding of German medical science, together with his language skills and professional ambitions, made him an ideal expert who was able to supply the prosecution and the court with valuable information regarding the ethics of human experimentation. In the second half of the trial the question of what constituted ethical and legal experiments on humans became of paramount importance. Eventually, the judges themselves interviewed some of the witnesses to find out what the accepted medical ethics principles in the Western world actually were. For this reason, I will examine the step-by-step evolution of the Nuremberg Code, and offer a tentative response to controversial questions regarding its authorship.

In Chapter 8 I look broadly at the effectiveness of the Code in influencing Anglo-American research culture from the early days of the Cold War in the 1950s to the 1970s, when issues surrounding bioethics began to dominate the political and scientific debate. I also examine

Alexander's theoretical work on the psychological causes of war crimes and his charitable work for some of the victims of Nazi human experiments. Broadly speaking, this concluding chapter focuses on social and political forces that shaped post-war biomedical research. For a long time the Code was seen as 'A Good Code for Barbarians', that is for German medical scientists, and was given little serious consideration in the Western scientific establishment.[52] I look at the way in which the international medical profession revisited the issue after the war by establishing the World Medical Association (WMA) and by promulgating a watered-down ethics code at the beginning of the 1960s, the so-called Helsinki Declaration. The Helsinki Declaration was one of many strategies developed by the medical profession to ensure that the level of legal liability – and indeed public embarrassment – of researchers and their institutions would be kept to a minimum at a time when civil liberty and human rights groups were exposing medical ethics violations in the United States and elsewhere. The chapter concludes with some of Alexander's reflections about his role at Nuremberg in the late 1970s. The exchange of ideas and information between Alexander and the New York psychiatrist Robert J. Lifton provides insight into the construction of historical narratives, and thus into the historiographical origins of one of the first major studies on Nazi medicine.

In this study, I argue that a social history of modern medical ethics and an understanding of the value of the Nuremberg Code, irrespective of the fact that it needed to be modified to take account of modern biomedical research, can make a valuable contribution to the future protection of patient-subjects in human research. A comprehensive study of the Nuremberg Doctors' Trial and the Nuremberg Code cannot be limited to the genesis and implementation of modern biomedical research ethics; rather, it must also engage with the wider history of international law and the development of human rights in medicine and science. International public outrage over Nazi atrocities stifled the political will and determination for compromise in the United Nations that led to the Declaration of Human Rights in 1948. The Nuremberg trials, including the Doctors' Trial, constitute in many ways the organisational and legal predecessor of the current war crimes tribunal in The Hague, where perpetrators can be tried, for example, for crimes against humanity, a legal concept that was applied in Nuremberg for the first time in history. The Hague Tribunal and the newly established International Criminal Court (ICC) only represent the tip of the iceberg in what is an important, though in many ways long and protracted process towards a more globally defined, international civil, human rights, and patient law that one day might be enforceable in concurrence with national bodies. This would mean that human beings would at last become the subject of medical research and practice, protected by national and international law against professional, economic or institutional abuse and exploitation. This would also mean that some lessons may have been learned from Nazism and its destructive effects on medical morality. Benjamin B. Ferencz, one of the prosecutors of the Nuremberg trials and a passionate expert in international law, recently said in an interview: 'The true sovereign of international law, that becomes more and more clear, is the human being. Only his or her protection matters.'[53]

Human research is – or should ultimately be – a dialogue between two equal subjects, and should remain so even if this exchange causes progress to be slowed along the way. Unless we see this dialogue as an essential part of the research process, and unless we are willing to pay a certain price for this dialogue to take place, medical ethics codes and other professional regulations amount to little more than lip-service. There is a continuing need (perhaps never more pressing) to balance the advancement of medical science with the protection of human and patient rights. In 1963, Bradford Hill remarked that the 'ethical obligation always and entirely outweighs the experimental', but in order to negotiate these two equally important values, which often stand in juxtaposition, researchers need to comprehend their own moral and ethical obligations, and also understand their evolution over time.[54] Doctors need to acknowledge that moral codes are formulated by man and thus subject to change. At the same time, however, they should be constantly mindful that both medicine and society must always uphold certain universal principles, including respect for the inviolability of patient-citizens and the right of the individual to self-determination. A social and political history of modern medical ethics in the twentieth century can, I believe, contribute to a balanced and rational decision-making process in order to face the moral challenges that lie ahead in the area of genetic engineering. An informed historical discourse can perhaps also make the case for changes in the research environment that would ensure that patient-subjects come to realise that research is not therapy, and that trust in the doctor–patient or investigator–subject relationship results from the conduct of the physician-investigator. In short, we need to improve the public understanding of the historical processes at work in medical practice, lower public expectations regarding the effectiveness of certain treatments and outcomes of research, draw attention to the risks involved in experimental studies, and reduce the level of uncritical trust that patients may place in the therapeutic quality of experimental research. Ultimately, as Jay Katz has pointed out, doctors have to learn, and perhaps be educated, 'to respect patient-subjects as persons with minds of their own and with the capacity to decide for themselves how to live their medical lives. The choices may or may not include a willingness for altruistic self-sacrifice, but such choices must take precedence over the advancement of science.'[55]

This book traces the history of how medicine became the subject of greater accountability and scrutiny through the medium of the biography of Leo Alexander. In doing so, it explores the social and political forces that called for the protection of subject-citizens in experimental research. The international medical community has come a long way in realising that medical progress is itself of little value if the people who practise it sacrifice the lives of those for whom it is intended along the way. A book about the Nuremberg Code can perhaps remind us that only the protection of human beings, their lives, dignity and human rights, really matters.

2
The Austrian Jew

Alexander's Vienna

Hitler and Alexander probably never met, though it could have been possible. For some time during the first two decades of the twentieth century, both lived in Vienna. The city was as influential in shaping the incipient prejudices and phobias of the former as it was in determining the religious and cultural identity of the latter. One can hardly over-estimate the influence that Alexander's upbringing and childhood in the capital of the Austro-Hungarian Empire had on his social conscience, on his devotion to art and German culture, on his interest in music, theatre and science – in short, on his character. While not always noticeable, his Viennese background was always present. In his speech and gestures, hobbies and professional interests, Alexander always remained firmly bound to his roots. Born into an Austrian-Jewish family, he was assimilated and educated, multinational and open-minded. Alexander and his siblings fit the stereotype of the hardworking Western Jew who began climbing the social and professional ladder after Emperor Franz Josef granted the Jews some legal protection in the late nineteenth century.[1]

Turn-of-the-century Vienna was a melting pot of different nationalities and religious beliefs; it was a city of profound contradictions, and social and political tensions. The capital was a microcosm of the empire's national and ethnic conflicts. To the outside world the city radiated imperial grandeur, artistic and cultural creativity, scientific progress and technological advances. Foreign visitors saw Vienna as a centre of modernism, the pinnacle of cultural and intellectual innovation. But behind the great splendour of royal palaces, parks and modern architecture, the city was strained by growing poverty and social frictions. Prostitution, infectious diseases and criminality were on the rise. For the ruling classes the growing number of radical political movements posed a threat to the old political and social order. Small traders and craftsmen feared the growing competition from large department stores, mostly Jewish-owned. The atmosphere was one of doom and cultural pessimism (*Kulturpessimismus*). Many felt a sense of decay, or experienced feelings of impotence when confronted with the modern technological age and the unpredictable social and political conditions that accompanied it.

The climate was a fertile breeding ground for racial fanatics and anti-Semites, many of whom stirred the phobias and social prejudices of the population. Anti-Semitic attacks against Jews were commonplace in the daily press. Vienna's mayor, Karl Lueger, an early admirer of Hitler, spear-headed a campaign against all alien and Jewish elements in society. In 1890 the capital had almost 120 000 religious Jews. Twenty years later, in 1910, their number had risen to more than 175 000. Compared to other major European cities the proportion of Jews living in Vienna was high.[2] As in Germany, the Jews showed a marked tendency to assimilate. The relative security that the Jews enjoyed during the long reign of Habsburg Emperor Franz Josef encouraged many of them to strive for social status and wealth. They aimed to become respected members of society, emancipated, educated and assimilated. At the same time they also sought acceptance and recognition from the bourgeois elite for their achievements and their role in public life. The importance that many Jews placed on education often gave them a head start in the struggle for status and resources. The term 'Jewish intelligence' became synonymous with the possession of unusual skills or expert knowledge. The number of Jewish students in Vienna was about three times higher than their overall percentage in the population.[3] For secondary schools the proportion of Jews was even more significant. In 1912 almost half of all pupils were Jewish. Medicine and law were the most popular subjects among Jewish university students. Statistics from 1913 show that 40 per cent of all medical students were Jewish.[4] Whether in language or literature, science, art or culture, Jews adopted German as their preferred cultural and national identity. Many Jews, for example, admired the composers Richard Wagner and Gustav Mahler, the latter being one of Wagner's most famous interpreters and a frequent visitor to the Alexander home.[5]

Most assimilated Jews, including the Alexanders, favoured liberal or social democratic politics, which allowed them to obtain influence faster than other political camps. What mattered was achievement and skill, not privileges based on noble birth and patronage. In 1908 the social democrat Benno Straucher told the Reichsrat: 'We Jews were, are, and will remain democratic, we can only flourish in democratic air, for us, reactionary air is stuffy, we subscribe to a free, democratic *Weltanschauung*, therefore we can only pursue truly liberal policies.'[6] Doctrines such as Zionism, the Jewish national movement, appealed to large sections of the poorer, mostly Eastern European Jewish community or to those searching for their Jewish ancestors. Theodore Herzl, the literary critic and founder of Zionism, had grown up in Vienna and rediscovered his Jewishness when the plight of the

Eastern Jews stirred his compassion. In his 1896 novel, *The Jewish State*, Herzl's vision of Palestine promised a solution to the oppression of the Jews through social discrimination, intimidation and racial hatred.[7] In response, wealthy assimilated Western Jews were asked to fund his project through the purchase of land in Palestine. Such ideas, however, widened the gulf between differing Jewish factions and stirred outside resentment against Eastern European Jews.

Although the federal authorities tried to keep anti-Semitic diatribes under control, the Emperor himself sometimes remarked in private conversations 'Who really is not an anti-Semite?'[8] Slogans such as 'Don't buy from Jews' appeared in the window of department stores and small shops alike. The Pan-German *Yearbook for German Women and Girls* advised customers not to shop in Jewish stores. Christmas presents bought from Jews were seen as a 'disgrace' that would dishonour the family and taint the holy night. As early as 1877 German fraternities introduced the 'Aryan Clause' and others followed suit.[9] No matter how hard they had worked, nor how successfully they managed to inculcate a German identity, neither baptism and conversion, nor marriage and money could protect the Jews from feelings of insecurity. To counter these feelings and preserve their hard-earned possessions, some Viennese Jews, especially those in the upper levels of society, like the Alexanders, attempted to further assimilate and integrate themselves into the Austrian-German establishment. They wanted to become almost indistinguishable from the upper bourgeoisie, a tendency that guided the education and family values that shaped the first twenty-five years of Alexander's life.

The shadow of the father

While Alexander's ancestors can be traced back to places in Austria and Hungary, Russia and the United States, most of his family background is poorly documented and largely based on hearsay, as passed on from generation to generation. His great-great-grandmother on his father's side, Julia Singer, née Steiner, was born in Vienna in the early 1800s into an educated Jewish family, and apparently used her spare time to translate the Bible from Hebrew into German.[10] After marrying Adolf Singer, she moved to Raab, Hungary, where they established a small textile business. When Adolf died of cholera, Julia took over the family business and single-handedly raised their six children: Carl, Ignaz, Samuel, Fanni, Leni, and Sophie, Alexander's great-grandmother. Julia's relative wealth allowed her to send Carl to Vienna to study at the Polytechnicum. He later supported the growing family business, which traded in paper and grain. Her son Ignaz also moved to Vienna where he first worked as a journalist and later founded the newspaper *Wiener Extrablatt*. His interest in charitable work compelled him to distribute coal and wood to needy people and to organise fundraising events such as concerts and theatre performances. Highly decorated by the city's dignitaries, the Emperor awarded him the 'Knightcross of the Franz Joseph Order', which ennobled him.[11] Alexander's great-grandmother, Sophie, married the Viennese jeweller Bernhard Friedman (1817–87). Friedman was apparently the first Jew in his line whom city authorities granted the right to open a business.[12] They had five children, the first of whom was Caecily (1846–1936), Alexander's beloved grandmother. In marked contrast to Alexander's assimilated parents, Caecily is said to have been very religious: she practised her Jewish faith by keeping a kosher diet and by celebrating the start of the Sabbath on Friday evenings.[13] The bond between Alexander and his grandmother seems to have been close: following tradition, he later named his daughter Cecily in remembrance of her.[14] In August 1870 Caecily married Leopold Alexander (1840–1903), a goldsmith from Rechnitz.[15] Together, they had three children: Sophie (1871–1936), who married and moved to Slovakia, Gustav (1873–1932), Leo Alexander's father, and Robert (1883–1966), a musician.[16] To earn a modest living, Robert once worked as an organist at Augustin Chapel in Vienna. Like his nephew Leo, Robert emigrated to the United States when life as a Jew in the Austrian capital became too dangerous.

Gustav Alexander, Alexander's father, was born in 1873. He studied medicine at the University of Vienna, where he received a doctorate in 1898.[17] He first worked as an assistant at the Anatomical Institute under Emil Zuckerkandl and Eduard Albert, and later at the clinic of Adam Politzer, the Royal Ear Physician of the City of Vienna. One of Gustav's colleagues in the tightly knit Viennese medical community was Julius Tandler, who later became one of Austria's key promoters of social hygiene and eugenics. In 1903 Gustav completed his *Habilitation*; a year later the Seventh International Congress of Otology awarded him the Lenval Prize.[18] It was around this time that he married Gisela Rubel-Schäfer, Alexander's mother.

Information about Gisela Alexander and her family is scarce. She was born in 1876 in Galicia, in a place called Strzyleze on the eastern border of the Austro-Hungarian Empire. Her surname was Schäfer, neé Rubel *recte* Schwitkes. Apparently she was once married to a man named Schäfer, and may have been an adopted child of the Rubel family. The name given to her at birth was Schwitkes.[19] According to family recollections, she inherited a substantial fortune, probably from her first husband. The money afforded both Gisela Alexander and her new husband a comfortable lifestyle. At the beginning of their marriage, she apparently explained that he would never have to worry about financial matters, and that she would always take care of them both. It was a promise with far-reaching consequences. More immediately, however, Gisela's economic independence allowed her to pursue her studies.[20] In the winter semester of 1898/99, she began to study philosophy. Four years later, in 1903, Gisela Rubel-Schäfer became one of the first women to be awarded a doctorate in philosophy at the University of Vienna.[21] Two years later, on 11 October 1905, she gave birth to the first of five children, a son, named Leopold. Leo was named after the Austrian Emperor Leopold I, a gesture meant to suggest the family's commitment to the monarchy. Neither Alexander nor his siblings were given traditional Jewish names. Rather, they were given names that emphasised the family's loyalty to Austro-German culture: Anne (1908–90), Alfred (1909–83), Helene (1914–65), and Theodore (1919–94); their names worked to camouflage the family's Jewish roots.[22] In a climate of growing ethnic and religious tensions Alexander's parents tried to ensure that their children's lives would be as little compromised by their Jewish ancestry as possible. In this respect, they were far-sighted. It was the inconspicuous Germanic name that allowed Alfred to conceal his Jewish background when he emigrated to Great Britain in 1938 in order to escape Nazi persecution.[23]

Gisela Alexander's wealth allowed Gustav to pursue his medical research without many of the mundane worries that accompany modern academic life. His marriage gave him the financial independence and security that he needed to devote himself fully to his research. In 1907 he was promoted to head of the Ear Department at the general polyclinic in Vienna. After several unsuccessful attempts, he was awarded the title Extraordinary Professor of Otolaryngology in 1909.[24] Ten years later, in 1919, he earned the rank of full professor for his work on ear diseases. He was also elected president of the welfare association for deaf, dumb and blind children in Austria. Gustav Alexander's medical and charitable work, together with his military service as a high-ranking medical official, an *Oberstabsarzt*, during the First World War, further enhanced his social and professional reputation and ensured the circulation of his name in the uppermost echelons of society.

By the time of Leo's birth, Gustav Alexander had published more than eighty scientific papers, ranging from studies on pathological anatomy and evolutionary biology to work on deformities and surgical techniques.[25] He was most interested, however, in the anatomy, physiology and pathology of the ear, and the diagnosis and treatment of ear diseases. Within expert circles, he was credited with initially postulating what would later become known as the Alexander Law.[26] As a consultant to the court of the Emperor Franz Josef, and the editor of the widely read 'Alexander Text of Otolaryngology', Gustav Alexander enjoyed social and academic standing as a distinguished scholar in the Austrian capital. In 1923/24 he published the classic textbook on the neurology of the ear in collaboration with Otto Marburg, the head of the neurological institute in Vienna and Leo Alexander's first employer.[27] Nonetheless, Gustav's work was not free from ideas pertaining to race and racial hygiene. Like many of his contemporaries he was interested in phrenology and in researching the hereditary defects of adults and children.[28] In 1930, for example, he published a racial anthropological study about the role of the temporal bone of the American Indians.[29]

For Leo Alexander the work of his father always remained the foremost point of reference in his life. In 1954 he recalled that one of the 'strongest, unconscious motives for becoming a physician was the strong bond of identification with my father, which I am sure in the long run tipped the scales of my occupational choice in medicine's favour'.[30] Alexander greatly admired and in many ways idealised his father. At the time of his death, Gustav had published approximately 220 academic articles, a record of publications that would both challenge and haunt Alexander. Throughout his life he attempted to escape the long shadow cast by his father.[31] When Alexander died in 1985 he had published more than 280 scientific papers and had given hundreds of public lectures.[32] He once said of his father:

> My father was one of those successful and happy physicians to whom doctoring was the essence of supreme satisfaction and who had the happy capacity to transmit his enthusiasm to others. It is therefore no accident that two of his three sons and one of his two daughters became physicians. The other daughter married a physician.[33]

Art, literature and old clocks were particularly close to Gustav's heart. Over the years he bought a great number of paintings from Viennese and foreign artists, some of whom he met in his capacity as their doctor.[34] The walls of the family's spacious flat, located at Skodagasse 15, in a wealthy district close to the centre of town, were covered with works of art, sometimes up to the ceiling. Old black-and-white photographs show its rooms and corridors, which were filled with sculptures and expensive furniture. Still-lifes and gold-framed portraits hang on the walls of the rooms in which Gustav conducted his private medical practice.[35] Such images convey much about this educated bourgeois family, whose desire for art and literature was an integral part of its cultural and social identity. Members of the family saw education and social representation as a precondition for cultural and national assimilation.

The Alexanders' home was a place in which Jewish intellectuals, doctors and artists could socialise, and at the same time receive professional advice and medical treatment. Artists and musicians such as Gustav Mahler visited Gustav Alexander, who was known as one of the most respected ear, nose and throat (ENT) specialists in Vienna. Sigmund Freud and the writer Arthur Schnitzler were also among the regular guests and patients of Alexander's father.[36] This extraordinary community of scientists and artists first introduced the young Alexander to intellectual debates about medicine and philosophy. On occasional Sundays, the Alexanders hosted lavish lunches for dozens of people, most of them well-known members of Viennese society.

Sometimes Gustav invited his friends and colleagues from the clinic to their holiday resort in the wealthy suburb of Baden. There the group would spend the weekend, enjoying chamber concerts and literary debate. The house had an expansive lawn decorated with live peacocks, evidence that it must have been quite an extravagant place. The Alexanders enjoyed a privileged lifestyle with much travelling, social networking and entertainment.[37]

Of course, most of the discussions centred on the latest developments in medical science. Gustav appears to have been an early advocate of psychoanalysis, and was especially impressed by men like Paul Federn, a Freud disciple who had a considerable success as a practising psychotherapist. On Sunday mornings, the two men occasionally met at one of the modern art exhibitions at the 'Secession', a fashionable place where the cultured elite of Vienna took in the latest political and social gossip. Here they would engage in lengthy discussions about the value of psychoanalysis. Through these discussions, the young and impressionable Alexander was able to familiarise himself with the basic elements of cutting-edge medical discourses. These informal intellectual debates stimulated his lifelong interest in the workings of the brain.

Yet, in general, the education of the children was governed by iron rules. Alexander's father is known to have been authoritarian and often insensitive. He demanded hard work and good performance from his five children in whatever they undertook. During the family's formal Sunday dinners, he questioned the children about what they had learned at school in the past week. He is said to have told them: 'I work in the clinic, you work in the school, and I never want to hear any complaints. You must do what you must do.'[38] Throughout the week the children did not see much of their parents, only on weekends. 'They had to behave in a certain way', Alexander's daughter Cecily recalled, 'they had to do very well in school, they had maids, nannies and people like that.'[39] It was expected that each of the children would learn to play a musical instrument such as the piano or cello. Occasionally, when the family entertained guests, Alexander and his siblings were asked to perform. By looking at the way in which Alexander later brought up his own children we can get a fairly good idea about his own education and upbringing:

> He patterned family life on what he remembered of his own life, of his upbringing, which was much more formal than by American standards. Children should be seen and not heard and well behaved. And when they entertained we would be introduced and shake hands and have good manners, and if we were asked to do something, to play the piano or do a little concert for the guests, we were expected to do that.[40]

Gustav Alexander's children were instructed in foreign languages and cultures, and were taught to ride. Alexander learned French, English and

Italian as an adolescent, and studied Latin and Greek in high school. In 1922, at the age of seventeen, Alexander travelled with a friend to Poland to learn about the country's culture and architecture.[41] Whereas the values of education and assimilation dominated Alexander's child-hood, religion seems to have played an almost negligible role, with a few exceptions. Alexander is said to have had a bar mitzvah ceremony at the age of thirteen to mark the point at which he, as a Jewish adolescent, was obliged to follow the Jewish Law.[42] This also meant that he had to learn to read Hebrew.

Alexander's upbringing allowed him to develop a keen interest in the history of ancient societies and monuments. Between the ages of ten and fourteen he dreamed of becoming a historian of antique civilisations, a passion that he further developed during an extended stay in China in the 1930s. His love and talent for meticulous detective work gave Alexander an extra edge not only in his work as a scientist, but also as a war crimes inves-tigator: 'The fascination of tracing and revealing hidden facts has remained one of the motivations of my scientific interests and has added motivation and satisfaction to my work with Army Medical Intelligence and the Office of the Chief of Counsel for War Crimes at Nurnberg [*sic*] after the Second World War.'[43] At the age of fifteen Alexander seems to have toyed with the idea of becoming a doctor. On Sunday mornings he was permitted to accompany his father on his informal rounds of the hospital wards:

> Afterwards we used to go for walks in the country, or to museums or exhibits of art, natural history or anthropology. It was on these Sunday mornings that I became increasingly impressed with and interested in the creative challenge of saving life and re-creating the health of living human beings, as compared to the more static creative accomplishments exhibited in the museums and galleries.[44]

For Alexander these mornings were an 'unbelievable thrill', particularly when his father would tell him about the 'intricate examination and reasoning that had to precede therapeutic action'.[45] These mornings left him with nothing less than a romantic desire to save human lives, to heal, and to see patients restored to full health. This captivated him. Alexander began to realise that doctors needed to have a 'creative capacity'. They were not pen-pushers, but stood at the crossroads between life and death, like gods and priests rolled into one.

While Alexander's mother seems to have run the household most of the time, she too was subordinate to the autocratic rule of her husband, and apparently discontinued her philosophical studies as a result. Later, in the 1920s, she was often ill, suffering from diabetes and occasional depression. Such a grand-bourgeois household demanded the presence of servants who helped with the children's education and the day-to-day management of the estate. The children's loyal nanny Trudl, their female cook Marianne, and the concierge Toni, made sure that all instructions were executed exactly according to the father's wish.[46] He wanted them to be well fed, properly dressed, clean, and well behaved, mirror images of young, bourgeois adults who represented a prosperous and wealthy family.

But the First World War and subsequent inflation also affected the upper-middle classes. Many lost most of their capital and savings. Apparently Gisela Alexander lost so much of her fortune during and after the Great War that she had to sell some of her property in the Ukraine. To preserve their bourgeois lifestyle and finance the children's university studies, she turned to the stock market and began speculating, but without success. Things worsened when the family of one of Gustav's former patients, who had been hospitalised and declared insane, began to blackmail the Alexander family.[47] Threatening to ruin their reputation, Gisela Alexander saw no alternative but to meet their financial demands for years, whilst hiding her secret from everyone except her twelve-year-old daughter Anne. Ten years later, in 1932, the same patient murdered Gustav Alexander in cold blood in the middle of Vienna.[48] It is possible that the flow of payments had dried up during the depression. The tragedy suddenly left a large family without a father and a husband. As the eldest of five children, Leo was expected to follow the same path as his father. He was expected to take responsibility for his younger brothers and sisters, and become a respected and successful physician. The first twenty-five years of Alexander's life closely mirrored the life of the father whose shadow continued to determine his career path long thereafter.

Becoming a doctor

Alexander started his professional life at a time when the national economies of Austria and Germany were in turmoil, hit by hyperinflation, mass unemployment and the humiliation of national defeat. The countries witnessed a rapid increase in infectious diseases caused by a lack of sanitation in over-populated and largely impoverished urban areas. The authorities desperately needed to accommodate the thousands of war veterans pouring into the city, many of whom were suffering from battle wounds and mental exhaustion. Shell-shocked soldiers and those returning from the trenches, the so-called 'war-neurotics', exhibited a whole range of new psychotic phenomena, which opened up an entirely new field of medical study. Within the medical profession ideas about racial hygiene and eugenics were becoming increasingly popular, not just in the field of research, but also as part of the medical curriculum. As a result, some professors argued that the mentally and physically handicapped should be sterilised, prohibited from marrying, and forced to undergo abortions. Rising numbers of the mentally ill in state-funded institutions prompted calls for reform in the asylum system and encouraged the exploration of innovative therapeutic methods. Within the context of controversial debates about the organic and psychological origins of mental diseases, Alexander's interest in neurology and psychiatry stood him in good stead for a fast-track career as a medical scientist.

In 1923 he passed his *Abitur* (A-levels) at the Piaristengymnasium in Vienna. We know little about his overall performance, but evidence suggests that he probably ranked in the top half of his class, not brilliant but certainly hard-working and ambitious. Upon entering Vienna's Medical School, Alexander found his passion in the fields of psychology and psychiatry: 'The fact that people could be suffering and ill in spite of apparently healthy physique impressed me as a particular challenge to medicine because of the apparent paradox implied', he once remarked.[49] He wanted to find out 'how the mind and/or the brain worked within the fabric of human health and disease'.[50] Jumping ahead of the medical curriculum, Alexander attended lectures by the social hygienist Julius von Wagner-Jauregg and the psychoanalyst Paul Schilder. In the 1920s doctors saw many cases of encephalitis epidemica, which suggested that a disease of the brain could simultaneously affect both the mind and the body. Neuropsychiatry, so it seems, was regarded as an innovative, modern scientific discipline that attracted young researchers who were eager to link the latest discoveries in heredity and infectious diseases with wider demographic and sociological developments.

At the age of twenty-one Alexander began to publish in academic journals such as the *Anatomischer Anzeiger*, the *Deutsche Zeitschrift für Nervenheilkunde* or in the *Klinische Wochenschrift*.[51] In 1926 Alexander published his first academic article about the morphology of the cerebellum, work that he had carried out as a medical student at Marburg's neurological institute.[52] His research fit the approach of eugenically minded experts who wanted to locate the hereditary and organic causes of specific mental diseases, some of which Alexander linked to 'constitutional inferiority'.[53] Further research into hereditary defects and evolutionary biology paved the way for a fellowship award by the Austrian Ministry for Public Health to work at the Zoological Station in Naples, Italy.[54] Issues related to the evolution of the brain, both in man and animals, continued to fascinate Alexander throughout his life. The interdisciplinary nature of his work helped him build a network of contacts both within and outside Europe. In 1928 he received his first opportunity to study in Germany; he was invited to spend a semester at Oskar Vogt's prestigious Kaiser Wilhelm Institute (KWI) for Brain Research in Berlin.[55] The work at the KWI was an important step in Alexander's quest to qualify for a professorship, preferably at a German university. It also gave him contact with medical scientists like the neuropathologist Julius Hallervorden, who was involved in the 'euthanasia' programme he investigated after the war.[56] These connections to German

Plate 1   Leo Alexander as a young man.

scientists help explain why Alexander's relationship with the German medical establishment remained ambiguous throughout his life. He knew that he himself had once been part of this community.

In 1929 Alexander moved to Frankfurt am Main to begin an internship at the Municipal and University Clinic for the Emotionally Disturbed and Mentally Ill, headed by Karl Kleist, a distinguished professor of brain pathology.[57] Upon his arrival, Alexander wasted no time in competing for attention and responsibility in an environment that was dominated by young and ambitious doctors.[58] Many of his colleagues were Jewish, though not all, and some of the latter silently approved of the right-wing and *völkisch* ideas that permeated the universities of Weimar Germany at the end of the 1920s. When one of his colleagues, Eduard Beck, fell ill unexpectedly, Alexander was asked to oversee an entire ward. Although he was working long hours and well into the night, he used every spare moment to report back to his father about his activities, whether, for example, he had performed lumbar punctures or administered salvarsan injections to patients suffering from syphilis.[59] Kleist and the senior staff of the clinic were soon impressed by Alexander's work ethic and skill in handling two wards single-handedly. For Alexander it was only a matter of time before he would complete his *Habilitation*, another necessary hurdle on the road to a professorship. Everything was going according to plan.

To view Alexander as a 'control-freak' would be an understatement. Every inch of his career, every move that could possibly benefit or harm his professional reputation, every contact and potential friction, was meticulously monitored and weighed against his central goal – to become a medical scientist of the stature of his father. Three factors shaped his outlook in these years. For Alexander it was essential that the reputation of his father could not be construed to his disadvantage. In other words, he wanted to be sure that no one could have reason to believe that his father had paved the way for him. Alexander made skilful but judicious use of the family's contacts; it was important to him to earn his spurs as an independent medical scientist in his own right, one who 'deserved' his reputation through education and hard work.[60] Secondly, he avoided all activities that could alienate his host-country or produce unnecessary tensions. Whether it was his choice of music, art or literature, nothing was left to chance in his attempt to rise within the German scientific community. When, in 1929, his father suggested that he should travel to America, Alexander responded: 'Dear Papa, I believe that this is not very opportune in view of the current attitude of the Germans.'[61] At a time when Germany was dealing with massive reparation payments and economic depression, nothing was worse than being perceived as friendly to Anglo-American interests. And finally, there was another factor that always remained in the back of his mind. He knew that he had to assimilate into the German cultural context, avoid potential encounters with anti-Semitism, and make friends with those who showed a certain appreciation for *völkisch* and ultra-nationalist ideas. Yet anti-Semitic outbursts frequently left him with a sense of insecurity, not so much because of his strong religious identity, but because of their potential effect on his medical career. From early on Alexander developed a fine sense for professional politics.

After the construction of a new building complex by the Weimar Bauhaus architect Martin Elsässer, a facility in which the relaxing appeal of spacious gardens was combined with the latest therapeutic techniques, the Frankfurt clinic became internationally renowned for its research and teaching in the field of neuropathology and psychiatry. A special film studio, equipped with slow-motion facilities and single-frame projectors, together with state-of-the-art bacteriological laboratories, conveyed a sense of modernity and the belief in the constant progress of medical science.[62] Together with his Jewish colleague Ernst Herz, who was in charge of the film studio, Alexander developed an interest in film. In 1931 he presented his first medical film at an annual conference of the south-west German psychiatrists.[63]

Yet life in Frankfurt was not entirely dominated by research and clinical practice. Sometimes in the evenings, Alexander joined the Kleist family for dinner and demonstrated his musical talent on the piano. Kleist's daughters remembered him as a tall, large man who was also a gifted musician.[64] Alexander was a man who loved life; he enjoyed going to the cinema or to the latest theatre performances with one of his girlfriends, and later with his fiancée, Gisela Preitz.[65] His colleagues were also of great importance to him. His network of colleagues gave him crucial advice and moral support when the political storm gathering over Germany scattered them all over the world. Among his closest colleagues, most of them Jewish, were Alice Rosenstein, Hans Strauss, Ernst Herz and Arnold Merzbach. After 1933 all of them emigrated. Some fled to Holland or Hungary, but most of them, like Alexander, eventually emigrated to the United States.

Frankfurt am Main was Alexander's first intellectual home. Unlike other places, research and teaching were unified and co-ordinated by Kleist, a man whose mission was to improve the living conditions of his patients. He was the unchallenged authority of the clinic, a benevolent patriarch, completely devoted to his field. As an advocate for social and economic reform in the Weimar asylum system he promoted the development of outpatient provisions and occupational therapy.[66] Yet debate at the clinic also centred on ideas regarding eugenics and racial hygiene, concepts that strongly influenced Alexander's medical thinking at the beginning of the 1930s.

Eugenics

Aspects of eugenics held a certain appeal for young physicians, especially after the first university chairs were established. The founding of the

Kaiser Wilhelm Institute for Anthropology, Human Heredity and Eugenics in 1927 gave the German eugenics movement a respectable institutional base.[67] Despite drastic cuts in the German health system, triggered by the prevailing economic crisis, the Frankfurt clinic remained a model institution, a modern asylum, where reform psychiatry achieved a symbiosis with research into the hereditary and organic causes of mental diseases. Outpatient facilities and new somatic therapies were as much a part of this belief system as was the understanding that voluntary sterilisation and marriage control of the handicapped were necessary preconditions for a state-interventionist health policy.[68]

For Alexander, the genealogical study of families with hereditary and mental diseases and the analysis of brain specimens of former patients were integral components of his work. In order to foster relations between the Frankfurt clinic and the regional asylums of the Hesse-Nassau district, he initiated a large-scale demographic project to study the genealogy of schizophrenic patients in a Nassau village over an extended period of time.[69] During one research trip he found a family with over 100 living members, many of whom suffered from mental illnesses and had been institutionalised in one of the regional asylums. Building on work by racial hygienists such as Ernst Rüdin and his team of eugenic demographers in Munich,[70] these hereditary-genealogical studies enhanced Alexander's reputation and established new links to asylums in Hadamar, Eichberg and Herborn. Significantly, all of these institutions later became involved in the killing of tens of thousands of handicapped patients in the Nazi 'euthanasia' programme. After the war Alexander's first-hand knowledge of the German health system played an important role in his investigation of medical atrocities.

It is still unclear whether, or to what extent, Alexander shared his German colleagues' view of racial hygiene and medical ethics. Like many of the Nazi doctors, Alexander was trained in the 1920s by German professors whose utilitarian and paternalistic belief systems led them to regard patients as little more than objects of scientific curiosity and research. It is almost certain that Alexander failed to obtain consent from the members of the Nassau family who formed the basis of his schizophrenia research study. And not unlike Julius Hallervorden, whom he later interrogated about his involvement in the 'euthanasia' programme, Alexander made sure that he could use as many brains and body parts as possible in his neuropathological studies.[71]

However, to suggest that Alexander's medical ethics were also those of the Nazi doctors would be going too far. Medical ethics are not static; they are always subject to historical change. In the same way that science is a dynamic concept, capable of accommodating the transplantation and transmission of knowledge into different national and cultural contexts, medical ethics can be understood and practised differently in various institutional and cultural environments. In Alexander's case the process of acculturation into the Anglo-American scientific community, compounded by the experience of forced emigration, greatly influenced his attitude towards German medical research practices, as well as racial hygiene and eugenics. Alexander and some of the Nazi physicians probably underwent a similar socialisation process and received similar medical training. Before 1933 they may even have held similar ideas with respect to eugenics. This was certainly not the case, however, after Hitler came to power and began implementing his radical political ideas in German society.

The process of emigrating, first to China in 1933 and then to the United States, had a defining impact on Alexander's life and character, not only on his political consciousness and religious identity, but also on his view of medical ethics and eugenics. Even if answered inconclusively, the issue highlights some of the inherent tensions and ambiguities in Alexander's personality after the war. Following the unconditional surrender of Germany in 1945, he was asked to investigate the research practices of scientists whose basic understanding of the role of medicine in society was originally grounded in the same scientific and moral belief system as his own.

Alexander never completed his eugenics research. On 20 January 1933, eleven days before Hitler came to power, he concluded his second and last report on his research activities in the Hesse-Nassau region. Not without a degree of pride he told the authorities: 'On 1 February of this year I will start my eight month *scientific holiday* [emphasis added]. I have accepted the invitation to go for half a year to Beijing Union Medical College in Beijing (China) as an honorary lecturer in neurology and psychiatry.'[72] As a postscript he added: 'On 1 October 1933 I will resume my work at the regional cure and nursing homes.' It was a promise he would not and could not keep.

3
The Émigré

A scientific holiday

On 10 February 1933 Leo Alexander boarded the English steamer *Ranpura* in Marseilles for a month-long cruise to the Far East. It was the beginning of what was to be a six-month adventure trip, a 'scientific holiday'. Determined to document every step of the journey, Alexander took hundreds of photographs, many – if not most – of himself. Some photographs show him happily swimming in the pool on the ship's upper deck or standing by the railings; others show him dressed for evening dinner in a neatly ironed white shirt and tie.[1] He was clearly a proud man. Already anticipating his return to Germany, Alexander was preparing to apply for a suitable academic post, preferably a professorship at a German university, in Berlin or Frankfurt am Main, and begin to settle down with a woman he fancied, have children, and become a respected medical scientist not unlike his father. Yet the trip to China proved to be a watershed in Alexander's life.

In August 1932 Richard S. Lyman, newly appointed associate professor of neuropsychiatry at Peiping Union Medical College (PUMC) in Beijing, offered Alexander a six-month lectureship in China.[2] The offer entailed overseeing a small neuropathological laboratory at PUMC and thus promised the opportunity of gaining clinical experience with Chinese mental patients.[3] After colleagues assured him that the Rockefeller-funded medical college was one of the best in China, Alexander accepted the offer.[4] On 29 October Roger S. Greene, acting director of PUMC and Vice-President of the Rockefeller Foundation (RF) for the Far East, appointed Alexander as an 'Honorary Lecturer in Neurology and Psychiatry' for a period of approximately five months.[5]

Alexander knew that the visit to China was likely to enhance his professional career. At the same time, however, his decision to leave Europe was motivated by reasons of a much more personal nature. On 12 April 1932, Gustav Alexander was shot and killed by a former patient near the family's apartment.[6] The disturbed man, the same patient who had previously

Plate 2 Leo Alexander standing by the railings on board the English steamer *Ranpura*, travelling to Beijing, China, to begin a six-month 'scientific holiday'. He would not be able to return to Germany for another twelve years.

Plate 3 'The good ship Ranpura'.

blackmailed the family, apparently sought revenge from his former physician. The callous murder prompted widespread rumours that Gustav Alexander had somehow made a mistake in the patient's treatment. The damage to the family's reputation was considerable, and there was even talk of Alexander having to return from Frankfurt to Vienna. Alexander, however, kept a low profile and continued with his research. Six months later tragedy struck the family once again. This time his grief-stricken mother died after a prolonged illness. The Rockefeller Fellowship gave him an attractive opportunity to distance himself from family responsibilities, especially those involving the care of his relatively young siblings. After the deaths of Gustav and Gisela Alexander the financial situation of the family also worsened considerably.[7] To the outside world the trip to China looked like a career move; for Alexander it was also a flight from home to a place that he believed would be 'exotic and exciting'.[8]

In 1921 Rockefeller medicine was brought to Beijing. The Rockefeller Foundation established the PUMC, a complex of about twenty buildings with green-tiled Chinese roofs, located in the vicinity of the Forbidden City. With its introduction came an entire culture, as defined by John D. Rockefeller, Jr., only son of the oil tycoon, and the trustee of the Foundation. This culture included Western medical education and Christian missionary work, and the forging of business relations on the Asian continent.[9] Although the Rockefeller Foundation stressed intellectual co-operation and research, some members of the organisation were driven by the fear of the poor Chinese immigrating to America. Rockefeller, Jr., for one, was interested in the role of race and wanted to initiate eugenic research at the PUMC in order to draw biological comparisons between the Chinese and Westerners.[10] The PUMC became the centre of the Foundation's work in Asia, an 'American transplant' established to promote Western scientific medicine and commerce. The institution was a pioneer in the exchange of ideas and research, yet one that would also leave a legacy of cultural tensions.

At the PUMC the Chinese students were carefully selected from the upper echelons of society and were instructed in the English language. The standard of education was meant to be as high 'as can be found anywhere in Europe or America'. Established without regard to the socio-political and economic conditions of the host country, the PUMC became the model institution for Western medicine in China. It reflected the philosophy of the Foundation, as summarised by Bullock: 'educate at the top and the rest will take care of itself'.[11] Since 1914 Roger S. Green had acted as the Beijing middleman between the PUMC, the Rockefeller Foundation and the Chinese Medical Board (CMB). The years from 1927 to 1935 marked a period of intense administrative change in which authority was transferred from New York to Beijing. At the time of Alexander's arrival, the PUMC was going through one of its most critical institutional crises.

Plate 4 Alexander's first impressions of Peiping Union Medical College, Beijing, China, March 1933.

Plate 5 The buildings of Peiping Union Medical College, Beijing, China, March 1933.

Plans to expand the neurological unit at PUMC had been discussed since the late 1920s, and were finally realised with Lyman's appointment in May 1932.[12] Born in 1891, Lyman was educated at Yale and studied medicine at Johns Hopkins University. As an American elite scientist, one who had trained in psychiatry under Adolf Meyer, Lyman undertook the standard study tour of European capitals in the mid-1920s. Upon returning to America, he was appointed Associate Professor of Medicine at the University of Rochester. In 1930 he moved to Leningrad to work in Pavlov's laboratory, and then travelled to Munich to work with Walther Spielmeyer. Around this time he probably became acquainted with Alexander.[13]

For the PUMC Alexander was an 'extra gift', a highly qualified Austrian-German scholar who came at no expense to the college. Officially the college was told that 'through certain fortunate circumstances' Alexander could visit Beijing 'without any cost to the college either for salary or travelling expenses'.[14] The Rockefeller Foundation was informed that his expenses would be covered by 'private sources'.[15] As it turned out, it was Lyman who financed Alexander's entire stay and fellowship through private funds.[16] The use of private resources became necessary after Lyman realised that the PUMC had no fully equipped hospital ward for neurological patients. Apart from a small ward with a total of nine beds, a neuropathological laboratory, and an outpatient clinic, Lyman presided over an almost non-existent staff. The expansion of personnel was, therefore, one of his foremost priorities.[17] Lyman's other main objective was the improvement of sanitary conditions. By European standards – the basis on which PUMC was founded – the neurological department was modest at best, and substandard at worst. There was more evidence of a romantic notion of oriental medicine than actual work on the ground. Alexander's own cultural understanding of the country and its customs was uninformed and partly prejudiced towards the Chinese people. Convinced of the apparent superiority of Western scientific medicine, Alexander hoped that his work would contribute to comparative 'racial psychiatry' and eugenics.[18]

Elation and foreboding

Alexander arrived in Shanghai on 13 March 1933. From there, he took the steamer *Shengking* to Tientsin, not far from Beijing, where he was greeted by Lyman and his wife. Moments later, Alexander was rushed to the court of the British Consul General, where he was asked to determine the mental state of a British official who had murdered his Chinese wife.[19] He advised the authorities not to imprison the man, but to transfer him to the PUMC for a period of observation. Barely a day in China, Alexander was successfully promoting the new department of neurology at a medical college in a city he had yet to see. Alexander clearly appreciated the importance of maintaining good relations with the authorities. He first rented a small house in Tientsin, close to the south-east corner of the Tataren wall, but for someone accustomed to a bourgeois lifestyle the house proved too modest. After a week he moved into the Grand Hotel, which he felt was more in keeping with his social status.[20]

The practice of psychiatry in China was unlike anything Alexander had experienced in Europe. In the early 1930s, Western psychiatry had yet to be established as a scientific discipline in Chinese medical institutions. People regarded as a 'public nuisance or danger to others' or 'offenders in the eyes of the police' were segregated and confined in asylums in Shanghai, Nanking, Canton and Beijing.[21] Others were attended by Chinese physicians who, depending on local customs, favoured treatments involving acupuncture, traditional Chinese medicine, hypnosis, exorcism or shock therapy. Chinese doctors could draw upon a rich body of language to describe mental conditions as well as those suffering from them: for example, a person could experience *hu-tu* (confusion), *fa-feng* (excitement), and *men-ch'i* (worried depression), and it was possible to speak of a *feng-jen* (insane person).[22] Western psychiatrists soon realised that Chinese treatments carefully considered the patient's situation within the context of a larger social group. The family played a central role in caring for those suffering from mental disorders. Moreover, the mentally ill could turn to charitable organisations such as guilds and public health offices, Christian missionary institutions, and places of worship, such as Buddhist temples. In contrast, the Chinese viewed Western psychiatry and its institutions with great scepticism. When asked to choose, most patients preferred Chinese psychiatrists.

Such cultural differences were of little concern to Alexander. He saw himself at the cutting-edge of Western medical research, albeit in a foreign culture. He was an explorer of the human brain, ready to discover new and uncharted territory. Alexander's early correspondence to colleagues in Europe is filled with enthusiasm, a man pleased with his own achievements. His every impression, it seems, was worth being communicated to Europe, not only to keep friends informed, but also to describe his work environment and elaborate schedule.[23] 'We do see very many war injuries ... spinal cord injuries and lots of head injuries', he wrote to Kleist in March 1933. At the same time Alexander had just been put in charge of the neurological department of the relief hospitals where soldiers returning from the Chinese–Manchurian battlefields were given first aid.[24] In the course of his work Alexander encountered neurological symptoms that were entirely new to him.[25] Since Chinese writing consists of symbols, the effects of head injuries and memory loss were entirely different from those observed in the Western linguistic tradition. All Chinese symbols refer directly to objects and do not evoke any phonetic signal. This meant that reading without actually understanding the complete sense of the word or without remembering the complete word was impossible for head-wounded Chinese soldiers.[26] For Alexander, this phenomenon was interesting and complex. Aside from such observations, however, the war between China and Manchuria, later Manchuko, had little effect upon the lives of the scientific elite at PUMC. Occasionally there were troop movements from the Chinese and the Japanese armies through the city, but, according to Alexander, 'one doesn't notice the war'.[27]

Unlike Shanghai, where segregation policies hampered social interaction, Beijing was a cosmopolitan city with a bustling intellectual and cultural milieu. As a member of PUMC and as a Westerner, Alexander quickly gained entrée into the mostly British and German expatriate community whose cocktail parties brought him entertainment and amusement. Academically and socially he was part of Beijing's high society, in which Westerners mingled freely with the Chinese elite.[28] On weekends he often travelled to nearby palaces and temples or visited the Great Wall in the north of Nankau.[29] Like many visitors to Beijing in the 1930s, Alexander became an amateur collector of Chinese art.[30] The sculptures and artefacts still in possession of the Alexander family continue to bear witness to his passion for Chinese culture. Along with his flatmate, Arthur P. Black, professor of medicine and one of his father's former colleagues, he occasionally conducted chamber concerts, mostly Beethoven's violin sonatas. It kept his love of German music and culture alive.[31]

Yet reports and rumours about the new German government were not encouraging. At first newspapers reported that the Nazis had unleashed a wave of police terror against Jews, social democrats and communists. They were discriminated against, intimidated and held in 'protective custody' (*Schutzhaft*) in one of the many new prisons of the secret police (*Gestapo*). There they were generally beaten and terrorised or sometimes tortured or shot in cold blood. The country saw a wave of anti-Semitism and street violence of previously unknown proportions. Much of it was targeted against 'asocials', homosexuals, communists, gypsies and Jews. Nazi propagandists were frantically masterminding a nationwide boycott of Jewish businesses, doctors and other professionals. This was followed by additional discriminatory measures including the introduction of the 'Law for the Restoration of the Professional Civil Service' in April 1933, which dismissed all political opponents and 'non-Aryans' from their previous positions as civil servants. The law also applied to Alexander. Only those who had fought in the First World War were exempt from the law. Alexander was not.

In May 1933 the Jewish neurologist Arnold Merzbach told Alexander that all of the Jewish doctors at the Frankfurt clinic had been dismissed and that all personal and professional links to Kleist's institution had been severed. Among those who had lost their jobs were the psychiatrists Hans Strauss, Ernst Herz and Alice Rosenstein, not to mention Merzbach himself. 'We all are without hope. Our very existences are falling apart

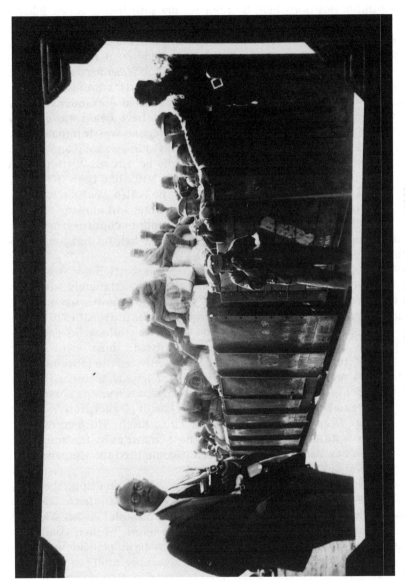

Plate 6   Leo Alexander and soldiers from the Chinese–Manchurian war, 1933.

[*gehen kaputt*], our youth has no hope in our homeland whatsoever', he told Alexander.[32] Those feigning ignorance about this government-led discrimination were the quiet beneficiaries; many showed no hesitation in assuming positions held by their former Jewish colleagues. Eduard Beck, one of Alexander's peers, was among them. As a supporter of Nazi racial policy he began lecturing at the SA Führer school in the Hesse-Nassau region and became a supporting member of the SS.[33] In the spring of 1933 he was promoted to 'head doctor' (*Oberarzt*), the position formerly held by his Jewish colleague Hans Strauss, who was forced to emigrate to the United States. In July Beck assured Alexander that any 'news of atrocities' (*Greulnachrichten*) he may have heard was entirely fabricated and untrue.[34] By this time the regime was internationally renowned for its ruthless and criminal behaviour, and someone who so vigorously defended its legality could hardly be trusted. Writing to his brother Alfred, Alexander noted that Beck's letter had been 'strikingly cold and I have the strong impression that he is also *gleichgeschaltet* [of the same mind]. This is how things change, times and humans.'[35] Many Jews decided to emigrate to neighbouring European countries, or to Asia and America. Others, mostly the elderly, stayed behind and sometimes committed suicide in total despair.

Nazi pressure on the Frankfurt clinic to 'cleanse' itself and dismiss its 'non-Aryan' staff was exceedingly – even disproportionately – high, as can be seen from nationwide statistics. Of the 614 university teachers who had been dismissed by 1934, members of the universities of Berlin, Frankfurt, and Breslau accounted for 40 per cent alone. In Frankfurt sixty-nine university teachers were dismissed; most went on to emigrate.[36] Indeed, the anti-Semitic and openly hostile attitude of the authorities made it increasingly difficult for Jewish doctors to earn a living under greatly restricted and often dangerous working conditions. In response to persecution, more than 300 Jewish physicians were forced to emigrate from Frankfurt during the Third Reich. Thirteen of them were later captured and killed in their host countries by the advancing German armies. Another fourteen doctors committed suicide in order to escape arrest or deportation.[37]

Shortly before Alexander moved into his new house in Beijing the previous owner, a German-Jewish scientist, cancelled the contract. The Nazi takeover had made his return to Germany impossible. Jewish scientists were suddenly stranded in China, unable to return to their country of origin and without sufficient contacts to establish permanent careers there.[38] Slowly, but unmistakably, the world was beginning to turn on its head. Whereas Jewish scientists wanted to return from China to Germany, but could not, dozens and later hundreds of Jewish scientists wanted to emigrate from Germany to China, but could not, at least not very easily. A sense of anxiety was beginning to permeate Alexander's correspondence. In

May 1933 the family's lawyer, Maximilian Friedmann, warned Alexander about the political developments in Germany:

> Since you have left Europe there have been great changes in the society; I do not know the angle from which newspapers at hand in China report about the current events. It is extremely difficult to report, especially since we in Vienna do not yet know precisely what the situation is in Germany and how the future fate of Austria will turn out. Even assuming ... that a lot of news about Germany is exaggerated, it is for certain under cool and rational consideration that for our professions especially, for intellectuals in somehow prominent positions, and also for university academics, lawyers, well-known doctors, teachers etc. the prospects in Germany are most unfavourable.[39]

Although the situation in China looked increasingly unstable, Friedmann advised Alexander not to return to Germany but to establish a career in China or America. In his opinion there was 'little room for the middle-European intelligentsia in the middle of Europe'.[40] The 'numerical advance of National Socialism', Friedmann explained, would bring about similar conditions in Austria sooner rather than later. As a trusted family friend, Friedmann's assessment of the situation mattered greatly to Alexander. It was a powerful warning that Jewish medical scientists no longer had any prospects in Germany, nor indeed in Austria, given that the political situation of that country was moving in a similar direction.

The rest of Alexander's family concurred with Friedmann. 'The fact is', Alfred told Alexander, 'that the Hitler regime has removed all Jews in some exposed or state positions, and that therefore the situation frequently resembles one of pogroms, especially during the orchestrated "days of boycott" against Jewish entrepreneurs.'[41] Jewish lawyers were prohibited to appear in court, Jewish doctors were prevented from practising, and all Jews had been removed from the clinics. If Nazism triumphed in Austria, he warned, it would be foolish to return. Even the well-known surgeon Ferdinand Sauerbruch had been forced to move to Zürich, and Alfred himself thought of emigrating to Italy. Alexander's eighty-five-year-old grandmother, Caecily, described the prospects in Germany, a country she had adored all her life, as 'horrible', and had little hope that the situation would change. For Robert Alexander, his elderly uncle, German culture had 'succumbed to the swastika'.[42] Yet the central question for friends and colleagues was whether Alexander would return to Germany, especially after a Viennese newspaper had printed a flattering account of the young scholar.[43] Otto Marburg, a friend in Vienna, believed that Alexander should 'thank God' for being in a 'relatively bearable situation'.[44] Alfred agreed with his assessment: 'Everyone thinks that it is great luck that you are currently in China, where you seem to have the possibility of easily finding yourself a permanent position in America.'[45] In his own mind, however, Alexander hoped that things would sort themselves out and that he could return to Germany. When the news arrived that he could not, his shock was profound.

Shock and disillusionment

On 10 July 1933 at approximately 11.30 p.m., an officer from the Chinese Government Radio Service received a short radiogram from Frankfurt, which he was ordered to deliver quickly and directly to 'LC Alexander Medical' in Beijing. The text comprised only seven words: 'Advise continued employment Beijing. Letter follows. Kleist.'[46] During and after the war these words had an almost prophetic meaning for Alexander, who believed that the radiogram had saved his life.[47] 'Leo said many times that that telegram saved his life', his daughter recalled. 'He said that it was a great disappointment ... He felt that he was safe. He knew that there were things going on in Germany, but he felt he was above all of that, he was a physician and well connected and so on, that he would be safe.'[48] Kleist's cryptic warning made it impossible for him to return to Germany, even if he wanted to. Finding himself a permanent position in China, emigrating to a different country in Europe, or moving to America were his only alternatives.

Kleist's follow-up letter reached Alexander at the beginning of August. Kleist made it plain that any return to Germany would be in vain, if not 'totally impossible'.[49] Alexander's case was 'twice as difficult'. He was not only 'non-Aryan' but also 'non-German'. 'You, as a Jew, if you have not served as a soldier in the First World War, cannot be state employed', he told Alexander.[50] He advised him to apply for an extension at PUMC and to make good use of his contacts in Beijing's Anglo-American scientific community, especially Richard Lyman and Roger Green, either of whom might be able to find him a post in the United States. There is no doubt that Kleist was fond of Alexander. As a well-educated, well-connected, serious researcher, he was ideally suited to the Frankfurt clinic. At times patronising, at other times warm and far-sighted, Kleist clearly wanted to give Alexander clear, direct and solid advice: 'My feelings for you, my wishes and my task, to continue to support you in your work, remain unchanged. I feel, however, obliged to ensure that you have no false hopes and instead lead you clearly onto another path.'[51] Kleist's letter came as a shock to Alexander, whose exceedingly high self-esteem had led him to clearly overestimate his 'market value'. Alexander was forced to realise that the world, particularly Britain and the United States, was suddenly flooded with highly trained German and European medical scientists, a situation that allowed universities and research institutions to pick and choose the best people for the lowest possible price.[52]

While the Jewish community in Germany was the target of government-sanctioned anti-Semitic diatribes and racial hatred, the German expatriate community in Beijing joined the crusade by directing unprecedented hostility towards Jews in their midst. For Alexander this meant further isolation in a foreign culture that he barely knew. He advised colleagues to exercise caution in coming to China. In some of the larger hospitals practically 'all Germans (and there are practically no Jews [in these hospitals]) are extraordinarily fierce anti-Semites. I therefore socialise very rarely with Germans.'[53] To disabuse members of Germany's Jewish medical community of their false illusions, Alexander compiled a small manual called 'Rules for Emigrating to China' which he distributed through his Frankfurt colleagues. It gave potential émigrés an overview of rules and regulations, provided information on finances, warned against common pitfalls, and listed useful contacts in China.[54] Cities in which it was relatively safe to establish a private medical practice were Shanghai, Nanking, Canton, Tientsin and Hankow. According to Alexander, Beijing was the last place in which Jews were advised to settle down. The Germans had made themselves 'unbelievably unpopular in the entire world and are regarded as real barbarians', he told his brother, 'and the peculiar thing is that compared to a British citizen or a good type of American, this is the social impression that they make upon others'.[55]

The experience of German anti-Semitism and Chinese militarism left Alexander with a bitter and distorted view of Chinese politics and culture. A country that taught visitors to 'endure the blows of fate with equanimity and looks in all situations for that which is valuable and important'[56] was now perceived as a war-stricken nation, filled with corruption and hypocrisy.[57] 'There is no country in which there is so much lying as in China', he told Alice Rosenstein, 'and where this is all right. It can bring one to despair, also in interacting with Chinese colleagues, who indulge in this country's malady with a masterly skill.'[58] The Chinese–Japanese conflict gave Alexander a welcome opportunity to vent his anger and frustration over his situation. It also became clear that the PUMC could not extend his contract indefinitely. He wanted to leave China. But that was easier said than done. By October 1933 none of his applications to American universities had been successful.[59] He was ready to accept any form of employment, whether in a state or private hospital, research institution or mental asylum, so long as it allowed him to emigrate to America. A sense of urgency began to appear in his writing. Now 'any doctor' who might have the 'odd idea to need a neurologist' was a potentially valuable contact. By 11 October 1933 Alexander was at the end of his tether: 'I find myself in a real mess', he told one of his American colleagues.[60]

And there was another pressing problem: women, particularly American women. Knowing that rumours travelled fast in the Anglo-American expatriate community, he did not want to risk losing his chance of emigrating by appearing to be the womaniser that he in fact was. He avoided being seen with women in American circles and limited his outings with one particular American woman for fear that any kind of gossip might jeopardise his chance for employment oversees. At the time Alexander led a relatively isolated life, which, in his view, was even somewhat monastic.[61] Alexander's keen sexual appetite and need for frequent affairs continued throughout his life, earning him the title of philanderer from friends, colleagues and relatives.[62]

Eventually Alexander fell into a deep depression. After years of meticulous control over his fortune, his life was suddenly disintegrating. Only few could imagine, he told a friend in Italy, how it felt to find himself 'suddenly sitting on his arse' after the start of a promising career.[63] He continued, 'The primitive brutality and unfairness of the events barely justifies any serious description: Jewish intellectuals are being expelled and imprisoned, but the money of the deceased James Loeb from New York is accepted by German scientific institutes with open arms.'[64] Yet Alexander conceded that he had not taken National Socialism seriously for a long time and that he had under-estimated its popular appeal and far-reaching consequences. The events in Germany left him with a sense of personal failure and great uncertainty about the future. The experience of having been 'ripped out' of the German medical community, and the hopelessness and professional humiliation that followed, seem to have remained suppressed until a decade later, when he was commissioned to investigate German medical war crimes. It allowed him a sense of retribution for some of the personal suffering he had endured.[65] The feelings of loss and frustration that he endured in China were clearly traumatic for Alexander. The longing for revenge became a reality, no matter how hard he tried to suppress these feelings after the war.

The crisis he endured in China awakened Alexander's sense of responsibility for the Jewish community and shaped the formation of his Jewish identity. 'Has the Jewish national sentiment increased in Germany under the outside pressure?', he asked his brother. 'I myself have experienced a small rise. It is interesting how such things always keep the Jews by the flagstaff, which they are just about to leave.'[66] Nazism made Alexander acutely aware of his Jewish roots. Although he had never been a practising Jew, nor would he ever become one in a strict sense, he was beginning to feel drawn to the idea of a Jewish people. This spiritual home was the only one left to him at the time. It was a particular bond; one that had grown from necessity and spiritual suffering rather than inner conviction or lifelong practice. For Alexander a 'scientific holiday' had turned into an uncertain journey, a life of permanent transience, rooted in multiple cultures, but also strangely disconnected and detached. By moving closer to his Jewish roots he may have tried to compensate for the sense of loss and loneliness that he was experiencing. After the war he told his daughter that 'he could never not be a Jew'.[67]

Despite this crisis, Alexander managed to continue with his research and publish a number of scientific papers, work that provided him with excellent credentials in America.[68] For most scholars emigration entailed both difficult personal adjustments and great professional challenges; they had to sever ties with home and family, and adapt to a new cultural and professional environment. Emigrating to America, Palestine or Britain, however, could also mean that young scientists would find better career opportunities than they had experienced in their native country, even under peaceful conditions. For some medical émigrés the experience of leaving home played a crucial role in defining their identity. As one Austrian psychologist put it: 'For me my Jewishness only became part of my identity because of Hitler.' This kind of experience explains Alexander's commitment to the Jewish cause and his critical attitude towards the German medical profession for nearly the rest of his life. At the same time it also made him appreciate the contacts he had established during his prolonged 'scientific holiday' in China. Alexander's mentor, Richard Lyman, had encouraged his interest in sociology and its use in psychiatry. 'This stood me in good stead on active Army duty overseas', he recalled in 1954, 'and in my studies of War Crimes and of the social psychological aspects of totalitarianism.'[69] The 'Chinese Connection', so it seems, allowed Alexander to acquire a unique type of expertise that was needed after the war.

Forced migration

'He has youth, energy, high standards of work, unusual training in a high speciality and excellent personal habits – there is no doubt at all that he will prove to be a definite asset for America.'[70] Lyman's carefully phrased letter of December 1933 marked the successful outcome of a long and protracted immigration procedure through which almost all potential émigrés were channelled by the American authorities. For the most part, however, Alexander's experience was atypical for German and Austrian medical émigrés. Certainly his port of embarkation was unusual, but he also emigrated much earlier than most, well before the mass exodus of Austrian physicians at the end of the 1930s.[71] Alexander departed at the beginning of the Nazi regime, under privileged conditions and in a climate that was supportive of Jewish refugee doctors. Like other Jewish doctors, he was fleeing persecution, but among them, he was in a relatively privileged position. He was young, highly educated, well-connected, unmarried, and he could speak the language. Additionally, the fact that he was coming from China, and not directly from Germany, may also have eased the pressure for the few available 'non-quota' visas. Last but not least, Alexander was coming from the PUMC, an 'American transplant' and elite institution, whose members provided him with references, contacts and financial resources. Alexander's professional and personal experiences say much about the kaleidoscope of factors that shaped the process of acculturation and adjustment of émigrés to their host country. In this respect his experiences also provide insight into the sociology and day-to-day politics of emigration.

According to a government census from July 1933, the German Reich had a total of 51 527 doctors (4395 female doctors), of whom 5557 (10.9 per cent) were identified as Jewish.[72] The figure was probably higher because hundreds of Jews had already emigrated by the time of the census. The Reich Representation of the German Jews estimated a total of 9000 'non-Aryan' doctors; about 17 per cent of all German doctors were therefore considered to be Jews.[73] Compared to the number of Jews in the German population as a whole, which amounted to little more than 1 per cent in 1933, the Jews had acquired disproportionate representation in the medical and legal professions, in banking and the arts. Jewish physicians were generally concentrated in large cities such as Berlin, Frankfurt am Main or Breslau. In Berlin, for example, more than half of all doctors were Jews. Nazi propagandists used such figures to attack the German medical profession for being 'infiltrated with Jews'. More often than not they called for the wholesale expulsion of Jews from the German body politic. In response to the systematic persecution of the Jewish community the country witnessed its first wave of medical emigration. The second wave occurred after 1938, when almost all Jewish physicians in Germany were prohibited from practising, except for some 700 'healers' (*Krankenbehandler*) who were permitted to treat only Jewish patients. Those between twenty-one and thirty years of age, primarily medical students and junior doctors, and those belonging to Alexander's generation, between thirty-one and forty, amounted to almost 70 per cent of all doctors in the first wave of medical emigration.[74]

Medical students generally emigrated to Switzerland, Czechoslovakia or Austria with the intention of completing their studies. Most trained physicians, on the other hand, emigrated to Palestine in order to re-establish their professional careers. Compared to the small number of doctors who left for America in 1933, a total of 58 per cent of all German-speaking doctors emigrated to Palestine. Yet after a massive influx of highly trained physicians, the authorities of the British mandate introduced strict immigration regulations to stem the rising tide of medical refugees who were perceived as posing a threat to the resident medical community. Medical émigrés therefore viewed America as the most promising alternative to Palestine. Despite its distant geographical location and restrictive immigration and employment regulations, 50 per cent of all German-speaking doctors emigrated to America, making it the leading destination, followed by Palestine (22 per cent) and Britain (12 per cent).[75] By 1937 an estimated 5500 doctors and thousands of medical scientists had been forced to leave their country. The total number of émigré physicians may have been as high as 10 000.[76]

On 20 July 1933 the Emergency Committee of the Rockefeller Foundation launched an initiative to support German scientists. Their primary goal was to select and secure the best scientists for the American academic community. Another objective was to identify the specific parameters for future research.[77] The Foundation's interest in 'humanitarian aid' stemmed from the realisation that the global circulation of the scientific elite could potentially alter the composition of entire disciplines in America and elsewhere. The effective control and careful selection of scholars was therefore of the utmost importance. A representative of the Foundation was immediately despatched to London to establish the necessary contacts between Germany and America.[78] Alexander was keenly aware of these developments. He advised his Jewish colleagues in Germany that the Americans had no interest in doing anyone a personal favour but that they had 'an interest to catch, from the great mass of broken intelligentsia in the middle of Europe, the best for America and for the benefit of their institutions, preferably cheap'.[79]

At the end of 1933 more official steps were taken to provide a safe haven for distinguished medical scientists. In October, the president of the New York Medical Academy, Bernhard Sachs, announced the establishment of the 'Emergency Committee in Aid of Displaced Physicians' to provide Jewish émigré doctors with temporary employment in the health system.[80] Supported by Christian and Jewish doctors, the Committee avoided being drawn into any political debate about the effect of foreign doctors on the domestic job market. The creation of the Emergency Committee signalled a shift towards a more active policy to help persecuted Jewish scientists from Europe. For Alexander the change of climate occurred at exactly the right moment.

The breakthrough came when Lyman approached a colleague at Worcester State Hospital, near Boston. In his reply, the head of the department of mental disease, Roy G. Hoskins, included a robust account of the situation in America. According to Hoskins, America was 'flooded with people out of jobs, including a rather large number of well-trained individuals. I have, for example, on my own staff two girls, each with a PhD ... who are receiving a stipend slightly less than our coloured maid. The times are truly out of joint.'[81] He proposed to 'squeeze' Alexander in under the condition that he would accept room and board only. 'He would live in the hospital with some hundreds of other employees ... If the economic situation improves, we might, within a few months, be able to add a stipend, but that cannot be promised at this juncture.'[82] And then came the crucial sentence: 'This may be construed as a definite offer to Dr Alexander, if you will vouch for his being of pleasant and cooperative personality. Our group is selected with congeniality as one of the primary requisites and we do not care to introduce a disrupting factor.'[83] The need to integrate himself into the American culture and community as fast as possible, and please everybody around him, shaped Alexander's life for the next couple of years.

'Happy news! I have a post in America', was Alexander's joyful reaction.[84] Things were finally moving in the right direction. Additional references by one of Alexander's well-to-do friends, Arthur P. Black, Associate Professor of Medicine at PUMC, who personally guaranteed that Alexander would never become a 'public charge', probably by means of a 'large sum of money',[85] were essential in fulfilling part of the visa requirements.[86] At last the way was clear for his emigration to America.[87] He was scheduled to start work at Worcester Hospital on 1 January 1934. Only weeks after receiving the job offer Alexander boarded the steamer *President Jackson* to sail via Japan to America's west coast.

Having secured his professional life Alexander now wanted to stabilise his personal life as well. He decided to get married, that is, he wanted to persuade his one-time German girlfriend, Gisela Preitz, to follow him to America.[88] Everything was to be arranged as inconspicuously as possible. The plan was as follows: she would travel to America under a false pretence, perhaps to do some work of potential interest to the new regime. Alexander's suggestion that she should study 'American work camps' or 'female prisons' was not without a certain degree of black humour with respect to the situation in Germany. Once in America she would fall in love with an American citizen – 'who I guess would be me' – and marry him. 'It would be no one's business', Alexander plotted, 'whether this man would be a Buddhist, Taoist, Lamaist, Agnostic, Christian or, like him, a Jew.'[89] But there were three questions she had to honestly ask herself. First, was she willing to become an American citizen? Second, did she think she could be happy in America? And finally, was she free from all anti-Semitic feeling? Although he himself was free of 'old atavisms' and 'educated prejudices', he wondered if Preitz was indeed independent and strong-minded enough to have remained untouched by the anti-Semitism that engulfed Nazi Germany. The plan was nothing but wishful thinking. Preitz never embarked on a journey to marry her one-time lover. The relationship lasted for another year until her parents intervened in November 1934 to preserve the alleged purity of their daughter's German blood.[90] The affair, however muddled or naive it may have been, speaks to the thousands of relationships that were profoundly affected by Nazism and European anti-Semitism in the 1930s.

Acculturation

We had just been on deck when it happened, playing 'Shuffleboard', when we saw the large wave coming. The boat slowly travelled up the steep hill, further and further, until it was at the top. Suddenly, nothing. Behind the top there was nothing, that is to say a steep slope, and the ship almost fell, bow pointing towards the valley of the waves, plunging deep into the water. The impact was hard, it splashed to all sides, and things fell to this side and that in the kitchen and community rooms. Fortunately the ship quickly found its balance and could immediately continue its journey; only some plates on the bow had become loose. The whole thing happened unbelievably quickly. When everything was over, I said that one now can understand the meaning of how it is when the ocean opens up and swallows you.[91]

While spending time on deck after days of stormy weather during the trans-Pacific crossing, Alexander witnessed a phenomenon that few will ever see: a tidal wave. In his description of the event, included in a letter to his brother, Alexander found a poignant, and probably unconscious, metaphor for his own sense of loss and uncertainty. The image of the tidal wave – how it had risen, leaving the massive ship and its passengers in total limbo before releasing them into a free fall – symbolised his own experience of emigration, an event that left his life in turmoil.

While Alexander's experiences shaped his own individual identity as an émigré medical scientist, others in his position also shared many of the same feelings. All had to make innumerable adjustments: institutional, intellectual and cultural, in order to re-establish careers in America. For many the foremost feeling was one of loss. Sometimes it was one of anger. Émigrés had every reason to be frustrated by the extent to which external political developments had shaped the course of their lives. Most had been left with no choice but to emigrate. All of a sudden they were thrust into an entirely different culture, with different traditions and local customs. They had little contact with family and friends. From that point on they spoke a language that was not their own. But forced migration was both a challenge and a unique opportunity for people like Alexander to establish their careers anew. In some cases emigration made it possible for them to have careers in the first place. The idea that the careers of medical scientists would have continually progressed if Hitler's Germany had not forced them out of Europe is a counterfactual claim that cannot be taken for granted. Even for Alexander, with his extensive academic network, his career as a medical scientist could have turned out quite differently. Emigration often encouraged greater intellectual innovation, for scientists encountered new university systems that were less restrictive than those on the European continent.[92] The need to adapt to new environments led many scholars to reassess their own cultural and intellectual heritage, and, in most cases, they benefited from linking 'old' traditions with 'new' ideas and value systems. For Alexander the experience of emigration led to a profound shift in his intellectual and scientific perspective.

Alexander's adjustment was made easier by his Chinese and American colleagues who introduced him to the New England community. But these contacts also carried significant social and professional pressure. While friends were concerned about Alexander and his career, they were also anxious about their own social status, and did not want to jeopardise it by bringing émigré scientists into the country. While the economic depression and the general employment situation in the United States prevented the wholesale immigration of medical scientists, university administrators competed for the best and most distinguished scholars for their own institution or field. A shifting and, at times, hostile public could also influence the direction of university policies toward émigré scientists, particularly during election periods. All of these factors led to increased selectivity with regard to émigré scientists. By forcing Alexander to acculturate, his personal and institutional contacts wanted to ensure that he would become one of the few 'selected' scholars who deserved émigré status and was welcomed by American society.

Alexander arrived in Seattle in January 1934 with little more than a suitcase.[93] In Chicago a colleague of the architect Frank Lloyd Wright gave him a guided tour of the city. This left him 'deeply impressed' about the size and aesthetics of modern American architecture. In New York a representative of the Rockefeller Foundation advised Alexander to be cautious in exhibiting attitudes that could be regarded as 'European'. Alan Gregg, director of the division of medical science, told Alexander that Americans attached more importance to 'team work and that he [would] be wise to make himself as useful as possible, not only to his chief, but to his colleagues'.[94]

The beginning was tiresome and frustrating. Overcoming language difficulties in a totally different environment was one thing. Realising that many Americans were prejudiced towards Europeans, ignorant about the current political situation, or simply not interested, was quite another. Apparently a number of hospitals had already expressed dissatisfaction with the ability of Europeans to integrate into the working community. Others complained about the degree of co-operation shown by some émigrés. Their tendency to oppose and protest was regarded as a bad character feature. A person 'who disagrees [was] considered disagreeable'.[95]

Many Americans were baffled by the intellectual views of their new European colleagues,[96] and Alexander began to realise that one needed considerable flexibility and effort to adapt to the new culture. He also needed a symbolic bridge, an assignment, or a kind of mission that would help him overcome his longing for the past. Whenever possible, he participated in public lectures and conferences and corresponded with those who could bring him into contact with others in the field. Like most Europeans, he also struggled with his Austrian-German accent. Understanding and accepting certain idiosyncrasies was another lesson in the process of acculturation. 'One typing mistake, one crossed-out word, or a corrected letter in a formal letter will be regarded as a personal insult overhere [sic]', he told a colleague in Germany. 'That is a peculiarity of the American formalism, which you have to know before you come here. Trivial things, no one in old Europe would bother [about], such as dandruff on the top of your suit

or ... unironed trouser[s] are an adequate reason overhere [*sic*] for dismissing a university professor.'[97]
Yet, despite his efforts to integrate, the past frequently caught up with him. Poised between the past and the future, he existed in two different worlds, and each was filled with different types of thoughts. He oscillated between memories of what life had been like in Germany[98] and China[99] and projections of what it would be like in America in the future. Alienated from his cultural and professional roots, he sought a place of refuge, a new home. For someone with such strong connections to the European cultural tradition, it is hardly surprising that after a brief period of excitement, Alexander fell into depression once again. For many émigrés depression was followed by homesickness and plans to return.[100] By the end of March 1934, he was forced to take to his bed with scarlet fever; this was followed by weeks of isolation and reflection. Accustomed to company and social interaction with people who admired him, the feeling of loneliness became almost unbearable. On 25 April, he wrote to his brother:

> I am not well ... the external conditions are turning out very badly (poor facilities, poor and limited possibilities to work and exert influence, unpleasant and cold people, total loneliness) so that I have, for the second time in my life, become dreadfully homesick. How are the conditions in Austria? Do you think that I would have a chance to practise or get a position as a neurologist in Vienna? Please answer immediately. How is our financial situation? Can we open a private sanatorium in one of [our] ... houses (presuming there are some left)?[101]

The idea of returning to family and friends was nothing but wishful thinking, a kind of nostalgia that had nothing to do with political and social realities. It was the lack of 'spiritual and material satisfaction' that made him homesick, the 'coldness of the North Americans' and their apparent lack of cultural understanding.[102] 'Here in America one is very lonely', he wrote to a friend in Austria, 'even people who have been here for a long time feel the same; one realises this especially when one is ill, and torn out of the general day to day work. But even in the work one finds a lot of difficulties, thematic and personal.'[103] According to Alexander a 'chilling wind' was blowing in America, 'one cannot choose'.[104] At the same time he hoped that his brother would reassure him that emigration had not been a mistake. For Alfred nothing was easier to do. 'It is a strange play of events', he wrote to Alexander in May 1934, 'that just as you are thinking of returning, all our colleagues are saying, "he is lucky, he emigrated just at the right time and will succeed". Just a couple of days ago your former friend E. Gold visited me and could not stop envying and congratulating you on your position.'[105] This was the kind of moral support that Alexander desperately needed.

As was the case in Germany, the Austrian government was becoming increasingly dictatorial. In February 1934, the authoritarian regime of the Austrian Chancellor Engelbert Dollfuss (1892–1934), who governed by means of emergency decrees, had quashed the attempted revolt by the social democrats. Bans on political parties now extended from social democratic and socialist parties to trade unions and the Austrian Nazi party. The February uprising resulted in widespread political unrest and terror campaigns that eventually led to the failed *putsch* by the Austrian Nazis in July. The attempt left Dollfuss dead and the country in a state of civil war. In Vienna the atmosphere was on a knife-edge. Free medical practice had ceased almost completely. Fear and suspicion reigned among Alexander's Jewish friends and colleagues. The family's influential friends now stayed at a distance. Others lived in constant fear of forced 'retirement' or awaited the closure of their institutes. According to Alfred, Alexander's chance of re-establishing his career there was 'less than small'. It was much better, he argued, to persevere under the most difficult and unpleasant conditions than to return to Austria at that critical juncture.[106]

Such accounts gave Alexander a sense of perspective and made him realise that the 'pull from the past' was counterproductive, and offered no help in overcoming his existential fears. Rather than looking backwards and mourning the past, he needed to adopt a more forward-looking perspective. News about the continued persecution of the Jewish community fuelled his desire to sever his intellectual and cultural ties.[107] He was also beginning to make plans to bring family members to America should the political situation worsen.[108] As the 'outpost' of the family and the first point of call for Jewish colleagues in need of advice[109] Alexander started to acquaint himself with America. He was beginning to live beyond the present.

'Here in America it is of vital necessity to be in a good mood – smile', he told his brother with a sense of irony. In June 1934 he made plans to move to Boston State Hospital where the neuropsychiatrist Tracy J. Putnam had offered him a full-time position.[110] Before the offer was even finalised, influential friends from PUMC had also managed to secure him a part-time teaching post at Harvard Medical School. His contacts from China, and his Rockefeller connections in particular, were valuable assets in Boston's close-knit society, where personal friendships mattered greatly in the constant game of social tennis.[111] According to his daughter Cecily, Alexander's trip to China gave him a fair amount of 'social mileage'.[112]

Yet it was in the midst of New England's scientific community that Alexander first encountered American anti-Semitism. Because he had come from a former missionary hospital in Beijing, many people believed that he was Christian, and they would frankly exchange their views about the Jews during dinner and cocktail parties: 'I am well informed since many people here ... do not regard me as a member of the uniquely blessed confession.

On those occasions one hears surprising things. Who knows whether [He]lene with her Palestine plan has not chosen the better path', he told his brother in June 1934.[113] For some time he considered Palestine as a genuine alternative to America after realising that it would take years to establish himself. The demand for trained German-Jewish immigrants was still great in Palestine. He thought of going there as a neurologist, or at least encouraging others to do so. Palestine was the only place in the world where, according to Alexander, a Jew could 'hold his head up high. And that will mean something.'[114] He was disappointed by the way in which American Jews had responded to the plight of their fellow European Jews. There was little sense of solidarity and almost no feeling of belonging to a community, least of all to a common people. He believed that only the 'most faithful unity and a rapid development of Palestine' could support the Jewish cause. In Alexander's view, the Jews had not learned lessons from the past, from violent pogroms and repeated expulsions; otherwise they would have invested their money in Jerusalem, rather than giving it to the now 'Jew-free' (*judenreinen*) German universities.[115] For America the situation did not look promising. Here the Jewish community was following a 'vain and hopeless dream of assimilation'. Alexander had become, in his own words, an 'unconditional follower' of the plan to develop Palestine into a Jewish state. 'Even if all do not go, it provides those Jews living outside Palestine with status and a spine.'[116]

Alexander's frustration about the societal forces that had brought Hitler and the Nazis to power simmered underneath such rational reflections. In February 1934 he told a friend in Italy that he hoped their 'old Jewish God' would eliminate the 'Prussian pigs' (*Saupreussen*) and protect the 'chosen children'.[117] He regarded the developments in Germany as repulsive, but far worse was the 'half-conscious support' that similar tendencies received in other countries. 'The complete and utter failure of the German system would be of great importance for the civilisation of the whole world', he told a colleague from Poland.[118] Forced emigration not only transformed Alexander's attitudes towards Germany and the Jewish national cause, it also changed his perspective on racial science and eugenics.

Anti-eugenics

'I am just receiving word ... concerning your success in having received funds for the study in [*sic*] sterilisation laws and related problems of heredity', Alexander wrote to Abraham Myerson, director of the Research Division at Boston State Hospital, in July 1934.[119] One of the most outspoken representatives of the American anti-eugenics movement, Myerson was notorious for bitter irony with which he mocked the underlying scientific assumptions of negative eugenics and racial anthropology. In particular, he attacked the feasibility of the existing sterilisation laws.[120] At the annual meeting of the American Neurological Association (ANA) in June 1934, Myerson criticised the proposed 'ideal' sterilisation laws, and ridiculed the work of American eugenicists. Leading proponents of eugenics such as Harry H. Laughlin and Charles B. Davenport were accused of being racist, anti-democratic and irrational, especially with respect to the potential outcome of their proposals. According to Myerson these researchers over-estimated the importance of sterilisation on the nation's body politic, and at the same time overlooked the environmental and social factors that influence human behaviour. He regarded the eugenics movement as biased, arrogant and vague, mainly because its proponents lumped together various groups of medical conditions under a crude utilitarian concept of society. Myerson enjoyed attacking 'harebrained' eugenic ideas that called for the sterilisation of all 'potential parents of socially inadequate offspring'. Future eugenicists, he argued, would need to be clairvoyants with supernatural powers to detect whether someone fulfilled the criteria. He felt that the proposal to sterilise people on the assumption that their future offspring might be socially inadequate was 'naive beyond [the] ... powers of expression'. 'Imagine the graft, the blackmail and the generally muddled and corrupt social reactions involved in this proposal!', he told his audience.[121] Every scientist was therefore obliged, in his view, to challenge eugenic proposals before they could be moulded into laws that would destroy freedom and individuality.[122]

Eugenic sterilisation had been introduced in the United States at the turn of the century. The first sterilisation law that was passed by an American legislator was in Pennsylvania in 1905, and was subsequently vetoed by the governor. Two years later, in 1907, Indiana began to support the sterilisation of the mentally handicapped on a voluntary basis. By the beginning of the 1930s, sterilisation laws had been introduced in almost all of the states, and approximately 15 000 procedures had been performed throughout the country. In Germany, American sterilisation laws served as a model, and were used to justify the introduction of negative eugenic measures. Nazi eugenicists frequently pointed to America when asked to link their government's programme to the international eugenic movement, and thus provide their racial policy with an aura of scientific legitimacy.[123]

The introduction of Germany's compulsory sterilisation law, officially enforced as of January 1934, gave the ANA a pretext to investigate the role and effectiveness of sterilisation laws more generally. Myerson was asked to chair the inquiry and was assisted by Alexander. Although other medical scientists such as James Ayer, Clyde Keeler and Tracy J. Putnam made critical comments, the overall scope and nature of the study bore the hallmark of Myerson and Alexander. In 1935 they submitted their report to the ANA and in 1936 they published the tract 'Eugenical Sterilisation, a Reorientation of the Problem'.[124] The 1935 report constituted one of the most sophisticated and comprehensive rebuttals of claims that had been made for years by the international eugenics movement. The report showed that sterilisations often originated as eugenic measures, but ended up as social ones.

In the eyes of the authors, the concept of eugenics was riddled with methodological errors and it was lacking scientific support from modern genetic studies. Evidence from countries like Germany, where sterilisations were carried out with 'characteristic thoroughness', also showed that in many cases eugenics was linked with Aryan racism and Nordic mysticism.[125]

Myerson and Alexander concluded that 'the scientific day [was] past when the germplasm and the environment are to be considered as separate agencies or as opposing forces'.[126] The ways in which these factors operated in the development of a person's character were 'mostly in the country of the unknown'. On the whole, however, the race was not rapidly 'going to the dogs'.[127] Myerson and Alexander argued that, if enacted at all, sterilisation legislation should only be introduced on a voluntary and regulatory basis and not enforced against a person's will, as was done in Germany. Sterilisation could only be recommended in a few select cases, and only if the consent of the patient (or his or her legal guardian) was obtained.

Myerson and Alexander maintained that sterilisation programmes would not radically change the complexion of human society. The compulsory laws enacted by Nazi racial hygienists constituted an over-reaction to a social and biological problem that did not exist: 'We do not believe that society needs to hurry into a programme based on fear and propaganda' was how the authors summarised their findings.[128] In the place of negative eugenics both recommended fresh air, sunshine, exercise and healthy food. Above all, Alexander's work on sterilisation laws made him more sensitive to the principle of voluntary consent, an issue of central importance during the debates on the Nuremberg Code.

Alexander's own eugenic work had stopped with his emigration. But this did not prevent others from wanting to use it. Kleist hoped that Alexander would leave the work with him 'so that either I or an assistant at the clinic … will complete your research'.[129] Kleist knew that Alexander's work on heredity was of interest to Nazi medical science. Alexander first wanted to avoid the whole matter. The realisation that his former mentor appeared to be collaborating with the new regime was just too distressing.[130] '[Kleist] now wants to have well-behaved Aryans complete my unfinished drafts of earlier work', Alexander told Rosenstein in August 1934. 'Otherwise I don't hear anything from Frankfurt.'[131]

The situation with Kleist provided yet another reason to sever ties with his professional past. In the autumn of 1934 Alexander's relationship with Gisela Preitz ended when her parents refused to allow their marriage. The parents' response was typical of many ordinary Germans who believed that their nation needed purification from all alien and Jewish elements. Doubting whether Alexander would be able to look after their spoiled daughter, whom they described as a 'fastidious and wholly wasteful house-wife', the Preitzs were also afraid that Alexander would gain access to some of their 'German wealth' and damage the 'German economic politic'. Herr Preitz was especially appalled by the prospect of race mixing. This, he claimed, would lead to self-destruction. His 'völkisch confession of faith' (*völkisches Glaubensbekenntnis*) and the 'blessing of the national awakening' (*Segen des nationalen Aufbruchs*) had convinced him that the marriage of the two was doomed from the outset: 'The thought alone that there should be grandchildren somewhere out there in the world, blood of my wife and of my blood ... who would serve our German *Volk*, yet would be lost, would just be unbearable to us, to our son, and to our entire family and kinship.'[132] If this did not suffice to convince Alexander that he was the wrong man, a comment made in passing by Herr Preitz did. Their daughter had apparently considered marrying Alexander only under the condition that she would sacrifice future offspring.[133] No longer confined to his scientific and professional life, eugenics had entered into his personal life as well.

Fortunately, Alexander did not suffer for long. On 28 November 1934, about a week after his marriage proposal had been rejected, he met a twenty-five-year-old American woman, Phyllis Elora Harrington, a social worker at Boston City Hospital.[134] They bumped into each other during one of Alexander's daily rounds as a visiting neurologist.[135] Besides their mutual interest in social psychology and medicine they shared a passion for classical music and culture. In April 1936 they were married. Less than a year later, in March 1937, Phyllis gave birth to their first child, Gustave[136] Osgood, named after Alexander's father. He was followed by Cecily Kate, born in November 1938, and Jonathan Harrington, born in April 1940.[137] For Alexander, having a family facilitated his integration into American society and made him more at home. It was almost ten years before he set foot on German soil again, this time as an Allied investigator charged with documenting the devastating effects of Nazi racial policies.

For Alexander the 1930s were a period of stability and confidence, one in which he found the 'courage to be', as the German émigré philosopher Paul Tillich pointed out in 1936.[138] He was beginning to identify with the American way of life. By the end of 1934, Alexander moved to Boston to work on problems related to multiple sclerosis, and he and Myerson started in-vestigative research on sterilisation laws.[139] The move to Boston was another step forward in gaining a foothold in the American medical establishment.[140] Until 1941, when America joined the war, Boston was his intellectual home. In little more than six years he published more than fifty scientific papers on subjects relating to neuropathology, anatomy and psychiatry.[141] In 1940 Alexander made his most important scientific contribution to date: he showed that Wernicke's disease, which is often observed in chronic alco-holics, results from a vitamin B1 deficiency. He had first recognised the disease in vitamin B1 deficient pigeons and was able to reproduce the disease in animals.[142] He also conducted research on the central nervous system with Putnam and published on various subjects including alcoholism and cancer, dysentery and industrial hygiene, toxicology and eugenic sterilisation. An obsessive and slightly eccentric researcher, Alexander attracted the attention of the media and the public. Local and regional newspapers began talking about the 'Vienna native'. In November 1935, he was asked to participate in a public debate with a leading social activist about professional opportunities for women in the field of mental disease and social work.[143] Through these types of appearances, Alexander learned the intricate art and rules of propaganda, performance and persuasion that he so successfully applied later at the Nuremberg Doctors' Trial.

On the eve of the Second World War Alexander travelled to London to visit his brother Alfred, who had managed to escape from Austria in 1938, only seven days after German troops had marched into Vienna.[144] He also planned to attend a conference with Myerson in Copenhagen. Little did he know what would happen in the weeks to come. On board the ship he organised a forum on foreign affairs to study the current political climate. Interested in the surrounding environment, he documented the psychological and political make-up of his fellow passengers, some of whom wholeheartedly supported the Nazi dictatorship. Whereas some of his reflections warrant further analysis, particularly those concerned with the extent to which moral belief systems shape the individual and society, his assessment of the larger political and military situation was less than accurate. Although Alexander had noticed the posters urging Londoners to be prepared in case of war, he was convinced that 'war will not come this year or in any of the next four years'.[145] Fourteen days later Europe was at war with Germany. It was one of many cases in which he misjudged the international situation.[146]

War and psychiatry

Since the late 1930s Alexander wanted to join the US army to fight the Nazis on the front lines. His was the patriotic dream of thousands of émigrés who wanted to play an active role in the coming battle against Hitler's Germany; it was a way of paying their dues to the country that had given them hope and shelter at a time of crisis. Joining the armed forces was more than a matter of pride; it was a chance to identify more strongly with American patriotism and the country's national interests. For some émigrés, it was also an opportunity to fight their own enemy, Nazi Germany. In 1938 Alexander tried to join the Army Medical Corps Reserve, but was judged physically unfit because his weight was over the maximum limit. When he was eventually permitted to join the armed forces, he had to sign a waiver.[147] Comrades remembered Alexander as a corpulent man, with a good sense of humour and an obsessive work ethic, yet with few friends among fellow soldiers. Some regarded him as sloppy and clumsy, with a talent for annoying people.[148] He was seemingly unable to conform to army rules and regulations, and official inspections of his ward generally led to some kind of censure. At the same time he is said to have treated his nurses and support staff in a distinctly authoritarian fashion. It is difficult to estimate the extent to which the wartime memories of fellow soldiers can be taken at face value, especially when so many years have passed. It is likely, though, that Alexander's age (he was significantly older than his comrades), his physical stature, his refugee status and language problems (apparently he was unable to understand jokes), his obsession with research, and, last but not least, his Jewishness contributed to his reputation as an eccentric outsider. While people may have envied him, they also kept him at a distance.

By the time Alexander joined the US army in 1943, the war was being fought in forty different places. As in the First World War, soldiers suffered from a great variety of mental and physical conditions, ranging from fatigue and nervous exhaustion to severe anxiety, hysteria, tremors, deafness, blindness, paralysis and attempted suicide. For much of the Second World War Allied military neuropsychiatry was based on drug-based methods to cure the 'war neurosis' that had caused such acute problems in the previous war.[149] Physicians espousing the nihilist approach, including Sir William Osler and his colleagues from Johns Hopkins University, viewed drugs as more harmful than beneficial to the body. Instead they stressed the role of the physician in the psychology of healing. Yet their approach gave way to new biochemical treatments. The development of new drugs like sulphonamides, antibiotics and penicillin ushered in a period of medical activity that greatly influenced military psychiatry. Doctors applied new methods such as insulin coma, cardiazol- and electroshock therapy to induce artificial fits in order to relieve patients from states of anxiety. By the end of the 1930s more than forty different drugs, most of them barbiturates, had been used to treat mental disorders. Chemical and therapeutic tools ranged from prolonged narcosis or 'deep-sleep therapy', narco-analysis and narco-synthesis, to barbiturate abreaction, insulin subshock treatment and 'truth drugs' such as sodium pentothal. One of the most commonly used drugs for treating mentally exhausted soldiers was sodium amytal, introduced by William Sargant and first produced in 1923. Sodium amytal helped mentally exhausted soldiers retrieve suppressed, traumatic memories. As a result, they were able to work through these memories, and often improved. This form of treatment became known as 'Sargant's method'.[150] Military experts were able to call upon an extensive repertoire of drugs and treatments (most were not without substantial health risks) to help soldiers overcome their mental confusion, at least temporarily, and return to military duty.

In the first half of the war, British and American military neuropsychiatry differed significantly.[151] From 1938 British specialists had focused on the lessons of the First World War. In particular, they wanted to prevent tens of thousands of 'shell-shocked' soldiers from receiving wartime pensions. In this war, British authorities were taking a no-nonsense approach. The term 'shell-shock' was banned from all official correspondence.[152] Government officials hoped that a robust policy of both recognising and downplaying psychoneurosis, together with the announcement that no pensions would be paid to those suffering from the condition, would keep the number of mental breakdowns in the armed forces low, or at least consistent with their occurrence in the civilian population. The Americans, on the other hand, assumed that their screening tests had eliminated most potential problem cases. As a result, the US military was badly prepared for battlefield psychiatry. Relatively inexperienced psychiatrists like Alexander were sent to Britain for training at base hospitals, often with the result that comparatively minor incidents were treated as psychiatric casualties. American authorities only gradually realised that prevention could reduce the rate of war neuroses. Applied to the logical extreme, the new 'preventive psychiatry' could lead to a kind of circular reasoning. In his acclaimed novel *Catch-22*, Joseph Heller vividly portrayed the vicious circle that American pilots faced when showing signs of mental exhaustion from flying endless combat missions:

> There was only one catch and that was Catch-22, which specified that a concern for one's own safety in the face of dangers that were real and immediate was the process of a rational mind. Orr was crazy and could be grounded. All he had to do was ask; and as soon as he did, he would no longer be crazy and would have to fly more missions. Orr would be crazy to fly more missions and sane if he didn't, but if he was sane he had to fly them. If he flew them he was crazy and didn't have to; but if he didn't want to he was sane and had to ... Yossarin saw it clearly in all its spinning reasonableness. There was an elliptical precision about its perfect pairs of parts that was graceful and shocking, like good modern art.[153]

Psychiatrists like Alexander, who had a striking affinity to Heller's psychiatrist Major Sanderson, were ordered to keep the total number of neuropsychiatric patients as low as possible. Interestingly, it is conceivable that Heller might have modelled aspects of Major Sanderson on Alexander, whom he could have met while serving in one of the bomber squadrons. There simply were not that many American psychiatrists in the European theatre of operation, and even fewer who exhibited such a marked degree of eccentricity.

As a staff member of Duke University in Durham, North Carolina, where he had moved in 1941, Alexander was assigned to the 65th General

Hospital and sent to Fort Bragg, North Carolina during the spring of 1943. His position was Chief of the Section for Neuropsychiatry.[154] Alexander appears to have enjoyed his training, especially the moments of excitement when he climbed over barricades 'to the tune of the machine gun barrage'.[155] At the end of October 1943 he arrived with the 65th General Hospital in the west of England at Blackmoor Park, near Malvern, where the autumn air and the foliage reminded him of New England: 'I trust we shall live up to expectations in terms of performance of work and contribution to the war effort', he told his wife upon arrival.[156] He was full of praise for the British. England was simply a 'grand country'. Alexander welcomed the co-operation of the local townspeople with their bands, chess games and boxing matches, and commended the efficient British war effort: 'There is a complete and real blackout here at night, and boy it is dark ... The rules are strictly laid; these people here in England mean business and are extraordinarily efficient; they work hard too. And get things done.'[157]

To overcome the lack of communication with American medical scientists Alexander attempted to enter the British research community. In November 1943, for example, he attended a joint British–American meeting on aviation psychiatry at the Royal Society in London. His brother Alfred's involvement in the Emergency Medical Service (EMS) also helped him to become part of the military medical establishment. Contacts with Rockefeller scientists soon made him feel at ease in his new environment: 'Science and enterprise does not need marble, it grows quite well in Nissan huts ... Neuropsychiatry is doing extraordinarily well here in the European Theatre of Operation (ETO), I find, particularly in view of advances made by the British, but taken up immediately and carried further by us. There is first rate stuff going on that nobody [would dream] about at home.'[158] His contacts quickly extended to the leading personalities and institutions in the field. By the end of the war he was invited to Cambridge University for special investigative work, and there met with the fellows of King's College in Cambridge.[159]

Alexander and his fellow medical scientists of the 65th General Hospital saw the war as a period of medical discovery, a time of excitement and optimism that would help them to understand the aetiology of neurological conditions: 'I have learned a lot and am learning a lot more about the psychodynamic mechanism of the origin of neurosis ... I think I have made and am making new discoveries here ... scientist-soldier is not a bad combination', he wrote to Phyllis in January 1944.[160] The development of the electroencephalogram (EEG) and brain wave studies significantly improved the availability of diagnostic techniques for certain mental conditions. Likewise, the standard use of drugs transformed the treatment of battle wounds. Any knowledge about a new diagnostic tool or form of medical treatment, unless it was secret, was passed on to his colleagues in America.[161] Whenever possible, he exchanged ideas and research with

British and American colleagues at conferences.[162] For Alexander the war created an exciting intellectual climate, one that, in his eyes, encouraged medical progress.[163]

Since almost all of Alexander's wartime correspondence with his wife has survived we have a fairly good idea about his thoughts and activities throughout the war, as far as censorship regulations permitted. A meticulous note-taker, he constantly urged Phyllis to file every scrap of paper, and every letter, no matter how trivial. For the most part, he was proud of his military work. At the same time, however, he struggled to fulfil his role as a father and husband. Sometimes he was overly concerned with the day-to-day rearing of the children – 'give the children their cod liver oil daily, and file all my letters'. At other times he scolded his wife for using only two-thirds of the space on the V-mail paper.[164] 'Mail was very difficult', his daughter Cecily remembered, 'we would get no letters for a long time and then we would get five, six or seven in a little package ... Everything was rationed and the children in school were saving string and fat and so forth to help the soldiers and so we always imagined that we were helping our father in particular.'[165] For Alexander it was essential that his family, and his wife in particular, believed in his war mission. In a classic psychological twist he sometimes projected his own occasional lack of morale and confidence onto her: 'The key to your sustained morale and happiness is to be found in your firm belief in the importance of my assignment and mission', he told her in October 1943.[166]

The correspondence between Alexander and his wife never went far beyond the daily routine, rationing and air raids. Most of the time it was trivial. At times he was grateful for boxes of brownies; other times he requested more cigars and chocolate. Only rarely did Phyllis comment on the war situation – unless, for example, there were issues that concerned the well-being of the children or the financial situation of the family. Their communication was effectively one-sided; Phyllis was his sounding-board. Yet there was considerable warmth and affection between them. He wrote about the plays he saw, the music he heard and the friends he visited. And, of course, he described how much he loved her and how faithful he was. On 23 January 1944 he told her that she 'and the children are the source of the greatest happiness' he had ever known: 'And I am here in the ETO [European Theatre of Operation] with my comrades in arms to see to it that their future will be one of freedom, human dignity and happiness.'[167] Ten days later he wrote to her: 'I [would] love to have you here with me and spoil you some more, right now. I need a fling too, and a fling with you only would do. You are the only woman who really fascinates me, and as a consequence to [sic] this interesting fact I am faithful to you too. Of course I, and I suppose everybody else, always expected you to be faithful; but in my case it comes as a surprise to me and I suppose to you too.'[168] With regard to his actual medical work, the correspondence between Alexander and his wife remains conspicuously oblique, not because he did not wish to communicate such facts, but because army regulations demanded strict secrecy.[169] For example, it was prohibited to mention names and places of hospitals and other locations, or to discuss research that could be of strategic value to the Axis powers. But these rules also made the exchange of ideas with his American colleagues difficult.

By the early spring of 1944 the 65th General Hospital was suddenly transferred to East Anglia, apparently after President Roosevelt's son had complained to his father that British bomber pilots received better psychological care than their American counterparts.[170] The move was meant to boost morale in the American armed forces. The 65th General Hospital became the centre for the 8th Air Force. It could accommodate up to 1400 beds, and was staffed by a group of highly motivated, university-trained doctors. Before long, the US army took notice of Alexander's ninety-bed ward. On 18 April the Chief of the Neurology Branch of the Office of the Surgeon General, Major William H. Everts, invited Alexander to 'direct everything and anything' about neurological illnesses and forms of traumata to the Surgeon General.[171] A few days later, two leading air force psychiatrists made an impromptu visit to the hospital and, according to Alexander, 'saw things which interested them'.[172] His work involved 'appraisals of normality' for fighter pilots and 'disease studies', so-called Rorschach tests for severe neurological cases. Alexander was determined to record his observations for the 'quiet years of contemplation after the War': 'Since such work will probably not be duplicated, nor the material seen for a long time, many useful observations are bound to be forgotten as if they never existed ... this has happened to a good many observations and techniques in the last war.'[173] By the middle of 1944 he was beginning to feel 'useful' to the army:

I have so far succeeded in keeping records which meet my obsessive scientific standards and keep my typewriter clattering while I listen and talk, and while I think and summarise. It is an old British typewriter, but it is serving me well, and my dexterity has risen to the occasion. I am typing on it at present, at ten o'clock p.m., in my examining room, and while a patient, whose headache and tension I just successfully cured under sodium amytal and a resounding flow of my old hypnotic technique ('strong, happy and well; for the duration of the war and forever thereafter'), is snoring soundly behind me on my examining bed. The deeper and more complex anxiety states, associated with exhaustion and loss of weight, are treated with modified insulin (Sargant's method), with or without an initial period of sustained narcosis protracted over a number of days. And then there are the more purely sociological problems which are handled with pure psychotherapy or common sense rather, and the jaunty behaviour problems requiring merely disposition, some of which [are] associated with incidents which are a welcome, though rare, comic relief from the seriousness of the essential aspects of the work. I find the Rorschach test extraordinarily revealing in regard to prognosis and choice of treatment, above and beyond its uses in civilian therapy.[174]

At the beginning of 1944 Alexander was given an assistant after noting that he had temporarily lost his 'supply of horselike energy'.[175] The young captain, Nicolas Camera-Peon, was a Mexican native who had graduated from Johns Hopkins University and trained with the psychiatrists Adolf Meyer and John Whitehorn before becoming a flight surgeon. For Camera-Peon the war was a 'tremendous opportunity' to enhance his professional career. He was broadly educated, interested in German music and culture, knowledgeable about Chinese art, and multilingual – all of which warmed Alexander to him.[176] They frequently spoke German with each other and intensified their personal bond. Camera-Peon, who today lives in Washington DC, remembered Alexander vividly: 'He was an imposing person because he was very corpulent, but he was a kindly man and you got that impression from the beginning. So I was very well impressed. I liked him. And apparently it was mutual because he liked me too. And we got along quite well.'[177]

Alexander's second, but unofficial, assistant was David B. Vinson, an energetic young psychologist who used the neurological ward for his own professional training. Vinson was stationed at a different base, yet visited the 65th General Hospital almost every evening in order to work with Alexander and Camera-Peon throughout the night.[178] Exhibiting a certain gung-ho patriotism, Vinson liked to spend his leave at the front where he enjoyed blowing up German fortifications and tanks. Returning to the ward, he often brought souvenirs, like a captured aviator's cap, which Alexander sent to his son. Once he surprised Alexander with a box of German cigars, which he had stolen from a defeated German field headquarters during one of his crusades.[179] The charged, male-dominated atmosphere of the war certainly appealed to Alexander. The war allowed for a laboratory situation in which few outside factors interfered with his research, in which heroic narratives alternated with comradeship and excessive work. Here Alexander could be the scientist through and through.

But the sheltered, and at times jovial, atmosphere changed when the number of soldiers suffering from flight fatigue or from severe head and brain injuries continued to rise. The pressure on air crews was terrifying. Losses and the occurrence of mental breakdowns became extremely high. More and more soldiers showed aggressive behaviour and, as a result, were court-martialled.[180] Alexander generally followed a biological approach in his expert assessments. Those attacking their fellow men, or assaulting women whilst intoxicated, apparently suffered from a combination of 'biological abnormality and emotional stress'.[181] He also addressed issues of 'morale' and 'leadership', especially when it turned out that many neuropsychiatric patients came from certain combat units. Alexander's study of leadership structures of fighting units revealed that morale was a key factor in determining the average rate of mental breakdowns.[182]

War crimes

News about Allied losses was always depressing. But even more depressing was information about German war crimes, particularly the wholesale shootings of civilians that were being reported. Since the outbreak of war, eye-witness accounts suggested that the German military was waging a ruthless and brutal campaign that ignored the customs of established warfare and violated the international conventions, treaties and laws to which Germany was a signatory. As early as November 1940, the Polish and Czechoslovak governments-in-exile jointly declared that the 'violence and cruelty' to which Germany was subjecting her neighbouring countries was 'unparalleled in human history'. This allegation, made against one of the most modern and economically powerful nation-states, was so dramatic that many believed that the two governments-in-exile were overstating their case. Among other crimes, Germany was accused of 'banishment of hundreds of thousands of men and women to forced labour in Germany, mass executions and deportations to concentration camps, plundering of public and private property, extermination of the intellectual class and cultural life, spoliation of treasures of science and art and the persecution of all religious beliefs'.[183]

Intelligence reports and other sources of information seemed to confirm most of the allegations. On 25 October 1941 President Roosevelt issued a stern warning to the Nazis that their crimes would one day bring frightful retribution.[184] On the same day Churchill told the public that Nazi atrocities, especially those being committed behind the German lines in Russia, surpassed 'anything that has been known since the darkest and most bestial ages of mankind. They are but a foretaste of what Hitler would inflict upon the British and American peoples if only he could get the power ... Retribution for these crimes must henceforward take its place among the major purposes of the war.'[185] These declarations reflected the growing concern among the major Allied powers that Germany was committing grave offences against the common law, and against national and international law, a situation that not only demanded the firm condemnation of the horrors, but the creation of a judicial machinery to hold those responsible accountable after the war.

An attempt to establish the legal and theoretical underpinnings of such an enterprise was made by Raphaël Lemkin, a distinguished Polish scholar of law and adviser to the US authorities. In 1944 Lemkin published *Axis*

Rule in Occupied Europe, a book that examined the system by which Germany and her allies were subjugating the European people. His book also included a section called 'Proposals for Redress'.[186] Central to Lemkin's argument was his point that the law of military occupation did not grant the invader 'unlimited power over the inhabitants temporarily under his control'. Lemkin meticulously documented the numerous instances in which Axis powers had grossly violated the laws and customs of war as codified by the Hague Conventions of 1899 and 1907.[187] Lemkin's analysis revealed that Germany had 'embarked upon a gigantic scheme to change … the balance of biological forces between it and the captive nations for many years to come', a policy of extermination and destruction of nations and ethnic groups for which he coined the term 'genocide'. The term derived from the Greek word *genos*, meaning tribe or race, and the Latin word *caedo*, meaning the act of killing or slaughter; it was coined in analogy to words like homicide or fratricide.[188] As a result of the murder of entire national, religious and ethnic groups, and as a result of the 'grave dislocation of demographic, economic and cultural values', Lemkin campaigned for the establishment of an international system that would permit the trial and punishment of perpetrators of such crimes, not only in their own country but also in their place of refuge or in the country in which the crime had been committed. Lemkin had proposed such a system as early as 1933 at the Fifth International Conference for the Unification of Penal Law in Madrid, but it was rejected. Now was the time, he felt, to renew his call for the international community to realise that Nazi Germany posed a grave threat to international peace and civilisation.

An émigré scholar, Lemkin had worked on his book since 1940, first in Sweden and then, in 1941–2, at Duke University, where Alexander taught in the Department of Psychiatry. The two seem to have become acquainted during this period.[189] Alexander's interest in devising a similar, all-encompassing, theoretical construct for the Doctors' Trial, one that was specifically applicable to medical war crimes, may have originated in discussions with Lemkin at Duke. Alexander certainly seems to have become more conscious of the international political situation during that time. In February 1944 he expressed, for the first time, a certain degree of gloom about the military and political situation; he felt that Nazi Germany was threatening to destroy the core values and institutions of 'Western civilisation' and of America in particular. To his six-year-old son Gustave, he tried to explain the moral justification for the war:

Some day you and they [his siblings] will be grown up, and will have to stand together in defence of each other's rights, lives, liberty and pursuit of happiness; as fellow citizens certainly, as fellow soldiers – like your father and his comrades – possibly. What your country stands for has to be constantly worked for and, if necessary, fought for. We must remain constantly worthy of what those before us have achieved. That goes for us, your father and his friends and for you and your friends. This letter has turned rather serious, but I feel serious, my dear son.[190]

The more Alexander became aware of German atrocities the more he wanted to play an active role in any post-war policy that aimed to bring the perpetrators to justice. It was the paradox of an amateur philosopher whose political judgement had frequently proved him wrong on almost any issue of national policy, but who was realistic and far-sighted about Germany. National Socialism and European fascism were unacceptable for human society and needed to be defeated on principle.

During the war Alexander had little insight into the complexities of Allied policies that laid the foundation for future war crimes investigations and war crimes trials. He certainly had no idea that he himself would eventually become involved in exposing Nazi medical atrocities. However, he knew that the Germans were committing atrocities on a previously unimaginable scale. At one point his brother's Viennese cook, who had managed to escape to England, told him that her Jewish husband had been imprisoned by the Nazis, and had probably been killed. '[It] is awful to think that people I know may be in an abattoir', he told Camera-Peon.[191] Information about Nazi war crimes, however small and unconfirmed, fuelled his desire to publicise the extent to which the Nazi regime was destroying the Jewish people and the values of modern civilisation. His aim was nothing less than to expose the effects of German fascism on humanity. He therefore decided not to volunteer for an army of occupation, but to return to America after the war with 'some fairly definite ideas as to how to prevent the German danger in the future'.[192]

On 20 July 1944 members of the German Army High Command launched an unsuccessful attempt to assassinate Hitler. For Alexander the failed coup d'état nevertheless signified a major turning point in the war: 'The war teaches us to respect realities and not to be gotten down by them. Today's interesting news of the first sign that the Germans are getting upset about the realities they have brought about, may be portentous indeed. Lord Haw-Haw no doubt will go to great lengths to explain things away, but the handwriting is undoubtedly on the wall.'[193] In spite of this, any sign of exuberance would have still been premature. The Allies still needed to defeat Japan 'after Germany folds up', as he told his wife. On 18 September 1944 he could barely suppress his anger after receiving press releases that called for early demobilisation in America: 'As long as soldiers are still fighting, dying, suffering from wounds and from nervous exhaustion over here, it is frivolous to talk of demobilisation, as if all but the shouting were over. It is not.'[194] The issue had obviously touched a raw nerve.[195] The war not only shifted Alexander's research towards military and aviation medicine, it accelerated the development of his political consciousness, and strengthened his commitment to fighting the German aggressor at all costs. Alexander's experience of forced emigration fuelled his determination to support any initiative that was designed to investigate, prosecute and ultimately punish those guilty of war crimes. This can hardly be said of the Allied governments.

For a long time the more general question of what to do with Germany as a whole was left in limbo. It was not until the Casablanca Conference in January 1943 that the Allies declared that nothing short of Germany's unconditional surrender was acceptable.[196] The Allies were determined to establish a more co-ordinated policy of occupation and supreme authority in order to make sure that the fiasco in punishing German war criminals after the First World War would not be repeated.[197] Since 1942 the punishment of war crimes had been a major war aim, formulated and endorsed by the representatives of nine governments-in-exile in the St James Declaration. The innovative dimension of the St James Declaration was in making responsible not only those who had committed war crimes, but also those who governed or commanded those who carried them out. The Declaration was a major warning to the Germans that international action was anticipated to bring war criminals and the Nazi leadership to account. How this goal would be achieved, however, remained unclear; there were no lists of names of alleged war criminals and no investigative and judicial machinery to make such pledges a reality.[198]

There was certainly no lack of innovative ideas or far-reaching proposals that were made by international legal experts. In 1942 the London International Assembly, for example, an unofficial body that had been created under the auspices of the League of Nations Union, set up a Commission to study not only the issue of war crimes, but to make recommendation to the Allied governments for the establishment of an International Criminal Court (ICC).[199] For some time a 'Draft Convention for the Creation of an International Criminal Court' was given serious consideration. It was envisaged that the jurisdiction of the court would be 'defined in the widest possible manner and should cover crimes hitherto unlisted as war crimes'; these included crimes committed by heads of state who had drawn up plans of 'racial extermination, systematic terrorism, mass murder, deportations, economic looting in Axis and occupied countries, and the establishment of concentration camps'.[200] Hitler was the obvious choice for such a charge. The ICC was to apply international criminal law that was to be codified by the United Nations, and a Chief Prosecutor, acting on behalf of the United Nations, was to be given the power to ensure that 'only heinous crimes with grievous consequences were tried'.[201] The subsequent controversies about the remit and jurisdiction of the ICC continue to this day.

One of the essential problems in establishing an infrastructure for gathering evidence was the lack of commitment of Allied intelligence officials in believing that Nazi atrocities had been committed on a vast scale. For members of the British Joint Intelligence Committee, for example, information from Polish or Jewish sources was simply unreliable; its chairman, Victor Cavendish-Bentinck, believed that both groups, in particular the Jews, were primarily interested to 'stoke [the Allies] up'. Although information from top secret German decodes revealed that the Nazis planned to murder the European Jews one way or another, he felt that it would be 'a mistake in publicly giving credence to this gas chamber story'.[202] This position only changed slightly after the Allies received the Riegner telegram in August 1942, which revealed that the Nazi leadership was accelerating the process of murdering European Jews.[203] But at the time most officials had neither the techniques nor the inside information which would have allowed them to fully assess and understand the context of the telegram. Although attempts were made to discourage Germans from committing further atrocities by letting them know that they would be brought back to the scene of their crimes, and judged by the people they had outraged, the general attitude towards a uniform war crimes policy remained primarily focused on the period after the war.

One of the first, but half-hearted practical attempts was the creation of the United Nations War Crimes Commission (UNWCC) in London in October 1942. The brief of the Commission was to gather and collate evidence on war crimes and war criminals. In collaboration and under pressure from the exiled governments not to ignore the mounting evidence of the Final Solution, the British and American governments drafted proposals for the UNWCC.[204] The Commission was made up of representatives from seventeen nations. Only the Russians were excluded: they had deliberately been omitted from the negotiations between London and Washington over the exact wording of the goals of the Commission, and were informed about it only at the last minute. It was a bad start. Mistrust and tensions in inter-Allied intelligence sharing were to become recurring features in the months to come.

Early in November 1943 the three foreign ministers, Cordell Hull, Anthony Eden and Vyacheslav Molotov, reached agreement in Moscow to punish Nazi atrocities by holding war crimes trials in and by the countries where the atrocities had been committed. In the Declaration of Moscow the Allies committed themselves to the point that the major Axis criminals whose crimes had no particular geographical location would be judged by 'joint declaration' by the Allied governments, while those responsible for massacres and executions would be sent back 'to the countries in which their abominable deeds were done in order that they may be judged and punished according to the laws of those liberated countries'.[205] The Moscow Declaration became the theoretical cornerstone for Allied war crimes policy after the war. But what exactly 'joint declaration' would mean in practice, whether it would be the wholesale shooting of some

10 000 leading officers, as suggested by Stalin, court martials, summary executions, a series of show trials, or a political indictment by the international community, remained entirely open. Another option was, of course, to do nothing at all, to take the moral high ground and wait until the victims took matters into their own hands and lynched the suspected war criminals. After all, a desire for lynching was what many expected would be the instinct of the masses after the war, including that of Allied soldiers liberating the concentration camps.[206] It was for precisely that reason that the St James Conference called for concerted international action to prevent revenge and to satisfy a sense of justice.

By the end of the war the Allied governments had not progressed beyond the St James and Moscow Declarations. Apart from two vaguely defined categories of criminals, minor and major, the question as to how the major criminals in particular were to be punished and on what kind of evidence continued to be ignored. In the complex political battles over the shape of the post-war world, especially over the Allied occupation policy of Germany, which included issues of massive social restructuring, demilitarisation and dismemberment, the issue of war crimes had a relatively low priority. This began to change when the Allied armies advanced further into German territory and discovered that tens of thousands of people had been worked, starved and gassed to death. Jews, gypsies and Slavs, prisoners of war, soldiers and civilians had not been killed in the heat of war, but systematically, in a co-ordinated fashion.[207] Masses of documents chronicled the organised plunder of whole peoples, of slave and forced labour, and of wholesale barbarities of previously unimaginable proportions. Tens of thousands of handicapped patients had been killed in places such as Hadamar, near Limburg, in Hartheim, near Linz, in Grafeneck, near Munsingen, in Sonnenstein, near Dresden, in Bernburg, near Halle and in Brandenburg on the Havel. From every corner of the former Reich details of atrocities left investigators and soldiers in shock.

But there were few revelations which outraged the American public like the news of the Malmedy massacre: the murder of seventy-two unarmed American soldiers at a road crossing in the Belgian town of Malmedy in December 1944 during the Ardennes offensive. Responsible for this cold-blooded killing spree were members of the First SS-Tank-Division 'Leibstandarte Adolf Hitler', who were sworn to total secrecy regarding these acts, a fact which made it extremely difficult for investigators to find out what had actually happened. The public demand for justice carried substantial symbolic and political weight, and it was therefore not surprising that forty-three out of seventy-three defendants were later sentenced to death.[208] It was felt by many that the cold-blooded mass murder made swift and international action of paramount importance.

While journalists and newsreel crews alerted the world to slave labour and the horrors of camps, Western governments were suddenly waking up to the immediacy of the war crimes problem. Following the liberation of Buchenwald in April 1945, newspapers were reporting the piles of corpses, gassing facilities and the mass murder of mental patients. Investigations into the 'euthanasia' programme, that is, the systematic murder of handicapped infants and adults, were stepped up. Eyewitness accounts and testimony from survivors gave graphic details of torture and degradation to a public which struggled to comprehend the extent and brutality of the crimes committed. The first photographs documenting the conditions in the camps were believed to have been manipulated for Allied propaganda purposes. Survivors were thought to be exaggerating. But after weeks of sustained press coverage, US officials called for the work of the UNWCC to be speeded up. Previously it had been furnished with little status and power. Specially arranged tours through Bergen-Belsen, Buchenwald and Dachau by newspapers editors, and visits by senators and congressmen, further stiffened public opinion. By the beginning of May, *Life* magazine reported under the headline 'Atrocities' that the capture of German concentration camps piled up 'evidence of barbarism that reaches the low point of human degradation'.[209]

The mass of incriminating material pouring out of Germany forced Allied military officials to confront the realities of German occupation. They had to decide what to do with the major war criminals once they had been apprehended or had surrendered themselves. They also had to investigate the crimes and collect as much evidence as possible to mount war crimes trials in the future, assuming that they would still be politically opportune. One of the central preconditions for such trials was the process of interrogating the leaders of the regime. It was into this highly charged atmosphere of conflicting political, military and judicial priorities, together with a lack of inter-Allied co-operation, that Alexander was catapulted. At the beginning of May 1945 he was ordered to become a war crimes detective in the American zone of occupation.

4
The War Crimes Investigator

Assignment

The city of Lübeck on the Baltic Sea, north-west Germany, was effectively cut off from the remainder of the Reich when the first reconnaissance troops of the British forces reached the city on the evening of 3 May 1945. For the Gauleiter of Hamburg, Karl Kaufmann, this was the signal to announce the capitulation of the city over the radio; shortly afterwards Hitler's successor and head of state, Karl Dönitz, decided to discontinue further fighting in the north. In England, Alexander followed the events on the BBC. On the evening of Friday, 4 May, at around 8.30 p.m., he could hardly believe what he heard on the radio, and immediately wrote to his wife: 'The news is grand. I just heard the news of the surrender of Northwest Germany and Denmark and Holland to General Montgomery's Army Group. VE day can't be far off. Admissions have fallen off.'[1] Yet while the people of Denmark, and indeed elsewhere, went on to the streets to celebrate, Alexander was continuing his research on combat personnel.[2]

Three days later, on Monday, 7 May, reports of Germany's unconditional surrender were coming over the air force teletype. Work became increasingly impossible for Alexander. Air force crews were setting off 500-pound bombs as firecrackers on fields around the air base while free beer and Scotch were handed out to all officers and enlisted men. The time for collecting research data on flight fatigue was clearly over. Back in America, Alexander's wife was equally overwhelmed about the news, telling him that it was 'incredibly wonderful that [the] people of Europe [were] now at peace and that the war is really really over and that countless lives are to be saved and countless people do not have to be hurt. I am very happy tonight and more tomorrow.'[3] Phyllis wanted to visit a church and thank God for having made this day possible and for all the people who brought it about, including her husband. Coincidentally, Alexander had leave commencing the very moment that the war was over. On 8 May, at 5.30 a.m., he arrived in London, just in time for the VE day celebrations. After more than two weeks of silence, on 22 May, he described to Phyllis how he had felt: 'What a day it was! It was like a fourth of July celebration in Squantum, multiplied a thousandfold. I was among the crowd before Buckingham Palace at 11 p.m., staying til 12 ... I stayed in London three days, then went off on my leave to Torquay. When I returned I found most interesting and exciting orders, and I am on my way to carry them out.'[4]

Alexander's carefully worded notion of the 'most interesting and exciting orders' marked the beginning of his war crimes investigations which for the next two months would bring him into contact with almost all of Germany's leading research institutions and scientific experts. Originally the assignment was scheduled to last no longer than ten to fourteen days.[5] The aim was first and foremost to make a comprehensive assessment of German military neuropsychiatry by interviewing individual researchers, by investigating their methods and techniques, and by assessing (and confiscating) their research data. In short, to evaluate the quality of German medical science, and exploit the results for the Allied military machinery.

In contrast to the efficient exploitation of German science in the operation code-named 'Paperclip', planned with military precision and staffed with almost 3000 'T-Force-experts', Allied war crimes investigations were lacking a co-ordinated approach, staff and direction.[6] The investigative machinery was haphazardly organised, fraught with inter-Allied jealousies, and lacklustre political support from many of the national governments. But agents of task force organisations such as the Field Information Agency, Technical (FIAT) or the Combined Intelligence Objectives Sub-Committee (CIOS) which had been established to assess and exploit advances in German science and technology, frequently came across war crimes which lay outside the purview of the original brief. Alexander's order was likewise limited to the evaluation and exploitation of scientific data and equipment. The chaotic conditions on the ground nonetheless provided considerable independence.

Much has been written on the shortcomings of Allied war crimes investigations, bad preparation and communication, and subsequent results in the denazification programme, including the Nuremberg trials.[7] Underlying such arguments are sometimes counterfactual claims as to what Allied politicians and those in authority *should* have done, or what they *could* have done better.[8] Little work, however, has been undertaken on the men on the ground, the 'foot soldiers', and their methods of improvisation and informal means of communication. Rather than blocking the investigations, the uncoordinated policy decisions seemed to have produced a 'controlled vacuum' which skilled and energetic investigators could fill with their own initiatives and ideas. Far from fulfilling their duty aimlessly in the unstable and constantly changing political situation, investigators like Alexander often showed a large degree of flexibility and ability to improvise. Their work evolved from the constant exchange of information with military officials of the same or similar rank. Of their conversations and informal conferences during joint travels or over dinner, under time pressures and extraordinary external circumstances, understandably only a few records were ever produced and probably even fewer survived. It is the social history of the first groups of investigators that remains largely oblique and difficult to assess. Alexander's detailed diary entries and reports provide insights into some of this work.

Officially, American war crimes investigations were meant to focus exclusively on cases involving Allied nationals; only in July 1945 were cases of non-US nationals included in the inquiry. But in the conflicting realm of directives and counter-directives, American investigators possessed substantial discretionary powers. From the start, they investigated not only crimes committed on non-US nationals and mass atrocities in concentration camps, irrespective of nationality, but also crimes and persecution on racial and religious grounds that had occurred since 1933. Many of the investigators were European refugees, who simply ignored calls by the Judge Advocate General (JAG) to limit their investigative work. Often they would persist in researching a particular atrocity or war crimes site, irrespective of whether the material would eventually be useful in a war crimes trial. In retrospect their work is of immense historical importance, mainly because it was not restricted to the narrow focus of military law and policy objectives. Alexander's war crimes work conveys a brief period of determination to bring German perpetrators to justice rather than high-level political and administrative tensions which began to dominate the Nuremberg trials. But it also highlights the great difficulty in establishing the degree of complicity and guilt of those who simply had knowledge of the atrocities and remained silent, of those who had abetted and initiated policies, or collaborated and participated in the crimes. The overall extent and variation to which the professions, organisations and individuals within German society were implicated constituted a situation which was far beyond the investigative scope and power of the occupying forces.

There were two important alterations to Alexander's original assignment which happened as a result of the conditions in the Allied zones of occupation. Authorised to investigate everything and everyone of interest, Alexander broadened the scope of the inquiry extensively. In addition to German neuropsychiatry, he explored the field of neuropathology, neurosurgery and aviation medicine. He also gained an insight into the extent to which the Nazis had actively carried out the killing of handicapped children and adults. He was well informed in all of these areas, had published and lectured in these fields, and had previously criticised Nazi racial policies. Alexander also wanted to learn about those who had made their careers under the Nazi regime, for example by denouncing and intimidating colleagues or by filling the vacancies created by Jewish émigré scholars like himself.

Stemming from the first change to his assignment came a second alteration. Having broadened the initial inquiry, Alexander discovered numerous instances of deliberate medical wrongdoings. There were hundreds of cases where German physicians had performed experiments on concentration camp inmates under appalling, unhygienic conditions and without the subjects' informed consent. Someone other than Alexander, concentrating on German neuropsychiatry alone, may not have come across, or indeed documented, war crimes at all. Alexander consequently shifted his focus towards investigating, and ultimately exposing German medical war crimes. The countless stories of victims of medical atrocities, human suffering and of the places where these horrors were committed, fuelled Alexander's sense of outrage and stiffened his resolve that those who were responsible had to be held to account. Alexander's war crimes investigations can only be understood from the perspective of someone who was deeply shocked by what he saw, and who had the executive power and knowledge to expose the perpetrators in the immediate aftermath of the war.

Yet there were substantial shortcomings and legal problems related to the independent and unauthorised broadening of the investigations by men like Alexander. First, Alexander had relatively little legal or investigative expertise. Like hundreds of soldiers who were expected to become detectives overnight, he was not adequately prepared for his assignment. One of the British investigators involved in the Bergen-Belsen case recalled: 'We were not geared, or trained or qualified or had enough resources to do the job. It was a makeshift, hurried and ad hoc decision and we had to do the best we could.'[9] Alexander's medical training and language skills, together with his knowledge of the German cultural and scientific environment, certainly qualified him for the job. However, he had no idea of how to take depositions from witnesses and victims, nor how to ask the right questions which would be admissible in court. His interviews and subsequent notes were never checked, read or certified by the witnesses themselves before or after he produced the CIOS reports. The JAG office demanded sworn, typed and signed statements, which meant that much of the evidence was in essence worthless, at least from a legal perspective. For Allied prosecutors the material constituted little more than useful background information, but was inadmissible in any future war crimes trials. Alexander's reports were also overtly biased and riddled with personal comments. In that sense, Alexander was representative of other investigators, often European refugees or military personnel, who in the post-war euphoria combined military duty with a personal desire to settle old scores.[10]

'A grand scale post-mortem'

In January 1944 a war crimes office was established as part of the JAG of the US army. It was this office which at the end of the war was put in charge of establishing cases of torture and atrocities in concentration camps liberated by American troops (Dachau, Mauthausen, Ebensee), and tried cases of murder and maltreatment of US soldiers (such as the Malmedy massacre) as well as other war crimes committed in the American zone of occupation. Since February 1945, US army groups were ordered to establish war crimes investigation units which were responsible to the JAG.[11] Initially, there were nineteen investigation groups authorised, with teams consisting of four officers and five non-commissioned officers (NCOs) backed up and advised by about thirty legal experts from the JAG office at Eisenhower's European headquarters.[12] The man in charge of the American prosecution was the Iowa lawyer Colonel Clio E. Straight, who in March 1945 was ordered to establish SHAEF's war crimes section in Paris. The city was also host to the newly developed and computerised Central Registry of War Criminals and Security Suspects (CROWCASS) which produced detailed lists of wanted Germans who were likely to pose a security risk to the occupation forces.[13] CROWCASS, once its duties had been modified and its offices moved from Paris to Berlin, became a valuable resource in tracking down war criminals and in preparing individual cases for the Allied prosecution.

In charge of the 7th US Army war crimes group, to which Alexander reported and delivered his documents, was Lieutenant-Colonel Paul Rigby.[14] At the beginning of April, Rigby had been told to 'recruit whomever he could' after alarming reports of atrocities had been received from combat units. By the end of May, he had most of the twenty-two men together whom he had mainly selected from record files. Their expertise ranged from legal and administrative to scientific or investigative training. Highly motivated and efficient, Rigby's teams collected incriminating evidence for a total of 120 cases within the first four weeks, implicating hundreds of German officials. There were many cases involving forced and slave labour as well as cases of concentration camp atrocities, areas which the American prosecution wanted to exclude from the investigation at that point. Yet such fine legal and political points were of little concern for most of the two dozen investigators.

Alexander arrived in Germany on Wednesday, 23 May 1945, via Brussels, where Lieutenant-Colonel John Barraclough was establishing the British war crimes programme.[15] It is possible that he was briefed on his way to Germany, since his arrival coincided with the arrest of all members of the Dönitz government in Flensburg. The Third Reich had virtually ceased to exist and supreme authority over the whole of Germany had now passed to the Allied authorities. Flying low over the suburbs of Munich, he could see the smoke still rising from some of the buildings burned in the concentration camp of Dachau. Surviving inmates of the camp were waving and cheering at the plane, and he could see two American field hospitals being set up near the camp grounds. One of the hospitals was the

Plate 7 Dachau concentration camp after liberation by American soldiers, April/May 1945.

16th Evacuation Hospital. In one corner of the camp he spotted the national emblems of the liberated nations, painted in multiple colours over the concentration camp walls. Upon arriving in Munich, the sight of the enormous destruction in the camp became apparent, 'a fitting end of the Sodom and Gomorrha which it was in its heyday. Driving through ruined streets dust of the rubble still fills the air.'[16] Overall an intense sense of place and time was responsible for Alexander's shifting moods over the following weeks of the investigation. The places he saw shaped his understanding of the crimes being committed. A feeling of outrage at the German people was his natural response, but there were countless questions raised by these places. Who were the people who had been worked and starved to death in these camps? Who had been in charge? When had these camps been constructed and for what ostensible or real purpose? Who was ultimately responsible for such places?

As far as the victims were concerned, Alexander did not have to wait long; he would see them, or would meet them on the streets of Munich. They were wandering around in small groups and enjoying their recently acquired freedom; some were proudly wearing parts of their prison garb in order to exhibit to the German people their very existence. Their emaciated bodies were a chilling physical reminder that the Nazis had failed in their task of annihilating them. Talking to a group of fifteen-year-old Jewish boys from Hungary was particularly upsetting for Alexander. Although they were looked after in a special camp by the American army and had gained considerable weight since the liberation, some still looked frightfully thin. Most important, though, was that 'their eyes were bright again', he noted. Conveying a sense of satisfaction, he told his wife on 26 May: 'The Germans have been thoroughly and soundly beaten and they seem to know it.'[17]

Those military units liberating and taking over the administration of the Dachau camp were so shocked about their discoveries that they produced an immediate report on the camp, the town and its citizens. Based on evidence from the Office of Strategic Services (OSS), the Counter Intelligence Corps (CIC) and other units, the report provided a first analysis of the history and conditions at Dachau.[18] One chapter dealt with the question many American soldiers like Alexander were asking themselves. What and how much had the citizens of Dachau known about the camp and what had they done about it? A preliminary survey revealed that the rhetorical question *Was konnten wir tun?* (What could we do?) was the townspeople's standard response and most of them wanted to be seen as the victims of political oppression rather than as indifferent bystanders. Another section of the report included the diary of a prisoner and the testimonies of survivors. Written by Dr Ali Kuçi, sections of *The Last Days of Dachau* were circulated by the International Prisoners Committee the day after Alexander arrived in Germany. He immediately mailed a copy to his wartime comrade

Ivan Brown in England to let him know that the news about Nazi atrocities was indeed based on facts.[19]

Under special orders from SHAEF, Alexander was given an extensive briefing of his assignment in a large camp of G-2 investigators near Munich. His task was to make a 'complete survey of the neuropsychiatric work of the German army and *Luftwaffe* (German air force), as well as of civilian agencies'. His powers were clearly substantial. Alexander had 'full powers to investigate everything of interest, and to remove documents, equipment, or personnel, if deemed necessary'.[20] The well-known research institutes in Munich, especially the German Research Institute for Psychiatry (*Deutsche Forschungsanstalt für Psychiatrie*, DFA), one of the centres of German race research, were first on his list. Here he hoped to find further leads for other military and civilian installations, perhaps even information which might corroborate rumours that the German government had intentionally murdered tens of thousands of mental patients. The overall aim was nothing less than a comprehensive assessment of the scale, methodology and quality of German medical science: 'We are doing a grand scale of post-mortem[s] of the Third Reich', he told Phyllis a few days after his arrival in Germany.[21]

German neuropsychiatry

Work began on Monday, 28 May 1945, at the German Research Institute for Psychiatry. Upon the arrival of the American troops in April 1945, Ernst Rüdin, director of the DFA and an influential theoretician of Nazi racial thought, had apparently fled to Switzerland.[22] Other sources suggest that he remained in Munich, physically weakened and suffering from a heart condition.[23] Alexander therefore needed to deal with the acting director and serologist Franz Jahnel, an established scientist with, as it later turned out, a good knowledge of some of the criminal human experiments which had been conducted at the Ravensbrück concentration camp.[24] Such information, however, was not relayed to Alexander. Alexander and Jahnel instead discussed the thousands of serological examinations that Jahnel's laboratory had performed for military and civilian hospitals. As far as war neurosis was concerned, Jahnel was of the opinion that the problem had been solved in the Second World War by means of suggestive therapy or 'painful electric currents', together with a policy of 'not letting the patients attain the goals which the illness served'.[25]

It was a rather lacklustre start, prompting Alexander to requisition Rüdin's files in the Genealogical Department of the KWI for Psychiatry. It appeared that Rüdin was probably keeping a low profile because of the part he had played in the killing of the handicapped. Alexander realised that Rüdin must have feared that some of the relatives of the murdered patients might come back and exact retribution. It quickly transpired that in the course of the programme not only incurable defectives had been killed, but also patients suffering from remedial illnesses, such as depression or brain tumours. Rüdin's files, however, revealed no incriminating evidence whatsoever, and Alexander was told by Jahnel that he had destroyed all damaging evidence.[26]

Alexander then moved on to interview Kurt Schneider, the consultant psychiatrist of the German army in Poland, France and Russia, and now in charge of clinical psychiatry at the DFA.[27] He was surprised to find that Schneider had never heard of abreaction treatments, and that he rejected the use of drugs offhand. The German researchers had apparently linked a number of deaths to an overdose and excessive repetition of sedatives. Schneider had likewise never heard of insulin subshock treatment, a modified form of insulin coma therapy which Anglo-American psychiatrists applied to schizophrenics. Psychotherapy was also not used in the German army, except in the air force where it was applied as part of the neuropsychiatric rehabilitation process. Such treatment was provided by lay therapists who were trained at the German Institute for Psychological Research and Psychotherapy in Berlin, headed by the psychotherapist Matthias Heinrich Göring, a cousin of the Reich Marshal Hermann Göring.[28] In general, German military psychiatrists had resorted to some of the crude methods of treatment used in the First World War which included Friedrich Panse's modified 'Kauffmann treatment' where the patient is given a series of painful and strong galvanic currents. One of Alexander's interviewees later admitted that he regarded the treatment as 'pure and unadulterated sadism'.[29]

Nazi military psychiatrists such as Schneider were faced with the problem that the term 'neurosis' carried extensive moral connotations. Labelling soldiers as 'war neurotics' implied that they were 'morally objectionable'. Schneider and his colleagues therefore attempted to limit the number of soldiers who were diagnosed as neurotics by narrowing the clinical definition. But by doing so, they had lost sight of the overall extent to which war neurosis was affecting the armed forces. This explains their surprise when the total number of soldiers diagnosed as neurotics turned out to be only about 1 per cent compared to those in the First World War. Their clinical approach had clearly distorted the statistics. During further interrogation, Schneider admitted the existence of 'psychosomatic disorders in patients who showed no other obvious signs of emotional distress and the postconcussional headache states were not included under the diagnostic category of neurosis'. Alexander wanted to know what had happened to these patients. Schneider replied: 'Well, those people finally were always sent home one way or another. They were a considerable group.' The answer left Alexander with the feeling that Schneider's work was motivated less by therapeutic considerations than by considerations of fairness in the administrative procedure in a regime which had been totally devoid of fairness.

Following the exposure of dressing up statistics on war neuroses, Schneider attempted to salvage the reputation of the German army by stressing its apparent 'fair justice system'. Despite the fact that soldiers were being sentenced to death for a minor offence or self-mutilation, they could apparently 'redeem themselves in combat'. For Schneider, military justice was the 'only clean and honest justice' in the Nazi regime compared to what he saw as the 'completely corrupt' civilian justice system. He obviously could not recall any trials where racial questions had played a meaningful role, except in one instance where an SA officer had been sentenced to several years' imprisonment for a case of *Rassenschande* (racial disgrace) in Poland.[30] This raised the question of anti-Semitism and the 'euthanasia' programme of which Schneider revealed little more than the name of the SS psychiatrist Werner Heyde. As it later turned out, Heyde had been one of the most forceful advocates of state-sanctioned murder.[31]

German neurosurgery

Determined to press on, Alexander left Munich on the next day, 29 May 1945, with two British military officials for Bad Ischl, Austria, in order to investigate the German army and air force medical centre, headed by the chief consulting neurosurgeon of the armed forces, General Wilhelm Tönnis.[32] Tönnis' neurosurgical centre had formerly been located in Berlin-Reinickendorf, but was evacuated to Bad Ischl in October 1943. One of the military experts accompanying Alexander was Dennis Williams, Wing Commander in the RAFMC, the other was Major George Smyth from the RAFMC.[33] Travelling in a heavily armoured car, the three men observed the columns of retreating and disowned German troops on their way back to their occupied country. Upon arrival, Tönnis gave them a cordial reception and immediately arranged for rooms in one of the hotels which had been taken over for use as 7th Army Hospital, prompting Alexander to record in his diary the same night: 'Thought to myself what a crazy world: the Germans took previous occupants to conc.[centration] camps, now we take present occupants to prisoner of war camps.'[34]

In the evening Tönnis entertained his guests with food and wine while his wife, a 'very self-obsessed' woman, went on to complain that the leadership had failed but not the people. This was to become one of the standard apologies, and indeed post-war myths, which allowed many Germans to ignore their past for years to come. For Alexander and the two British investigators the behaviour of the couple was a bit much: 'The Germans are taking defeat just as poorly and abjectly as they took victory; they are falling all over themselves to please us', he told his wife.[35]

But Alexander conceded that Tönnis was obviously a good politician who quickly adapted to a changing military and political situation. Shortly before the arrival of American troops, Tönnis had the Gauleiter of

83

Plate 8 Leo Alexander, war crimes investigator for the Supreme Headquarters Allied Expeditionary Forces. During his six-week tour of duty in May/June 1945 he discovered many cases of Nazi medical atrocities and criminal experimentation on humans.

the area arrested to prevent the destruction of bridges or any last ditch defence by the German forces. He then went alone to the local concentration camp of Ebensee and took about 750 of the most severely ill victims to his own hospital.[36] The whole venture had been a masterstroke. Even the inmates in the camp mistook Tönnis for the advance party of the Americans since his uniform exhibited no signs of the swastika.[37] Not without a certain degree of irony, Alexander remarked that 'his wife must have done a good repair job'.[38]

As far as medical evidence was concerned, Tönnis and his group were forthcoming in imparting information; they supplied the investigators with their publications and those of their colleagues, handed over unpublished statistics and showed them motion picture records about methods of neurosurgical treatment.[39] The material revealed the extent to which German soldiers suffering from brain injuries had been subjected to comprehensive programmes of rehabilitation. These included the use of athletics, water sports or speech training. With more than 10 000 soldiers passing through Tönnis' rehabilitation centre during the war and a total number of about 50 000 soldiers suffering from injuries of the brain, spinal cord and peripheral nerves, the organisation had been set up as a research, testing and teaching centre of the highest order, and was equipped with the most advanced medical technology. Yet, despite extensive research on battle-wound infections, Alexander realised that German scientists had no, or only partial knowledge of penicillin. Spot-checking of files, however, was not possible since Tönnis had sent all his official records on gunshot wounds to a colleague in Zürich where they remained inaccessible to the Allies.[40] Switzerland, at this point, seems to have served as a refuge to suspected Nazis and their personal files. The revelation left Alexander with a sense that Tönnis was a sophisticated and sly politician, 'although I hear that he was quite as good at roughness the German way in his own setting'.[41] It also transpired that one of Tönnis' close collaborators was a man called Hans Pittrich, a young Nazi psychiatrist and supporting member of the SS who had trained with Karl Kleist in Frankfurt am Main.[42] Pittrich had made his career by taking over the position of a Jewish colleague, who had been forced to emigrate in 1933. This man was none other than Alexander himself.[43] History had come full circle.

Ebensee and medical crimes

On 5 May 1945 the American 11th Armoured Division was inching its way along the Danube towards Linz, Austria; the soldiers had absolutely no idea of what they would find in the main concentration camp of Mauthausen and in its system of fifty satellite camps. Radiating from Mauthausen had been an extensive system of sub-camps of which Ebensee and Gusen were the two major ones. Established in 1943, Ebensee had been predominantly a slave labour camp for the construction of underground tunnels and various SS enterprises which included the production of rockets. Yet by the end of the war the camp had become one of the many centres for dying prisoners.[44] The images of living skeletons and the smell of death and disease surpassed everything American soldiers had encountered so far.[45] Between January and May 1945 approximately 40 000 people had died in the main camp of Mauthausen. A report written in June 1945 by Arthur Truner from the Chief Medical Intelligence Branch, Office of the Surgeon General, stated that 'at the time of uncovering, the Camp could be described as utterly without sanitation. Water power had been off for weeks, and conditions were indescribable.'[46] Truner was particularly shocked to discover that the eleven-year-old son of the camp commandant 'had been allowed to amuse himself by shooting residents of the camp with a rifle from the porch of the main administrative building'.[47] The historic cruelties exposed in *Schindler's List* apparently were no isolated incidents.

While Alexander was still under the impression that he would have little more than another 'weekly investigation' to do, his wife sensed that he would not return to America for some time. 'With your last news of order and what is happening now in Germany and the War Crimes Commission about to function, it seems logical that you have been chosen and may be busy for [a] long time', she told him on 2 June 1945.[48] She was right. After completing the interrogations of Tönnis and his staff on 31 May, the three investigators travelled to Ebensee to gain an idea about conditions within the camp. Here, for the first time, we hear Alexander's outrage about the crimes and a vivid description of the hypocrisy and ignorance which he felt some of the Germans were exhibiting. His reflection of the situation included those medical experts he had left only hours before. In the evening, after their arrival, he recorded in his diary:

Ebensee Concentration Camp: A real inoculation against the German deference and charm which they are turning on. Grim. 18,000 people (a large portion of Hungarian Jews taken from Hungary a year ago), under the whips of SS men and of 2,000 convicts (mostly crimes of violence such as murder and robbery) who acted as foremen. The mortality was 300 per day, rising to 1,000 a day for one week. Now, after 24 days of American care, the mortality is down to 70 per day. We saw the bodies of 3 people who died today in a large hall at the crematorium. Two extremely emaciated, literally skin and bones; the third severely emaci-ated, with hunger oedemas of the legs. None died from diseases; all of pure malnutrition and *incubation*. There were never a significant number of typhus cases in the camp, only 8 existing now. Inmates interviewed: 2 more 16 year olds, Hungarian Jewish boys. 1 year in camp, now active as workers. One gained 25 pounds since the liberation. A 41 year old lawyer from Vienna, 4 years in various camps, *wing*; energetic; shows the mental strain, expressing a harangue about Palestine. The administrative assistant, of partly English ancestry. The guide, by name of Sebastian, from Rumania. Very impressive Jude Katz; Jew from Hungary. One year ago the Germans came to his village, singled out the Jews, told him that they are going to take him to work in Germany: that he and his wife are going to work; that his aged parents would take care of his two daughters, aged 6 and 8, while they worked. When they arrived, an officer standing in the main square at the camp would scan the columns over, would pick out men who seemed capable of work and send them to the right; the others to the left. The latter were taken directly to the gas chamber and gassed. His wife, two children, and his parents were taken to the left and he never saw them again, while he was sent to slave labour. The doctor whom we saw later (Dr. Tot) told us that he saw 3,000 women and children killed by gas in one night, in groups of 200; that he and the others had to carry out the bodies to pits; he cried when he recalled it. On rainy days when trains arrived and the officer did not want to stand in the rain, all arrivals went into the gas chamber.[49]

'I will never forget it', Alexander told his wife a couple of days later. Heading back to Munich from this place of unimaginable horror, the three investigators interrupted their frenzied research with a stopover at Hitler's mountain chalet high up on the Obersalzberg near Berchtesgarden which had been heavily bombed by the Allies. 'The outlines of the place with the big windows', Alexander noted, 'from where he threatened the world, are well preserved, in ... ruins'. Sitting on the stone edge outside, looking into the empty, ruined room inside, Alexander felt like Seipia on the ruins of Carthaga.[50] It was the feeling of victory which for a moment made these men enjoy their journey through a devastated landscape. To his teenage son Gustave he wrote: 'You would find it most interesting here. The disorganised reminiscence of the German Army are being driven to PoW-centres, broken German airplanes in rows by the roadsides, bombed towns in rubble. The end of a great war.'[51]

Hans Luxenburger, chief consulting neuropsychiatrist to the Surgeon General of the German Air Force, was next on his list. He was interviewed at the Air Force Hospital in Possenhofen, Bavaria.[52] Asked about the selection process, Luxenburger revealed that in 1941 all psychological tests for flying personnel were abandoned on Göring's personal order. Apparently a number of former Nazi youth leaders with good party credentials and the sons of important party functionaries had been rejected.[53] From then on fighter pilots were selected on the basis of 'character' rather than on the basis of intelligence and aptitude for flying. Since the summer of 1943 the number of neuroses suddenly increased when wholly unqualified soldiers were accepted and sent without adequate training – for reason of gasoline shortage – to the Eastern front. In Luxenburger's view 'the material [sol-

87

Plate 9 Broken German airplanes in rows by the roadside. The woman standing near one of the planes is probably Phyllis, Alexander's wife, 1945–7.

diers] became poorer and the need greater'.[54] Treatment consisted of psychotherapy and included the use of persuasion, hypnosis, suggestion and psychocatharsis. Apparently no drugs were used. Therapeutic methods such as narcotherapy, insulin subshock or abreaction treatments were unknown to Luxenburger. In contrast to Allied flying personnel, German pilots had no operational limit; every flyer had to continue with his duty until he was either killed, severely wounded or until he showed signs of neurosis and was considered *abgeflogen* (to be through as a flyer). Yet even then, not one of them was discharged. Attempting to exploit the interview situation, Luxenburger criticised the conduct of the recent chief consulting psychiatrist to the German army, Maximinian de Crinis.[55] However, what Luxenburger and the investigators did not know was that de Crinis had committed suicide on 2 May 1945 because he was on the list of wanted war criminals for his role in the killing of handicapped people. Less than twenty-four hours later Alexander was to find out what had happened in German asylums.

On Saturday, 3 June, Alexander, together with Major Rudolf J. Baruch of the 93rd Evacuation Hospital, visited the Cure and Nursing Home Eglfing-Haar, near Munich. Allied forces had been tipped off that the acting director, Anton Edler von Braunmühl wanted to volunteer information about the killing of handicapped children and adults which he had discovered among the secret files of Hermann Pfannmüller, the former director and early participant in the 'euthanasia' programme.[56] Pfannmüller had tried to escape but was captured and imprisoned. From the documents it was apparent that between January 1940 and June 1941 more than 1800 non-Jewish patients had been transferred to one of the killing centres. In addition the salvaged transport lists included 213 children whose murder had been authorised by the organisers of the programme in Berlin. The children were killed separately in specially designed children's wards, generally by means of overdose of a common drug to camouflage their unnatural deaths. For example, barbiturates, hyoscin and a special sedative called modiscop which was manufactured and used as an anaesthetic in Vienna were used on the children.[57] On 20 September 1940 a special transport of Jews was dispatched to Lublin, Poland, for extermination, but their files contained no information about the overall number or identity. Only the correspondence with the relatives who were enquiring of their whereabouts suggested that at least thirty-one Jews were on that transport. Shortly afterwards Pfannmüller prided himself that his institution was free from Jews.

Von Braunmühl's information was invaluable in gaining detailed insight into the functioning of the 'euthanasia' programme, and in understanding the secret system of cover organisations that were affiliated with the operation codenamed 'Aktion T-4'. Pfannmüller's files implicated dozens of state officials, fellow doctors and nurses in participating and benefiting from the first systematic programme of mass murder. However, as it turned out, von

Braunmühl had volunteered the information for quite specific reasons. Knowing that the killing of infants would be revealed sooner rather than later, he wanted to strike a deal with the Americans to pre-empt negative publicity for the Eglfing asylum. He wanted the Americans to shift publicity about the killings to institutions such as Kaufbeuren, which had also been involved in the programme. Any news that patients had been murdered at Eglfing would interfere with his plan to establish a new institution for the mentally ill.[58] Since having turned over most of the evidence on his own initiative, von Braunmühl argued that there should be some consideration for his own institution.[59] While the bodies of the victims were still warm, this asylum director was already plotting his post-war professional career.

The next day Alexander handed over the evidence to the 7th Army document centre and informed Captain Barbour, the officially designated Counter Intelligence Corps (CIC) investigator of the 9th Air Force, about the conversation which he had had with von Braunmühl. Alexander left it to the CIC whether they wanted to 'play ball' with von Braunmühl and continued his tour of duty. Now the hunt for war criminals was on. Whereas the investigation had previously focused largely on German neuropsychiatry, and had recorded certain crimes more or less by chance, it now shifted towards a more systematic approach to uncover the involvement of physicians in Nazi atrocities.

Ludwig Hochapfel, for example, was questioned by Alexander about the selection of concentration camp personnel.[60] As it turned out, Hochapfel divulged some quite extraordinary details about the process of finding 'well performing' concentration camp commandants, especially those regarded as 'bullies', like the notorious 'Beast of Belsen'. Alexander was told that the relevant Nazi authorities had realised early on that psychopathic personalities were unsuited for the job. According to Hochapfel the personalities had to be 'particularly reliable and stable'. Only in a second stage were they brutalised during a special training period: 'Their brutal performance pattern was then established and further fortified by practice.' In his diary Alexander jotted down in German that the aim had been to create *Gewohnheitsrohlinge*, people who by the force of habit would exhibit brutal character traits.[61] So rather than looking for 'natural psychopaths', the Nazi administration believed that the environment in which the camp officials worked and lived would sufficiently brutalise and desensitise them, whilst at the same time retain their sense of loyalty and obedience towards the authorities. Once again, and in a rather twisted way, the Nazis contradicted themselves about the biological selection of the fittest. It was at this point that Alexander began to reflect about the psychological make-up of Nazi personalities, their motives and patterns of behaviour. Some of the more theoretical questions and subsequent attempts at finding explanatory models about such human behaviour would continue to intrigue him for the rest of his life.[62]

Aviation medicine

On 5 June 1945 Alexander visited the Institute for Aviation Medicine, headed by the former radiologist Georg August Weltz.[63] Part of the institute had been moved to a dairy farm in Weihenstefan because of heavy Allied bombing. Originally it had been located in barracks on the grounds of the physiological institute at the University of Munich. Research was carried out on small and large animals to study the effects, and possible treatment, of exposure to cold and low pressure. The basement of the dairy farm also contained a state-of-the-art low-pressure chamber. Weltz and his group of medical scientists had become interested in resuscitation from exposure to cold, especially in water, during the Battle of Britain in 1940, when German fighter pilots downed in the freezing North Sea subsequently died of hypothermia. His group included the pharmacologist Robert von Werz, the chemist Karl Seelkopf, the military physician of the air force Wolfgang Lutz, and the technical assistant Gertrud Schumacher.[64] Together they had made a startling discovery. They had realised that a large number of hypothermic animals could be revived by placing them in a hot bath of 40°C, although it was previously believed that such a procedure would produce a 'rewarming collapse'. An increase in temperature resulted in a further increase of animals that survived. The method had first been suggested by the Russian scientist Mikhail Lapchinksi in 1880, but was subsequently discarded because it was believed to be the source of the 'rewarming death'. Weltz and his group had rediscovered this life-saving method without understanding its physiological aetiology. According to Alexander, their over-enthusiastic search to find a scientific explanation for organic disturbances in hypothermic animals was, on the whole, characterised by an 'ingenuous bent for amateurism', even though their original observation was sound.[65]

Lutz then elaborated that the fundamental approach of the group had been to see whether death from exposure to cold was a result of anoxia. Tests had been carried out with small mice, rabbits, guinea pigs and pigs, sometimes in conjunction with low-pressure experiments. Theories as to the causes of death from hypothermia varied greatly in Germany. According to the physiologist Hermann Friedrich Rein from Göttingen it was due to a paralysis of the central nervous system. Others believed it to be tissue damage, and yet another theory suggested that it was due to an increase of the oxygen saturation of the venous system. However, none of the models had proven death from exposure to cold conclusively. Asked by Alexander whether their group had applied their findings to men, especially in experiments on humans, Lutz side-stepped the question and referred to the work of the armed services. Apparently he 'knew of no experimental studies on human beings'.[66] While they had no data on humans, he told Alexander that his group could provide experimental data on large animals that were somewhat comparable. But when Alexander wanted to inspect the place of the experiments, he was told that they had been carried out on an estate near Freising, which apparently was too far away to visit. Alexander replied that it was not too far, and so the party left for Freising.

Realising that the estate was marked by the conspicuous absence of any equipment useful for experiments on large animals, Alexander enquired about its whereabouts and was finally shown two cracked wooden tubs in a shed behind the stable. The wooden tubs had apparently been disposed of after the experiments had finished. Asked whether any of their ideas, methods or recommendations had been applied to human beings, Weltz denied this on two occasions, but indicated that the German Air Force Sea-Rescue Service in France had applied his method and sent him reports. The examination of these reports, however, revealed that the patients had all been treated according to the traditional methods of rewarming. Weltz was simply unable to produce any records which showed that his method had been applied. In a private conversation Weltz attempted to strike a deal with Alexander by asking him whether he should close the institute and dismiss his staff, or whether there was a chance of working under the auspices of the US military authorities. He hoped to receive funding from an American research organisation such as the Rockefeller Foundation. Alexander responded that no such plans existed and that Weltz should preserve all the material, equipment and staff in order to provide further information to other agencies. Asked again whether any work on human beings had been carried out, either by himself or by anyone he knew, Weltz was 'quite positive in denying the question'. The obvious attempts to conceal vital evidence convinced Alexander that medical war crimes had apparently been committed. About a month later he noted:

> I came away from all these interviews with the distinct conviction that experimental studies on human beings, either by members of this group themselves, or by other workers well known to and affiliated to the members of this group, had been performed but were being concealed.[67]

There were three reasons why Alexander had gained this impression. Firstly, the instruments for large animal experiments had been so strikingly absent in an environment where every piece of equipment for every mouse or guinea pig was meticulously preserved, independently of whether the experiments had been completed or not. Secondly, the fact that Weltz was unable to produce any reports on any humans at all, who had been rescued or treated by his new method, suggested that such data had been filed with material which he wanted to conceal. Finally, by attempting to persuade Alexander to authorise the closure of the institute, Weltz wanted a *carte blanche* to hide or dispose of further records. Yet Alexander felt it best to suppress his suspicions. He wanted to leave these men under the impression that he had been satisfied with their performance, hoping that they would not remove or destroy any records. Aware that his knowledge of the experiments was limited at this point, he planned to return to the scene after having unearthed more evidence.

Euthanasia

Moving back and forth between the different subjects of his investigations, Alexander now turned his full attention to the killing of handicapped children and adults. On 7 June 1945 experts from the 7th Army document centre in Munich briefed him with background information on various people who were implicated in the killings, mostly asylum doctors and nurses.[68] His interview with the chief consultant to the Army Medical Corps in Munich, Oswald Bumke, therefore concentrated mostly on the 'euthanasia' programme.[69] Bumke was a distinguished neuropsychiatrist who in 1934 had offered his resignation in protest against the Nazi sterilisation law, but the regime decided to keep him for public relations purposes. Bumke was frank in discussing the killing of the insane. Although supposed to be a top secret operation, 'the sparrows were whistling it from the rooftops', he told Alexander; it was a tragic crime, which had destroyed the trust of the public in the psychiatric profession. According to Bumke, psychiatrists had always been suspected of 'putting people away' but now they were actually killing them. When asked by the authorities whether there were any foreseeable problems with the relatives if their kin were transferred, he had replied that they would be 'afraid that this means that their [sic] being transferred from life to death'.[70] Intrigued by these revelations, Alexander set out to investigate the programme comprehensively.

Together with Major Baruch, Alexander left for Heidelberg. There, on 9 June he interviewed the director of the Wiesloch asylum, Wilhelm Möckel. It was an experience Alexander would never forget.[71] Having left the interrogators waiting in the conference room for some time, when he eventually appeared Möckel represented little more than a frightened man. He was pale, sweating profusely and was shaking all over his body. Only when Alexander reassured him that they had come for information and not to arrest him did he calm down. Shortly afterwards he stopped trembling, excused himself and went into his office to phone his daughter, telling her in German – but overheard by Alexander – 'that it was not what he had feared'. Returning to the meeting, Möckel then readily disclosed vital information about the killing of the handicapped in his institution. All confidential and secret documents about the programme had already been turned over to the American authorities and passed on to the war crimes section of the JAG.

Apart from the transferral of handicapped Jewish patients, there had been about 800 handicapped asylum inmates transferred to one of the killing centres. In addition, Möckel added sheepishly, the asylum had a children's ward for 'intensive treatment' of mental defectives, the result of which was that the children were generally 'put to sleep'. Established in early 1941, the ward had existed for about half a year; eleven children eventually died as a result of the 'special treatment' which was applied by Josef Artur Schreck, the deputy director of the asylum, and his nurses. Apparently Schreck refused to perform further killings after three children had been killed, stating that 'a hospital is not the appropriate place'. Apparently the assignment was then passed on to a young doctor from Eglfing-Haar.[72] Following the closure of the ward, the notorious 'euthanasia' doctor Carl Schneider established a 'research house' and arranged that the killing of patients would in the future be carried out in institutions other than Wiesloch, for example in Hadamar or Grafeneck.[73] According to Möckel about 600 patients were sent to Hadamar to be starved to death. Some patients were also sent to Brandenburg or Vienna. In the end, Möckel could not endure the transferral of patients any more. Instead of declining participation or refusing to authorise the transports, he found an ingenious way of dealing with a problem which obviously 'nauseated' him: 'Whenever a transport was to leave at night, I usually left the institution at noon and did not come back until the next day.' Only rarely would Alexander hear such a confession of deliberate and premeditated ignorance again.

However, there were some at the Wiesloch asylum who could not look away. One of the nurses, Amalie Widmann, had become especially attached to the patients. Like a caring mother, she could not live with the idea that her patients were transferred to an unknown institution where they were killed.[74] Therefore, in July 1940, she decided to visit the killing centre of Grafeneck. Her testimony not only gave startling insight into the extent to which the local population knew what was going on, but shows a degree of courage only a few Germans exhibited at the time. Arriving at the train station in Marbach near Münzingen, the local townspeople looked at her in disbelief when she asked them the way to Grafeneck. Most of the inhabitants apparently knew full well what was happening in the vicinity. Finding the place closed, with a sign saying that entrance was strictly prohibited, because of 'danger of infections', she became frightened and ran into an open field when heavily armed police officers turned up in green uniforms. There she was picked up by a local farmer, who told her that she should 'not go there. One must not say anything.' Shortly afterwards she was imprisoned by the SS guards of the asylum and interrogated. She told them that she wanted to see her old patients and inspect the conditions in which they lived. Responding angrily to her request, the commanding officer told her that the patients in Grafeneck liked it so much 'they ... never want to leave again'.[75]

Another staff member of Wiesloch, Alfred Schenninger, reported that Möckel had been a Nazi faithful from the beginning and had wholeheartedly supported the extermination of the handicapped. Möckel's close connection with some of the key organisers of the 'euthanasia' programme, for example, men like Paul Nitsche, Carl Schneider and Werner Hyde, clearly implicated him. Schenninger could also recall that he had once 'met the whole gang' and there was evidence that the organisers had frequently met for consultations at Wiesloch. But during the second interview, Möckel revealed more about his other activities, quite apart from overseeing the murder of patients. The Wiesloch director was, as it turned out, an enthusiastic horticulturist. His office was full of graphs about the progress of horticulture and fruits, planted on the asylum ground. Proudly he showed Alexander his latest variety of plums. Möckel was also a prolific writer for horticultural magazines and had recently published an article about its value in bringing delight and joy into the lives of the mentally ill (at least for those who remained alive). For Alexander the meeting with Möckel was an extraordinary experience, especially after having seen the places of atrocities of which this was an integral part. Later he recalled:

I came away from the interview with Möckel with the feeling that here was something that had no place in the reality of life at all, but something that was part of the famous stage play 'Arsenic and Old Lace'. This 'Arsenic and Old Lace' atmosphere pervades a good deal of Nazi Germany. In a way they were all 'Brewsters', faithful to the setting of the play. There was no point in deciding which Germans in positions of authority had committed atrocities and who had not, but rather, who had committed them with an air of innocence like the two old ladies in the play, and who had committed them with overt aggressive brutality, like one of the nephews. There were few people around of the type of the good nephew who looked on in horror, but without energetic determination or effective ability to put a stop to it. The Brewsters family of the famous play is indeed symbolic of the state of affairs psychological and factual which had existed in Nazi Germany. Giving him all the benefit of the doubt, the least that can be said about Dr. Möckel is that he was the sweet old lady type of killer.[76]

For the moment Alexander needed a rest from the investigations. He decided to spend the weekend in Frankfurt am Main, and visit his former professor, Karl Kleist. A stopover at SHAEF in Frauenthal am Main near Wiesbaden was accompanied by the visit of Montgomery and Zhukov. Yet the presence of the two military celebrities meant tight security and blocked roads for many hours. Arriving in Frankfurt on 10 June he immediately searched for the place where he had once lived before being forced to emigrate. The house at Feuerbachstraße 44 was totally destroyed. Only a wall, a chimney, and a few partitions of stones were sticking out of the rubble. Reflecting about his sense of *déjà vu*, he later noted in his diary: 'Had a hard time finding the place, strange thing about memory after twelve and a half years.'[77] He then went to the Römerberg, where almost all buildings were submerged in a sea of ruins.

One of the places where he had once spent his evenings with friends was nothing but earth and brick, with long grass growing all over it, 'on the edge of which sat a German sailor and a girl, playing gay old songs on two accordions. If you closed your eyes, you could think the Appleweinstuben[78] were still there, but when you opened them it was all ruins, with some of the spirit emerging, Poles, GI's. The men who brought Applewein out of his house.'[79] Like searching for his own past, he also enquired what had happened to his one-time girlfriend, Gisela Preitz, who now lived in Kiel, was married, and had two young children.[80] Coming back to the city in which he had laid the foundation of his professional life evoked feelings of nostalgia and a sense of sadness about the enormous destruction in a country he had once admired for its civilised culture.

Meeting Kleist the next day on 11 June was a pleasure for Alexander, although one not without tensions.[81] Kleist had just been reinstated in his former position as director of the Frankfurt clinic after having been dismissed by the Allied authorities for his membership in the Nazi party, for his role in the Hereditary Health Courts, and for his advisory function in the Nazified Reich Institute for Film and Picture in Science and Education.[82] Throughout the war he had also been chief consulting psychiatrist to the 9th (Kassel) Corps Area. Appearing overly defensive, Kleist told Alexander that he had given up his attitude of 'passive objection' to the regime after the successful invasion of France in 1940 because he believed that the war was effectively won, 'and that he had to come to terms with the [Nazi government] in order to be able to continue [with] his research'.[83] The *Blitzkrieg* victories had apparently convinced Kleist that he needed to collaborate with the regime if he wanted to use the war for his scientific work.

Kleist's explanation also revealed some of the motives as to why he had consented to the dismissal of his Jewish staff in 1933. Alexander himself had been severely affected by the dismissal and, in a sense, had come to hear from Kleist the underlying justification for the action at the time. To continue and expand his research activity had always remained Kleist's goal which apparently warranted concessions to his personal integrity. Kleist then stated that he had used his position to exercise a 'moderating influence' on the Nazi 'euthanasia' programme; he had apparently criticised the government 'without committing suicide'.[84] Yet as far as the killing of the handicapped is concerned, the historical record is conspicuously silent about any overt form of opposition from Kleist, except for a number of critical but unpublished reports from the 1930s about the condition of patients in the asylums of Weilmünster, Herborn and Eichberg.[85]

Kleist used the meeting with Alexander to construct a post-war myth which depicted him as one of the few who had actually opposed Nazi policies; this appeared all the more credible since most of his colleagues were deeply involved in medical war crimes. Kleist and Alexander also spoke about their mutual wartime experiences, especially about the treatment of war neuroses. According to Kleist, most neuroses were 'masked', that is, psychosomatic illnesses which were overlooked and treated as purely disciplinary problems, or in special field formations.[86] One of the most striking changes in the mental constitution of the civilian population had been what German psychiatrists had labelled 'egotistic regression' (*egoistisch zurückgeschraubtsein*), a neurotic behaviour which manifested itself when people began focusing entirely on their individual and personal problems. This resulted in incidents where citizens publicly rejoiced if their houses had been spared during the bombing raids on Frankfurt am Main, for example in March 1944, although most of the city had been razed to the ground.[87] Such apparent changes in the attitude of the civilian population are relevant in so far as they can shed light on some of the actions and inactions during the killings; although the murder of the handicapped was officially a top secret operation, it became generally known to the public. Kleist also revealed the extent to which he was informed about the 'euthanasia' programme.

Kleist saw the operation as a 'state organised lie' which depended on enforcing 'silence by tyranny'. Saying anything against the programme was apparently equivalent to suicide; a word about it 'meant concentration camp, and concentration camp meant death'. Not only did Kleist reveal unintentionally that he knew of the exterminatory function of concentration camps, but indirectly admitted his deliberate decision not to raise his voice on behalf of the victims for fear of personal retribution. Indeed, for a man in his position such opposition could have been a calculable risk. Kleist protested on behalf of patients, but only before the war while he was inspecting the asylums of the Hessen-Nassau region in 1938. He described the conditions as appalling, with patients sleeping on straw bedding, undernourished, and with no clothing or shirts. Kleist subsequently resigned from his supervisory post. Despite the criticism against the authorities, one needs to question why, after having witnessed that the German government showed no respect for the welfare of the mentally ill whatsoever, Kleist joined the Nazi party little more than a year later.

Three days after Alexander had spoken to Kleist, on 14 June, the latter was dismissed for a second time by the military authorities as the director of the Frankfurt clinic. Whether Alexander had recommended his dismissal to the authorities is not known. By August 1945, Kleist was also suspended from his university post.[88] But with the help of the mayor of Frankfurt and the notorious *Persilscheine* (certificates of innocence) from fellow scientists, Kleist was eventually able to re-establish his position in post-war Germany.

Neuropathology

While the Allied powers established an increasingly efficient system of occupation, Alexander submitted his investigative material to SHAEF[89] and completed another interview with a military psychiatrist who expressed the rather unconventional view that flight fatigue could be overcome by stimulating soldiers' ambition for decorations.[90] He then embarked on a journey to Hadamar, one of the most atrocious of the six main killing centres of the 'euthanasia' programme.[91] Since the acting director, William Altvater, had little information about the killings, Alexander questioned the head nurse Irmgard Huber.[92] She stated that after the outbreak of war the asylum had been turned into a military hospital of which sections had been reserved for British and French prisoners of war. Only some of the patients remained, mostly those who had been working on the nearby farms. After the transformation of Hadamar into a killing centre at the end of 1940, new doctors, clerks and drivers had arrived from Berlin. About forty to seventy patients were killed each day. Huber recalled that the patients were taken to a special wing in the cellar, where they had to undress and be examined, before being killed by poison gas on the same day or during the night following their arrival. In July 1941 the whole set-up disappeared. A year later, the killings resumed on a much smaller scale; this time the victims were emaciated Russians and Poles who were supposedly suffering from tuberculosis, but never coughed. When Alexander inspected the site, he found that workmen had attempted to cover up the installation with fresh masonry, though traces of the crematorium chimney were still visible. The killing chambers had also been closed by masonry. Only the autopsy room was still accessible. It was a grim place. Russians and Poles were literally starved before being killed by injections in semi-private rooms in the women's wing. This programme continued up until eight days before the Americans arrived in 1945.

Hadamar clearly left a deep impression on Alexander. On the same day, 14 June, he drove to Dillenburg to visit the laboratory of the neuropathologist Julius Hallervorden at the KWI for Brain Research.[93] The laboratory was found in an impeccable condition and fully operational. Most of the vast collection of histopathological specimens, including Max Bielschowsky's valuable collection, had been evacuated from Berlin to Dillenburg during the war. There were more than 110 000 preparations from 2800 patients at Hallervorden's disposal, together with several thousands of preparations from the State Hospital of Görden, another of the many killing centres. Two of Hallervorden's research associates, Hugo Noetzel and Eduard Welte, had been arrested by the Allied authorities in the meantime.[94] Hallervorden was quite forthcoming in showing Alexander his histopathological preparations, and in discussing his latest research.

Alexander was shown a series of confidential reports which covered the years from 1940 to 1942. These revealed the number of cases which Hallervorden had examined each year. The reports included hundreds of gunshot wounds of the brain, but also 1500 brains of patients who had died from typhus, 185 of which had been sent from the Jewish hospital in Warsaw, and seventeen Jewish-Polish cases from Lublin.[95] Hallervorden strongly denied ever having received brains from concentration camps, a statement which may have been true since he might not have received them directly. But Hallervorden then admitted that he had initiated the collaboration with the organisers of the killing programme in order to exploit the brains of the victims for his research. On 20 July Alexander noted:

> Dr. Hallervorden had obtained 500 brains[96] from the killing centres for the insane. These patients had been killed in various institutions with carbon monoxide gas. Dr. Hallervorden himself initiated this collaboration. As he put it: 'I heard that they were going to do that, and so I went up to them and told them "Look here now, boys, if you are going to kill all these people, at least take the brains out so that the material could be utilised". They asked me: "How many can you examine?" and so I told them an unlimited number – the more the better. I gave them the fixatives, jars and boxes, and instructions for removing and fixing the brains, and then they came brining them in like the delivery van from the furniture company. The Gemeinnützige Krankentransport Gesellschaft (the Public Ambulance Society) brought the brains in batches of 150–250 at a time'.[97] The man who organised this service was Dr. Hegener, a paediatrician from Berlin, whom Dr. Hallervorden remembers as a 'crazy and arrogant fellow, who talked all the time about himself'. 'There was wonderful material among those brains, beautiful mental defectives, mal-formations and early infantile diseases. I accepted those brains of course. Where they came from and how they came to me was really none of my business.'[98]

In addition to the unethical and criminal origin of the material there is the problem of collecting this kind of data in the first place. With tens of thousands of patients being killed, it had become unfeasible to perform autopsies. Even Hallervorden acknowledged that this fact reduced the 'scientific value of the material'.[99] Since in all cases the killing of the patients interrupted the 'natural course' of the disease, there would not be any comparative material at a later stage, nor is it clear how the disease would have progressed in the patients, if they had been kept alive. Most of the patients were starved prior to being killed and it is likely that this affected the brain specimen. Not a single case can be compared with specimens obtained from patients who died after the normal course of their illness. Thus, any conclusions based on the material in later publications was not only ethically highly problematic, but scientifically flawed.[100]

Hallervorden's utilitarian approach to human subjects separated the method of scientific enquiry from any kind of ethical consideration. When he was offered the brains of schizophrenics and epileptics, he refused to take them, not for moral reasons, as he maintained, but because he felt that they were of little relevance for his research projects. Hallervorden may have opposed the psychological effects of the programme, which 'brutalised' the nursing personnel and 'nauseated' himself, but the knowledge of the immorality of the killings, least of all their criminality, did not change his desire to exploit the apparent opportunity for his research. In short, Hallervorden wanted to use the 'euthanasia' programme for his professional interests. At the same time, he was aware that in 1945 psychiatry as a discipline had lost the respect of the German people, and probably that of other nations as well.

Interviewing Hallervorden in the summer of 1945 constituted something of a dilemma for Alexander. Both men not only shared similar approaches and interests as researchers, but were scientists in the same medical discipline who interacted with some of the same international colleagues. Alexander probably knew Hallervorden from the 1920s as part of his teachers' generation. Exchanging pleasantries and information about colleagues in England, for example about émigré scientists such as Max Bielschowsky, Alfred Meyer or Karl Neubürger, was part of the scientific etiquette to show mutual respect to each other.[101] A substantial amount of Hallervorden's work was closely related to Alexander's own research interests. This fact undermined his otherwise rational and relatively detached approach when interviewing German physicians. Whereas he felt the moral duty to report and condemn the use of brain specimens which had been obtained from the victims of the 'euthanasia' programme, he was genuinely fascinated with the work of an expert whom he regarded as a 'thorough, accurate and ingenious observer'. Alexander's diary entries and his subsequent CIOS report reflect this ambiguity. The interview marked a key moment in the investigation where the boundaries between investigator and interviewee became significantly blurred. Alexander's objective and, for the most part, impartial reporting about the violation of patient rights and lives was temporarily suspended, entangled in a web of conflicting personal, scientific as well as professional interests.

Breakthrough

On 14 June 1945, while on his way from Frankfurt to Göttingen, a coincidence played into Alexander's hands which precipitated an unexpected turn in the investigation. Meeting the army chaplain Lieutenant Biegelow over dinner at the officer's mess of the 433rd Battalion in Rennerod, the latter enquired about Alexander's views on the Dachau human experiments.[102] Only days ago Biegelow had heard the testimonies of some of the witnesses and survivors of the experiments being broadcasted over Allied radio.[103] Biegelow was particularly shocked about the nature of the experiments which involved prisoners being placed in tubs of ice-cold water while their suffering was recorded by EEG-instruments attached to their bodies. For Alexander the radio broadcast about Dachau was interesting news. He immediately realised that the experiments were 'strikingly similar to the animal experiments performed by Dr. Weltz and his group'.[104] Unfortunately, the chaplain could not remember any of the names of the prisoners who had been broadcast on the radio. Yet Biegelow's information was the missing link in the investigation.

On arrival in Göttingen, Alexander questioned Hubertus Strughold, the former director of the Aviation Medical Research Institute of the German air force and professor of physiology.[105] Throughout the war, Strughold had pioneered equipment which allowed German pilots to reach higher altitudes, and developed means for them to adjust to speed, temperature and oxygen deficiency. Strughold was forthcoming in admitting that he had knowledge of the experiments from the Nuremberg conference in October 1942 which had taken place at the Hotel Deutscher Hof. Because the doctor in charge, Sigmund Rascher, had used 'criminals' for the experiments, Strughold expressed his strict opposition to such research on principle. He told Alexander that he had 'always forbidden even the thought of such experiments in [his] institute, firstly on moral grounds, and secondly on medical ethics. Any experiments on humans that [were] carried out were performed only on [the] staff and on students interested in [the] subject on a strictly volunteer basis.'[106] Shortly afterwards Strughold was visited by the surgeon of the US 8th Air Force, Colonel Harry Armstrong, who recruited him for 'Project Paperclip'.[107]

Equally forthcoming with information was the distinguished Göttingen professor of physiology, Hermann Friedrich Rein. Like that of Strughold, Rein's role during the Nazi regime is ambiguous and subject to dispute. Rein was critical of Weltz and his group; he felt that the trained radiologist was not qualified to explore complex physiological problems 'beyond a certain intuitive knack'. It may also have been professional jealousy which tempted Rein to oppose the work of a colleague and shift attention away from the Göttingen scientists. Alexander was given no further clues beyond the name of Rascher, a 'nasty fellow', whose experiments had not yielded 'any decisive new findings'.[108] Rein apparently never saw the experimental design, but spoke to Rascher during the Nuremberg conference in 1942. The impression Rascher had made on his colleagues was far from flattering. In a semi-drunken state, Rascher is said to have challenged the scientific basis of Rein's work in the most appalling way by saying to Rein:

You think you are a human physiologist and you have just published a book entitled Human Physiology, but all you ever did was work on guinea pigs and mice. I am the only one in this whole crowd who really does and knows human physiology because I experiment on humans, and not on guinea pigs or mice.[109]

There were no witnesses to the conversation, and it is possible that Rein invented or greatly exaggerated what was said in retrospect. However, Rascher's overall mediocre character and his overt careerism are beyond reasonable doubt. The statements by Rein and other distinguished researchers reveal that the German medical and scientific elite were closing ranks to place responsibility and blame squarely on the one person who was known to have been disreputable and criminal. It was a strategy that had potential, not least because Rascher was dead and could not defend himself.

Further interviews about the Dachau experiments at the Institute for Physiology in Göttingen produced no new evidence, except that each of the men vouched for the scientific integrity of the other, whilst blaming Rascher.[110] It was a vicious and frustrating circle, and Alexander knew he was making no progress. There was one detail, though, mentioned by Rein in passing, which sounded promising. It appeared that Rascher had been a member of the SS. On 17 June[111] Alexander proceeded to the 7th Army Document Centre in Heidelberg, where he hoped to find new leads following the discovery of Himmler's secret files by the US army in a cave in Hallein, near Strasbourg. There, all of a sudden, things fell into place. Himmler's papers turned out to be one of the most important collections of incriminating evidence in post-war Germany, revealing in minute detail the political rationale, development and findings of the Dachau experiments. Himmler's near-neurotic obsession to preserve every scrap of paper, which he meticulously annotated in green pencil, was pervasive throughout the files. The man who had ordered his underlings to destroy all material related to the SS had ironically become the best source for Allied war crimes investigations. His papers also became one of the cornerstones in the Nuremberg Doctors' Trial. 'If history sets him down as one of the worst of barbarians, he has only his penchant for paper work to blame', one commentator noted in 1947.[112]

Together with Lieutenant Boulton and Hugh Iltis, who were among those who discovered the material, Alexander searched for reports and correspondence about the experiments. Classified 'top secret', the material exposed the entire system of Rascher's dealings with the head of the German SS and police, Himmler. Their communication provided insight into the mentality of the people who had initiated and carried out the experiments, but also revealed the professional animosities, threats and means of influence at the top of the German medical hierarchy. Rascher and his wife[113] both had a tendency to scrounge for favours and positions by denouncing other scientists.[114] By the end of the war both were executed on order of Himmler, because they had become a security risk as far as their knowledge of the camp experiments was concerned. What is more, the material exposed the extent to which the SS and the German Air Force had collaborated in the experiments. It exposed the large number of people who had ordered, abetted and participated in the research. Even this group constituted only a fraction of the German medical elite, who had silently consented to the experiments. Assessing accurately the degree of complicity in German medicine and society was not yet within the scope of Alexander's research. One of the main findings was that Rascher had not carried out the experiments alone. The immediate collaborators included the physiologist Ernst Holzlöhner from Kiel University and Erich Finke, Holzlöhner's assistant. The cold-water experiments had developed out of low-pressure research in the same experimental block five at Dachau. These had been carried out by Hans Wolfgang Romberg and Rascher under the supervision of Siegfried Ruff, one of Strughold's collaborators and director of the German Research Institute for Aviation. The findings raised serious doubts about the accuracy of Strughold's testimony. He had been well acquainted with all of these men, and had been present, together with Rein, during the presentation of research at the Nuremberg conference in 1942. For Alexander it was 'revealing to realise that only Dr. Rascher was named by Dr. Strughold and Professor Rein, while their colleagues Holzlöhner, Ruff, Romberg and Finke, whose participation in the human experiments was then not yet known to us, were still being covered up'.[115] Slowly but consistently, the fine net of complicity was beginning to unravel.

Now it was time to confront the Weltz group with the evidence. On 19 June Alexander set off to Munich. Arriving late at night, he first held a conference with members of FIAT.[116] On the evening of 20 June, after having inspected the charred remains of Weltz barracks, which included a burned-out low-pressure chamber, he visited Lutz in Freising for a second time. This time Alexander came unannounced. He found Lutz in the laboratory, unprepared, and slightly nervous. Alexander first engaged Lutz in a trivial conversation before shifting the subject to the Dachau experiments. Lutz knew that any further cover-up was pointless, admitted his SS membership, and responded to Alexander's suggestion to 'let down his hair' by telling him what he knew about the experiments. It turned out that Weltz had offered him the 'human' job, but that he had declined it for 'being too soft'.[117]

Some of the participating researchers attempted to justify the ethics of the experiments by drawing from comparisons in history; both Romberg and Holzlöhner had tried to explain their participation by pointing to the conditions in shipbuilding wharves in the Middle Ages, when the workmen assigned to remove the forward support of the hulls, which frequently crushed or killed them, were selected from prisoners sentenced to death. According to this view, it seemed legitimate to subject a prisoner on death row to suffering, if it served some broadly defined higher purpose especially in a national emergency. Another of Holzlöhner's rationalising models stressed the importance of the expert (*Fachmann*) to ensure that the project would not fall into 'uncontrolled hands'.[118] Such obvious attempts at denying the criminal nature of the experiments disintegrated the moment the war was lost. After a visit from a British intelligence official in the summer of 1945, Holzlöhner must have felt exposed and committed suicide in order to escape prosecution.[119]

On 21 June Alexander interviewed, for the first time, some of the witnesses of the experiments with the help of American officials stationed at Dachau.[120] Among the witnesses was John Bauduin, chairman and founder of the 'International Investigation-Office for Medical SS-Crimes in the German Concentration Camps, Dachau'. The office had been set up on 11 June 1945 to secure the imprisonment and prosecution of the perpetrators, the confiscation of their property and the compensation of the victims and their relatives. It also distributed a questionnaire to all concentration camps in order to establish the extent to which medical experiments had been carried out, and ascertain the specific nature of criminal human experiments.[121] The Czechoslovakian philologist Paul Hussarek from Prague and the German ex-prisoner Oscar Häusermann from Stuttgart also offered vital information about the survivors of the experiments, the selection of victims as well as details about three assistant doctors and eight camp assistants.[122] Yet relatively few victims were later called upon to give evidence in the Doctors' Trial. Their testimony confirmed suspicions, however, that Rascher had not worked alone. One of Rascher's assistants was a Dr Castelpietro, who had organised the selection of experimental subjects to create the greatest degree of rivalry and disunity among the camp inmates. At the top of the list were Jews, gypsies and stateless persons, followed by foreign Catholic priests, 'criminals' and political prisoners. Whereas Polish Catholic priests were largely selected for the poison-bullet experiments, the German researchers seemed to have preferred Polish Jews for the cold-water experiments. The witnesses could name only a single person who had survived the medical torture. His name was Leo Michałowski, a Polish priest.

The thirty-year-old Michałowski had been in charge of two religious schools in the small village of Sweecie (Swiccic), near Chulm on the Vistula, when the German army had invaded, shooting 192 of the 570 priests, whilst torturing others. This was followed by the arrival of the SS, who sent Michałowski along with 198 other priests to Dachau for five and a half years.[123] Altogether about forty survived. Michałowski was one of the few survivors of the malaria and cold-water experiments, and was able to give a detailed account of the conditions and atmosphere that pervaded the research. After repeatedly protesting against the involuntary and forced nature of the malaria experiments, the doctor in charge replied: 'I am responsible for your life, not you.'[124] By the end of 1942, Michałowski was taken to the 'Aviation Room' in block five, which was sealed off by a wooden fence, and immersed in ice-cold water until he lost consciousness. After half an hour he was forced to smoke a cigarette, then ordered to drink a glass of schnapps, before the physicians cynically enquired how he felt. Michałowski's testimony later became one of the most poignant moments at the start of the Nuremberg Doctors' Trial.[125]

Upon Alexander's return to the 7th Army Document Centre in Heidelberg the staff had in the meantime found the complete and final fifty-six-page report on *Freezing Experiments on Humans*, written by Holzlöhner, Finke and Rascher in October 1942. It is the only existing copy ever to be discovered, and Alexander later published the report in its entirety.[126] The report gives a detailed insight into the rationale and technique of the experiments, the clinical picture produced by intense chilling, the theoretical and practical causes of death, and various methods of resuscitation. The data provided was extremely detailed and thoroughly prepared. Graphs and statistics provided ample evidence about the criminal nature of the experiment. One of the experiments recorded that the time it took to kill people by means of intense chilling varied between 53 and 106 minutes. To the war crimes authorities Alexander reported: 'This table is certainly the briefest and most laconic confession of 7 murders in existence!'[127] Alexander's war crimes investigations had been successfully concluded. It was time to return home to his wife and children.

5
The Road to Nuremberg

Assessing German medical science

On 26 June 1945, after weeks of silence, Alexander wrote a long and impassioned letter to his wife in which he outlined his views on Nazi medicine and policy. Written the day before he was leaving for Paris to brief the American prosecution about medical war crimes, the letter conveys a sense of finite condemnation about the state of affairs of German medical research and practice:

German medical science presented a grim spectacle. Grim for many reasons. First, because it remained essentially static and became comparatively incompetent, and second, because it was drawn into the maelstrom of depravity of which this country reeks – the smell of the concentration camps, the smell of violent death, torture and sufferings of muted victims will not rot of one's nostrils. Their really depraved pseudo-scientific curiosity went so far as to carry out vivisection and similar experiments involving extreme suffering, mutilation and death in human beings, large numbers of human beings, in concentration camps. The evidence is clear cut and admitted; and although one suspected the worst, the reality, as revealed, still surpasses the worst expectations.[1]

As far as plans for re-educating and denazifying German society were concerned, Alexander was pessimistic. He felt that the moral sense of the German people and of the inner circle of the regime had been 'completely perverted'. For the moment he was content with the privileges which resulted from the Allied occupation and enjoyed a good swim in the pool near the Neckar river which had been reserved for non-Germans only.[2] He also had no problem with the policy of non-fraternisation.[3] Germans, on the whole, were seen as guilty and lesser guilty criminals who needed to be 'rehabilitated'. In a letter to Phyllis he described the Germans as 'these people', alien yet strangely familiar people he had once admired. Stopping short of advocating that Germany as a whole was collectively guilty, and needed to be punished, his position remained firm over Allied policies towards the German people. Like many in 1945, Alexander saw the task of the Allies as preventing Germany from ever again becoming a threat to world peace.

Alexander's war crimes investigations fuelled his support for trials and severe punishment for the principal perpetrators. At the end of June he was impatiently waiting to analyse the 'most remarkable facts, documents and admissions' which he had collected in his diary, together with photostats and microfilms, and to produce a complete report at CIOS headquarters in London. Instead of one report on German neuropsychiatry, he would eventually write seven.[4] By now he was also beginning to look forward to seeing his wife and family after almost two years of overseas service, and to breathe their 'clean air and spirit'.[5] Such notions reflected his sense of 'stain' which resulted from the in-depth investigations. The brief tour of duty changed his perception of medical science and greatly influenced his later position on human experimentation. His outspoken advocacy for future medical ethics standards which called for voluntary consent by the subjects can be explained by the violations of patients' rights and lives he had documented.

Arriving at London CIOS headquarters at the beginning of July, Alexander was based at the Chief Surgeon's Office amongst other intelligence officers who were frantically writing up their findings for SHAEF. As far as the quality of German research was concerned, Alexander could offer relatively little information that was of use to Allied medical science. In the field of neuropsychiatry, he had found only two methods which appeared to be worth further investigation: the German intensive rehabilitation programme for brain-injured soldiers which had been established in Berlin-Reinickendorf, and the 'special training and redemption battalions for psychopaths'.[6] Of practical use in neurophysiology was an 'ingenious device' which could signal the slowing of the cerebral electroactivity from anoxia or intense fatigue, and thus could indicate whenever a person became 'inefficient'. The device was especially useful for bomber pilots. The machine had been developed by Alois Eduard Kornmüller in collaboration with the Phillips company in Chemnitz. According to Alexander the device 'should be obtained'.[7] As it turned out, the village where the device was kept was occupied by the Russians; US intelligence agencies were nonetheless interested 'in picking it up'.[8] Seizing the opportunity of increased public interest in German research, Alexander later gave an extensive report to the media, entitled 'Ringing Bell When Brain is Tired'.[9]

A substantial amount of intelligence gathering was conducted for the prosecuting authorities who were conferring in London to prepare the International Military Tribunal (IMT). Yet Alexander's findings contained relatively little material for the American prosecution, at least it seemed so at first. The fact that neuropathologists had initiated and used the brains of 'euthanasia' victims for their research did not constitute a war crime, and was left to the national and international body representing the medical profession to tackle as a matter of medical ethics.[10] German neurosurgery and neurophysiology appeared to be 'as good as' these disciplines could have been without penicillin, and generally showed a preoccupation with problems of infection.[11] There was, of course, the issue of the 'euthanasia' programme which Alexander had addressed in his report on public mental health practices. But this was of less immediate concern to Allied prosecutors because the crimes had been committed mostly on German nationals, and therefore constituted a difficult legal issue in any prospective trial.[12]

The most important of Alexander's seven CIOS reports was his sixty-eight-page report on *The Treatment of Shock from Prolonged Exposure to Cold, Especially in Water*.[13] The report not only provided original scientific data but contained hard evidence that war crimes of a medical nature had been committed. This evidence was further substantiated by a report on German high altitude research in which Alexander outlined some of the preliminary work which had led to the Dachau experiments.[14] The material later became an integral part of the indictment against the defendants in the Doctors' Trial. Alexander described the contents of the report on the Dachau freezing experiments as 'red hot' and the nature of the crimes as utterly shocking. '[It] would make your eyes pop out and your hair stand on end', he told his wife, 'and it will, after it will be released for publication.'[15] He was certain that the authorities would want to publish the evidence to alert the public about the criminal nature of German medicine. Nevertheless, the report fell under SHAEF's strict security rules. It remained classified until the authorities knew whether the scientific data was sound and could be applied to the US Air Rescue Services.[16]

According to Alexander, two groups of German researchers had proven that for the treatment of shock produced by exposure to low temperature the method of rapid and intensive rewarming by means of a hot bath of 45°C was superior to all other known means of resuscitation. The credit for rediscovering Lapchinksi's forgotten method belonged undoubtedly to the Munich physiologist Weltz and his co-workers. Alexander documented all those individuals who had ordered, initiated or collaborated in the experiments on human beings; he was convinced that the authorities would 'find that the manner in which these experiments were performed constituted a war crime'.[17] Although accepting in principle that voluntary experiments, which involved the suffering and even death of humans, might be justified in 'national emergencies' if the question was of 'military-medical importance' – a position which he changed in later years – Alexander maintained that the Nazi medical experiments could not be considered 'voluntary'. The experiments had been conducted with such a degree of brutality and 'callous waste of unnecessarily large numbers of human lives' that all criteria of war crimes appeared to be fulfilled. At the same time, Alexander conceded that the principal investigator, Sigmund Rascher, 'although he wallowed in blood ... and in obscenity ... appears to have settled the question of what to do for people in shock from exposure to cold'.[18]

This statement was bound to lead to controversy about the ethics of medical research. Alexander therefore wanted to qualify his conclusion. Since Rascher had been unmasked as a fraud, the question arose as to the overall reliability and scientific quality of the research. With regard to the work by Weltz and his group, it was apparent that some of the preliminary animal experiments had not been sound and therefore warranted scepticism. However, the main data and the final report, written by the senior physiologist Holzlöhner, Rascher and Finke, satisfied 'all the criteria of objective and accurate observation and interpretation'.[19] In conclusion, the scientific data convinced Alexander that the rationale for the method of intensive rewarming of hypothermic victims was sound and should immediately be introduced as the treatment of choice by the Air–Sea Rescue Services of the US army.

It was this conclusion which was to become a dilemma for Alexander and many medical ethicists for decades thereafter. Is it legitimate for medical scientists to 'use' scientific data which had been generated under unethical or even criminal circumstances? Do researchers retrospectively sanction such research, and exculpate the researcher by using and citing such data? These questions, however relevant, can easily detract from the fact that Allied military authorities 'used' the data gathered in places such as Dachau from the moment it became available to them. The OSS and other intelligence agencies compiled detailed information about German scientific research long before the end of the war.[20] The main objective of the FIAT commission was to evaluate and exploit the scientific achievements of German scientists and technicians. More than fifty volumes, ranging from biophysics to viral disease, give evidence about the extent to which the exploitation of German science was seen as an integral element of reparations. Alexander's report likewise supplied the military with information considered relevant to both war crimes authorities and military experts. Only days after the report was completed, the information facilitated the ongoing investigation of German aviation researchers.[21]

Alexander's CIOS report had clearly caught the attention of the Allied authorities. In September, the UNWCC commented that it contained a 'narrative of skilful detective work', and the US navy immediately launched a second investigation into the nature and potential use of the Dachau experimental data. The Office of the US Chief of Counsel War Crimes Commission, the 3rd Army Intelligence Centre and Counter Intelligence Corps, the 7th Army Document Centre and the medical officer in command at the Dachau camp all collaborated in the preparation of a second report on the subject which became known as the 'Naval Report'. Less than three months later in October 1945, the US Naval Technical Mission in Europe presented the 300-page report No. 331–45 on *German Aviation Medical Research at the Dachau Concentration Camp*.[22] On the first page Alexander's CIOS report is mentioned as the main point of reference. The introductory paragraph of the Naval Report states: 'This report is an attempt to present objectively the aviation medical research studies made in the Dachau concentration camp. This research extended into that extremely critical realm of human physiology never before investigated in which the life of the experimental subject is compromised.'[23] As far as the use of data was concerned, the Naval Report concluded that 'upon appropriate evaluation the information reported may contribute materially to the present knowledge of physiology and through practical application may be the means of saving lives'.[24]

Since the IMT was in full preparation the investigators realised that this conclusion might be a potential cause for concern if the information was readily applied by the US military. They therefore decided to include a disclaimer into the analysis, arguing that by using the data to save human lives the victims would not have died in vain: 'This report is not intended to condone to any degree whatsoever the violations of the Oath of Hippocrates and the flouting of humanitarian principles which occurred during the courses of the researches described. It is believed that a moral responsibility exists to make available the information gained through the sacrifice of lives and sufferings of the prisoners who served as experimental results.'[25] What is more, the Harvard anaesthetist and member of the planning committee of the National Research Council, Henry K. Beecher, who in the 1960s exposed violations of medical ethics standards in the United States, was asked to comment on the scientific validity of the Dachau research. He appears to have confirmed the soundness of the research.[26] The US naval investigation concluded that 'some of the experimental data' had indeed been inaccurate, as had been pointed out by Alexander, and that 'all of the experimental data' would be subject to very critical evaluation. Aside from these limitations, the investigators strongly believed that the data which was sound could be an 'important complement to existing knowledge'.[27]

The research was not only seen as valid and readily applied by the Americans, but the researchers who had participated in the work were recruited by the US air force into 'Project Paperclip' to conduct aviation research at Heidelberg. From 1945 up until 1955 the Americans employed a total of 765 German and Austrian scientists, physicians and engineers in their attempt to exploit the best brains of the former enemy countries. Among those hired were Hermann Becker-Freysing, Konrad Schäfer and Siegfried Ruff, who had supervised parts of the Dachau high-altitude experiments. A year and a half later all three would find themselves 'in the dock' at Nuremberg.

Someone who slipped through the investigations was Hubertus Strughold, a pioneer in aviation medicine who had pursued his career with a team of thirty-three scientists in Los Antonio, Texas. During an interview in June 1945, Strughold had given Alexander the impression of someone with high moral principles and personal integrity. Apparently he had 'always forbidden even the thought of such experiments' in his institute for reasons of medical ethics.[28] However, up until the late 1970s repeated allegations surfaced which suggested that Strughold had, at least in part, been connected with the Dachau experiments. None of the allegations, however, was ever substantiated to warrant prosecution proceedings by the US Office of Special Investigation.[29]

The only existing evidence shows that Strughold was present during the Nuremberg conference in 1942, when the leading German scientists were being informed about the Dachau experiments. He thus had been given full knowledge that the experiments were being performed. After the presentation by Holzlöhner on 'Prevention and Treatment of Hypothermia in Water', the minutes record that Strughold raised the following question: 'With regard to the experimental scientific [human] experiments, but also for the orientation of the Sea Rescue Service, it is interesting to know what kind of temperatures one has to anticipate in the relevant seas during the different seasons [for our downed Luftwaffe soldiers]?'[30]

Other scientists present during the conference later recalled that they had been 'shocked' by Holzlöhner's talk, but did not recall Strughold raising the question. This is probably true only for some scientists. Becker-Freysing, for example, felt encouraged by the presentation and initiated a set of experiments in Dachau himself.[31] Stughold's question, if it was raised, which is likely, was probably directed towards the following two aims: firstly, to encourage the researchers to repeat the series of human experiments under real-life conditions in order to account for factors such as wind, waves and the freezing of humans in a certain type of water; secondly, to find out about the temperature at which 'German aviators' would die. Strughold's question seems to convey his distrust of the reliability of the data after realising that the physical conditions of the Dachau experimental subjects would not allow comparison with 'German aviators' whose health was in a much better condition. Strughold appears to have wanted to repeat the experiments with German soldiers in order to obtain more accurate medical data. But his suggestion was encroaching on an absolute taboo in 1942, namely the use of German aviators for potentially fatal human experiments. It could be that it was Strughold's proposal which 'shocked' the other participants, and led to their amnesia about Strughold's question because it indicated his complicity and willingness to expand the human experiment to a field in which 'German scientists' would not want to participate. All this is speculative, and the existing evidence is far from conclusive. Legal proceedings against Strughold never got under way. The case, which had been meticulously prepared by the Office of Special Investigation, headed today by Eli Rosenbaum, was closed after Strughold became unfit to stand trial. The man who had recommended Strughold for the American 'Project Paperclip' was none other than Leo Alexander.[32] The apparent contradiction and inconsistency in exploiting the research of German scientists, on the one hand, while prosecuting them, on the other, exists mainly in the retrospective analysis. In the summer of 1945 there were few people for whom these two lines of action would have presented an immediate conflict of interest, or indeed a moral dilemma. Whereas the former was seen as a substitution for Allied reparation, the latter had been announced in various declarations throughout the war. Both were major war aims, and part and parcel of the same objective – to ensure that Germany would be for ever unable to become a threat to world peace again. These goals were promoted and pushed forward by different Allied departments and interest groups, whose political influence fluctuated considerably. As far as the aim to prosecute war criminals was concerned, the Allies were making substantial progress during the London Conference in the summer of 1945.

Mounting the IMT

On 26 June, the day Alexander concluded his war crimes investigations in Germany, the representatives of the four Allied powers met in London to discuss the idea of holding an international war crimes trial against the major Nazi perpetrators whose crimes had no geographical location. Key to the American initiative for an international trial was Robert Jackson, a New York lawyer who had advanced to Attorney General without ever having attended law school. In May 1945 President Harry S. Truman had appointed him the United States Chief of Counsel with extensive powers to hammer out an agreement with the four powers for a trial. In preparing the case, his staff could call upon experts from any department for help, but he was answerable to none, except the president. His British counterpart, Sir David Maxwell-Fyfe, later commented that for Jackson the vocation of the lawyer caught the 'full wind of the traditions of natural justice, reason and human rights'.[33] When Roosevelt died in April 1945, Jackson told the American Society of International Law that it would be better to shoot Nazi criminals than to destroy the belief in the judicial process by creating mere show trials. 'You must put no man on trial before anything that is called a court ... if you are not willing to see him freed if not proved guilty. If you are determined to execute a man in any case, there is no occasion for a trial.'[34] During the London Conference the Allies were not in agreement about the basic principles of the trial and its objectives. The Russians took the view that the chief war criminals had already been condemned and convicted; what was left was to determine the measure of guilt and the form of punishment. This ran against all elements in the Anglo-Saxon legal tradition, and would almost have prevented the trial from happening. Negotiations continued for more than six weeks to find a compromise on various issues related to the different legal traditions. Finally, on 8 August, the heads of the delegations signed two documents. The first was the London Agreement, which announced the intention to mount an International Military Tribunal (IMT) to fulfil the wishes of the United Nations and of the signatories of the Moscow Declaration. The second was a comprehensive document which laid out the general jurisdiction, composition and powers of the Tribunal. The London Charter, as it was called, listed four main points which would constitute the basis for the indictment.[35] Count one was the crime of planning and waging aggressive war. It had been given a new name, Crimes against Peace. For Jackson this was the 'crime which comprehends all lesser crimes'. Jackson's aim was nothing less than declaring once and for all that aggressive war-making is illegal and criminal. Count two addressed war crimes, a less innovative charge, although by definition it suggested that responsibility for war crimes ultimately rested with those who had governed those who had committed the crimes. Holding high office thus implied greater guilt, rather than being useful as an argument for defence. Those directing medical and other atrocities from their office desks now had to fear for their freedom. The final count of the Charter was that of Crimes against Humanity. It was another innovative charge which had been suggested by Hersch Lauterpacht, the top expert of international law, who wanted to include the persecution of racial and religious groups, especially of the Jews, and the subjugation of the European people.[36] The charge was designed to give expression to the strong revulsion against Nazi atrocities and terror. The Charter also recognised, for the first time, crimes against humanity as a separate type of offence and as part of international law. All crimes within the jurisdiction of the Tribunal had to be directly connected with the war, and thus had to be committed after September 1939. The London Agreement and the Charter became the central cornerstones of the IMT and the subsequent Nuremberg proceedings. Most of the achievement of the trials, as well as their shortcomings, have their roots in the Charter.[37]

In addition to inter-Allied tension there were a number of practical problems which had to be resolved. First of all it had to be decided where the trial should take place. Berlin and Munich were overcrowded by Allied forces and totally destroyed. Leading war crimes officials also regarded Berlin as a place of reconstruction and development but not as 'the right place for a punitive expedition'.[38] General Lucius Clay, Military Governor of the US zone of occupation, suggested Nuremberg, because the courtroom in the Palace of Justice had miraculously survived the sustained bombing campaign on the city. There was also sufficient space for up to 1200 prisoners and adequate housing facilities for the large numbers of trial staff, legal experts and journalists who were expected to attend such a historic event. Most importantly, however, the city had significant symbolic character. For over a decade Nuremberg had hosted Hitler's infamous Nazi rallies, and had witnessed the promulgation of the Nuremberg Race Laws. It was a fitting place to hammer home to the Germans that the regime had been utterly mistaken in its 'visionary' policies. What is more, Nuremberg was in the American zone of occupation, where food rations, materials and equipment were in better supply than anywhere else. The Americans had the financial and human resources to stage such a major trial. Predictably, the Russians were not enthusiastic about the idea. Berlin therefore became the 'permanent seat of the Tribunal' where the judges first met, before travelling to Nuremberg to hold the trial. It was one of many compromises in inter-Allied power politics at the dawn of the Cold War.

The list of major war criminals was published at the end of August 1945 when Alexander was about to return to America. For the next year and a half he became an observer rather than an active participant in the developments, mainly because he had returned to America. Among the defendants in the IMT were Göring, Ribbentrop, Heβ, Kaltenbrunner, Rosenberg, Frank, Bormann (*in absentia*), Papen, Sauckel, Dönitz and Albert Speer. On 19 October they were served with the indictment. The *Glasgow Herald* poignantly commented that 'of all these men, who but a year ago enjoyed wide influence or supreme power, not one could find a refuge in a continent united in hate against them'.[39] *The Times*, however, questioned the inclusion of Gustav Krupp, who was neither a Krupp by birth nor the owner of the family shares. Since 1940 he had been removed from controlling the company and was seriously ill and unlikely to stand trial. The man who had been in charge of weapons production and the use of slave labour was his son, Alfried Krupp. Yet the indictment listed his father, Gustav. It was an embarrassing slip of the pen (earlier lists of defendants had listed Alfried) which led to one of the first defeats of the prosecution after requesting that either Krupp should be tried *in absentia* or his son should be added to the indictment. It was plainly asking to substitute Alfried for Gustav, a practice unacceptable in almost any court of law. Both motions were rejected out of hand. The French immediately wanted to announce a second trial of leading German industrialists, one in which Alfried Krupp was among the key defendants.[40] Thus, in some sense, the error increased the political pressure to establish further Nuremberg trials.

The charges against the defendants had by now been expanded to four major counts. Count one, drafted by the American prosecution, was concerned with a Common Plan or Conspiracy. This was a 'catch-all' construct to cover almost all Nazi crimes, including those which had been committed before the war. There had been many declarations by the Allies to punish those who had committed crimes, but there had been no warning of the intention to do the same with those who had conspired to commit them like a group of gangsters. The concept of the Common Plan or Conspiracy in international law was *ex post facto* law, that is, law which retrospectively identifies acts as unlawful which were not illegal at the time they were committed. During the IMT this concept produced many legal problems for the prosecution, and was largely abandoned in the subsequent Nuremberg proceedings. Count two constituted Crimes against Peace. Drafted by the British, it introduced for the first time Lemkin's concept of 'genocide' into the legal context, as well as into the English language. Working as an adviser on foreign affairs at the US War Department, Lemkin had felt the need to find some all-encompassing concept which would cover the destruction of a nation or of an ethnic group, and which would be particularly applicable to the murder of European Jewry.[41] Counts three and four on War Crimes and Crimes against Humanity were drafted by the French and the Russians, and included detailed information about a regime that had violated almost every conceivable principle of human civilisation.

By the time the chief prosecutors met in London on 23 August to formulate the indictment and begin selecting evidence for the prosecution, Alexander had completed his work and was about to go back to America. In the last six weeks he had written seven CIOS reports, totalling more than 1500 typewritten pages. For weeks he had not written a single note to his family. Phyllis had become exceedingly concerned, so much so that she had contacted the Red Cross to search for Alexander.[42] In May she had told him: 'Is one (1) letter each month to your family all you can manage? Or could your work day, leisure hours and fatigue component be reevaluated thoughtfully by you? This is the only cut back in rations I find too hard to live with.'[43] Attempting to explain his silence, he told her that the work was 'a hard grind' which had required his total commitment. Two of the reports had already come out as restricted publications. The others he wanted to publish as fast as possible: 'I am trying to arrange through the Surgeon General's Office to have them released for open publication, and to bring them out in book form (as two individual books).'[44] In the meantime, he sent copies of the report to Abraham Myerson, Richard Lyman and Tracy Putnam. All three of them were authorised to read restricted publications. Aware of the historical importance of the material, he sent another set of copies home for archival purposes.[45] His final comment before departure revealed the extent to which the war had shaped his religious feelings:

> It looked like a long up-hill job then, and it was up-hill a good deal of the way, and many have not been fortunate enough to come back from it. We all must give thanks to the Lord for having blessed our cause, and for giving victory to our arms. We must now strive to safeguard our victory and peace maintained by laws of God. That is the work of the future in which all who survive must share.[46]

Beneath the religious rhetoric the statement conveyed his concern for the future of the world after the first atomic bombs had been dropped on Hiroshima and Nagasaki in the summer of 1945.[47] But it was also meant as a vow to examine the causes which had led to National Socialism and do all in his power to prevent it from ever happening again. Part of this commitment was aimed at studying the character of the major German perpetrators.

Studying the German character

When the IMT opened on Tuesday, 20 November 1945, Alexander was approaching various government departments in Washington to offer his services to the authorities that were co-ordinating the German occupation. After his return at the end of September, Alexander was faced with the prospect of unemployment. His plan was to return to his former post at Duke University, but Lyman wanted him to postpone a return until the summer of 1946.[48] Alexander therefore suggested to Lyman that he would work on a study of German mentalities until the position at Duke became available. His idea was to conduct personality studies of some of the key German war criminals, not as a military investigator, but as a consultant, arranged and supervised by any interested government agency. Lyman was to facilitate this research through his contacts with the OSS.[49] As it turned out, Lyman had apparently no connections with the OSS any more and could not raise any hopes for Alexander at Duke. What Alexander perceived as a cold shoulder, lay first and foremost in the lack of financial resources which Lyman had at his disposal, together with his intention to resign from Duke and return to China.[50] The future was looking increasingly bleak.

By November 1945 Alexander started on a personal crusade to offer his expertise to the American military and civilian authorities. He was convinced that either the Rockefeller Foundation, the State Department or the War Department would be interested in studies on the German character.[51] On 1 November he approached Gregg of the Rockefeller Foundation and told him that for the last three and a half months he had been detached from the 65th General Hospital to do special intelligence work for CIOS. According to Alexander, 'more investigative work of a neuropsychiatric nature should be carried out in Germany, including, if possible, personality studies of the war criminals'.[52] Alexander wanted to enlist the support from the Rockefeller Foundation and from Tracy Putnam, his former boss, for a broadly defined study on German medical war criminals. On 5 November he therefore met with Robert A. Lambert, one of the officers of the Rockefeller Foundation, for lunch at the latter's home. Lambert recorded the essentials of the conversation:

A.[lexander] feels strongly that the psychological study of war criminals should be pursued further and he would be interested to participate.

This study should be done through the State Department. He has offered his services but doubts if he will be given an assignment, as other men still in the service are available.[53]

Alexander's doubts originated from rumours that the State Department had apparently been reluctant in putting war crimes on the political agenda during the war, in particular with regard to the extermination of the Jews. His suspicions were not unjustified. The response he received from most departments was friendly, but uncommitted. On Friday, 9 November, he left for Washington DC to sound out whether any prospective position was on offer. He first met with members of the OSS, followed by discussions with representatives from the Central Affairs Division (CAD) in the Pentagon, who promised to forward his application to the relevant authorities in Germany.[54] The last meeting on that day was at the Surgeon General's Office where he was greeted by an unpleasant surprise.

Alexander's CIOS report on the Dachau freezing experiments had been released to the press, and had been given extensive coverage in some of the leading American newspapers. With the IMT about to begin in a couple of weeks, American news coverage on the major German war criminals had risen to unprecedented levels. The public was following the creation of the IMT via radio broadcasts and news bulletins, while film crews were setting off to record the event for the cinema. What is more, the trial against forty SS members of the concentration camp of Dachau was scheduled to commence on 15 November.[55] In this climate a detailed report on some of the Dachau freezing experiments was a major newspaper scoop. On 4 November George Connery from the *Washington Post* reported that Nazi medical science was aimed at torture and death of the experimental subjects.[56] Quoting long passages of Alexander's report, Connery stressed that only one known living survivor of the experiments had been found, and that the death toll was estimated to reach hundreds. Three days later the *Washington News* published a similar article, which made the publication of his report less newsworthy once he been granted permission to do so.[57] Alexander was furious.

The decision to release the report to the public had, in the meantime, been reversed by the War Department after it had become apparent that the report contained sensitive material for the prosecution of German doctors.[58] A few days later, on 13 November, Alexander again stressed the importance of further intelligence work at the Surgeon General's Office. James W. Riddleberger, the official from CAD, explained that OSS had been disbanded at short notice in September when no further funds were available to take over the work. Those people who had been appointed were not always the best; some had hardly any knowledge of the German scientific or cultural context, or were unable to speak German. Overall there was a sense that departmental infighting had produced 'poor planning' with regard to investigative and intelligence work in

Germany.[59] Neither the US government departments nor the Rockefeller Foundation seemed particularly interested in investigating the psychology of German perpetrators any further.

By December 1945 it transpired that he was unable to resume his peacetime activity at Duke University before the summer of 1946. Unaware of the fact that Lyman himself was intending to leave Duke, Alexander was greatly disappointed.[60] Yet his former colleague, Abraham Myerson, received him 'with open arms' and offered him a part-time position as Associate Director of Research at Boston State Hospital. In addition, he decided to open up his own private practice which allowed him to pursue some of his medical research. Expanding research at Boston State Hospital, however, failed since the Rockefeller Foundation declined to provide the necessary funding for what Alexander had hoped would become a thriving neurological department.[61] The reason for this setback was probably rooted in the fact that some American medical scientists had observed Alexander's career, and were now spreading rumours about his suitability as a departmental head. Only a couple of days after Alexander's visit to the Rockefeller Foundation, on 13 November, it became clear that some medical scientists regarded him as a loose cannon. After a conversation with Theodore J. C. von Storch, Associate Professor of Neurology at Albany Medical College, the officer at the Rockefeller Foundation recalled:

> Leo Alexander has apparently been a rather prominent figure in military neurology and his career has given rise to a large number of apocryphal stories, not all of which are flattering. V.[von Storch] confirms my opinion that A.[lexander]'s enthusiasm and energy are assets in a large clinic, but his lack of common sense and good judgement makes him questionable as a department head. There seems to be a large measure of doubt as to his security at Duke, and it would be nice to arrange a suitable position for him. V.[von Storch] thinks well enough of A.[lexander] to offer him a position on his service if he had the means.[62]

It is difficult to assess the degree of professional jealousy and departmental politics which may have prompted von Storch to make these remarks, but it is almost certain that Alexander's emotional nature and his quick temper, together with his reputation as a philanderer, provided potential material to blacken his name in the tightly controlled American medical establishment. It also shows the extent to which the Rockefeller Foundation took an active role in shaping the American scientific landscape in universities and research laboratories.

But back on the European continent the Office Chief of Counsel for War Crimes was taking notice of Alexander as a competent and highly determined medical investigator. Since April Jackson had been preparing his opening speech for the IMT with masses of intelligence material.

Alexander's account of the Dachau experiments attracted his attention, and he used it to graphically display the callousness and brutality of the Nazi regime. It was merely one small piece in the grand scheme of the American conspiracy charge, but it had a significant effect in the courtroom, and was reported in the international press.[63] Jackson's speech left observers with little doubt that the men in the dock had been responsible for the great misery their country had brought to other nations. Whatever the setbacks in 1945, Alexander had firmly established his credentials as someone eager to collaborate with the US war crimes authorities, a key factor which influenced his appointment as the medical expert in the Doctors' Trial.

Planning the subsequent trials

Since the days of preparing the IMT the question had arisen of whether the four powers should mount a second or even a third international trial. During the London Conference the issue had appeared and reappeared when lists of potential defendants were produced and discussed. Those standing on a separate list were likely candidates for a second international trial, and the Charter later took due notice of this intention.[64] The French and the Russians, in particular, pushed for a series of Nuremberg Tribunals in parallel sessions. While the prosecutors were preparing one case for trial, it was thought, they could prepare the evidence for a second. Defendants in the second tribunal were likely to include either further generals or, more probably, a trial against German industrialists and financiers for supporting and benefiting from Germany's aggressive war. Jackson opposed this approach and refused to commit the US to a second international trial, arguing convincingly that it was first necessary to see whether the first could be successfully completed.[65] From the start the insistence by the French and the Russians for more than one trial was instrumental in mounting the subsequent Nuremberg proceedings. Ironically neither country would later be party to them.[66]

One month after the formal opening of the IMT in November 1945, the Allied Control Council in charge of overseeing Germany's occupation passed Control Council Law No. 10 which introduced a uniform legal basis for the prosecution of war criminals other than those dealt with by the IMT.[67] Law No. 10 provided the legal framework for all subsequent military trials. Article III granted each of the major Allies the right to try war criminals in their zone of occupation before an appropriate tribunal. The law also allowed for the provision, if authorised by the occupying authorities, that German courts could deal with crimes committed by German nationals against German nationals or stateless persons. During the Doctors' Trial the latter part of the law became a major sticking point in the debate on whether or not the prosecution should pursue 'euthanasia' which had been aimed at and conducted mostly on German nationals.[68]

Based on the Moscow Declaration and the London Agreement, Law No. 10 recognised the following four acts as a crime: Crimes against Peace referred to the initiation of invasions of other countries and wars of aggression in violation of international laws and treaties. War Crimes referred to offences against persons or property which violated the laws or customs of war, including murder, ill treatment, deportation to slave labour, the killing of hostages, plunder of public or private property, or the deliberate destruction of cities, towns and villages. Crimes against Humanity included, but were not limited to, the extermination, enslavement, deportation, imprisonment, torture, rape, or other inhumane acts committed against any civilian population. It also covered the persecution of civilians and soldiers on political, racial or religious grounds. The final category was membership in a group or organisation judged and declared criminal by the IMT. Persons involved in any of these acts would be held accountable for initiating, ordering, abetting or taking a consenting part in committing these crimes, or if they were connected with plans involving their commission, or as a member of a group or organisation connected with such a commission, or if the person held a high political, civil or military position in Germany or in one of its allies. Those found guilty could be punished by death, life imprisonment, fines, hard labour, forfeiture of property, restitution or deprivation of civil rights. In short, Law No. 10 was drawn up to ensure that German war criminals would not escape Allied prosecution.

Law No. 10 was in large part based on broad precedents both in terms of German criminal law and international laws and treaties, of which Germany had been a signatory. It reflected the attempt by Allied legislators to prosecute and punish German war criminals according to the nation's own existing law, and thus to counter from the start the charge that the tribunals stood in violation of the *ex post facto* principle or that the proceedings were nothing but 'victor's justice'. Although international law had previously not codified specific war crimes, most of the offences with which the defendants were charged were illegal under German criminal law. The crimes specified in the London Charter and in Law No. 10 for the most part repeated the 1907 Hague Regulation on Warfare, which Germany had signed. Article 46 stressed that during war 'family honour and rights, the lives of persons, and private property, as well as religious convictions and practice, must be respected'. What is more, Germany was signatory to the Kellogg–Briand Pact of 1928, which condemned aggressive wars, and had signed the Geneva Convention a year later which laid out the rules for the protection of prisoners of war. It was in the tradition of staying close to existing German laws and regulations that Alexander later drafted some of the elements of the Nuremberg Code. He wanted to show that almost all of the offences were not only crimes according to German law, but that the doctors had violated their own professional codes of conduct which existed in Germany at the time.

Although Law No. 10 obviated the necessity for a second international trial, several attempts were made to establish another four-power trial, some less half-hearted than others.[69] For the most part a second IMT lacked political support from the national governments which perceived Nuremberg as an increasingly antagonistic institution in the rapidly cooling climate between the four Allies. Another four-power trial also lacked key support from Jackson, who became disillusioned by the performance of his Russian counterparts during the IMT. After his disastrous and widely publicised failure to cross-examine Göring, he had become a bitter and greatly disappointed man. Journalists and legal experts had seized the opportunity to expose his professional weaknesses in front of the world; one of the judges described him after the episode as 'sitting by, unhappy and beaten, full of a sense of failure'.[70] Another commented that '[Jackson's] instinct is to run away from the scene of his failure'. As a consequence, he became impatient with the trial, made life difficult for his staff, and was longing to leave Nuremberg. It therefore came as no surprise when on 29 March 1946 Jackson appointed the charismatic and hawkish lawyer Telford Taylor as Deputy Chief of Counsel, thereby placing him in charge of organising the prosecution in the subsequent Nuremberg trials.[71]

During the war Taylor had worked in London as Chief of the Military Intelligence Service, Special Branch. Born in 1908 in Schenectady, New York, he had graduated from Williams College before going to Harvard Law School where he received his law degree in 1932. Multi-talented, ambitious and impatient, Taylor constantly changed jobs. He worked as an instructor in history and government at Williams College (1928–9), as a law clerk (1932–3), an assistant solicitor in the Department of Interior (1933–4), a senior attorney in the Agricultural Adjustment Administration (1934–5), an associate counsel in the US Senate Interstate Commerce Committee (1935–9), a special assistant to the Attorney General (1939–40), a general counsel of the Federal Communications Commission (1940–2) and, from 1943 to 1945, as Chief of the Military Intelligence Service, for which he was awarded a Distinguished Service Medal. He was married and had two daughters at the time of his arrival at Nuremberg.[72]

The planning of further trials in the American zone got under way with the establishment of the Subsequent Proceedings Division in the Office of Chief of Counsel for the Prosecution of Axis Criminality. The question of whether the trials would be held in Nuremberg hinged on whether there would be another international (quadripartite) trial. A number of options and places were under consideration.[73] Taylor knew that another international trial in Nuremberg would make it impossible to mount 'zonal' trials in the same place simultaneously. Other places needed to be earmarked. In case there was no second international trial, or if that trial was held in another place (Berlin was under discussion), the zonal trials could be held in Nuremberg. Logistical issues were paramount. To complete the prosecu-

Plate 10 Brigadier General Telford Taylor, Chief of Counsel for War Crimes, pictured in his office at Nuremberg, where he was directing the prosecution of war criminals for the Office of Military Government for Germany (US). Taylor succeeded Supreme Court Justice Robert H. Jackson, who returned to Washington upon completion of the trial against the leading Nazi defendants at the International Military Tribunal. Nuremberg, Germany, 1946/7.

tion of war criminals as expeditiously as possible, the Office Chief of Counsel was anticipating a total of 800 staff members to run as many as six zonal trials simultaneously, some in Nuremberg, others in places like Bamberg, Ludwigsburg or Regensburg.[74] What the American authorities – and indeed British officials – were unlikely to accept was an international trial in the Soviet zone of occupation, presided over by a Russian judge.[75] Even worse was the prospect of permitting an international trial against German financiers and industrialists in the Soviet zone, as it would have provided the Russians with the perfect platform to stage a show trial against the capitalist system as a whole. At the end of January 1946, Taylor was nonetheless anticipating that 'the shape of things to come' included another international trial, with a focus on German industrialists and financiers, as well as a series of military tribunals in the American zone of occupation.[76] At this point a trial against German doctors does not seem to have figured predominantly in the minds of the American prosecutors.

By May 1946 Taylor met with representatives from Britain, France and Russia to sound out whether a joint trial against leading German industrialists would be feasible. Considerable disagreement existed over the selection of the defendants. Support from the American prosecution for a trial against financiers was low-key after they had realised that the case against Hjalmar Schacht was difficult to prove. Jackson had warned the other chief prosecutors in April 1946 that there would be no point in mounting a trial against industrialists should Schacht be acquitted. After Jackson's poor cross-examination observers were, for the first time, anticipating this outcome.[77] While American financial leaders were beginning to lobby against a trial of German industrialists, British officials let it be known that they were also 'not enthusiastic' about a second trial, although the government did not want to be seen as opposing it. 'The official attitude [of the British] is rather cool', Taylor told Howard Petersen, the Assistant Secretary of War.[78] Petersen's response on 17 June was likewise cool, informing Taylor that the US government was 'opposed to another international trial'.[79]

Yet the argument about the issue was far from over; at the end of July Taylor was still recommending to the Secretary of War that the US should 'publicly agree to participate in a second international trial'.[80] However, in his final report to President Truman in October 1946, Jackson made it clear that he would discourage another Allied trial and instead hold individual trials in each zone of occupation.[81] A second international trial was seen not only as too expensive but also as too inefficient in prosecuting large numbers of alleged war criminals. Moreover, the existing inter-Allied frictions made the establishment of a second four-power trial increasingly unlikely on the eve of the Cold War. When it became apparent in autumn 1946 that the United States was not going to participate in another international trial, Taylor urged Jackson to advise the president to phrase his public announcement 'so as to do no damage to the prestige of the London

Agreement or to the "international" character of our war crimes program'.[82] He knew that the question of a second quadripartite trial was intricately connected with the development of international law. In January 1947 the formal invitation by the French for a second IMT was officially rejected by the American government.[83] As a result, the Nuremberg Code probably never received the international recognition which it could have had, had it originated within an international trial.

Whereas a case against German finance and industry had encountered great obstacles from the start, a trial against the major medical perpetrators became all the more likely. In the meantime, a good deal of expertise had been gathered in previous trials involving medical murder. From September to November 1945 the British had staged the Bergen–Belsen trial and in March 1946 they had tried Bruno Tesch for his role in supplying Zyklon B to the concentration camps. From 18 March to 3 May 1946 the British had also established the first of a series of war crimes trials in the Curio-Haus in Hamburg, mostly against the guards and personnel of the Neuengamme concentration camp. In the course of the trial it became apparent that Nazi physicians had carried out tuberculosis experiments. Since the beginning of 1946 British prosecutors were also preparing a trial against the staff of the Ravensbrück concentration camp which included the indictment of key medical personnel from the nearby SS sanatorium in Hohenlychen. Finally, the IMT had drawn attention to the fact that a large number of doctors appeared to have been involved in crimes against humanity.

During the IMT a certain amount of evidence appeared to implicate Göring as the head of the German air force in the Dachau high-altitude research. When Göring called Field Marshal Erhard Milch as a defence witness, the prosecution realised that Milch was implicated more heavily than Göring.[84] Later in the trial, chance played once again into the hands of the prosecution. During the cross-examination of Wolfram Sievers, the official of the SS-Ahnenerbe (Ancestral Heritage) Society who had been called as a witness to speak on behalf of the SS as an organisation, the British prosecuting lawyer, Lord Elwyn-Jones, produced the most damning documents which implicated Sievers in the 'Jewish Skeleton Collection'. This was a collection of heads and bodies of murdered Jews, compiled by the anatomist August Hirt at the Reich University of Strasbourg for anthropological purposes.[85] Both incidents shifted the attention of the prosecution to explore this area more closely and assess whether there was a systematic approach to the crimes. A trial against doctors appeared feasible from the American perspective since many of the persons implicated in the crimes were in either British or American custody. A trial against German physicians was also a means to re-educate and denazify German society and explain to the world why and how things had happened.

Experts not officially charged with war crimes policies, like the representatives of FIAT, had also come across evidence that experiments on living humans had been performed under barbaric conditions. To explore this material further, however, was outside the agency's jurisdiction. On Wednesday, 15 May 1946 at 10.30 a.m., nine British, four American and two French representatives of FIAT met for the first time at Hoechst in Wiesbaden to discuss how the material should be handled. No Russian representative had been invited. Among those present were the Canadian medical officer and wing commander John W. R. Thompson, the British forensic pathologists Sidney Smith and Keith Mant, as well as the bacteriologist Pierre Lépine from the Institute Pasteur in Paris. The meeting was chaired by the British brigadier R. J. Maunsell, intelligence expert and head of the British section of FIAT. The conference attempted to co-ordinate the different war crimes branches and agencies whose responsibility was limited to the economic, technical and scientific exploitation of Germany. Although Britain and France disagreed over the extent to which medical war crimes should be morally condemned – with France wanting to condemn them more widely and more strongly – both nations agreed that further investigations should be undertaken by scientifically qualified experts.

France was given the task of compiling a survey of experimental work conducted during the war that involved the abuse of human subjects for research purposes. The plan was to evaluate German medical science, although it was generally believed that only a small portion of it had produced any valuable scientific data. The participants agreed further that each of the countries present should prepare a specific medical war crimes case. Individual zonal trials were given preference over another international trial. The meeting showed that concerted efforts were being undertaken to co-ordinate Allied war crimes investigations and that each of the three Allied nations planned to prepare its own trial against the German medical profession. The Americans were preparing a case for the Dachau high-altitude and freezing experiments. The French were building up a case on typhus, and the British favoured the case against the Ravensbrück experiments concerned with gas gangrene.[86] British experts suggested a four-pronged approach to further investigations, including the confiscation of all facilities of the researchers, the reconstruction of experimental procedures, witness testimonies and full interrogation of the accused to establish the motives of the crimes. They were of the opinion that the Ravensbrück investigations would also uncover evidence about other human experiments, including bone transplantation, sterilisation, artificial insemination and various gynaecological experiments performed by the notorious Auschwitz doctor Carl Clauberg.[87]

As a result of the conference it was recommended that a four power commission for the investigation of medical war crimes should be established which would involve both medical and legal experts. The proposal became the basis for an International Scientific Commission (for the Investigation of War Crimes of a Medical Nature), in short ISC (WC).[88] Weindling has suggested that the participants wanted a four-power trial in conjunction with an international commission, and that the meetings of this group of scientists constituted 'a potential alternative to a military trial'.[89] However, the legal and political realities in the various zones of occupation, the actual jurisdiction and authority of the FIAT group, and the legal expertise of individual members does not warrant this conclusion. The group had almost no official standing with the Allied Control Council, something the head of FIAT readily admitted during the conference in May.[90]

The FIAT conferences were made up of mid-ranking soldiers, most of them physicians in civilian life, who saw themselves as self-appointed prosecutors and judges. The British displayed a combination of a gentlemanly attitude and self-righteousness, whereas the French wandered off into the realm of medical ethics and criminal philosophy. The British head of FIAT, Maunsell, was primarily concerned that 'the winter [was] more or less over' so that one could 'tackle this matter in earnest'.[91] At the same time he acknowledged that the investigation of war crimes was 'not within our terms of reference as far as FIAT (British) is concerned'.[92] The British were primarily interested in assessing and exploiting the results of German experimental work for strategic purposes. Other members of the group were unprepared. During the FIAT conference in May 1946 Sidney Smith was asked how one should deal with the problem of medical atrocities. His response was symptomatic for the conference: 'Well, Sir, I don't know that I can contribute anything very useful at present.'[93] However, his colleague, Major Keith Mant, apparently could. He had investigated medical experiments in the concentration camps of Ravensbrück and Auschwitz, and had made up his mind that those involved in the work were guilty: 'I am afraid I am not a legal expert but ... if a person carries out an experiment or group of experiments [where] there is death, he is guilty of manslaughter or murder. In fact rather worse than murder ... I shall attempt to see that no one gets away.'[94] This kind of amateur approach fell far short of the need to select a number of medical cases which could be prosecuted and put on trial expeditiously, or gather the defendants and give them a fair hearing. At one point the French representative asked whether 'experiments [must] be fatal to be illegal', whereupon the chairman's patience snapped: 'I think that we can not [sic] discuss what is [a] crime and what is not.'[95]

During these informal sessions the Americans disclosed hardly any of their material and generally referred to the ongoing Nuremberg proceedings. Though the meetings were important as far as discussions about the ethics of medical research on humans was concerned, the FIAT conferences and the ISC (WC) had almost no political weight. For the Americans it was, and remained, a side-show, especially after August 1946. They were hardly interested in letting the initiative pass over to the French or the British once they had decided that they were going to prosecute German doctors in one of the Nuremberg trials. The Americans were also unimpressed by the unprofessional handling of witness testimonies by men like Mant. On 26 October 1946 Alexander G. Hardy told James M. McHaney, chief prosecutor in the medical case, that his 'opinion of Major Mant's work is not too good' and that one could 'readily see from reading his report on the Ravensbrück case that our hope of obtaining any real evidence from this source is dark'.[96] The performance of the French was not much better. Moreover, by October the Americans thought that the French did not have much to contribute to the Doctors' Trial. 'I made every attempt to obtain whatever evidence was available in the French War Crimes Division', Hardy told McHaney, 'I must admit that they do not have much of value.'[97] Yet Taylor's office monitored the activities by British and French war crimes experts, mainly because the British had amassed a considerable amount of incriminating evidence. Whether it could be used in a court of law was obviously another matter. Most of the potential defendants were also in British custody, which made continued co-operation necessary.

In mid-August 1946 it became clear that President Truman for obvious political and ideological reasons wanted to take an executive decision about the subsequent Nuremberg trials.[98] On 17 August Taylor therefore proposed to the War Department that they establish six courts which would prosecute the representatives of certain segments of German society in an expeditious fashion, including German physicians involved in medical experiments. The proposed starting date for the first of the trials was 15 October 1946.[99] The original plan to mount eighteen zonal trials in the six courts in Nuremberg was later reduced to twelve; it involved the prosecution of representatives of the judiciary, of I. G. Farben, the Einsatzgruppen, the ministries and the German High Command. As a matter of expediency the prosecution decided that a trial against German doctors was most likely to succeed, given the available incriminating evidence, and that it therefore was to become the first of the trials. Overall, the establishment of the Doctors' Trial was a matter of high politics and decided by the US Office of Chief of Counsel for War Crimes in close co-ordination with Washington.

On 25 October the United States indicted twenty German doctors and three bureaucrats for crimes against peace, war crimes, and crimes against humanity. The indictment was issued only four weeks after the conclusion of the IMT and only one week after the Office of Military Government for Germany, United States (OMGUS) had issued the Ordinance No. 7, which gave American military tribunals the power to prosecute those indicted under Law No. 10. The Americans thereby signalled that they would go ahead with the establishment of the first of the subsequent Nuremberg proceedings, the Doctors' Trial.[100] All twelve subsequent Nuremberg trials, which involved a total of 184 defendants, were to become American trials rather than four-power trials.[101]

Gathering the accused

A key issue in the preparation of the trials was gathering the accused. Speed was of the essence. Those apprehended at a later date often stood a good chance of escaping prosecution, especially if they had used the lapse in time to destroy as much incriminating evidence as possible. In March 1947, while the Doctors' Trial was entering into its second phase, the US authorities realised that a number of physicians had been captured 'who would have been defendants had they been apprehended soon enough'.[102] Allied investigators were literally looking for a needle in a haystack. British intelligence was tracing war criminals under the eloquent code-names 'Operation Fleacomb' and 'Operation Haystack'. Small teams of specialists 'with a talent for this type of work' were given all the available information about the alleged criminals. Their task was to find them, something that proved to be increasingly difficult with the passage of time.[103] Whereas some doctors, like the notorious Josef Mengele, had gone into hiding, others were likely to escape criminal prosecution after being released from prisoner of war camps.[104] Some of the major criminals accused of medical crimes had committed suicide or were believed dead. To dispose of vital evidence, Himmler had ordered the execution of Sigmund Rascher shortly before the end of the war.[105] The rate of suicide in the weeks leading up to Germany's defeat had been staggering. Ordinary Germans and party functionaries had decided to end their lives to escape feelings of personal guilt and collective shame about Germany's world standing. By the end of April 1945 the Reich Physician of the SS and head of the German Red Cross, Ernst Robert Grawitz, killed himself by detonating a bomb in his house in Berlin-Babelsberg. Maximinian de Crinis, head of the psychiatric clinic at the Charité and one of the main organisers of the 'euthanasia' operation, shot himself on the outskirts of Berlin. Even in custody, some of the doctors with blood on their hands decided to escape trial. By October 1945 Leonardo Conti, the Reich Health Leader, hanged himself in his cell at Nuremberg.[106] All of the above-mentioned individuals would have been defendants in the Doctors' Trial, and were therefore called the 'missing defendants' by some American newspapers.[107]

Other physicians were fortunate enough to escape attention, at least momentarily. Fritz Fischer, for example, who had experimented with sulphonamide drugs on mostly young Polish girls at the Ravensbrück camp, was overlooked when Allied investigators arrested the historian Dr Fritz Fischer, the future world-famous author of *Griff nach der Weltmacht*, translated as *Germany's Aims in the First World War*.[108] It took Fischer, the historian, a considerable amount of time to convince the authorities that his identity had actually been mistaken. A month later, on the evening of 4 August 1945, the 5th Counter Intelligence Corps arrested Fischer, the Ravensbrück doctor in Rosche, near Uelzen.[109] Fischer was first transferred to Neumünster, then to Nuremberg to serve as a witness in the IMT. By September he told his wife that he was 'under arrest to answer for actions' which he had carried out during the war 'on orders from above'.[110] This became his standard line of defence. He was in good spirits and lectured her about God, humanity and purity as the basis for the education of their children.[111] Fischer seems to have been unaware that the military authorities saw him as a key defendant in a British-led Ravensbrück trial. His inclusion would probably have resulted in him being sentenced to death.

Fischer was part of the 'Hohenlychen Group'. These included the head of the SS sanatorium in Hohenlychen and Fischer's superior, Karl Gebhardt, who was arrested on 16 May in Flensburg-Mürwick. Like Fischer, he was brought to Nuremberg as a witness in the IMT. His staff member and assistant in the criminal experiments was Herta Oberheuser, the only woman in the Doctors' Trial. On the evening of 20 July 1945 she was arrested by members of the British Secret Service in Stocksee, near Ploen, and brought to Bad Oeynhausen where the British war crimes headquarters was located. Oberheuser served as a witness in the IMT before being charged with multiple crimes.

One month earlier, on 20 May, the American Counter Intelligence Corps (CIC) arrested a man called Hermann Ober near Stuttgart.[112] In June Ober was discharged from a prisoner-of-war camp, but again taken into custody in Traunstein and later in Moosburg. At the end of the summer his real identity was established: Victor Brack, a bicycle enthusiast with no medical expertise whatsoever, and one of the leading figures in organising the murder of tens of thousands of handicapped in the 'euthanasia' programme. Pseudonyms had always been one of Brack's specialities. While the killing programme was in progress, he had called himself 'Jennerwein', referring to a notorious eighteenth-century poacher. Applying expertise gathered in the 'euthanasia' programme to the Final Solution, Brack had proposed to Himmler in 1942 that one should sterilise two to three million Jews out of the 10 million Jews consigned to death and use them as slave labourers. He had every reason to disguise his identity. Throughout the pre-trial interrogations and the Doctors' Trial he perjured himself many times, which did not help him, as he was eventually hanged.

On the same day that Brack, alias Ober, was captured, the 3rd Counter Intelligence Group arrested Rudolf Brandt around lunchtime at a British control point near Bremervörde, midway between Hamburg and Bremen.[113] He was accompanying Heinrich Himmler. Brandt was chief of Himmler's personal staff and had passed on the orders for some of the most atrocious medical experiments. Himmler and his adjutants had disguised themselves as members of the *Geheime Feldpolizei* (Secret Military Police), not knowing that the organisation was on the Allied blacklist and that all sergeants were subject to automatic arrest. Whether Brandt was also travelling in disguise is not known. Himmler, at first, was not recognised. The men were driven to Westertimke, near Bremen, where they were searched and questioned. British intelligence had been tipped off by the Danes that Himmler was on his way to Bavaria to join with other SS leaders. Further interrogations were conducted at Barfeld, near Lüneburg. On 23 May Himmler finally 'snapped' and revealed himself. Shortly afterwards he committed suicide.[114] Then there was the air force group. The group included numerous physicians who had initiated, supervised and participated in various Dachau medical experiments, men like Siegfried Ruff, director of the German Research Institute for Aviation in Berlin, Hans Wolfgang Romberg, Ruff's assistant researcher and collaborator in the experiments, Hermann Becker-Freysing and the Austrian doctor Wilhelm Beiglböck. The latter had been arrested in March by the British in Linz and was about to be put on trial in Graz when the Nuremberg war crimes authorities became aware of his whereabouts.[115] Whereas Romberg was arrested in October 1945 at his home in Gilzum near Braunschweig, Ruff and Becker-Freysing enjoyed their freedom and considerable status as aviation scientists until shortly before the trial. Both were employed by the US air force in the Aero-Medical Centre in Heidelberg until the authorities realised that their charge could become a potential embarrassment. By mid-September 1946 CIC finally arrested both of them and brought them to Nuremberg.[116] Another physician imprisoned as one of the first suspects of the Dachau experiments was Georg August Weltz. On 21 June 1945, the same day that Alexander interviewed some of the few survivors of the experiments at Dachau, CIC arrested him in Munich. Weltz was detained in the same prison complex in Dachau where the subjects of his research had once suffered.

There was one group of potential defendants that was easy to find: the last German government under Admiral Dönitz which had established its headquarters in the north-German town of Flensburg in Schleswig-Holstein, near the Danish border. Within a week of taking office Dönitz had accepted Germany's unconditional surrender,[117] but throughout most of May his government was allowed to exist. Although the military government had been imposed around 10 May in Flensburg in the north of Germany,[118] SHAEF had a conceptual problem as to how one handled the surrender of a government that had ceased to exist as a consequence of its unconditional surrender? On 19 May Churchill finally gave the go-ahead to arrest the so-called German government: 'All this should be very popular with the papers right now. It seems a notable step in making sure we have no-one to deal with in Germany.'[119]

Among those arrested by the British forces in Flensburg was Karl Brandt, the key defendant in the Doctors' Trial. Born in 1904 in Mühlhausen, Alsace, Brandt had been one of the most influential and powerful physicians in the Third Reich. Brandt was the only son of Julius Brandt, a major of the reserve army and later a police officer. On his mother's side, he came from a family of doctors from Thuringia. It was an environment of conservative, mid-ranking civil servants and state-employed physicians, loyal to the monarchy and the authorities, which inculcated Brandt early on in a sense of duty towards the state and the nation. Brandt studied medicine at the University of Jena, Freiburg i. Br., Munich and Berlin. In 1928 he graduated and started an internship at the Bergmannsheil Hospital in Bochum. In 1935 he transferred to the Surgical University Clinic in Berlin. Brandt became a member of the NSDAP in 1932 (No. 1,009,617) and joined the SA in February 1933. In March 1934 he married Anni Rehborn. After providing emergency treatment for Hitler's adjutant Wilhelm Brückner in August 1933, he was appointed Hitler's escort physician in June 1934. Throughout the middle and late 1930s, Brandt was constantly in Hitler's entourage and enjoyed the 'ear of the Führer'.

From the beginning, Brandt was involved in the planning and organisation of the Nazi 'euthanasia' programme, the murder of tens of thousands of handicapped children and adults. In autumn 1939 Brandt and Philipp Bouhler, head of the Chancellery of the Führer, were appointed to oversee the introduction of the programme. Following the end of the centrally organised 'euthanasia' programme in 1941, the killings continued under the code-name 'Aktion Brandt' on a more decentralised level to free hospital bed-space for war-wounded soldiers and civilians. The 'euthanasia' programme provided the Nazi leadership with technical expertise and personnel for the systematic mass murder of large numbers of people in the Holocaust. In August 1942, Hitler appointed Brandt as General Commissioner for Health and Sanitation to co-ordinate the military and civilian sectors of the health system. Brandt's position allowed him to become the dominating personality in the German health service at the expense of the Reich Health Leader, Leonardo Conti, who was increasingly marginalised. Brandt was answerable only to Hitler directly. In 1944 he was promoted to Reich Commissioner for Health and Sanitation, and thus became the highest medical authority of the German Reich. He was also put in charge of medical research and became Hitler's plenipotentiary for chemical warfare. Brandt was involved and implicated in numerous medical experiments carried out by German doctors on concentration camp inmates, especially those concerned with epidemic jaundice and chemical warfare agents.

In early May 1945 Brandt secured accommodation with his friend Albert Speer in a sixteenth-century waterside castle in Glücksburg.[120] On the morning of 23 May, a unit of British soldiers armed with anti-tank guns finally surrounded the castle to arrest Speer and his staff. Whether Brandt was arrested within the castle-walls or in some nearby living quarters is not known, but his detention report lists the same time of arrest as that of Speer: 9.30 a.m.[121] Both Brandt and Speer were taken into custody and brought to Flensburg prison where all prisoners were thoroughly strip-searched for poison capsules, a treatment some of the former high-ranking ministers later described as 'undignified'. Three of Brandt's staff members, Paul Rostock, head of the surgical clinic at the Charité, Siegfried Handloser, Chief of the Army Sanitary System, and Kurt Blome, Deputy Reich Health Leader had already been arrested days earlier in Garmisch, Flensburg and Munich respectively.[122] They would all meet again in the Nuremberg dock.

Brandt was first flown to Luxembourg, and whisked off to Mondorf to be reunited with the leading politicians, diplomats and military men of the Third Reich in the prison camp called 'Ashcan'. His registration number was 31G 350020.[123] The Allies had selected the small town of Mondorf near the River Mosel on the border with Germany for security reasons. Located on a plateau, the town was strategically well placed to be controlled and guarded by the army against all kinds of unwelcome visitors. Made up of vineyards and patches of woodland, the surrounding countryside could be patrolled from almost every position in the town. Military planners anticipated attacks from hard-line SS fanatics and feared that released concentration camp victims might go on the rampage and take revenge on their former tormentors. For Speer it may have been 'a moment's pleasure' to find Brandt in Mondorf, but it soon became clear that Brandt was anything but optimistic about the future. He knew that his involvement in the 'euthanasia' programme would cost him dearly.[124] Brandt was later transferred to 'Dustbin', the VIP de-briefing centre for scientists and technicians which was located at Kransberg Castle.[125] Here he was extensively de-briefed about the German medical system and his own role in medical atrocities.

Although Allied intelligence was in possession of unconfirmed reports about the killing of handicapped children and adults, hard evidence was first gathered and evaluated in the spring and early summer of 1945 by specially assigned war crimes investigators. Having distanced himself from the actual killing operations, Brandt was almost never mentioned when witnesses testified about the systematic murder of handicapped patients. Those implicated were mostly doctors and nurses, asylum directors and government officials, rather than those in charge of overall directions of the programme. Alexander's CIOS report on 'Public Mental Health Practices in Germany' provided the American and British authorities with substantial information about the methods and procedures in the 'euthanasia' programme. Brandt's name, however, was totally absent.[126]

The first suspicions about Brandt cropped up in the late summer and autumn of 1945 when the United Nations War Crimes Commission listed him among potential war criminals wanted for trial by various national and military authorities.[127] Charges included mass murder, massacres and medical atrocities. In these early investigations two factors worked against Brandt. He was constantly confused for the next two years with Dr Rudolf Brandt, chief of Himmler's personal staff and high up on the

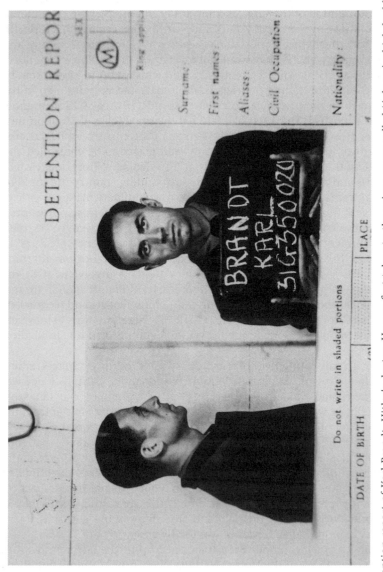

Plate 11 Detention report of Karl Brandt, Hitler's doctor. He was first taken to the prison camp called 'Ashcan' which had been reserved for leading Nazi officials. His registration number was 31 G 350020.

list of wanted criminals.[128] Alexander's report on cold-water experiments mentioned an 'Obersturmbannführer Dr Brandt', who, it was assumed, was Karl Brandt.[129] The fact that Rudolf Brandt carried almost the same SS and military rank and was equally involved in criminal medical experiments turned against Karl Brandt. Special scrutiny was exercised whenever his surname was mentioned. One British intelligence report devoted a whole section to the 'Identification of Karl Franz Friedrich Brandt', and tried to establish the links between the two men.[130] By April 1946 Brandt had been listed four times by the Central Registry of War Criminals and Security Suspects (CROWCASS), as security suspect, a witness of crimes, or as actually wanted for trial by nations such as Czechoslovakia. Even if some of the charges were unfounded, the sheer amount of evidence now beginning to appear made it increasingly unlikely that he would escape trial. Having been apprehended by the British, the Deputy Judge Advocate General (DJAG), British Army of the Rhine (BAOR), was also preparing a case against him while at the same time allowing Allied prosecution teams to question him as a witness in conjunction with the start of the IMT.[131]

At the end of 1945, British agencies discussed the possibility of charging Brandt with war crimes committed at the concentration camp of Sachsenhausen-Oranienburg. The co-ordination between the various British and Allied departments was characterised, however, by confusion over general policy direction and a lack of political commitment.[132] By April 1946 Brandt was scheduled to be released after having been transferred from Nuremberg to Dachau, where the American 3rd Army had established an extensive prison camp for thousands of alleged war criminals. Brandt's release was stopped only at the last minute when the Belgian member of the UN War Crimes Commission, M. de Baer, who just happened to be at Dachau, discovered that the detaining authorities had not been furnished with the Commission's list of war crimes suspects. The authorities had apparently 'been unable to find anything with which to charge him and he would probably have been released'.[133]

In May 1946 the US attorney Alexander Hardy produced a comprehensive report about the 'Individual Responsibility of Prof. Dr Karl Brandt'.[134] After having studied the bulk of the evidence he had reached the conclusion that Brandt was more closely connected with criminal experiments on humans than it was possible to prove at the time.[135] Hardy believed that further interrogations of Brandt and his subordinates, together with documentary analysis, would 'place Brandt in an unhealthy position' and in all probability 'establish Brandt's guilt for war crimes'.[136] By August 1946 it had been decided to turn Brandt into defendant number one in the forthcoming Doctors' Trial. One of the US prosecutors made his robust line of investigation clear: 'It is my desire to place him as top man on the totem pole as of the earliest possible date.'[137]

Planning the prosecution

On 17 July 1946 one of America's most distinguished medical scientists, the 'conscience of US science', as some would call him, left his Chicago home to travel to Washington DC. There he leafed through the files of the War Department on German medical war crimes for a couple of days before taking off for Wiesbaden, Germany, where he arrived on 27 July for what was originally designed as a fact-finding mission for the Secretary of War. Yet his involvement was to become crucial in the prosecution of Nazi physicians. The man who had left Chicago to advise the Office of Chief of Counsel for War Crimes on its forthcoming medical case was Andrew Ivy, vice-president of the University of Illinois, a respected professor of physiology and newly appointed Special Consultant to the Secretary of War.[138] Ivy's trip to Germany and France, which lasted from 18 July to 12 August 1946, shaped the strategy of how the prosecution should tackle the medical case from a legal, ethical and public relations perspective. His recommendations also ensured the recruiting of a German-speaking medical expert, limiting the potential damage to Allied – especially American – medical science, and called for written medical ethics guidelines on human experimentation.[139] Ivy's role, like that of Alexander, was central to the origins of the Nuremberg Code.

Born in 1893 in Farmington, Missouri, Andrew Conway Ivy grew up in the state of Missouri. A gifted musician with a natural talent as a baseball player, Ivy studied medicine and physiology in Chicago before teaching medicine for some years at the Northwestern University. In 1939 he became a member of the National Research Council and advanced to become one of the central advisers to the US military establishment, for example to the quartermaster general of the US armed forces and to the US navy. He also became the head of the Naval Medical Research Institute. His scientific work centred around questions that were of immediate concern to the US armed forces in the war, particularly in the field of physiology and clinical medicine as well as in submarine and aviation medicine. Like his German counterparts, he and his colleagues studied methods of how to make seawater palatable and assessed the clinical effects of high-altitude flying. As a result of this work fighter pilots were obliged to wear oxygen pressure masks. A year after the end of the Doctors' Trial, in 1948, President Truman honoured Ivy for his 'outstanding fidelity and meritorious conduct in World War II'. Yet Ivy's work went beyond that of a laboratory researcher. He was extremely media conscious and knew how to control the agenda of journalists and film crews who were covering the Allied occupation of Germany. Ivy's desire for publicity backfired in the mid-1960s when he supported a quack cancer treatment called Krebiozen.[140] However, a media-conscious medical expert, who had no qualms in being economical with the truth in order to hold Nazi physicians to account and ensure that American medical science would be seen as ethical and legal, was exactly what the prosecution needed in the run-up to the Doctors' Trial in 1946. Indeed, Ivy was the ideal choice. Throughout 1946 American attorneys had conducted preliminary investigations about the character of German experimentation. They wanted to know whether the experiments had really been necessary, adequately designed and carried out, and whether they had produced any valuable results. Since many of the experimental victims had allegedly been condemned to death, they feared that the use of such prisoners in human experiments could be sanctioned legally. If this was the case, it was likely to cause significant legal problems in the trial. Taylor's office had also received intelligence that American researchers had performed experiments on themselves and on human subjects during the war and thereafter. Of particular concern to Ivy and the prosecution were a series of malaria experiments which had been conducted on hundreds of American prison inmates, reported in *Life* magazine in June 1945.[141] It also turned out that the British forces were supporting Robert Alexander McCance (1898–1993) from the British Medical Research Council in carrying out experiments on infants suffering from meningomyelocele, a birth defect that is commonly known as spina bifida. McCance had asked the authorities 'to make some tests on these children, which will not in their experience do them any harm, but which they do not feel quite justified in carrying out on perfectly healthy children'.[142] These cases raised the question whether American and perhaps British researchers were likewise guilty of professional misconduct, and if not, why not. The evidence suggests that neither the prosecution nor the judges, nor anyone else involved in establishing the trial, had a clear idea at this point what the main legal and ethical issues were that the trial needed to address. 'If we had been able to do it over again three years later', Taylor mused in 1976, 'we would have done it in a much more sophisticated way ... with greater awareness of the implications of the positions we were taking.'[143] Upon his arrival in Germany, Ivy found that the prosecution appeared to be 'somewhat confused' about the legal, ethical and indeed scientific dimensions in the forthcoming trial.[144] Taylor put it more diplomatically: 'We were educated in large part by our opponents.'[145]

After a stop-over at Hoechst in Wiesbaden for discussions with Thompson from FIAT (British), Ivy visited the Kaiser Wilhelm Institute in Heidelberg on 30 July where the US air force had assembled German aviation scientists as part of 'Project Paperclip'. Ivy found that the group was conducting experiments 'of great value to our Air Forces at a time when aviation medical research is relatively dormant because of rapid demobilisation'.[146] He then flew on to Paris to attend the inter-Allied conference on medical war crimes on 31 July and 1 August at the Institute Pasteur. The French authorities, seizing the opportunity to make an impact on international opinion, had established the ISC (WC) in June, headed by the bacteriologist René Legroux. Little had been achieved so far, except that the British appeared to have collected more evidence than the Americans.

The purpose of the ISC (WC) was twofold: to assist in a medico-legal manner the prosecution of German medical war crimes, and to prepare and publish a report, a so-called 'white paper', on the subject for the purpose of informing the scientific and medical world of the type of experimentation that the Nazis had carried out. Another of the Commission's aims was to condemn the illegal and indeed criminal use of human beings for experimental research.[147] The leading medical and scientific organisations of the four powers were encouraged to issue a public statement in this regard.[148] Each of the four powers was also advised to appoint a national commission. France took the lead because its government had already appointed one before the Paris meeting took place.[149]

The Paris conference revealed the ambivalent nature of the tasks ahead. For example, Ivy insisted that the proposals regarding the ISC (WC) '*should not be permitted in any way* [emphasis added] to delay the preparation for the prosecution of the defendants who committed War Crimes of a Medical Nature'.[150] This was to ensure that the Americans were left with a free hand as far as the prospective Nuremberg trials were concerned. They were in no way obliged to co-operate with the other powers in putting German doctors on trial. Although international condemnation of medical atrocities was desired, 'the publicity of the medical trial should be prepared so that it will not stir public opinions against the ethical use of human subjects for experiments', a point pressed by Ivy who feared that a trial against German experimenters could jeopardise research on humans and thus prevent medical progress.[151] 'Therefore', the minutes record, 'Doctor Ivy felt that some broad principles should be formulated by this meeting enunciating the criteria for the use of humans as subjects in experimental work.'[152]

Here, in August 1946, we find the rationale for the creation of principles for permissible experiments on humans in embryonic form. The principles resulted, to a great extent, from Ivy's strategic approach to human experimentation and from his knowledge of the subject matter. He knew that a trial of German doctors, and an international condemnation of the crimes by the four powers, could lead to calls to prohibit experiments on humans once and for all. This was the worst-case scenario. All the proposals made by Ivy and the other members of the Commission over the following months have to be seen in the light of attempting to prevent this outcome. In order to prosecute doctors for unethical behaviour, but ensure that the international medical community could continue to use humans in experimental research, a 'pragmatic instrument' was needed to label the German experiments as 'unethical' and those of the Allies as 'ethical'. Ivy's 'broad ethical rules' which he subsequently produced constituted this 'pragmatic instrument', 'adopted and publicised for the purpose of contrasting ethical and unethical experimentation of [*sic*] human subjects'.[153] The origin and primary objective of Ivy's medical ethics principles was to make human experiments possible in the future. All other issues, like the protection of human and patient rights in medical science, or the role of the informed consent principle, were secondary to this overarching objective. This had significant implications for the strategy of the prosecution and the origin of the Nuremberg Code.

In 'Appendix B' of the report on the Paris conference Ivy included an 'Outline of Principles and Rules of Experimentation on Human Subjects'. He listed three major principles:

I. Consent of the subject is required; i.e., only volunteers should be used.
(a) The volunteers before giving their consent should be told of the hazards, if any.
(b) Insurance against an accident should be provided, if it is possible to secure it.
II. The experiment to be performed should be so designed and based on the results of animal experimentation that the anticipated results will justify the performance of the experiment; that is, the experiment must be useful and be such as to yield results for the good of society.
III. The experiment should be conducted
(a) So as to avoid unnecessary physical and mental suffering and injury, and
(b) By scientifically qualified persons.
(c) The experiment should not be conducted if there is *a priori* reason to believe that death or disabling injury will occur.[154]

The requirements were far from specific. There was no mention of what 'consent' meant, how it would be obtained and by whom, or what kind of information the subject was entitled to receive. There was also no reference to vulnerable groups like the mentally handicapped and children, nor did the rules explain what 'for the good of society' actually meant. Whilst claiming that the principles applied 'in all countries of the world' which had contributed to the 'progress of medical science' in the past, Ivy had kept them deliberately vague in order to allow room for interpretation and discretion for medical scientists in the future. On his return to the United States, he submitted a comprehensive report which included his three ethics rules to the AMA Board of Trustees. These 'inadequate' guidelines, as Katz has called them, were subsequently adopted in a shortened and significantly modified form by the AMA House of Delegates on 10 December 1946, one day after the opening of the Doctors' Trial.[155] Ivy had probably realised that any future expert testimony by the prosecution would be strengthened if the witness could refer to some written, and indeed published, medical ethics rules. Ivy's ethics rules were written in anticipation of his own role as an expert witness in the trial, something he only admitted during cross-examination by the defence.[156] Ivy's report on 'War Crimes of a Medical Nature Committed in Germany and Elsewhere on German Nationals and the Nationals of Countries by the Nazi Regime During World War II' was probably written between 9 August and 16 October 1946 after his return to the United States and before the forthcoming conference in Paris at the Institute Pasteur. The report developed many of the key arguments later used by the prosecution in the trial, anticipated most of the counter-arguments which the defence would eventually advance, and provided ammunition against the counter-arguments. It summarised almost all of the main issues raised and debated in the course of the Doctors' Trial. Ivy also advanced the grand claim that human experiments 'without consent, or by coercion' were 'contrary to the laws of humanity and the ethical principles of the medical profession which have been in practice for 22 centuries'.[157] From this premise everything else followed. The 'Ethical Rules for Human Experimentation', that is Ivy's three principles, were intended to show that German physicians were guilty, both ethically and legally, because they had 'ignored these ethical principles and rules, which have been well established by custom, social usage and the ethics of medical conduct'.[158]

The legal value of the 'ethical rules' lay in their pragmatic character. They provided strong legal, cultural and historical arguments against the anticipated line of defence. The defence would claim that the experiments had been conducted for the good of society and the nation, that is, that the 'end justifies the means'. They would also argue that the accused had acted 'under orders from superior authority' and that the experiments were carried out on human beings who had been condemned to death and were likely to be killed. Hence, the argument would run, 'some good should be derived from their death, even without the consent of the persons concerned'.[159] Yet since there was no law in any country which permitted the exploitation of condemned prisoners the argument could be discarded. Another expected argument was that if experiments on humans were conducted under the aegis of Himmler and the SS, they should at least be performed by 'trained scientists' in order to ensure the validity of the results. This line of defence suggested that 'if a crime is going to be committed, the scientist should be an "accessory before and to the fact" to insure that the crime will be committed so that knowledge accrues therefrom'.[160] All of these arguments were later propounded in a number of ways by the defendants during the trial.[161]

The principles of consent and safety were singled out as essential to the case. In all civilised societies, Ivy claimed, it had 'always [been] possible to secure volunteers' without coercion. Voluntary consent and 'complete cooperation' of the experimental subject were paramount in obtaining reliable results. Yet Ivy's main priority was to ensure that the public would not lose confidence in the medical profession.[162] The world's medical profession, above all, had to be protected from coming into disrepute. This included manipulating the outcome of the Doctors' Trial as a whole. It was the assumed 'duty of Society' to protect the achievements of medicine and prosecute medical scientists whose conduct was contrary to the 'laws of humanity and human rights'. The timeless existence of professional standards of conduct for physicians, outside socio-political and cultural influences, was taken for granted. A case in point was the German doctors themselves, who responded by saying 'No' when asked whether they would treat their children, their wife or themselves in the manner they had treated their experimental subjects, 'regardless of their overt support of the ideology of the *Herrenvolk*'.[163]

Another major issue was the attempt of the prosecution to base most of its legal argument on German laws and regulations in order to forestall accusations of *ex post facto* law in the trial.[164] They wanted to show that Nazi doctors had violated the laws of their own country. For example, there was no provision in the German penal code which permitted the use of human subjects 'without their consent where death or prolonged suffering is likely *a priori* to ensue'. On the contrary, German regulations from 1931 stated that 'experimentation shall be prohibited in all cases where consent has not been given'.[165]

Ivy recommended the following course of action: first, the authorities were asked to try an estimated 60–70 leading medical and non-medical officials and medical scientists, who were involved in 'mass killings' of a medical nature, including experiments on humans without their consent. This was to be followed by prosecuting those implicated in less serious crimes, 'for the sake of justice and the wholesome moral effect of example and precedent'.[166] Third, the interrogation of witnesses should be conducted to obtain as much scientific data as possible 'since the only good ... which may be derived from the experiments is scientific data'.[167] Ivy's fourth recommendation was Alexander's job description for Nuremberg, that is, the proposal to appoint a German-speaking medical expert to the prosecution who would work full-time in Taylor's office, collect evidence and interrogate witnesses in preparation for the trial.[168] Originally, two medical experts were seen as the absolute minimum for the trials and doubts were raised whether this would be adequate.[169] By the end of the year, though, the prosecution was glad to have one expert at all. Points five and six of Ivy's recommendations had far-reaching implications for the way in which the prosecution approached the Doctors' Trial. They facilitated the writing of the Nuremberg Code and ultimately influenced the conduct of the trial:

5. It is recommended that the official in charge of the publicity of these trials should be cautioned to release the publicity in such a form that it

will not jeopardise ethical experimentation on human subjects; i.e. the publicity should be pointed to emphasise the contrast between the unethical and illegal experimentation of the Nazis and the ethical experimentation conducted in Allied countries, and even in Germany before and during the war.

6 It is recommended that the various crimes of a medical nature be collected and published in book form along with a code of ethical rules for human experimentation with the idea of preventing recurrences of Nazi crimes and providing a basis for an international legal convention.[170]

Finally, all officers of the German Medical Association (GMA) who were implicated in crimes, whether by ordering, abetting or condoning them, were to be prosecuted to show the Germans that 'incorporated bodies' should 'at least' have protested against the commission of illegal acts by its members.[171] All of Ivy's recommendations and the report on the Paris conference were classified as secret.[172] Further proposals were scheduled for another conference at the Institute Pasteur in mid-October 1946 when, it was hoped, the British, American and the Russians authorities had reached a decision with regard to the creation of the International Scientific Commission (for the Investigation of War Crimes of a Medical Nature), the ISC (WC).[173] Apart from the British none of the other powers had made any provisions. The Americans were not only half-hearted about committing themselves to the ISC (WC) but remained doubtful whether the Commission could produce anything of value for the forthcoming medical trial.

At around the same time the US prosecution had to deal with practical matters after realising that a large number of the accused doctors were in British custody. Collaboration with the British was essential for the Americans to amass a substantial body of incriminating evidence. In the autumn of 1946 Britain placed the entire 'Hohenlychen Group', including Karl Brandt, as well as substantial documentary evidence, files and expert reports, at Taylor's disposal. These men and women would otherwise have been prosecuted in the British Ravensbrück trial which was held in Hamburg from 5 December 1946 until 3 February 1947.[174] While tensions with Russia were mounting, American demands were given high priority in London on the eve of the Cold War. On 30 September Taylor was in a position to inform the Assistant Secretary of War, Howard Petersen, that the prosecution had assembled 'plentiful and quite sensational' evidence against the defendants in the Doctors' Trial, adding that out of all the subsequent trials the trial against the German physicians 'should be a rather easy case to try and to decide, and therefore I think a good one to start with'.[175] For once, Taylor's assessment of the situation was way off the mark.

On 25 October 1946, the Chief of Counsel for War Crimes filed the indictment against the defendants in the Doctors' Trial. On 5 November the indictment was served to the defendants, giving them thirty days to prepare their defence.[176] It listed the accused according to the position that they had held in the Nazi medical hierarchy. The defendants were charged with a common design or conspiracy, with war crimes, crimes against humanity and membership of an organisation declared criminal by the IMT, particularly with criminal experiments in the concentration camps of Dachau, Sachsenhausen, Natzweiler, Ravensbrück, Buchenwald and others. In the course of the experiments hundreds of inmates had experienced extreme suffering, torture and death. Some experiments were carried out in order to study the limits of human endurance at extremely high altitudes, others to find an effective rewarming method for persons suffering from severe hypothermia. Malaria and mustard gas experiments had been performed to develop effective new treatments, sulphonamide drug experiments at the concentration camp of Ravensbrück to test the effectiveness of that drug, to name but a few.[177] Several of the defendants were also charged with murder, torture and maltreatment of people that were not related to medical experiments, for example with participation in the 'euthanasia' programme. All of the twenty-three defendants (see Table 5.1) pleaded not guilty to the crimes they were charged with, yet were soon about to come face to face with the four men who had been seconded to Nuremberg to pass judgement on them.

The tribunal arrives

Information about the judges in the subsequent Nuremberg Trials is relatively scarce, particularly in the Nazi Doctors' Trial. Yet we know a little bit about the recruitment process. In August 1947 officials from the War Department noted that 'the judges for the Zonal trials should be so far as possible of standing and prestige equal to that of the Nuremberg judges' and that therefore the selection process would 'require exceptional care and review by the most responsible authorities in the department'.[178] The recruitment of the judges was co-ordinated in the war crimes branch of the War Department. Legal consultants were delegated to 'tour the country to interview persons who are selected as the judges whom the Secretary of War would like to nominate'.[179] High-ranking military persons, circuit and district court judges, state court judges and experts working in the judicial field such as 'members of the bar and law school professors of high standing' were potential candidates. The law schools of Michigan, Chicago, California and Texas were regarded as the best places to recruit able judges. The lawyer Charles Horsky was appointed by the Secretary of War as an unpaid emissary to select and interview shortlisted candidates.[180] The War Department proposed its candidates to General Lucius Clay, who conferred with the Office of Chief of Counsel and the Legal Division of OMGUS.[181]

Plate 12 The defendants in the Nuremberg Doctors' Trial. Nuremberg, Germany.

Table 5.1 Defendants in the Nuremberg Doctors' Trial

Name	Position
Karl Brandt	Reich Commissioner for Health and Sanitation
Siegfried Handloser	Medical Inspector of the Army and Chief of the Medical Services of the Armed Forces
Paul Rostock	Chief of the Office for Medical Science and Research under the Reich Commissioner for Health and Sanitation
Oskar Schröder	Chief of the Medical Service of the Air Force
Karl Genzken	Chief of the Medical Department of the Waffen SS
Karl Gebhardt	Chief Surgeon of the Staff of the Reich Physician SS and Police and President of the German Red Cross
Kurt Blome	Deputy Reich Health Leader and Plenipotentiary for Cancer Research in the Reich Research Council
Rudolf Brandt	Personal Administrative Officer to Reichsführer SS Himmler and Ministerial Counsellor and Chief of the Ministerial Office in the Reich Ministry of the Interior
Joachim Mrugowsky	Chief Hygienist of the Reich Physician SS and Police and Chief of the Hygiene Institute of the Waffen SS
Helmut Poppendick	Chief of the Personal Staff of the Reich Physician SS and Police
Wolfram Sievers	Official of the SS-Ahnenerbe (Ancestral Heritage) Society and Director of its Institute for Military Scientific Research and Deputy Chairman of the Managing Board of Directors of the Reich Research Council
Gerhard Rose	Vice President, Chief of the Department for Tropical Medicine and Professor of the Robert-Koch-Institute and Hygienic Adviser for Tropical Medicine to the Chief of the Medical Service of the Air Force
Siegfried Ruff	Director of the Department for Aviation Medicine at the German Experimental Institute for Aviation
Hans Wolfgang Romberg	Doctor on the Staff at the Department for Aviation Medicine at the German Experimental Institute for Aviation
Victor Brack	Chief Administrative Officer in the Chancellery of the Führer of the NSDAP
Hermann Becker-Freysing	Chief of the Department for Aviation Medicine and Chief of the Medical Service of the Air Force
Georg August Weltz	Chief of the Institute for Aviation Medicine in Munich
Konrad Schäfer	Physician at the Institute for Aviation Medicine at the Reich Ministry for Aviation
Waldemar Hoven	Chief Doctor of the Buchenwald concentration camp
Wilhelm Beiglböck	Consulting Physician to the Air Force
Adolf Pokorny	Medical Officer of the German Armed Forces
Herta Oberheuser	Physician at the Ravensbrück concentration camp and Assistant Physician to the defendant Gebhardt at the SS hospital in Hohenlychen
Fritz Fischer	Assistant Physician to the defendant Gebhardt at the SS hospital in Hohenlychen

Source: NDT Records, fiche 3, frames 2–27.

On 15 August the name of the presiding judge in the Doctors' Trial, Walter B. Beals, was brought to the attention of the Secretary of War. By the middle of September Horsky interviewed him over the telephone and offered him the position. Many of the judges, however, including Beals, wanted to accept their appointment only under the condition that their family could accompany them to Europe. Some of the judges were also not fully convinced about the moral and legal justification of the war crimes programme.[182] On 21 September 1946 the Assistant Secretary of War conceded that there were great difficulties 'in securing the recruitment of able judges with sufficient prestige'.[183]

By the end of September the situation had improved. Three judges and one attorney had been selected to serve as judges in the Doctors' Trial. Walter B. Beals, justice of the Supreme Court of the state of Washington, Harold L. Sebring, justice of the Supreme Court of Florida, Joseph Moynihan, Presiding Circuit Court judge in the state of Michigan, and Victor C. Swearingen, lieutenant-colonel in the US army and former assistant attorney general of Michigan, had been nominated as judges.[184] Significantly, Sebring was interviewed by Swearingen who a couple of weeks later became his colleague in Nuremberg. On 26 September Swearingen interviewed Sebring in Tallahassee and arranged that he would be granted leave of absence by the governor of the state of Florida.[185] It is likely that Swearingen was also influential in the nomination of Joseph Moynihan, given that both of them had worked in the state of Michigan and probably knew each other. Moynihan, however, never took up his post. At the end of September he told Swearingen that his current workload and the state of health of his wife made it impossible for him to take a leave of absence for more than a year.[186] A couple of days later Johnson T. Crawford, Circuit Judge of the Oklahoma District Court of Appeals in Ada, accepted his nomination as a substitute for Moynihan. On 15 October the War Department informed Taylor that all of the judges had departed from Washington DC and that they would arrive, after a brief stopover in Paris, at Nuremberg. All of the judges asked for permission for their wives to accompany them to Nuremberg.[187] Swearingen even wanted to take his eleven-year-old daughter and his mother-in-law to Germany. Sebring only wanted his seventeen-year-old son in Nuremberg.[188] Each of the judges, except for Swearingen, so it seems, was given clerical support.[189] On 25 October 1946, the day that the tribunal was established and the indictment against the doctors was filed, General Clay appointed Beals, Sebring, Crawford and Swearingen as designated judges of Military Tribunal I.

Almost all of the judges took up their Nuremberg appointments at considerable cost, both personally and professionally. Their own knowledge of the historic nature of the tribunal, with its potential implications for the creation of new international law, found little support from legal colleagues in the United States. The American public was also beginning to lose interest in controversial military trials. Some federal judges were openly critical about the trials and questioned the underlying rationale of the war crimes programme. In September 1946 the circuit judge William Denman from San Francisco, California, who himself had been approached to serve as a Nuremberg judge, told the authorities that the American judges had a 'valuable duty to perform in impressing the German public with fairness and justice of [a] judicial system of a Western democracy' and that he and his colleagues had a duty to serve 'if we feel we can aid in accomplishing that result'.[190] However, Denman wanted to know whether the president knew of the fact that the War Department was 'accepting services of federal judges to perform functions not of their judicial office and outside the United States'. Most importantly, he questioned the legitimacy and impartiality of the recruiting process: 'If appointment of judges were to be by military commander, is it not open to suggestion that it is contrary to the American way of life for the prosecution body to choose the judges before whom the prosecution is conducted.'[191] In a letter to the Secretary of War, Robert W. Patterson, Denman expressed his concern over the public criticism which had been levelled against some of the Nuremberg judges in the past. The main problem was that the judges were appointed by the Zone Commander which meant that 'an executive officer creates a federal judge as a member of what appears to be purely a military court ... that is under the executive'.[192] Denman and his colleagues felt that the Nuremberg judges had to be authorised and appointed by the president, preferably with the approval of the Chief Justice. The Chief Justice, however, refused federal judges permission for leave of absence to serve on the war crimes tribunals.[193] The appointment of the judges in the Doctors' Trial was eventually confirmed by executive order No. 9813, signed by President Truman on 20 December 1946.[194]

The judges and legal experts who accepted their nomination knew that they would not necessarily receive any social or professional prestige in return. Most of them saw the assignment as a patriotic service to their country, and their appointments generally cut across party political lines. Whereas Beals was a Republican, Sebring and Crawford were Democrats.[195] Born in July 1876, Justice Beals spent most of his boyhood and high-school years in St Paul, Minnesota. After receiving his law degree from the University of Washington, he practised law in Seattle and in neighbouring King County, then served as a division judge advocate for the 81st Division during the First World War. Since 1926 Beals served as a justice on the Supreme Court of the State of Washington and acted as Chief Justice for that court from 1933 to 1934 and was reappointed as Chief Justice in 1945. His term was due to expire on 31 December 1946 when he was invited to serve as the presiding judge on Military Tribunal I. He asked to be relieved of his position in order to come to Nuremberg.[196]

Judge Sebring, the second most senior judge on the bench, was a man of the highest intellectual calibre and professional standards. Born in 1897, he came from Olath, Kansas, had spend his youth in LaJunta, Colorado, before graduating from Gardener High School and Kansas State College in Manhattan, Kansas. He first studied architecture, engineering and business administration, but then changed tack and entered the College of Law at the University of Florida.[197] From August 1934 until January 1943 he served on the bench of the Eighth Judicial Court at Gainsville, Florida. In 1943 he was appointed to the Supreme Court of Florida and became involved in a number of charitable and philanthropic organisations, for example, as the President of the Parole and Probation Association, as Director of the Children's Home Society, the Red Cross and the Tuberculosis Association. Another of Sebring's passions was American football and he became head coach at the University of Florida. After considerable debate he was permitted to take formal leave from his position on the Florida Supreme Court to serve on the Nuremberg tribunal. He became a key force in upholding strict rules of procedure; his ability not to lose sight of the overall task of the trial seems to have been greatly valued by Beals and the other members of the bench.[198] According to Tom Sebring, Nuremberg was one of the most stressful periods in his father's life, having neither known nor anticipated the workload and responsibility placed upon his shoulders.[199]

On the other two judges there is only a scarce amount of information available. Justice Johnson Tal Crawford was born in 1889 in Washington County, Arkansas. After receiving his law degree from Oklahoma University, he served for twenty-two years on the bench of the Oklahoma District Court in Ada, Oklahoma. In order to come to Nuremberg Justice Crawford resigned, but hoped to return to Ada and practise law after the conclusion of the war crimes trials. Victor C. Swearingen, the youngest of the judges, was born in 1899 in Kentucky where he graduated from the university in 1922. In 1925 he received his doctoral degree from Detroit College of Law and worked for a local law firm for over a decade. After a career as an Assistant Attorney General of Michigan and as a Principal Attorney for the Department of Agriculture in Washington DC, Swearingen joined the Pacific theatre in 1942, first as a combat intelligence officer, later as commanding officer of the 419th Troop Carrier Group. In November 1945, he returned to the United States and was assigned as an Assistant Staff Judge Advocate at the Air Transport Command HQ in Washington DC. In January 1946 he was promoted to Chief of Operations at the War Crimes Office in the Pentagon, where he helped to set up the military trials in Tokyo.[200] On 10 October he was discharged from the army and the following day was sworn in as Special Assistant Attorney General in the Criminal Division of the Department of Justice. However, for lack of suitable judges, the Department of Justice transferred him as 'a loan' to the War Department for the Nuremberg assignment.

On 26 October 1946, the day after their formal appointment, the four judges met for the first time with Charles E. Sand, acting Secretary General, to decide on the rules of procedure.[201] Sand, former probation officer of the Juvenile Court in Boston, Massachusetts, had succeeded Colonel John E. Ray, the Secretary General of the IMT.[202] It soon became clear that the organisational arrangements were far from ready for another trial. Major preparations were launched to establish a smooth-running trial machinery. The main courtroom, located on the second floor of the Palace of Justice of the easternmost wing, provided space for about 600 people, mostly Allied military officials, trial observers, journalists, film crews and specially vetted members of the German public, who would be seated in the gallery. Its entrance was heavily guarded by armed American military police who were advised to thoroughly check everyone's credentials. The building and courtroom needed major refurbishment and enlargement. For the subsequent Nuremberg trials rooms 70, 196, 295, 319 and 581 were to be transformed into courtrooms. The army worked day and night to install the necessary communication and simultaneous translation facilities for hundreds of lawyers and their staff, interpreters, defence counsel and the press. Air, rail and motor transport had to be organised, telephones and other means of communication with national governments had to be installed. A total of 124 miles of telephone wire were fitted into the court house alone. The press had to have access to special signal equipment in order to be able to forward their news reports; 240 seats were reserved in the courtroom for reporters. A hospital and dispensary provided medical care for prisoners and courtroom staff. The courtroom in the Doctors' Trial, room 600, had originally served as a recreation centre for US military personnel, who had used the judges' bench as a bar with pin-ups behind it. All the rooms therefore had to be repainted, and all the woodwork, including the wooden panelling, needed to be varnished.[203] Economists estimated the total cost at around 12 000 US dollars in addition to the cost for refurbishing the building at the start of the IMT.

On 8 November the judges had their first executive meeting.[204] These were sessions mostly held in camera, without no other personnel present except the Secretary General of the court or the head of the prosecution, Taylor. The framework of the trials as outlined in the charter required that the judgement in the trial had to be final and was not subject to review. There was no appeal procedure in place. Only the military governor had the power to alter sentences, but could not increase their severity. The execution of death sentences could be deferred 'if there is reason to believe that the testimony of the convicted person may be of value in the investigation and trial of other crimes'.[205] In their first session the judges noted that the indictment had been served to the defendants three days earlier, leaving them ten days to choose a defence counsel. One of the issues which had to be tackled more effectively than in the IMT was the compensation of the defence counsel. In any ordinary trial, the defendant would pay their defence counsel or the court would provide legal aid. Like all Germans awaiting denazification proceedings, the defendants had their bank accounts and assets frozen. As far as legal aid was concerned, no German state existed which could pay them. During the IMT the tribunal made one advance payment, believing that the trial would last no longer than a couple of weeks. By the beginning of 1946 some lawyers complained that whilst they were stuck in Nuremberg, they needed to pay the rents of their houses, office space at home, and the salary of their personnel. This time sufficient compensation was to be made available to the counsel, although the judges were careful to ensure that it would not exceed the amounts allowed by the IMT. Overall the US authorities were concerned that the defendants were given a fair trial 'which they, in the days of their pomp and power, never gave to any man'.[206]

There were dozens of practical matters that had to be resolved. These ranged from the appointment of defence lawyers (some of whom were known to have been former Nazi supporters)[207] to office facilities, equipment or transportation. Issues such as the judges' robes, especially flown in from Washington, mattered as much as the seating plan of the defendants. All of them were seated according to the order in which they were named in the indictment. The question of Oberheuser as the only woman led to some discussion. Some suggested that one should place her to the side of the dock so that she would 'not be crowded between two men'. The prosecution immediately objected, insisting that she should not be privileged in any way. Karl Brandt, defendant number one, was given the highly symbolic seat No. 13 in the far-left corner of the defendants' box, exactly the same place where Göring had sat a year earlier. Considerable debate also arose over the question whether Waldemar Hoven would be permitted to use an American lawyer from Boston. The request was turned down, as it might have postponed the expeditious start of the trial. The date for the opening of the trial was fixed for Monday, 9 December 1946, because the rules of procedure required that thirty days had to elapse after the serving of the indictment. Then there was the question where to place the press and other guests, especially VIP guests of the Allied Control Council. Another point of debate was whether the presiding judge would have to sit 'squarely in the middle of the bench'. All of the judges agreed unanimously.

Security fell into the hands of Colonel Burton C. Andrus, a meticulous, dark-haired, bespectacled and unobtrusive go-by-the-book officer, who was detested by many of the defendants for his unwillingness to recognise their former rank and status.[208] He had been in charge since the days when the major war criminals were detained in camp 'Ashcan' and throughout the IMT. Always concerned about formal matters, Judge Sebring complained to the Secretary General that none of the sentries 'comport themselves in a military manner'.[209] The way in which they had handled the inspection of passes had become 'progressively sloppy' since the conclusion of the IMT. Questions of translations and record-keeping had to be settled as well as the issue of who was permitted to interrogate the defendants. Whereas the tribunal had no objections to the fact that a member of the British prosecution would interview defendants for the forthcoming Ravensbrück trial, at first they rejected the idea that the French naval psychologist Françoise Bayle would be allowed to conduct physical measurements of the defendants and obtain handwriting specimens.[210] Most of the time the atmosphere in the executive sessions was stern and straight to the point, sometimes with brief discussion over a matter of contention before a motion was made. But there were also moments of humour, for example when Taylor, the 'left-wing political hawk', enquired whether one should introduce a forty-hour week for the Nuremberg staff. 'I did not think about a forty-hour week, I thought it was about eighty hours', Beals replied drily.[211]

The medical expert

Since Justice Jackson left Nuremberg the prosecution was under enormous time pressure. The Doctors' Trial was 'an improvised affair', as Taylor later put it, neither carefully prepared nor thought through.[212] Throughout the summer of 1946 Taylor tried to improve the quality of his legal staff, most of whom he regarded as ill-qualified. The army's ban on bringing spouses to Nuremberg made it difficult to recruit the most able legal brains, and this rule was progressively loosened. As late as September Taylor complained to the Assistant Secretary of War that 'with few exceptions' his men were 'utterly vacuous political hacks. They are of no earthly use to us and if they aren't very unhappy already they are going to be very shortly.'[213] Others were total eccentrics who thought they could sort out the war crimes cases in no time but literally fled from Nuremberg once they realised that it would involve a lot of work.[214] Taylor also desperately needed intelligent 'German-speaking research people' who could organise and interpret the mass of incriminating evidence.[215] Even so, the number of Taylor's staff was impressive. Compared to the small working legal team of the British prosecution at the IMT headed by Sir Hartley Shawcross, the Americans favoured quantity rather than quality. From May to July 1946 Taylor's staff increased from 25 attorneys to 113. By the end of October his team amounted to more than 400 American and Allied attorneys, interrogators, investigators and special agents of OCCWC.[216] 'The need for speed is the basic justification for employing a large staff to do this job', Taylor told Jackson.[217] In total the Americans employed a staff of 1776 people. Officials in Washington were nonetheless aware of the lack of legal and medical expertise in Nuremberg which increased the potential pitfalls in the case against the doctors.[218]

At the beginning of November 1946 Taylor cabled to the War Department that he needed an 'extensive paper on the history of medical experimentation on living human beings with particular emphasis on practice in US. Defendant Rose states that US doctors have extensively experimented on inmates of penal institutions and asylums, especially with malaria. Any truth in this? If so give us full facts.'[219] Taylor suggested contacting Ivy at the University of Illinois for further information whilst urging the military to fully explore this question, knowing that it was of vital importance in the forthcoming trial. In an encoded message from 16 November the War Department told Taylor that Ivy would be able to visit Nuremberg at the beginning of the trial and furnish the prosecution with all the necessary material about the history of human experimentation. The War Department had also recruited Morris Fishbein, editor of the *Journal of the American Medical Association*, to support the Nuremberg staff. The material shows that a great amount of background work was being conducted behind the scenes by the American military authorities to ensure that German doctors would be held accountable. Yet the intricate connection between the US military and the Nuremberg Doctors' Trial also meant that the trial became of less relevance once the strategic and political priorities of the day moved in a different direction. As long as Washington saw the Nuremberg trials as part of the overall aim to create a new post-war order, the prosecution and indeed the judges had little to worry about other than to establish the proper trial procedures. This naturally included the role of experts.[220]

On 15 November the issue of medical experts was briefly touched upon when Judge Sebring questioned whether the tribunal would want a medical expert.[221] Although all agreed that the tribunal probably would need an expert, the matter was not given much thought. The judges believed that the person would, in any event, be employed only temporarily. It was a misjudgement on the part of the tribunal, especially once it became clear that medical knowledge and a medical expert witness were much more essential to the trial than previously anticipated. For Taylor, speaking about the beginning of the trial decades later, the judges were 'just as green' to the inherent problems as some of his attorneys.[222] The prosecution, on the other hand, had understood the importance of medical knowledge in the forthcoming trial from the beginning. Backed by Ivy, they had therefore arranged the appointment of their own expert adviser through the Secretary of War.[223] Shortly after returning to America in August, Ivy had suggested to Taylor's office that 'unless expert witnesses among the Germans themselves can be found, the necessity may arise in some cases to introduce witnesses from other countries including our own'.[224] Who exactly proposed Alexander is not known, although his CIOS reports, which had attracted some attention during the IMT, and the familiarity of his name among the staff of the Pentagon and at Nuremberg, provides the most likely answer. Alexander was the obvious choice. On 7 November Taylor cabled the War Department: 'Urgently need information as to [the] probable date [of] arrival [of] Dr Leo Alexander. [The] indictment in [the] medical case has been filed and [the] opening of [the] trial [is] expected during [the] first week [of] December. Badly need Dr Alexander here two or three weeks in advance of trial for consultation and assistance in preparation of [the] case.'[225]

'When he left to go to Nuremberg my parents had a party', Cecily recalled, 'and there were farewell dinners for him and we were very sad to see him go, but thought that it was something very important.'[226] On the same day that the judges were discussing the matter, Alexander was already sitting in a military plane high above the Atlantic and was heading towards Paris en route to Nuremberg.[227] On 8 November the War Department had issued his travel orders: 'Dr. Leo Alexander, Expert to the Secretary of War, $40 per day, is hereby directed to proceed by air on or about 14 November 1946 from Washington, D.C., to Nuremberg, Germany, on temporary duty for approximately three (3) months, and upon completion thereof to return to Washington, DC'.[228] Four days later he was asked to report to the Pentagon where he was duly informed that Lemkin's concept of genocide would be the main basis for the trial.[229] The next day, on 13 November, the Jewish-born émigré lawyer Robert Kempner, a no-nonsense interrogator and staff member of the American prosecution, briefed him about his role as part of the prosecution. Alexander was answerable to General Taylor. Kempner criticised the overall planning of the trial and the quality of the indictment. 'Don't tell him [Taylor] that the indictment is sloppily drawn – you will see it yourself', Alexander recorded in his diary.[230] Alexander was advised to support Taylor's team in producing a good trial brief and lay out individual offences as much as possible in written form because 'the judges like to rely on written stuff'.[231] The prosecution apparently believed that the judges would otherwise be unable 'to grasp the whole offence', an assessment that was far from accurate.[232] Unlike others, the judges were under no false impressions about the gravity of the crimes that had been committed and were able to clarify the most contentious and difficult ethical issues in open court and under cross-examination.

Alexander left Washington on the evening of 13 November after 'the process of being processed', as he called it, had been completed. He had been sworn in, given the title of 'Expert Consultant to the Secretary of War' and promoted to lieutenant-colonel. Phyllis was told to frame the official document.[233] Before departure he watched a movie about safety instructions for transatlantic flights. Lagus on the Azores was his first stopover, where he was greeted with an evening dinner by members of the US navy. The next morning, at 7.30 a.m., he continued his flight high above a red sky, arriving in Paris at 5.30 p.m., then checked into the Hotel Napoleon.[234] Completely exhausted from the journey he slept until midday, did some sightseeing and went to hear an opera in the evening. Communication by telephone with Washington still proved problematic, especially when the weather was bad. In Paris he also visited the obvious tourist attractions: Les Invalides, Les Tuileries, the Louvre and Notre Dame. On 18 November, five days after his departure, he arrived in Nuremberg where he was cordially received at the Grand Hotel.[235] It would become his home for the next couple of months.

Alexander went straight to work the next day after realising that the prosecution was in a quandary. They did not seem to have sufficient written evidence to back up the case against the doctors. On the same evening he noted: 'Found them short of documents, called for my microfilm.'[236] The Palace of Justice appeared like a 'small town within a town'.[237] There was no time for sightseeing any more, except on the way to the court house. Nuremberg still looked like a 'heap of rubble'. Members of the court were also discouraged from walking alone unarmed through the inner walls of the city; apparently the ruins were 'hangouts for things of all kinds'. Alexander's daily routine involved leaving the Grand Hotel at around 8.30 a.m., when a bus would drive him to the Palace of Justice. There he would work until about 6 p.m. and return to the hotel. Then he would have supper, followed by 'talking shop' in the lobby to exchange ideas and notes. Back in the room, he would start writing summaries of interrogations from the preceding day, or make notes in his diary. A week after his arrival Alexander was satisfied that a substantial amount of material had been amassed since his investigations in 1945.[238]

Relations between the members of the prosecution were facilitated by a friendly and business-like atmosphere. Some, like Taylor and his assistant Erwin, had brought their spouses over to Europe. Alexander was trying to do the same with his wife and children. Many of the spouses also served in one way or another for the prosecution which helped to create an atmosphere of familiarity. Taylor's wife worked in the interrogation section, whilst Erwin's wife attempted to track down war criminals. 'In spite of an air of amateurishness and erudition, which would make a Boston cop's hair stand on end, her office works reasonably well. A very good job has been done in ferreting out missing war criminals', Alexander told his wife.[239] Some of the other staff members included James M. McHaney, a Southern lawyer from Arkansas, the chief prosecutor for Case 1. His assistant was Alexander G. Hardy from Boston, a smart and hard-working politician. Hardy's assistant was Arnost Horlik-Hochwald from Prague.[240] And then there was the interrogation department, headed by Walter H. Rapp, director of the evidence division. This was Alexander's first port of call.

Since the summer of 1946 the mission of the Interrogation Service Unit was to assist the prosecution in preparing the cases for trial by extracting pertinent information from defendants and witnesses. Any information found to be of value was to become part of the evidence in the trial.[241] All

Plate 13 The foyer of the Grand Hotel, Nuremberg, where Leo Alexander stayed. Nuremberg, Germany, 1946/7.

members were advised to create a constant stream of information so that other interrogators would improve on their techniques and quality of questions as rapidly as possible. There were about twenty-five German-speaking interrogators who produced Interrogation Report Summaries (IRS) and Staff Evidence Analysis (SEA) which summarised the main arguments and facts of a given interrogation. The methods of interrogation were to be kept flexible and adjusted as the different cases progressed. All interrogations were generally conducted in German with only the interrogator and the interrogatee present in the room. Alexander and his colleagues were asked to keep the number of VIP visitors, friends and 'curiosity seekers' to an absolute minimum. It was felt that the presence of anyone other than those involved in the interrogation would influence and distract the conversation and might seriously damage the quality of the evidence obtained. The interrogations were generally recorded on tape so that the interrogator did not have to take notes during them. In some cases there was a guard and a stenographer present.

The locations of the interrogations raised a number of questions. Interrogators needed office space and clerical staff; at least twenty rooms had to be reserved which were suitable for planting 'special recording devices', and met the tight security standards. All rooms had to be separated from the rest of the staff office and quiet. The expeditious handling of the cases made it necessary for up to twenty interrogations to be conducted simultaneously. That meant that five interrogators were kept in reserve, in case of illness, or to prepare material for the prosecution. Plans to organise the most effective methods of interrogation ran in many directions in the late summer of 1946; some floated the idea of establishing a kind of detention centre a couple of miles outside of Nuremberg where the Interrogation Service Unit would be relocated.[242] The plan never reached a serious stage. Others, like Ivy, proposed to use the latest lie detectors in the interrogations after having been informed that many Germans were 'covering up'.[243] In the end it was decided that the interrogations would take place in the Palace of Justice where the interrogators could stay in the 'closest liaison' with all staff members.[244]

Interrogations with those defendants sentenced to death or life imprisonment in the IMT were particularly sensitive. Each interrogator had to adhere strictly to the following rules. All interrogations had to take place in 'complete secrecy'. So-called 'side-shows', that is interviews which were not in direct connection with the cases under consideration, were strictly prohibited. The number of personnel cognizant of such interrogations had to be kept to an absolute operational minimum. The person conducting the interview had to keep a detailed record of all the people, including guards and monitoring personnel, who had knowledge that such an interview had taken place. This list had to be forwarded to the director of the evidence division: 'It is obvious that the Allied Control Council must have such a list

Plate 14   Leo Alexander interrogating the Nuremberg defendant Wolfram Sievers, who was responsible for criminal human experiments on concentration camp inmates. Sievers was sentenced to death and hanged in 1948 at Landsberg prison. Nuremberg, Germany, 1946/7.

Plate 15   Karl Brandt, Hitler's doctor, being interrogated by the US prosecution. Nuremberg, Germany, 1946/7.

since all the prisoners present a constant suicide threat and in case such a suicide should happen everyone concerned will be investigated.'[245] Rapp made it clear that unless everyone complied with these rules, it would probably be impossible to interrogate any of the sentenced major war criminals once they had been transferred to the prison complex in Berlin-Spandau.

Alexander was careful not to mention particular defendants in his personal correspondence, except on a few occasions. As it turned out, the defendant Wilhelm Beiglböck, who was accused of having been a leading participant in the seawater experiments, had been a classmate of his at the medical school in Vienna in the 1920s. Both lost contact when Beiglböck was discovered to have cheated in one of the exams. Although trying to impress Alexander with his love for literature and art history, Beiglböck could hardly conceal his deeply-rooted cultural and racial arrogance. 'There is one thing I am quite sure of', he told Alexander, 'that the Germans have culturally achieved more than the Polynesians.'[246] For Beiglböck black people were either porters in hotels or jazz musicians. To his wife Alexander confided: 'He did not recognise me, but I vaguely remembered him. He always was a Nazi rough-neck, and I guess he still is.'[247]

During the interrogations Alexander tried to retain a certain detached attitude towards the defendants. As if examining one of his air force soldiers about flight fatigue, like he had done during the war, Alexander took the position of the psychiatrist who would listen to his patients. Unlike interrogators such as Kempner, whose bullish way of questioning defendants was widely known in military circles, Alexander adopted a more pragmatic and sensitive approach.[248] He tried to create a friendly, almost intimate atmosphere in which the defendants were more inclined to talk about their motives and role in the experiments. He wanted to study the biographical and socio-psychological context in which the crimes had been committed. To do so, he needed to establish trust between himself and the interrogatee.

On 26 November Alexander interviewed Hans Wolfgang Romberg, one of Rascher's collaborators in the Dachau high-altitude experiments.[249] What interested Alexander were the motives of men like Romberg, and in particular their ways of justifying their silent approval and active collaboration. As a specialist in group psychiatry he wanted to know 'how these men had come into a situation of order and obedience ... and why certain other people, like Strughold, had kept at a distance'.[250] Did the accused know that they were committing a crime, and how did they sanction their role? Alexander wanted to explore the strong tendency among the defendants to subordinate themselves to existing authorities, the relevance of medical education and peer pressure, different forms of opportunism, idealism and careerism. More broadly, he was interested in how ideological and political formations shaped the understanding of ethics and the code of conduct of the medical profession. How could one explain that most of the doctors did not value the life of the individual higher than their duty towards the state, the community, the party or the Führer? When Rascher proposed using some of the experimental subjects who had been placed under Romberg's supervision, the latter successfully protested: 'These are my experimental subjects and I am responsible for them and nothing should happen to them. And here I was able to assert myself against him', Romberg told Alexander.[251] But Romberg was only able to assert himself when they were 'his' experimental subjects. All other experimental subjects, whom Rascher intended to kill for his research, do not seem to have evoked any sense of moral or individual responsibility in Romberg.

On 3 December, shortly before the start of the trial, Alexander conducted the first interview with the thirty-four-year-old Ravensbrück doctor Fritz Fischer.[252] Their discussion on that morning centred around Fischer's ideals and values which had not only shaped his thinking during his youth, but had influenced, if not determined, his overall mind-set and actions during the war: 'In school we were trained to believe in Hegelian philosophy and saw in the state the primary reality. We came to regard our duty to serve and obey in war as a virtue and a noble vocation.'[253] Three weeks later, at Christmas, Fischer repeatedly tried to justify his participation in the medical experiments by stressing that he had acted under military emergency orders (*militärischer Befehlsnotstand*). His statements revealed a certain kind of subservience to higher authorities which is one of the conditions in which people may commit crimes whilst believing they are carrying out orders: 'When war broke out, I knew that the only way we could overcome this bad situation for Germany [was] if we would cultivate the following two virtues: obedience and the acceptance of the community as the highest priority. This is where the great inner conflict between individualists and collectivists begins.'[254] Fischer was convinced that he was wrongly accused. Shortly after his arrest he had told his wife: 'Dearest Magdalene ... I am currently in custody in order to be held accountable for actions which I carried out during the war on orders of higher authorities.'[255]

On 4 December, the day after talking to Fischer, Alexander questioned the thirty-five-year-old Herta Oberheuser, who had been placed in solitary confinement. She felt that the trial was 'very bitter' for her as a woman. She refused to say why it was bitter, except that she had believed that all her actions had not been so severe as to warrant inclusion in the trial. 'For everything I did in the concentration camp I can take responsibility with my conscience', she later told Alexander.[256] Her philosophy in life had been 'to help human beings', she said, but her answers in the interviews raised serious doubts about her truthfulness. Born in 1911 in Cologne, she had studied medicine in Bonn and Düsseldorf before she worked as an assistant at the dermatological clinic in Düsseldorf. By 1940 she transferred to the city's health ministry. Responding to a newspaper advertisement, she

Plate 16 Women prisoners in the witness wing of the Nuremberg gaol. Left to right: Herta Oberheuser, defendant in the Doctors' Trial; and Theresa Reinwald, Dachau, secretary to Walter Busch, Nazi party judge. Nuremberg, Germany, 1946/7.

applied to work as a camp doctor at Ravensbrück and advanced to one of the most influential and closest associates of Gebhardt's group of doctors who were engaged in criminal research on humans. Early British investigators described her medical treatment and post-operative care as 'little better than sadistic'.[257] She withheld morphine and took no apparent steps to see that the patients were suitably nursed. She also admitted giving lethal injections of morphine or petrol to patients she regarded as incurably ill. 'What do you mean with [sic] lethal injections?', she asked her interrogators incredulously: 'The most we did was to inject (*einspritzen*) people shortly before their death on the order of the camp physician.'[258] One of the victims recalled: 'Dr. Oberheuser was very brutal to patients. When patients came sick to see her, she would be sitting on the examination table, and when they came up, she would kick them in the stomach, and send them away.' Oberheuser admitted that she used to sit on her office table and examine in that way 300 to 400 prisoners each morning and that she kept patients at a distance by means of an outstretched leg, apparently to see their 'whole body'. When the examination was completed she would push the patient away with her foot.[259] The doctor–patient relationship had eroded to an extent where doctors engaged in acts of human degradation rather than in establishing any form of interactive relation.

Creating a sense of trust with the defendants was facilitated by the fact that most of them were physicians. In some cases Alexander managed to establish a relationship not unlike that between professional colleagues. On 26 November Alexander told Brandt, for example, that all interrogations were voluntary, that he could refuse to give evidence, and that information obtained in the interview could be used against him in the forthcoming trial. This was news to Brandt. Apparently no one had yet informed him about the basic right to refuse giving testimony. Brandt replied:

I don't know what role you are playing. Since I know that you are a doctor, I am myself interested [in what happened], also personally. It is quite obvious that on a professional basis one can talk about things differently, and understand each other as when this is not the case and explanations are difficult, simply because the basic knowledge is not the same and may lead to misunderstandings.[260]

However, the extent to which the defendants attempted to disguise their deeds in a flood of verbose explanations or to argue that they had only followed orders or had no knowledge, made a broader theoretical analysis necessary. The constant flow of stomach-churning details of medical atrocities fuelled Alexander's desire to make sense of the unimaginable extent of criminal activity. Individual life stories about constant humiliations and the permanent fear of death, of young women and men mutilated and sterilised by means of X-rays, of priests subjected to medical torture, all this needed to be explained. The Doctors' Trial was about to begin.

6
Constructing the Doctors' Trial

Thanatology

In the weeks preceding the opening of the trial detailed discussions about the nature of German medical science and the principles of permissible and non-permissible experiments on humans emerged as a result of concerted efforts among the US prosecution to construct a legally viable prosecution case, and ultimately secure the conviction of as many of the accused as possible. The prosecution case was far from complete or satisfactory when Alexander and other senior members arrived at Nuremberg. The pressure for those on the ground at Nuremberg was enormous. To establish a trial with a shortage of qualified lawyers and staff, together with improvised organisational structures and communication facilities in an occupied zone where the population was more or less hostile towards the undertaking, was one thing; to constantly defend the rationale for the trials in a shifting political climate was quite another. While relations with the Soviet Union were deteriorating, support for war crimes trials was rapidly disappearing in Washington after the completion of the IMT. These factors contributed to a sense of emergency and need for improvisation among the prosecution team. Taylor and his staff knew that they had to 'win' the medical case if they wanted to hold further war crimes trials. They also knew that they were creating a precedent for future trials. Although the IMT offered them some guidance as far as the rules of procedure was concerned, the US prosecution found itself on quite unfamiliar legal territory in November 1946. Any idea members of the prosecution could come up with to secure the conviction of the defendants was given serious consideration, and not necessarily tested as to its legal practicability. One of these ideas was Alexander's concept of Thanatology, the systematic development of scientific, inconspicuous and effective methods to carry out the murder of other people.

Two interrelated factors triggered the debate about the nature of German medical science and the ethics of human experimentation in late November and early December 1946. First, the prosecution wanted to approach the medical case, as well as all the subsequent cases, as variations in the overall scheme of Lemkin's principle of genocide, that is, the intention and execution of murdering another people. Following lengthy discussions in the legal committee of the United Nations Assembly in November, it had become apparent that the genocide concept expressed not only the 'specific criminal intent' with regard to large victim groups, but, like the concept of crimes against humanity, it called for 'greater condemnation because it implied mass criminality and very great losses to humanity and civilisation'.[1] In January 1947, Lemkin formally informed the War Department about the need to 'develop the genocide concept in the doctors' case'.[2] While conducting interviews with the victims of Nazi atrocities, he had realised that the Nazis had not been interested in killing particular individuals, but in the systematic murder of ethnic and religious groups. The Nazis 'did not know the names of the victims but handled them by numbers. They did not hate nor had any particular interest to kill Mr. X, Y, or Z, but their acts were motivated by the desire to eradicate the particular national or racial group to which Mr. X, Y, or Z happened to belong.'[3] Lemkin and other officials wanted to use the stigma of the genocide concept as a means of preventing the defendants claiming that their work had been scientific in nature, and therefore apparently not criminal.[4]

The second factor was that the prosecution was expecting the defence to use the *tu quoque* argument, that is, that Allied medical scientists had conducted similar experiments, and that there were no grounds for the indictment. The defence was expected to argue that either doctors of both nations were guilty of violating principles of professional medical ethics, or none of them. Both factors convinced Alexander of the need for an explanatory framework that stressed the differences between Allied and German medical science. To back up the charges of genocide in the realm of medical science, and pre-empt the expected counter-attack by the defence, the prosecution invented and applied the concept of Thanatology. At the same time, it was addressing issues that went beyond the immediate scope of the trial. These issues were concerned with permissible experiments on humans, and with wider questions as to what constituted ethical and non-ethical experiments. The debate about the ethics of human experimentation and about the concept of Thanatology were mutually interlinked. One stimulated the other and vice versa. The core arguments in both debates were formulated by Alexander on the same day, on 3 December 1946, after having completed the bulk of his interrogations.[5] 'This dual focus', as Katz has pointed out, 'led the prosecution and its expert witnesses, in what otherwise might have been a murder trial, to defend ethical research practices in the non-Nazi world in ways that tried to deny any past ethical transgressions.'[6]

To understand the origins of the ten principles on permissible experiments on human subjects in the Nuremberg Code, one needs to look at how the debate developed at the beginning and in the course of the trial. Alexander's diary notes and memoranda are key in reconstructing this discourse, especially six of his unpublished papers that were directly related to both issues.[7] The Code evolved from these early debates and in stages throughout the trial.[8] Although there are still many gaps in the record in reconstructing the precise stages in its development and understanding the forces which pushed the debate forward, we do have a good idea about how the origin of the Code did *not* develop. The Code did *not* suddenly appear in the final judgement.[9] The Code was neither written on a particular day, nor was it created by a particular commission, organisation or individual person. The idea that 'medicine was not involved' in the drafting of the Code, as David J. Rothman suggests, cannot be sustained.[10] On the contrary, a number of medical experts and medical organisations, including Alexander and Ivy, influenced the conceptual outline and textual formation of the Code. Elements of the Code were at first shaped within the relatively confined realm of the prosecution. Future guidelines on human experimentation were also debated in expert circles like the ISC (WC) in Paris.[11]

Once the trial started, however, the debate on medical ethics and human experimentation became a public debate, with journalists, lawyers and medical representatives taking an active interest in expressing their particular views on the subject. Although the tribunal had underestimated the importance of medical expertise in the trial, the judges quickly realised the centrality of research ethics. Throughout more than 130 trial days the judges frequently interrupted the witnesses or the prosecution to clarify specific points relating to medical ethics. The discussions among the prosecution staff as well as those in open court are crucial in understanding the progress and character of the debate on human experimentation.

The suggestion that the Code evolved in stages throughout the trial proceedings is further corroborated if we look at the general Anglo-American court procedures applied in the Doctors' Trial.[12] As opposed to the German legal system, where judges studied all of the evidence for a particular case prior to the beginning of the proceedings, judges in the Anglo-Saxon legal system enter the trial proceedings with an open mind. Unlike their German colleagues, the judges will generally not have formed an opinion about the degree of culpability of the defendant. All this is to ensure the highest degree of impartiality towards the case in front of them. It is only during the actual trial that the judges begin to form their opinion about the issues at hand. Their opinion is being shaped by listening to what the witnesses say and by studying the trial transcript, by examining some of the witnesses themselves, and on the basis of the evidence introduced by both the prosecution and the defence. All this can sway the opinion of the judges, and it is only towards the end of the trial that they start to formulate the judgement.

The process in which the debate about permissible experiments on humans developed was multi-dimensional, with many twists and turns, and shaped by unforeseen incidents. Discussions on medical ethics could be triggered or revived by a testimony of one of the medical experts. A letter from an outside medical organisation, requesting information on future medical ethics standards, could intensify reflections to draw up a more elaborate system of ethics principles. A strong and convincing presentation by one of the defendants could initiate plans to bring in an expert rebuttal witness to counter the claims made by the defendant. All these 'events' shaped the debate behind the scenes and in open court. In other words, a perceptive lay observer of the Nuremberg proceedings would have been able, and without great difficulty, to formulate all, or most of the principles which experts regarded as mandatory for permissible experiments on humans. The language of the principles might not have conformed to the actual Code, but the gist and content of the principles would have been there. In short, by the end of the trial, the ten principles of the Code were extant as an integral part of the courtroom discourse. What remained for the judges to do was to write them down to give them the force of law, as they do when they weigh the evidence for and against the accused in their attempt to formulate the judgement.

Alexander first mentioned the concept of Thanatology in a memo to Taylor from 30 November 1946. The subtitle was 'Thanatology as a Scientific Technique of Genocide'.[13] On 5 December he submitted another memo to Taylor, entitled 'Suggestions for a Discussion of the Thanatology Genocide Angle'.[14] The Thanatology concept was applied specifically to the Doctors' Trial in order to explain medical atrocities and the techniques of genocide. Alexander had coined the term from the Greek word *thanatos*, meaning death. At the end of December Alexander redrafted his original memo from November.[15] The experiments showed that the doctors had not only developed a means of producing death, but an actual 'science of killing' for which Alexander coined the term Ktenology. He substituted the term 'Ktenology' for 'Thanatology' in his memo which was now subtitled 'Ktenology as a Scientific Technique of Genocide'.[16] However, he seems to have used both terms interchangeably. It appears that Alexander wanted to create a similar theoretical model that would complement Lemkin's widely-known concept, and boost his reputation as a theorist. There may even have been a degree of professional jealousy or competitiveness involved on Alexander's part. Both Lemkin and Alexander apparently knew one another after having worked together at Duke University in Durham, North Carolina, during the war. Unlike the concept of genocide, the story of the concepts of Thanatology and of Ktenology is one of failure. Their recognition or application by lawyers of international law and human rights experts is non-existent today, yet both concepts played a significant role within the parameters of the Doctors' Trial.

Under the statutes of the London Charter the *tu quoque* argument was inadmissible, but it had nevertheless played a major part in the IMT. The prosecution was expecting that the thrust of the defence team in the Doctors' Trial would be similar. They would argue, it was believed, that the same kind of human experiments had been carried out in America and in other countries, and on prisoners or asylum populations. For the prosecution it was, therefore, essential to show the differences in the nature of the experiments to the tribunal, from a legal, but even more so from a medical ethics perspective. They had to prove that according to German laws and regulations the experiments constituted a criminal offence as well as a serious breach of professional conduct. Arriving in Nuremberg, Alexander was promptly given an assignment to explore and point out the different characters of Allied and German medical science.[17] On 13 November Kempner had told him what could be expected from the defence:

Two main defence points ... expected: (1) experiments also in US and other countries. [Stress] Differences. (2) Under German medical, esp.[ecially] military law, they were allowed to do so. It should be made clear that according to German law it was a crime. Ask McHaney to send a cable to Kempner for the German law. Send a cable to this office. Sight should not be lost of that it is part of the general framework of genocidal activity.[18]

The conversation with Kempner seems to have prompted Alexander into action. On 13 November, he wrote to Clifton T. Perkins, Commissioner for Mental Health in the Commonwealth of Massachusetts. He told Perkins that the war crimes authorities felt that it would be important in the forthcoming trial 'to have evidence regarding the nature and procedural characteristics of the experimentation on human beings such as practised in institutions in this country including the State Institutions of the Commonwealth of Massachusetts in order to effectively contrast ethical with non-ethical experimentation on human beings'.[19] In particular, Alexander wanted to know what the 'conditions for approval of these experiments by the Research Council' were and how the voluntary character of the experiments was ensured. Alexander also approached officials at the Rockefeller Institute of Medical Research and a number of researchers at US universities and hospitals, asking them to send him an official statement which detailed

the general rules which govern such experimentation [on humans], any procedure for approval of particular experiments by a board of research scientists or officials of the hospital and the requirements laid down as to the need for consent of next of kin or guardian as well as for the consent and cooperation of the part of the patient.[20]

Thanatology was Alexander's answer to his assignment, a concept born out of practical necessity to counter the German defence and link the incriminating evidence in the medical case with the principle of genocide. On 21 November, three days after his arrival in Nuremberg, after a conversation with Taylor, Alexander mentioned the term Thanatology for the first time in his diary.[21] Throughout the following weeks he frequently referred to Thanatology in his reflections about the conduct of German scientists.[22] On 27 November he told his wife:

I have delved into that mass of material, and have finally grasped its meaning and have come out with an appraisal that makes sense. It is Thanatology pure and simple, and it is the technique of genocide. Thanatology is a word I have coined: *thanatos*, in Greek, means death. Genocide is the 'murder of peoples', a word coined by my old friend Lemkin. I shall send you the carbon of an appraisal of the whole problem which I have been writing for General Taylor, the chief prosecutor; and which I may publish independently, if the War Department approves.[23]

The origin of the concept of Thanatology thus stands in close connection with the preparation of the medical case by the American prosecution. Nazi medical experiments, some defendants argued, had been carried out to benefit the members of the German armed forces, to search for the most effective treatment of illnesses and offer solutions for aeronautical and naval combat and rescue problems. In its drive for *Lebensraum*, the German military had applied all means to achieve victory, irrespective of the countless loss of human lives. It was only when Alexander realised a marked discrepancy between the purpose of the experiments and their outcome that he approached the problem from a different angle. If one looked at the experiments from the perspective of 'usefulness', he argued, in contributing new knowledge to a certain scientific problem, the result was almost always negative: 'One cannot help feeling that the experiments were amateurish and poorly coordinated, that they failed to give the scientific information which was claimed to be desired, and that a unified policy was completely absent, except for the barbaric manner of their execution.'[24]

For Alexander the study of Himmler's 'field of science' warranted the conclusion that the main thrust of the research was aimed at finding methods to exterminate large populations by the 'most scientific' and 'least conspicuous' means. Experiments by the Ravensbrück physicians, like Fritz Fischer and Karl Gebhardt, exemplified the 'callous disregard' for the lives of the victims. It was this context, Alexander believed, which was so markedly different from the experimental environment of the Allies. Nazi doctors developed a new field in which the main objective was not to search for methods of healing, but for methods of producing death. Only in one case, namely in the study of hypothermia, had the Germans discovered useful but non-original information. Yet even here 'the only accurate statistical observation' concerned the length of time that was needed to kill humans by exposure to cold. On 3 December, six days before the start of the trial, Alexander recorded in his diary under the heading 'Further plans':

Many of these so-called experiments are frankly and openly devoted to methods of destroying or preventing life, namely to 'euthanasia' and extermination methods, and to methods of sterilisation. But the preoccupation with methods of producing death runs also through many of the other investigations like a red thread, irrespective of the ostensible other purpose of the experiment. The frightful body of new methods of killing – the new lethal injections, the new gases, the poison bullets, constitute a formidable body of new and dangerous knowledge, useful to criminals everywhere, and to a criminal state if another one is permitted to establish itself again, so as to constitute a new branch, a destructive perversion of medicine worthy of a new name, for which thanatology had been suggested by our medical consultant. This thanatological knowledge supplied the technological methods for genocide, a policy of the German Third Reich, which could not have been carried out without the active participation of its medical scientists. [25]

Taylor was the first to make use of Thanatology. On 30 November Alexander told him that the indictment offered no discussion about the motives that inspired the accused in ordering, abetting or performing the experiments. In case Taylor wanted to include 'such a discussion in the opening remarks of the prosecution', he might find the concept of Thanatology useful.[26] After having studied the experiments and Ivy's report on 'War Crimes of a Medical Nature',[27] Alexander came to the conclusion that there was 'another hidden meaning and research aim' which hinted at a common denominator and long-term policy, the search for scientific means of genocide:

In the light of all these facts, it becomes obvious that the difference between the German human experimentation and ours is not only the voluntary character and the safety which was always maintained in our experiments, and which Dr. Ivy stressed in his report, but far more fundamentally the main object of the entire research. This German research was not research for methods of healing, but for methods, mechanics and time factors of producing death by various non-obvious and non-conspicuous means.[28]

This was what Taylor needed. It allowed him to make a clearer division between German and Allied medical science. Unlike Jackson, the prosecutor in the IMT, Taylor did not write his opening speech by himself, but had the help of support staff, including Alexander. The workload during these hectic days was enormous. In little more than two weeks Alexander had produced a complete analysis of all the experiments and had studied the motives, techniques and personalities of twenty-three defendants. All this he had tried to put into 'clear and lucid writing' and submitted it, as it came off the typewriter, to General Taylor 'for inclusion into his opening speech'.[29] Shortly before the trial opened, Alexander was consulted over the actual drafting of the speech. On 5 December he submitted suggestions for a discussion about the 'thanatology genocide angle' to Taylor.[30] Two days later he 'corrected [the] General's opening address'.[31] One day before the trial opened, Alexander noted: 'Worked with General on opening address. He tied in a good deal of my material.'[32] Proudly he told his wife: 'He has used it well.'[33] Alexander was never credited for his contribution to the opening address which became renowned for its powerful rhetoric and use of evidence.

But there were obvious problems with the approach adopted by the prosecution. The main legal problem with the concept of genocide was that it focused on the murder of *another* people, especially on the murder of European Jewry. Hence the concept of genocide not only excluded the persecution of gypsies and other groups deemed 'asocial' but marginalised the issue of 'euthanasia', where a state had implemented a programme to systematically kill one section of its *own* people.[34] Kempner's view was that the 'euthanasia' programme was 'merely a training centre for killer personnel' of the Holocaust.[35] The role of sterilisation was neglected because it did not fall within the jurisdiction of the tribunal. Although there was much to be said about linking the various crimes and showing that the doctors had acted according to a common design,[36] the specific character, differences and stages of criminal medical conduct were likely to be glossed over. The judicial framework and the line of argument of the American prosecution explains why the War Department asked Alexander to 'play down euthanasia' in his assessment of Nazi medical crimes.[37] To stress the murder of German handicapped adults and children did not bolster the case of the prosecution, unless one could show that non-German nationals had been killed in the programme. Overall, the approach by the prosecution prevented, rather than facilitated, a full investigation of the first systematic mass murder of the Nazi regime during the Doctors' Trial.[38]

Thanatology was defined as being what Allied science was not, but like the principle of genocide, the concept of Thanatology had substantial shortcomings; it was likely to gloss over the specific character and stages of criminal medical conduct in Germany. The concept overlooked processes of cumulative radicalisation, and massive changes in administration and centralisation of resources, or the relation between modern medicine and the industry of war. Thanatology was an overarching principle that left little room for issues of individual responsibility and moral dilemmas. The dichotomy between 'human' Allied science and 'inhuman' German science may have been helpful for the prosecution in bolstering their case against the German doctors. It also may have illuminated the specific character of certain kinds of Nazi science, but as a theory to explain the complicity of medical science as well as the complexity of Fascist science, at best the analytical potential of Thanatology is limited.

Yet, at the same time, the concept of Thanatology reached beyond the immediate objective of the trial by defining ethical and non-ethical experimentation more clearly. The indictment provided an accurate account of the murders and atrocities committed in the course of the experiments, a graphic image of medical cruelty. Its aim was to establish the links between allegations and crimes, words and deeds. However, the indictment did not offer a discussion about the motives of the accused and the reasons which inspired them.[39] The trial raised profound questions as to how and why physicians were able to commit medical crimes: how men and women sworn to the Hippocratic tradition, trained as professionals in one of the world's most advanced scientific cultures, could commit such crimes, and whether they actually understood that they were committing a crime. What did knowing and not knowing mean in this context, individual responsibility and responsibility as a group or as a profession? Most of these questions were outside the scope of the trial. Thanatology offered one of the first, albeit simplistic attempts to address these issues.

Alexander saw the aim of the Doctors' Trial to stop any further development of 'Thanatological knowledge'. He wanted to introduce safety mechanisms and professional codes of practice which would make the reappearance of this form of 'science of killing' impossible forever. From the beginning the issue of informed voluntary consent was uppermost in Alexander's mind. On 23 November 1946, only days after his arrival at Nuremberg, Alexander advised the prosecution on how to counter the defence that only prisoners condemned to death had been used in the experiments. According to Alexander the evidence showed that the victims had been

> picked at random, that none of them was asked whether he was willing, that none of them signed any written agreement and that in a number of instances, especially in the case of the Polish girls at Ravensbrück, physical force had to be used to make them submit. That should explode the German claim that these experiments were voluntary, quite apart from the fact that a concentration camp was certainly no setting for anything voluntary ... It was not 'death penalty' or 'medical experimentation', it was death penalty plus cruel and unusual punishment in the form of 'medical' experimentation.[40]

On 3 December Alexander drafted a plan for a memorandum on 'Ethical and Non-Ethical Experimentation in Human Beings'.[41] The main question concerned the extent to which German experiments had been 'non-crucial experiments', inadequately prepared, therefore inaccurate, misleading and unnecessary. His examples were high-altitude and seawater experiments.[42] Alexander worked on the memorandum again three days later. On 6 December he recorded in his diary: 'Worked on "ethical and non-ethical experimentation on human beings" ... Dictated paper in the evening.'[43] On 7 December 1946, two days before the start of the trial, Alexander completed the first of two key texts on the ethics of human experimentation, which he addressed to Taylor. The second memorandum was completed in April 1947. Both memoranda contributed to the debate about human experimentation inside the prosecution team, and ultimately shaped parts of the Nuremberg Code.[44]

Alexander set out by outlining four crucial stages in scientific investigation in medicine. The first stage was what he called the 'thorough theoretical thinking-through of the problem'. All theoretical, experimental and practical knowledge first needed to be related to a given scientific problem. Many problems could be solved in this stage. The seawater experiments, for example, had been unnecessary and could have been easily solved by a trained investigator in a couple of hours.[45] The second stage, if existing knowledge proved insufficient, was a 'new investigation with the aid of simple physico-chemical systems'.[46] Often this stage proved more important and conclusive about the problem in hand than experimentation with the far more complex living organism. The third stage was concerned with experimentation on living animals, the so-called 'scouting' experiment, in which various approaches to the problem were tested. The fourth and final stage, after all theoretical and practical avenues had been explored, 'can sometimes be achieved by the crucial experiment', that is, an experiment on humans. This must be an experiment conceived so that its results are bound to be conclusive. According to Alexander there were cases where it was necessary to 'perform crucial experiments in human beings in order to settle certain problems as they apply to human beings, once and for all'.[47]

A valid example for a crucial experiment was Max von Pettenkofer's self-experiment which had furthered the understanding about the epidemiology of cholera. Pettenkofer knew about the history of the problem, that is, that cases of cholera increased in times of famine, and decreased or were insignificant during periods when there was sufficient nutrition in society. He also knew the nature and habit of the cholera bacillus (Stage 1), that it was unable to exist in an acid medium (Stage 2), and that he himself had sufficient secretion of gastric juices (Stage 3) in which the bacillus could not live. Pettenkofer was thus in a position to conduct an experiment on himself which was conclusive without endangering himself, the research subject.[48] Pettenkofer's successful self-experiment was well chosen. It allowed Alexander to choose not to question the professional authority of doctors to perform experiments on humans in general. Alexander believed that experiments on human beings were permissible if certain 'requirements' were fulfilled in three different 'spheres'. First, moral-legal requirements; second, medical-ethical (Hippocratic) requirements; and third, scientific requirements.[49] The conditions for these three requirements included some of the later principles of the Nuremberg Code.

In the sphere of 'moral-legal requirements' the following conditions needed to be fulfilled. The experimental subject had to be willing to undergo the experiment of his or her own free will, giving voluntary consent to the experiment. Legally valid consent could only be given if the person could properly understand the exact nature and consequences of the experiment, meaning the person was to be fully informed and in full possession of his/her mental faculties.[50] Examples that Allied medical scientists had adhered to these conditions were, for example, the soldiers and civilians who had participated in yellow fever experiments, the inmates of the Mississippi penitentiary taking part in pellagra experiments or the 'educated, high-minded and religious conscientious objectors' who volunteered for famine experiments during the war. Physicians and medical students were seen as the 'most competent' to give legal permission for experiments, because they would readily understand the technical problems and the risks involved. The decision by the German Reich Health Council in 1930–1 about informed consent, endorsed by Germany's legal theorists such as Ludwig Ebermayer, was seen as sound: 'Unless proof can be established that the person giving permission for an experiment had sufficient medical knowledge or was given sufficiently lengthy and complete explanations regarding the nature and consequences of the experiment, no permission could be held legally valid.'[51]

By drawing attention to the specific German regulation from 1930–1, the prosecution could point out that there existed sound written research standards prior to the Nazi takeover of power. Some ethical rules of a general nature had also been issued during the Third Reich, most notably in the 'Professional Order for the German Physician' from November 1937.[52] Significantly, the order stated that the duty of the German doctor towards the German people *did not exclude* his duty towards the individual.[53] The prosecution could then argue that German doctors had violated their own national laws and regulations of which they could scarcely claim to have been ignorant. If they had not known these regulations, the question would arise as to why they were not aware of these issues. If they had known them they would have to admit that they were guilty of professional misconduct. Alexander's moral-legal requirements were meant to hammer home some of the main charges against the Nazi physicians, namely that none of the experimental subjects in the concentration camps had consented to the experiments, that the experiments were far from voluntary, and that the persons undergoing the experiments were in no way informed about the potential risks involved in the research.

In the area of 'medical-ethical (Hippocratic) requirements', Alexander stressed the importance of the Hippocratic tradition in the doctor–patient relationship, irrespective of whether the physician examines the patient, treats the patient, or performs an experiment with his permission. The doctor should only do what is for the benefit of the sick, abstain from every voluntary act which he knows is harmful or do anything for ulterior motives. The Hippocratic Oath prohibited the giving of deadly medicine or poison to anyone, even when asked, or to suggest to others to give it. In other words, the Hippocratic tradition prohibits an experiment on humans 'if the foregone conclusion, probability or an *a priori* reason to believe exists that death or disabling injury of the experimental subject will occur'.[54] The 'spirit of the oath' also required, Alexander argued, that adequate preparations are made to aid the person against any remote chance of injury, disability or death. Finally, he drew attention to the risk–benefit relation, that is that the risk taken in the experiment should never exceed the 'humanitarian importance' of the scientific problem at hand.

Alexander's final area addressed 'scientific requirements'. Experiments on humans had to be based upon the results of the various stages of scientific enquiry previously outlined. The anticipated results had to justify the performance of the experiments: for example, it must yield 'decisive results for the good of society and should not be random and unnecessary in nature'.[55] The German doctors, it could be argued, had disregarded all moral-legal, medical-ethical, as well as scientific requirements. They were not only guilty of criminal offences, but guilty of professional misconduct and of violating the rights and dignity of human beings.

Alexander's concept of Thanatology and his first memorandum on human experimentation show that, two days before the trial started, the prosecution had not only developed a theoretical model to address medical crimes under the umbrella of the genocide concept, but had also laid down a number of 'conditions' which had to be met so that research on humans, if absolutely necessary, could be regarded as permissible. Most of the material had been haphazardly prepared and Alexander's theory was not fully thought through. The aim was to distinguish Allied from German medical science. This became the central issue as the trial progressed, but it also blurred the essential nature of the case, namely that the defendants were on trial for murder. By drawing attention to the destructive energy of German medicine, the prosecution hoped to counter any attempts of *tu quoque* in the trial; and by establishing certain standards of professional conduct in experimental research on humans, preferably based on existing German regulations, they wanted to show that Nazi physicians had not only committed a criminal offence, but had also violated the profession's own code of ethical conduct. Whether both concepts would actually stand up in trial, and whether the dual strategy of the prosecution would work, was far from certain when on Monday, 9 December 1946, Military Tribunal 1 convened its first session.

The opening of the trial

People remember that it was one of the coldest winters the country had witnessed for years. They found the entrance to the heated Nuremberg court house blocked by military police. Every visitor, however well connected, was meticulously checked for the relevant pass before entrance was granted. The procedure set down on the first morning remained the same throughout the next 139 trial sessions. The defendants were the first to enter the courtroom, always ten minutes before the opening of each session. At the back of the dock was a panel on one side with a wall-slide that allowed three to four people to enter at a time. Then they would squeeze their way through to their allocated wooden seats. The accused were brought up in small groups in a lift that was linked to the prison complex. All of the defendants had been sent to the barber and were properly dressed to ensure that they would not 'inspire pity'. Next came the prosecution and defence staff edging their way to the tables. Taylor and his staff had been allocated one of the tables in front of the public gallery. Old film footage from the National Archives in Washington DC still shows Alexander and the American legal staff sitting attentively at a long, wooden desk while Taylor delivers his opening speech to the international public. Finally the judges, led by Walter Beals, entered the courtroom. Once all were seated, at 10 a.m., the marshal of the court declared: 'Military Tribunal No. 1 is now in session. God save the United States of America and this honourable Tribunal. There will be order in the court.'[56]

The trial began with the presentation of evidence to sustain the charges contained in the indictment. For the entire first day Taylor delivered the opening statement before handing over to James M. McHaney, the chief prosecutor for Case 1.[57] Taylor started by outlining the responsibility of the trial. The defendants were charged with murder, torture and multiple atrocities in the name of medical science. Their victims numbered hundreds of thousands and only a few were still alive. The representatives of the United States, judges and prosecutors alike, had grave and unusual responsibilities towards the victims, to the parents and children of the victims, the 'nameless dead', the '200 Jews in good physical condition, 50 Gypsies, 500 tubercular Poles, or 1,000 Russians' who numbered among the anonymous millions of Nazi mass murder. Among the victims were countless Germans and nationals of countries overrun by Germany, prisoners of war, and Jews of many nationalities. Taylor made it plain that the 'mere punishment of the defendants, or even of thousands of other equally guilty, can never redress the terrible injuries which the Nazis

Plate 17 The judges of Military Tribunal No. 1. These four prominent American judges, appointed by President Truman, are shown listening to testimony of the trial against the twenty-three defendants. Left to right: Harold L. Sebring, justice of the Supreme Court of Florida; Walter B. Beals (presiding judge), justice of the Supreme Court of the state of Washington; Johnson T. Crawford, former justice of the Oklahoma District Court in Adam, Oklahoma; and Victor C. Swearingen, alternate member, former assistant attorney general of Michigan, from Detroit. Nuremberg, Germany, 1946/7.

visited on these unfortunate peoples'. One of the central aims of the trial was to establish these events by clear and public proof 'so that no-one can ever doubt that they were fact and not fable; and that this court, as the agent of the United States and as the voice of humanity, stamps these acts, and the ideas which engendered them, as barbarous and criminal'.[58] The prosecution had further responsibilities, Taylor stated:

> We cannot rest content when we have shown that crimes were committed and that certain persons committed them. To kill, to maim, and to torture is criminal under all modern systems of law. These defendants did not kill in hot blood, nor for personal enrichment. Some of them may be sadists who killed and tortured for sport, but they are not all perverts. They are not ignorant men. Most of them are trained physicians and some of them are distinguished scientists. Yet these defendants, all of whom were fully able to comprehend the nature of their acts, and most of whom were exceptionally qualified to form a moral judgement in this respect, are responsible for wholesale murder and unspeakable cruel torture.[59]

The accused were charged with murder, Taylor said, but this was no mere murder trial. 'It is our deep obligation to all people of the world to show why and how these things happened. It is incumbent upon us to set forth with conspicuous clarity the ideas and motives which moved these defendants to treat their fellow men as less than beasts.'[60] He was convinced that the trial also offered an opportunity for the German people to see and understand the causes for their current misery, the destruction of their cities and industry. The 'bold and lucid consummation' of these proceedings would also be of great importance for other nations to understand the 'sinister doctrines' of Nazism. It was the ideology of Nazism which 'sealed the fate of Germany, shattered Europe, and left the world in ferment'. The actual policy of mass extermination, Taylor argued, 'could not have been so effectively carried out without the active participation of German medical scientists'.[61] He also pointed out that only one of the defendants was directly responsible to Adolf Hitler himself, namely Karl Brandt.[62] He was the supreme medical authority in the Reich. None of the other accused had enjoyed such a direct and privileged relation to the centre of power.

Taylor then addressed each of the experiments in turn, the high-altitude, freezing and seawater experiments, the malaria and mustard gas experiments, the sulphonamide drug experiments, the epidemic jaundice experiments, the sterilisation, typhus and poison gas experiments, the incendiary bomb experiments, the Jewish skeleton collection at the University of Strasbourg and, finally, the 'euthanasia' programme.[63] It was a long list of unspeakable human degradation and stomach-churning horror. All of the defendants had shown 'an unprincipled willingness to abuse their power over the poor, unfortunate, defenceless creatures'. The experimental subjects had been deprived of their rights and dignity by a ruthless regime. All of the accused had violated the Hippocratic tradition, including the fundamental principle never to cause harm – *primum non nocere*.[64] One of them, Kurt Blome, had actually boasted in his autobiography *Embattled Doctor* that he had chosen a medical career in order to become a 'master over life and death'.[65]

Finally Taylor turned to the question of medical ethics as one of the most fundamental issues of the trial. Regardless of what they may have agreed to or signed at the time, none of the victims had been volunteers. Most of the victims had not been condemned to death, and those who had were not criminals, 'unless it be a crime to be a Jew, or a Pole, or a Gypsy, or a Russian prisoner of war'.[66] But most importantly, there had been no voluntary and informed consent prior to the experiments:

> Whatever book or treatise on medical ethics we may examine, and whatever expert on forensic medicine we may question, will say that it is a fundamental and inescapable obligation of every physician under any known system of law not to perform a dangerous experiment without the subject's consent.[67]

All of the accused had departed from 'every known standard of medical ethics'. For the prosecution the case against the doctors was 'one of the simplest and clearest', but it was also one of the most important because it epitomised Nazi thinking and Nazi way of life, the noxious merger of the German militarised state with Nazi racial policies.[68] Germany's leaders had failed to stand firm against the destructive forces of Hitler's party and their failure was the outcome of 'that sinister undercurrent of German philosophy that preaches the supreme importance of the state and the complete subordination of the individual'. In his concluding remarks, Taylor noted that a nation in which the individual means nothing will find few leaders courageous and able enough to serve its best interests.[69]

The use of Alexander's material for the overall thrust of the prosecution becomes apparent by comparing his notes with the text of Taylor's opening speech. Taylor adopted almost the exact line of Alexander's argument in those parts of the speech which dealt with the overall character of German medical science. The section was entitled 'Crimes Committed in the Guise of Scientific Research'.[70] He started by looking at the experiments as a whole. Most of the experiments appeared to be in relation to aeronautical and naval combat and rescue problems of the German armed forces. He drew attention to medical research concerned with treating diseases such as malaria, epidemic jaundice and typhus, or experiments related to finding treatments for war wounds caused by air raids and combat missions: 'To some degree, the therapeutic pattern outlined above is undoubtedly a valid one, and explains why the *Wehrmacht*, and especially the German Air Force, participated in these experiments.'[71]

Taylor then changed tack and told his audience that the prosecution would show that 'a quite different and even more sinister objective runs like a red thread through these hideous researches'.[72] The prosecution wanted to show that in some cases the true aim of the experiments was not to develop methods to rescue or to cure, 'but how to destroy and kill'. He specifically drew attention to the sterilisation experiments and to the use of poisoned bullets at Buchenwald concentration camp. For the prosecution it was proof that the experimenters 'really wanted to know how quickly the poison would kill'.[73] His concluding paragraph in this part of the speech addressed the concept of Thanatology:

> Mankind had not theretofore felt the need of a word to denominate the science of how to kill prisoners most rapidly and subjugate people in large numbers. This case and these defendants have created this grue-some question for the lexicographer. For the moment we will christen this macabre science thanatology, the science of producing death. The thanatological knowledge, derived in part from these experiments, supplied the techniques for genocide, a policy of the Third Reich, exemplified in the 'euthanasia' program and in the widespread slaughter of Jews, Gypsies, Poles, and Russians. This policy of mass extermination could not have been so effectively carried out without the active participation of German medical scientists.[74]

Taylor's condemnation of the Nazi regime and its corrupted moral value system was widely acknowledged by American, German and French news-papers as an impressive example of legal rhetoric, in which judicial and moral argument had been skilfully woven together with graphic detail.[75] The *Philadelphia Record*, for example, noted that the prosecution had out-lined its case 'in sharp, bitter tones' and asserted that Nazi Germany had 'died of its own poison'.[76] Some observers also commended the thorough-ness of the proceedings and the dispassionate way in which the prosecu-tion was handling the material. Others made a mockery of the defendants' line of defence. On 11 December the French papers *L'Ordre* and *L'Époque* reported that Brandt had objected through his attorney Robert Servatius that he was never Hitler's personal physician. 'You will prove in a short time', retorted the prosecutor to Servatius, 'that he was only his driver.'[77]

The response by the world's media to the daily revelations in the trial was one of shock. George C. Putnam from the UNWCC described the opening of the trial as 'showdown time' for the men of medicine who had ruled under Hitler's name: 'Tales of deliberately wanton killings, of so-called "mercy killings" by torture – they're all on the record tonight.'[78] An American physician expressed his anger over the lack of compassion and moral stature of the German doctors in a letter to the editors of the *New York Times*: 'Not a single word of protest or of indignation was heard from the so-called outstanding men at the head of the German universities nor from the German Medical Association. Nothing of that sort is heard even today. They probably have the nerve to claim they did not know anything about it.'[79] For David Willis from the UNWCC the demand to condemn the men as murderers was an 'eminently reasonable proposal'.[80] On 12 December the *New York Times* informed readers about a fifty-page report on cold-water experiments which was introduced as evidence by the prosecution as being 'the most startling and succinct report on murder in the history of criminology'.[81]

Many people were rather disconcerted when they first saw the defendants. The majority wore civilian clothes and those in uniforms had their decorations or insignia of rank taken off. Countess Alice von Platen, one of the German trial observers, perceived 'with horror the ordinary faces'.[82] She found it difficult to come to terms with the fact that 'no external features distinguished these twenty-three people from us ... The whole event would be easier to understand, if these were notorious sadists or psychopaths, but on the contrary they are men who for years filled the most responsible positions.'[83] The only woman on trial, Herta Oberheuser, attracted particular attention.[84] For many observers it was difficult to grasp that 'a woman' could have been involved in such heinous and brutal acts. Other spectators were plainly outraged that not a single one of the accused had pleaded guilty to the charges, something many felt was nothing but 'shameless and incredible arrogance'.[85] These accounts shaped the public image of the otherwise insignificant-looking men and the one woman in the dock.

The Ravensbrück witnesses

On the opening day of the trial Alexander was photographed together with Keith Mant, the British war crimes investigator, Françoise Bayle, the French navy psychologist and Alexander Hardy, a member of the prosecution team.[86] On 9 December he also gave an interview to the *New York Post*.[87] The trial was 'still going hectic', he told his wife. One of the greatest challenges for the prosecution staff was to find the right witnesses and documentary evidence to sustain the charges which Taylor had laid out so eloquently. The staff knew that the case of the prosecution would need to be constructed whilst the trial was up and running. The case of the prosecution was far from complete or secure when the trial started. Witnesses with second-hand knowledge were of little use to the prosecution because the defence would discredit the evidence during cross-examination, even if the witness knew exactly what had been going on in the camp. Any evidence based on hearsay or passed on by the people who had experienced the horrors was unlikely to stand up in court. Sometimes former camp inmates would invent events they had apparently

Plate 18 Herta Oberheuser, physician at the Ravensbrück concentration camp and assistant physician to the defendant Karl Gebhardt at the SS hospital Hohenlychen. Nuremberg, Germany, 1946/7.

Plate 19 War crimes investigators. From left to right: Leo Alexander, medical expert for the US prosecution; Alexander Hardy, assistant prosecutor in the Office of Chief of Counsel for War Crimes; Keith Mant, Royal Army Medical Corps (British Intelligence) and permanent delegate for the British commission; and Françoise Bayle, Médecin principal de la Marine and permanent delegate for the French commission. Nuremberg, Germany.

witnessed, believing that this would help the prosecution. On 10 December, for example, Alexander noted in his diary after having met the Dachau prison doctor Franz Blaha: 'A disappointment. An obvious faker.'[88] Alexander believed that it would all be over by February 'unless the defence springs a surprise'.[89] His estimates about the duration of historic events had never been particularly accurate. Behind the scenes the prosecution now shifted into a mode of frenzied activity. The aim was to keep ahead of the material before it was introduced as evidence in the trial. As in the spring of 1945, Alexander was obsessed with evidence and the running of the trial, especially with overcoming administrative obstacles to gain access to trial transcripts. He wanted to make sure that everything possible would be done to hold the German medical profession to account. A letter from 18 December to his wife gives poignant insight into the atmosphere during these hectic days:

> The pace of work is terrific. Sunday night [15.12.1946] four girls whose legs had been operated on and badly disfigured by experiments came from Warsaw. I had to examine them, take their histories, bring out the important points for interrogation, prepare complete experts statements regarding the examinations, all in three days. In addition to everything, three spoke only Polish, one spoke broken English and I had to work through a Polish interpreter who got them all involved in the lengthiest discussions. The work is finally completed today, Wednesday night, 6:00 PM and I have 31 pages of long, legal type completed. What a job! But it has got to be done and it has got be done right. The emergency of the situation and probably my obsessiveness just keeps driving me on, but my temper is getting short, so I noticed.[90]

The four women whom Alexander examined were Maria Broel-Plater, Władyslawa Karołewska, Jadwiga Dzido and Maria Kuśmierczuk. Their story resembled that of seventy-four women, who had been subjected to involuntary sulphonamide drug and bone transplantation experiments at the Ravensbrück concentration camp, except, perhaps, that theirs was one of the least repulsive.[91] The youngest of the women, who called themselves 'rabbits' (*Kanninchen*), was the sixteen-year-old Barbara Pietrzyk who managed to survive Ravensbrück but died of the after-effects in 1948. The oldest woman was Apolonia Rakowska, who was forty-five years old when she was executed by SS guards.[92] The scars that the experiments left on the survivors became a world-wide symbol for the appalling and inhuman character of Nazi experimental research on humans, one which the Polish authorities later comprehensively documented.[93] The life histories of the women made a deep impact on Alexander, so much so that he felt compelled to organise medical treatment for some of them in the United States at the end of the 1950s.[94]

181

Plate 20 Victims of Ravensbrück medical experiments arriving at Nuremberg. From left to right: French navy specialist Françoise Bayle (French trial observer); Leo Alexander (medical expert for the US prosecution); Jadwiga Dzido, Maria Broel-Plater, Maria Kuśmierczuk and Władysława Karolewska. These women were all operated on while held as political prisoners at Ravensbrück concentration camp. Nuremberg, Germany, 15 December 1946.

Maria Broel-Plater was the least severely injured of the four women. Born in Warsaw in 1913, she had trained and worked as a bacteriologist before joining the Polish resistance movement as a messenger. In June 1941 she was arrested by the Gestapo and taken to Ravensbrück where food provisions and living conditions were simple, but not bad at first. These worsened at the beginning of 1942 whenever more transports of prisoners led to an extensive overcrowding of camps, with prisoners suffering from malnutrition, severe diarrhoea and disease. Broel-Plater eventually lost part of her hearing ability as a result of being frequently beaten by some of the guards during the twelve-hour working shifts. In November she was briefly examined by Oberheuser whose only comment, 'that is good', assigned her to the group of experimental subjects. They were not asked to consent to the operations, nor were they given any information about what would happen to them. Broel-Plater's legs were shaved and she was given an injection until she lost consciousness. She was operated on on 23 November and re-operated on on 27 November 1942. When she woke up her legs were swollen and deeply discoloured and she had developed a high temperature. She received no care except from fellow prisoners. At one point she saw Oberheuser with a man whom she did not know at the time, but later identified him as Karl Gebhardt from a series of unlabelled photographs. In March 1945, while Germany was in the process of defeat, a list of names of all experimental subjects was read out in the camp, summoning them to the camp commander. Together with two other women, Broel-Plater was shown a piece of paper which stated that the scars on their legs had been the result of an accident which had occurred during their stay in the camp. She refused to sign the letter and, as a consequence, had to hide until the camp was finally evacuated at the end of April.[95]

The case of Władysława Karolewska was particularly shocking because she openly refused to participate in the experiment and was forcibly held down. Born in Zuromin in 1909, she had trained as a teacher in Opatowek Kaliski and later taught young children in the school of Grudziad. After having worked for the resistance for a year, she and her family were arrested by the Gestapo in February 1941 and imprisoned in Lublin. After two weeks the interrogations began. Her refusal to confess resulted in her being beaten by the Gestapo men with a leather strap with small metal balls on the ends for an hour in two sessions. Then she was taken to the cell where the beatings resumed until she could only lie on her stomach. This gruesome spectacle was repeated after two days, though she still refused to give the names of her accomplices. In September she was transferred to Ravensbrück. On 14 August 1942, together with eight other women, Karolewska was taken to the hospital where her legs were shaved before being brought to the operating room. Over the subsequent weeks several operations were performed which produced severe infections and pain in the swollen legs of the women. Whenever they were examined by

Fischer and the other camp physicians a blanket was thrown over the face of the women to ensure that they would not know what was being done to their legs, and by whom. Once Karołewska observed Fischer smoking a cigarette in his operating gloves whilst he was standing in front of the operating room between two operations. Post-operative care was totally absent. When some of the women asked why the bandages were not changed, Oberheuser ordered them to hop on one of their legs to the dressing room where the bandages would apparently be changed. With blood and pus flowing from their infected wounds the women could hardly remain conscious until they arrived at the dressing room, where Oberheuser was standing with a smile on her face, saying that 'the changing of dressing would not take place that day'.[96]

After refusing further operations in August 1943 Karołewska and some of the other women, including Jadwiga Dzido, were taken to the prison complex called the *Bunker*, a prison with thick walls and small windows closed by shutters to prevent the light from coming in. Here they would wait for hours in pitch-black darkness, without shoes and sweaters. The next day Karołewska was taken to a cell where a Dr Trommel asked her whether she would agree to 'a small operation'. She showed him her badly disfigured leg, told him that she had undergone two operations, and that it was actually prohibited 'to perform operations on political prisoners without their consent'. The last part of Karołewska's statement must have put the doctor in a real state of shock because he immediately disappeared from the cell; when he returned, he was accompanied by two SS guards, who forced Karołewska into the cell and threw her onto the bed. Screaming and kicking they eventually managed to hold her down by putting a rag into her mouth and by forcing her legs down on the stretcher. A German nurse quickly administered an injection whereupon Karołewska lost consciousness. The next morning she realised that another operation had been performed on both legs which were both seriously infected. In the operations that followed, the doctors removed pieces of shinbone from both her legs which left her severely mutilated. For more than half a year she was unable to leave the hospital and eventually had to hide from being executed shortly before the evacuation of the camp, like many of the other experimental victims. With dozens of women dying in the final months of the war, it had become relatively easy to change the prison number or to travel under false names once the evacuation transports were organised. Survival was fuelled by the burning desire to testify about these medical atrocities. At one point they told the camp commandant that they were not afraid of being executed if one of them survived to give evidence after the war.[97]

The third woman Alexander examined was Jadwiga Dzido, who was suffering from an acutely inflamed lesion at that point. Born in 1918 in Suchowola she had studied chemistry and pharmacy at the University of

Warsaw before she became a member of the Polish resistance movement
'Conspiracy' in November 1940.[98] Following her arrest by the Gestapo in
March 1941, Dzido was brought to Ravensbrück where she first worked
on a farm, and later sewing boots for the German army. On 22 November
1942 she was taken to the sick quarters with nine other Polish girls. Her
legs were shaved and two days later she was operated on. For five weeks
she was gravely sick, could not eat, had a high fever and was delirious.
After the war, Dzido only remembered the enormous pain she had
endured, having been sleepless and restless for most of the time. She
could not remember that the bandages or dressing were ever changed.
Together with Karołewska she was imprisoned in the *Bunker* on
15 August after having refused the continuation of the experiments.
Accompanied by Thea Bintz, the chief SS woman, the camp commandant
told them that they were 'rebels', that their behaviour was 'impossible'
and that they had to obey. If not, they would be shot. At that point one
of the women, who considered herself to be a kind of spokeswoman,
replied that as political prisoners they all preferred execution to further
operations. Realising that the camp commandant was backing down,
Bintz interjected that 'to give them death was to give them victory ...
they must suffer first and then die'.[99] Eventually no further operations
were performed on this group of women.

The pattern of humiliation and degradation runs through almost all of
the life histories of the women after having been captured by the Gestapo
and brought to Ravensbrück. The act of shaving the legs of the women
became a poignant reminder that another operation was about to be performed. Maria Kuśmierczuk, the last of the women Alexander examined,
was born in 1920 in Zamosc, the daughter of the factory owner Leon
Kuśmierczuk and his wife Nathalia Kuśmierczuk, née Dziubinska.[100] She
had studied medicine at the University of Wilna before being brought to
Ravensbrück. When the first operation was performed on her she was just
twenty-two years old. Of all four women she was the one most severely
mutilated because the doctors had peeled off her muscles on the shinbone,
leaving an ugly scar with a deep excavation. For more than one-and-a-half
years, until February 1944, she was unable to walk and had to remain in
the camp hospital. On 17 December 1946 Alexander recorded the following
conversation with Maria Kuśmierczuk:

Alexander: When did you first know that the operation was to be
            performed?
Kuśmierczuk: When they started to shave my leg.
Alexander: Did you then ask what was going to be done?
Kuśmierczuk: Yes, I asked a German nurse, but got no answer and was
            told to 'shut up' (*Halts' Maul*)
Alexander: Were you in perfect health at this time?

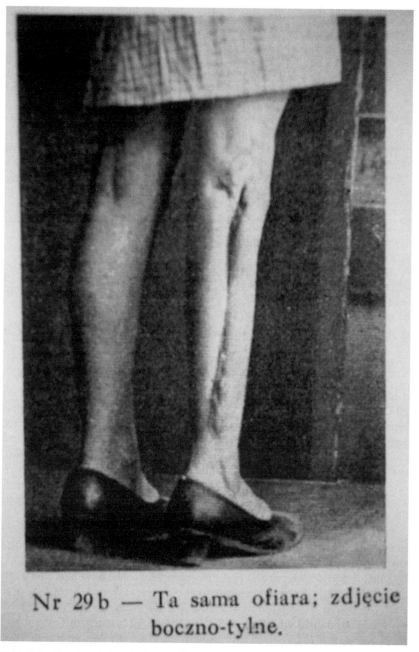

Nr 29 b — Ta sama ofiara; zdjęcie boczno-tylne.

Plate 21 One of the mutilated legs of the victims of medical experiments at Ravensbrück concentration camp.

Kuśmierczuk: Yes, perfectly healthy apart from the general state of malnutrition.

Alexander: Did you, at any time, say that you did not want to be operated on?

Kuśmierczuk: Yes, after the operation there was a petition drawn up by the prisoners and sent to the Camp Commandant, and I signed this paper protesting against the operation.

Alexander: Did you know, when you went under the general anaesthetic, that you were going to be operated on?

Kuśmierczuk: I did not know, but guessed this from the fact that my leg had been shaven.

Alexander: Had you seen other girls who had been previously operated on?

Kuśmierczuk: Yes.

Alexander: Did you say at any time that you would prefer to be shot instead of operated on?

Kuśmierczuk: Yes.

Alexander: Did you protest before the operation?

Kuśmierczuk: No.

Alexander: Why not?

Kuśmierczuk: Because of fear.

Alexander: Do you have any knowledge as to what happened to other girls who protested?

Kuśmierczuk: Yes, they were slapped in the face.

It was this evidence that was presented to a packed courtroom on Friday, 20 December 1946, one day before the court took its two-week Christmas recess. The preparation for the presentation had, in the end, become a 'race against time'.[101] Alexander's testimony was one of the most startling and emotionally disturbing, and thus, from the perspective of the prosecution, the most effective presentation of the entire trial. Learning from his previous, though not always successful contribution as expert witness, Alexander stage-managed the presentation of the women with meticulous detail.

Two days prior to his testimony he had given McHaney instructions of how the session should be choreographed.[102] The order in which the women appeared in court was to secure the greatest dramatic effect. Presenting Broel-Plater at the end, for example, would have been 'an anti-climax' because she was the one least severely injured. McHaney was coached to start the session by stressing that the women were 'nice, intelligent, educated girls' who had studied medicine, pharmacy and chemistry; these women were not at all 'sub-human', as the Germans asserted. 'They all have intelligence and charm and let them sparkle a little.'[103] It was this humane and emotive approach which Alexander hoped would make the strongest impact on the judges and the international press alike, in particular if it could be juxtaposed to what had actually been done to the women. In a second step he wanted the prosecution to point out the 'distinctly involuntary character of the experiments', exemplified by one of the women, who had openly refused but was physically forced to submit to the experiment.[104] All the other women had been bullied into the experiments. In one instance the experimental subject was asked to sign a faked statement to say that her leg injuries and scars had resulted from an accident, an indication that the authorities knew that a crime had been committed which needed to be covered up. McHaney was told to emphasise the history of the operations, 'who operated on them and which people they saw'. As it turned out, all of them knew Oberheuser, two of them knew Fischer (Dzido and Kuśmierczuk) and one could identify Gebhardt, Fischer and Oberheuser (Karołewska). Alexander assigned the role of the medical expert to himself. He would only talk about the technical aspects of the injuries, 'the various degrees of severe injuries to muscles, blood vessels, nerves and bones in addition to disfiguring scars and skin changes'.[105]

Alexander's expert testimony lasted the entire day.[106] After swearing the oath and establishing his expert credentials, he talked about his experience as an expert in both civilian and military courts and in teaching medical students about the principles of examination and trial testimony.[107] Most of his testimony was made up of technical language, interspersed with frequent references to the good character of the women. Psychologically Broel-Plater was 'of excellent quality, a woman of first rate intelligence and ability as well as character'. Karołewska was described as a woman of 'superior intelligence' who spoke fluent French and was well informed with a 'clear manner of expression'. For Alexander she was a woman 'of outstanding stamina and personality assets – in every way a highly useful citizen, both in peace and as a soldier in a time of war. She impresses me as the type of person who is naturally destined to leadership in any community.'[108] Stressing their social and intellectual abilities was meant to hammer home to the court that the experimental subjects were all but *Untermenschen*, that is sub-humans, and that the experiments went way beyond military or scientific necessity. The combination of raw facts, which every spectator could see on the legs of the women, together with Alexander's dispassionate medical expertise, left most members of the court in silent disbelief. Only rarely did the judges interrupt to ask a question. The case of Maria Kuśmierczuk was a particularly poignant example:

This patient's right leg is disfigured by a deeply scarred excavation (indicating), the bottom of which is the lateral aspect of the tibia bone (indicating) – this is hard tibia bone – from which the entire perennial and anterior tibia muscle groups have been peeled off or sloughed off. If you look at the other leg (indicating) what you see here is the tibia and

Plate 22 During his testimony at the Nuremberg Doctors' Trial, Leo Alexander, medical expert for the US prosecution, points to the scars on the leg of one of the victims of medical experiments at Ravensbrück concentration camp. Nuremberg, Germany, 22 December 1946.

perennial muscle, ante-tibia and ante-perennial muscle group. From this side (indicating) one cannot feel the bone directly; on this side (to the witness), will you turn around – there you see the bone is completely denuded. All this is hard bone surface, covered by skin only. This (indicating) is the bone directly, fibular bone and this is the tibia. You cannot normally feel these bones here (indicating) because they are covered by muscle. The muscle has been peeled off, leaving the bone at the bottom of the cavity. The lateral soleus muscle is likewise destroyed.[109]

The defendants and their lawyers were likewise awestruck by Alexander's powerful presentation. Throughout the entire day the defence counsel refrained from asking a single question, neither of Alexander nor of any of the Polish witnesses. The evidence was too overwhelming. The defence knew that whatever question they asked could backfire against their clients. Whenever Beals enquired as to whether the defence team wished to cross-examine the expert or the witnesses the courtroom fell into deep silence. For some of the defendants the façade of medical professionalism and righteousness had crumbled indeed, particularly for Fischer, who had performed most of the operations on the women. When Alexander interviewed him on 24 December he was still visibly shaken after having come face to face with his victims in the courtroom. 'I would have liked to stand up and say hang me immediately. I am finished', Fischer told Alexander.[110]

For Alexander the trial was the most important event he had ever experienced in his life. His obsession with collecting every scrap of paper, however relevant, reached new heights. Alexander 'the collector' was in his element. A sense of history in the making fuelled his determination to secure and preserve as much of the court evidence as possible, and create, while the trial was effectively under way, its own history. Whether diaries and personal notes, official letters and memoranda, transcripts and photographs, everything was neatly copied and filed for his 'personal collection' of documents about the Doctors' Trial. This material and his role in the trial were meant to secure his own place in history. On the other hand, he felt like a primeval 'hunter who suddenly finds himself in a swarm of the most amazing birds with only one gun in his hand and a limited number of bullets to bring those trophies home'.[111] Every letter Alexander wrote was constructed on multiple levels to ensure that he would be remembered as a leading force of the US prosecution. The day after his testimony he wrote to his wife:

This is the most tremendous thing I have ever gotten into. It is overwhelming; the wealth and importance of the material, from all points of view – medical, historical, psychological – is enormous; in all this maelstrom of the biggest, most hectically working legal machine ever assembled with inevitable improvisations, which drives one to

190

Plate 23 Fritz Fischer, defendant at the Doctors' Trial. Fischer carried out many of the medical experiments at the Ravensbrück concentration camp. Nuremberg, Germany, 1946/7.

distraction – the stream of documents coming in and being worked up, and in the shuffle of course much is lost or mislaid. I could kick myself for losing a rather rare find, namely, one of the strips of electrocardiogram which Rascher took while he killed people, by various means – low pressure, cold, shooting and hanging. I found it in a big box of material taken from Dr. Rascher's house. At that time I did not know its significance, and until proper identification was possible I left it in the box. In the meantime I got the story from one of the witnesses, Rascher's former assistant Neff, as to what it was. When I wanted to lay my hands on it again the whole box was gone because one document storeroom had been made over into an office and the material distributed to other storerooms – nobody knows where. I have been frantically looking for it, both to introduce it as a document in the trial and as a permanent museum piece either for the Surgeon General's museum or for the Smithsonian Institute. So far, no luck.[112]

During the following months the image of Alexander testifying at Nuremberg became a recurrent theme in addressing German medical atrocities. In March the magazine *Life* gave the story broad publicity under the headline 'Human Laboratory Animals'.[113] Among photographs of prisoners subjected to cold-water and high-altitude experiments, the article showed images of the legs of the Ravensbrück witnesses and of Alexander during his testimony. 'German medical men played an important part in the Nazi campaign to exterminate "inferior" peoples. Their special contribution was developing what the American Military Tribunal calls thanatology, the science of killing people by the millions', the article stated.[114] The *Newsweek* magazine called the Nuremberg defendants 'Thanatologists'.[115] In Germany, newsreels like *Welt im Film* and weekly news magazines published images of the Ravensbrück victims.[116] In February 1946 the journal *Heute* reported about Alexander under the headline 'Experiments'. The image of Kuśmierczuk's leg was the subject of particular outrage: 'it is the leg of a human being who was turned into a lifelong cripple by sadism and the brutal denial of basic human rights – disguised under the mantle of "applied military research" (*wehrwissenschaftliche Zweckforschung*)'.[117] 'Nazi medical researchers', the article stated, 'wanted to create monuments like those "Temples of Honour" which were destroyed a couple of weeks ago. The monuments which remained – as evidence and indictment, and as a warning and reminder – are those tragically mutilated limbs.'[118] On the previous page the journal had reported about the blasting of the two 'Temples of Honour' in Munich which had been little more than a façade for the Nazi cult of the dead.

Behind the public image of the trial, the different personalities of the prosecution team and its affiliated personnel from other nations needed to learn to work with one another. Tensions erupted apparently with

Plate 24 Leo Alexander testifying in the court with one of the victims of medical experiments at Ravensbrück concentration camp. Nuremberg, Germany, 22 December 1946.

Françoise Bayle, who was determined to conduct anthropological and psychological examinations of the defendants, and thus came into conflict with Alexander's own research interests. On 26 December Alexander recorded what must have been a kind of 'showdown' with Bayle, followed by talks with Erwin, Taylor and Rapp to establish who enjoyed 'the power behind the throne'.[119] Though the existing record does not show the outcome of the conflict, it was probably decided in favour of Alexander, who was better connected to the centres of power inside the prosecution team. Alexander also knew that the prosecution still needed his medical expertise and his ability to dig up more incriminating evidence. The next day, after McHaney had returned to Nuremberg, interrogations resumed. On Saturday, 28 December, Alexander began to prepare the cases for individual defendants, with Gebhardt, Fischer and Oberheuser at the top of the list. On Sunday, 29 December, after having worked almost non-stop since his arrival in mid-November, he enjoyed his 'first day of rest'.[120]

For many observers and political analysts the extent of stomach-churning evidence introduced in court soon became repetitive. Yet for those exploring and exposing the evidence there was no end in sight to the stream of revelations about medical crimes. Archivists, researchers and translators who had been ordered to prepare the material for the prosecution sometimes had to interrupt their work in total disbelief of the content of the evidence. For many the work would haunt them decades after the trial was completed. On 31 December 1946 Alexander told his wife:

> The mad old whirl is going on and more and more war crimes are unfolding. It sometimes seems as if the Nazis had taken special pains in making practically every nightmare come true. Some new evidence has come in where two doctors in Berlin, one a man and the other a woman, collected eyes of different colour. It seems that the concentration camps were combed for people who had slightly differently coloured eyes. That means people whose one eye had a slightly different colour than the other. Who ever was unlucky enough to possess such a pair of slightly unequal eyes had them cut out and was killed, the eyes being sent to Berlin. This is the carrying out into reality of an old gruesome German fairy tale which is included in the Tales of Hoffman, where Dr. Coppelius posing as the sandman comes at night and cuts out children's eyes when they are tired. The grim part of the story is that Doctors von Verschuer and Magnussen in Berlin did prefer children and particularly twins. There is no end to this nightmare, at least 23 are being tried now and, I trust, the others will follow later.[121]

Alexander was determined to help in the preparation of the trial against Field Marshal Erhard Milch, even if that meant that he would be separated from his family much longer.[122] Convinced that Nuremberg was 'a unique and momentous act in history' he hoped that the forthcoming trials would be 'instrumental' in preventing similar atrocities in the future.[123] On New Year's Eve he wrote a compassionate letter to his teenage son Gustave, conveying in a simple fashion what he thought about the German people and the German medical profession, and why he felt duty-bound to be thousands of miles away from home. After years of military destruction, racial hatred and death, Alexander wanted to contribute in whatever way to re-establish law and order in a post-war world, and ultimately play a part in creating a more civilised and humane society. The eventful days in December and his widely publicised role in the trial had given him the sense of a historic mission, one which he believed was aimed at securing a more lasting peace for the future. To his son Gustave, he wrote:

> I have a great deal to tell you when I come back and this is a real historical occasion. The people we are trying committed crimes during the war. All these crimes which the Nazis have committed consist in [*sic*] abuse of their power over people whom they unlawfully imprisoned. The particular group which is being tried right now are doctors who abused their skill for killing rather than for helping and healing people as they should have. They in turn were put up to this by a criminal government which fortunately and with God's help we have defeated by force of arms during the war. Now is the time to establish law and order for the future; I hope, for a long time to come. I am here to help in this task and after it is completed I shall come home.[124]

Observers and publicity

News coverage about the trial was not restricted to Allied media or expert journals interested in the legal aspects of the trial. About two-dozen German correspondents regularly reported the latest news from Nuremberg. The United States zone radio station broadcasted fifteen-minute commentaries on the progress of the trial, and occasionally the odd Nazi would pay tribute to the former medical elite.[125] By the beginning of March 1947 the Sunday edition of the *New York Times* carried the headline 'Nazi Medical Horrors Revealed at New Trials'. 'Nearly 100 German spectators observe the Nuremberg trials daily. They are checked only for criminal record before admission.'[126] Frequent requests by medical students for passes were generally granted as part of the ongoing denazification effort.

The German medical profession also sent a 'commission of doctors' (*Ärztekommission*) as official observers to the trial. Led by the distinguished Heidelberg psychologist Alexander Mitscherlich, the commission's objective was to report in medical expert journals about the extent of medical misconduct during the Third Reich.[127] Originally, the Reich Medical Association (*Reichsärztekammer*) – the renaming of the organisation was not yet completed

Plate 25 Brigadier General Telford Taylor, US Chief of Counsel for War Crimes, discussing the progress of the trial with the press. Nuremberg, Germany, 1946/7.

– had sent six trial observers to Nuremberg. Throughout January and February 1947 membership of the commission decreased to only three people. One of them, Wolfgang Spamer, felt that travelling in Germany had become 'grotesque'.[128] Conditions for Germans in the winter of 1946–7 were near breaking point; the search for coal, food and housing facilities determined the daily survival of thousands of people. Germany's infrastructure, communication and transportation system had almost completely ground to a halt. Countess Alice von Platen, one of three trial observers and a protégée of the psychiatrist Viktor von Weizäcker, experienced the time in Nuremberg as one of the most difficult periods in her life.[129] For example, she often had to face a rather hostile German public on her daily train journeys to Nuremberg. Critical reporting about the atrocities of German nationals could easily be seen as treacherous behaviour. As the only female observer, supervised and directed by Mitscherlich's rather autocratic style of leadership, von Platen had great difficulty in completing her work in Nuremberg.[130] She sometimes found herself entangled in conflicting political and scientific interests. Mitscherlich himself was almost never in Nuremberg and only kept himself informed through regular reports by Mielke and von Platen. The logistics, like access to a typewriter or trial transcripts, barely existed. Another problem for the commission was to get its articles published in expert medical journals, most of which feared that reports from Nuremberg would damage fragile post-war doctor–patient relationships or harm the reputation of the German medical profession.[131]

Contacts with Brandt's lawyer Servatius and with Alexander facilitated access to trial documents for von Platen.[132] Another valuable contact was Eugen Kogon, a former concentration camp prisoner and author of *Der SS-Staat: Das System der deutschen Konzentrationslager*, which he published in 1946 in the Verlag der Frankfurter Hefte, his newly established publishing house.[133] Kogon's publishing house later allowed von Platen to publish her account of the 'euthanasia' programme. By 1947 many people toyed with the idea of publishing their accounts and interpretation of the trial and explain what might have gone wrong with German medicine and society. Whether defendants like Rostock and Rose, observers like Mitscherlich, Mielke and von Platen, or expert witnesses like Alexander, they all knew that first-hand accounts of the trial would be of significant interest for future historians and policy-makers alike. Unlike the others, Alexander had easy access to radio broadcasts and other means of communication to report about the Doctors' Trial.

'This is Wolfe Frank calling Radio Newsreel from the Court Room Nuremberg', the broadcaster announced on 10 January 1947. For the people in London and throughout the German occupied zones it signalled the start of yet another bulletin about the latest developments in the Doctors' Trial. Since the case depended to a great extent on medical expertise it was hardly surprising that journalists increasingly turned to Alexander for his view about the case. Asked about the character and moral belief system of individual defendants, Alexander did not mince his words in condemning members of his own profession:

Twenty defendants are physicians. In their professional qualifications they range from first-rate leader of scientific medicine in Germany with excellent international reputations down to the dregs of the German medical profession, namely SS doctors assigned to concentration camp hospitals, those strange and ambiguous focal points in the jungle of concentration camp life with their special wards perverted to abattoirs, slaughter houses or clandestine execution chambers. All of them have in common a callous lack of consideration of, and human regard for, and an unprincipled abuse of power over the poor, unfortunate defenceless creatures who had been deprived of their human rights by a ruthless and criminal government. All of them violated the Hippocratic commands which they had solemnly sworn to uphold and abide by – such as the fundamental principle never to do harm.[134]

Of all the defendants only one had expressed regret and sympathy for the victims, but refused to be named for fear of appearing to break ranks with his peers. Most felt that they had acted according to higher orders from the authorities and that it was 'unfair that they and their good and useful experiments are thrown into such awful company as the atrocities committed by the others'.[135] Gebhardt admitted that the Ravensbrück experiments had served to clear his name of a serious charge of negligence.[136] Frank then enquired whether science had benefited from the experiments in any way. Contrary to what Alexander had expressed shortly after the war, his reply was unambiguous:

Alexander: Nothing that could not also be discovered with other means. Most of the stuff is [of] poor quality and in many instances the avowed purpose of the experiments is not the main purpose at all. The greatest advance lies in the perfection of methods of killing. With peculiar fascination research projects, which started with another ostensible purpose, gradually veered in that direction – providing information about death or sterilisation. This is the thanatological trend in the entire research work, providing the technique for genocide.
Frank: Thanatology, of course, is the science of inflicting death.
Alexander: Quite right. For instance an investigation was started by Mrugowsky quite innocently as an investigation of potential injuries effects of impurities added to vaccines. But it became the origin of the notorious phenol injection with which vast numbers of people were killed with unprecedented rapidity by concentration camp doctors and other doctors tied up with the SS machine.

Frank: You couldn't really call that useful, can you?

Alexander: No, but you might consider this polygal drug a perhaps useful blood coagulant. It was experimented with by shooting prisoners from the shoulder to the spleen and then clocking the time they took to die.[137]

A number of medical experts, including some of the defendants, like Gerhard Rose, could not have disagreed more with Alexander's evaluation of the experiments. Rose, for example, was convinced that a case could be made that Rascher's freezing experiments had produced 'highly important, revolutionary results ... with a minimum of expense for the sea-rescue service and the treatment of hypothermic individuals'.[138] Taking into account that hundreds of people perished in the experiments, his notion that the information had been procured with a 'minimum of expense' (*Mindestaufwand*) carried a certain sense of cynicism, and raised the question about the extent to which data can or should be used that has been obtained by criminal and unethical means. More importantly, the trial raised the question about standards of existing and future medical ethics.

7
The Nuremberg Code

Medical ethics

At the beginning of January 1947 questions about the ethics and quality of German medical science led to a controversy as to whether one should publish the results of Nazi experiments. The debate was triggered in the British journal *Lancet* and followed up by the *British Medical Journal*.[1] Although nothing had apparently been discovered which merited publication, the editors asked readers in January that if 'facts of real value to medicine were still to emerge from the records of the experiments – should they be published or not?'[2] In the ensuing debate some argued that publishers would become 'accessories to the crime' while others were adamant that scientists had a duty towards the victims to publish the results so 'at least their suffering was of some benefit'. Experts from the *British Medical Journal* wanted to know whether if the Nazis had 'discovered a cure for cancer would the rest of the world say that this information must be destroyed because of the manner in which it was obtained?'[3] Others thought that the controversy was unnecessary. Ivy, for example, believed that German medical science had made no significant discoveries during the war and that there was probably nothing 'worth publishing'.[4]

Unimpressed by some of the media hype and despite the constant need for improvisation, the prosecution was well aware that the trial was likely to make legal history. On 16 December Alexander told his wife: 'What a madhouse this is! I don't know what they would have done without me, the Snafu[5] is so terrific. I am working from 8.30 a.m. till 2.30 a.m. What a grind! But we'll come out with something really monumental, both historical and legal.'[6] Only three weeks later, in early January, he tried to persuade Phyllis to come to Nuremberg. Not without a certain degree of irony he told her that his 'little apartment consisting of one room and bath and ante-room is very adequate indeed, and I am sure you will love it. The furnishing is simple and the twin beds that are in it are military style but I am sure you will be very comfortable. The bath tub is tremendous, Göring's size and you could swim in it.'[7] For Alexander, Nuremberg was a 'unique and momentous act in history and you should be here to go through it with me. We can always make or save money but we couldn't go through this again no matter how much we made or saved. So I expect you soon.'[8] Nuremberg, his daughter Cecily recalls, was very exciting and very chaotic:

> nobody got any sleep ... there was often confusion, red tape, interruptions, and tremendous pressure ... they felt that they had a certain window of time, and also he spoke about that there was confusion and difficulty in finding witnesses so he used people he knew, connections. Perhaps that's why he invited my mother to come over, perhaps when he realised that he would be able to go to Holland because he had reason to consult with his relatives there.[9]

Alexander was not alone in his assessment of the importance of the trial for future research ethics. The prosecution and the judges are likely to have realised at this point that general guidelines for future research on humans were needed and, perhaps, codified as part of the Nuremberg judgement. Yet up until mid-January 1947, Alexander does not seem to have spent much time reflecting about how such guidelines should look in reality, mainly because he was tied up with interrogating defendants and ensuring the smooth running of the trial. The same appears to be true of the prosecution as a whole. Only after the meeting of the ISC (WC) at the Institute Pasteur in Paris on 15 January did the issue of medical ethics become a priority for Alexander and the prosecution. The conference intensified international discussion about the formulation of ethics principles. As a member of the US delegation, Alexander was expected and well-positioned to make an impact on the debate.

Whereas some Allied countries were excluded, others did not want to participate officially. The meeting was convened ad hoc, one day earlier than originally planned, thereby excluding the representative of the Danish medical profession, V. A. Fenger, who arrived too late to take part.[10] Both the Danish General Medical Association and French medical experts had proposed the creation of a scientific commission for the investigation of medical war crimes to the UNWCC earlier.[11] The decision by the French to move this crucial meeting forward was probably intended to confine membership in the commission to the four Allied powers. By now the commission had become a matter of national prestige and power politics. Unlike the Danish, who would have wished to participate, Taylor and Alexander had flown to Paris to take part as 'unofficial delegates of the Nuremberg War Crimes Tribunal' because Washington was reluctant to boost the status of the commission by despatching official representatives.[12]

The British commission was led by Lord Moran, Churchill's doctor and President of the Royal College of Physicians. It included, among others, the physiologist Sir Henry Dale, the forensic pathologists Sidney Smith from Edinburgh University and Major Keith Mant from the Royal Medical Corps.[13] In October 1946, after having been approached by the chairman of the UNWCC, Prime Minister Clement Attlee had told Moran that since the French had chosen men of 'very high standing' it was necessary that 'both for reason of prestige and also in order that the investigators should have the benefit of the best possible advice, that our Committee should be composed of men of equally high standing'.[14] Moran also recruited a number of experts who advised him on the scientific quality of the experiments, for example, the psychiatrist Aubrey Lewis, the bacteriologist Ronald Hare and the eugenicist Charles Paton Blacker, an ardent advocate of sterilising mental defectives. Blacker, for one, thought it 'deplorable' that eugenics had been linked to Nazi racial practices.[15] The French participated with René Legroux, Pierre Lépine, Françoise Bayle, A. Touffait and Paul Tchernia.[16] Thompson and Henry S. Leger were present as observers. Moran, after having being elected to chair the meeting, outlined three objectives of the commission: to work against the 'disregard for human life and for human rights', to 'aid and maintain the public's confidence in ethical research' by laying down 'criteria for the justifiable use of human beings as experimental subjects', and to 'evaluate the results of the experimental work in question'.[17] In addition, the Institute Pasteur was designated as the permanent repository for collecting documentation on these three issues.

Divisions among the members of the commission erupted over the question as to how to deal with the public. Alexander's presentation on medical war crimes was severely criticised by Lord Moran after the former had told the meeting that he planned to submit two papers on German medicine and on the Ktenology concept to the American medical press. Moran argued that this would 'undermine' the effective work of the commission. The minutes record that 'some discussion followed' which implies that the two men probably had a fierce argument over the issue.[18] Alexander's insistence that articles written by individual members of the commission would not be disadvantageous was rejected by the French and British delegates. They feared that the pre-publication of some of the results would make the commission superfluous in the eyes of the international community. They favoured the confidential handling and selective publication of the material in order to prevent any long-term damage to the world's medical profession. The French also ensured that information about the objectives of the commission would be kept confidential and restricted to its members. When Lecroux met with the Danish representative Fenger the next day, he gave Fenger the impression that 'the task of this committee was in fact very limited'.[19]

Finally, the commission endorsed its view that the membership of the United States was seen as 'essential', a position that was shared by Alexander. On 15 February he told the US War Department that 'it would be desirable for the United States to join this Commission', and recommended the appointment of a number of medical experts, including himself.[20] However, the official rejection of a second IMT by the US government in January quashed hopes of official US participation.[21] The US prosecution also felt that an American committee was only of limited value in the trial against the Nazi doctors. On 30 January Taylor told the United States Commissioner at the UNWCC, Robert M. Springer, that 'the committee would probably be of no material assistance in the trial now drawing to a conclusion, but that their work would be valuable in emphasising the results and increasing the effectiveness of the judgement'.[22] In the meantime Moran was trying to encourage the United States to participate in the commission. One of his proposals floated the idea that the American committee could effectively operate from the United States through a European liaison. 'Dr. Alexander, now at Nurnberg, might well be used as the person representing the committee in Europe', Moran told a US official.[23] By the end of February a final decision as to whether America would become involved was still pending. In the end the US authorities decided against it.[24] Officials from the War Department, in particular, felt that there were certain budgetary constraints and that the available personnel should be used for the prosecution of war criminals rather than as advisers in a commission that had been set up mostly by the French and the British.[25] This meant that the ISC (WC) had only bilateral and not international status, and that consequently any medical ethics code published by the commission would have limited international standing.

In 1949, still sulking over the lack of American interest in the ISC (WC), Moran, considering the extent of medical war crimes, published a rather brief five-page report on the 'Scientific Results of German Medical War Crimes' which concluded that the experiments were 'not only ill-designed but were ill-conceived, and in many cases were unnecessary'.[26] With no apparent scientific results identifiable from the experiments, and after having been snubbed by the Americans, the commission felt unable (or perhaps unwilling) to come to any conclusions with regard to the moral issues involved. The British felt betrayed that the Americans had unilaterally established the Nuremberg trials as a forum to publicly condemn German atrocities and claim the moral high ground. The initiative had by now clearly passed to the Americans.

Indeed, following the meeting of the ISC (WC), Alexander was homing in on the subject of medical ethics. He was determined to come up with a set of ethics guidelines which would supersede his own principles from December as well as those formulated by Ivy in the autumn of 1946 which had been adopted by the AMA in a modified version only a couple of weeks earlier. During the Paris conference Alexander had laid out his theory about the science of killing in his talk on 'Ktenology as a Scientific Technique of Genocide' and had announced his intention to publish his theory in two articles.[27] Shortly before his departure to Paris, Alexander had also welcomed Ivy in Nuremberg who had just arrived from the United States. Both met again on 21 January after Alexander's return from Paris and continued their conversation about a future medical ethics code.[28] The next day Alexander recorded in his diary: 'Discussion re[garding] Ktenology with Dr. Ivy'.[29] Ivy left Nuremberg the following day, on 23 January, to return to Chicago. A special press announcement from that day reveals that Ivy had recommended to the American military authorities that

an international, legalised Code of ethics should be published on the use of human beings as experimental subjects. Dr Ivy made this recommendation after spending the past ten days reviewing the record of the current war crimes trial of 23 doctors and scientists accused of conducting medical experiments on inmates of concentration camps.[30]

The discussions within the prosecution team throughout January as well as Ivy's public recommendations seem to have prompted Alexander into action. He wanted to become the author of Ivy's proposed medical ethics code. One day later Alexander recorded in his diary: 'Sent off Ktenology article. Finished the additions to the article re[garding] ethical and unethical experimentation.'[31] On or around 24 January Alexander therefore must have edited and expanded his three ethics principles which he had outlined in December. Finally, on 25 January, he wrote: 'Worked on Ethics article, drew up Affidavit.'[32]

These diary entries are important in many respects. First, they tell us that Alexander's article on 'Ethical and Non-Ethical Experiments on Human Beings' was formulated at the end of January. In the article, which has no date, and in the affidavit, which is dated 25 January, we find, word for word, Alexander's six ethics principles from April 1947.[33] The diary entries show that Alexander formulated these principles about three months earlier than scholars have previously assumed, because most concentrated on Alexander's memorandum from April 1947.[34] Alexander's principles stated the following:

1. Legally valid voluntary consent of the experimental subject is essential. This requires specifically:
(a) The absence of duress
(b) Sufficient disclosure on the part of the experimenter and sufficient understanding on the part of the experimental subject of the exact nature and consequences of the experiment for which he volunteers, to permit an enlightened consent.

In the case of mentally ill patients, for the purpose of experiments concerning the nature and treatment of nervous and mental illness or related subjects, such consent of the next of kin or legal guardian is required; whenever the mental state of the patient permits (that is, in those mentally ill patients who are not delirious or confused) his own consent should be obtained in addition.

2. The nature and purpose of the experiment must be humanitarian, with the ultimate aim to cure, treat, or prevent illness, and not concerned with methods of killing or sterilisation (ktenology). The motive and purpose of the experiment shall also not be personal nor otherwise ulterior.

3. No experiment is permissible if the foregone conclusion exists, or the probability or the a priori reason to believe that death or disabling injury of the experimental subject will occur.

4. Adequate preparations must be made and proper facilities be provided to aid the experimental subject against any remote chance of injury, disability, or death. This provision specifically requires that the degree of skill of all those who are taking an active part as experimenters, and the degree of care which they exercise during the experiment, must be significantly higher than the skill which is considered adequate for the performance of standardised medical or surgical procedures, and for the administration of well established drugs. American courts are very stringent in requiring for the permissible use of any new or unusual technique or drug, irrespective of whether this use is experimental or purely therapeutic, a degree of skill and care on the part of the responsible physician which is higher than that required for the purpose of routine medical or surgical procedures.

5. The degree of risk taken should never exceed that determined by the humanitarian importance of the problem to be solved by the experiment. It is ethically permissible for an experimenter to perform experiments involving significant risks only if the solution, after thorough exploration along all other lines of scientific investigation is not accessible by any other means, and if he considers the solution of the problem important enough to risk his own life along with those of his non-scientific colleagues, such as was done in the case of Walter Reed's yellow fever experiments.

6. The experiment to be performed must be so designed and based upon the results of thorough thinking-through, of investigation of simple physico-chemical systems and of animal experimentation that the anticipated results will justify the performance of the experiment. That is, the experiment must be such as to yield decisive results for the good of society and should not be random and unnecessary in nature.[35]

Alexander's affidavit seems to have had no immediate effects among members of the prosecution throughout February and March 1947. It seems to have been produced as part of Alexander's 'literary work' about ethically legitimate and illegitimate research on humans. It is not known what actually happened with the affidavit or who had access to it. Although the affidavit states that Alexander had been put under oath, this does not necessarily infer that he must have shared the information with others. As a member of the US prosecution he had been placed under oath anyway and had permission to draft legal documents, memoranda and affidavits. The affidavit therefore has to be treated with caution. It is quite possible that Alexander, after having made additions to his article, may have listed the six principles separately in the form of an affidavit in order to ensure that he would have to be credited with their authorship in the future. Alexander was clearly not shy when it came to constructing an image of himself as a man of historical importance.

The same appears to have happened with Alexander's article about the ethics in human experimentation. He does not seem to have shown the article to anybody, except that he submitted it to the Public Relations Division of the War Department to receive clearance to publish it. Publication of the article was approved on 17 March 1947 when he was touring Holland to find further witnesses of medical atrocities.[36] Only after his return in April did Alexander revisit the subject of a medical ethics code. It is at that point that he himself created some confusion with regard to the precise origin of his medical ethics principles.

The Leibbrand testimony

Prior to the presentation of the case for the defence the prosecution suffered a major setback when their medical expert witness, Werner Leibbrand, a psychiatrist and medical historian from Erlangen University, testified on 27 January 1947 on medical ethics and professional medical conduct – only two days after Alexander had formulated his six principles.[37] Leibbrand had been chosen for his immaculate credentials and because he was of German nationality. The issue of introducing a German medical expert for the prosecution had figured in discussions as early as autumn 1946 and had resurfaced in talks between Alexander and Taylor at the end of November.[38] Allied legal advisers believed that a German medical expert might not only strengthen the case of the prosecution, but facilitate the process of denazification. Leibbrand's testimony was meant to convey that the Allied authorities saw only a *minority* of German doctors as having breached professional standards and as being guilty of crimes. It was an attempt at reconciling the medical profession with the Allied military government. However, the prosecution underestimated the power of cross-examination. Leibbrand's testimony backfired and left Allied medical science to appear almost in the same moral category as German medical science. Although this defence strategy had been foreseen, the actual ramifications and public relations impact came as a shock to Taylor's team.

During the Third Reich Leibbrand had suffered discrimination and terror by the Gestapo for being a member of the Socialist League of Doctors, and because his wife was Jewish.[39] He had witnessed the unprecedented wave of violence against political opponents and Jews after the Nazi takeover of power.[40] Leibbrand pointed out that the German doctor at the beginning of the twentieth century had become a 'biological state officer' who saw the patient as a series of biological events, and as 'a mere object like a mail package'. German physicians had perverted traditional Hippocratic ethics by showing a 'lack of morality and reverence for human life'. He condemned human experiments without the subject's consent, and drew attention to the Berlin psychiatrist Albert Moll, who as early as 1902 had warned his contemporaries of 'medical immorality' in his book *Ärztliche Ethik*.[41] According to Moll every person faced with the possibility of performing unethical human experimentation should ask himself whether he would subject his own relatives or members of his family to such treatment, and never conduct experiments without the consent of the patient. Leibbrand's position was similar to that of Moll. For Leibbrand human experimentation was only permissible if the person had given voluntary, informed consent, was mentally capable of giving consent, and was not forced or in any way coerced. He categorically ruled out experiments on prisoners, infants or the handicapped.

When the hearing reconvened at 2.30 p.m. with the cross-examination, the defence lawyers attempted, and succeeded, in turning Leibbrand's testimony against the prosecution. Using the traditional technique of cross-examination, for example luring the witness to make general or false statements before presenting the court with hard evidence, Servatius, representing Brandt, carefully framed his questions. He wanted to ensure that Leibbrand would not sense the direction of the questions, using the word 'approval' instead of the more legally sensitive word 'consent'. Leibbrand confirmed that experiments on prisoner populations were not voluntary, because of the circumstances of arrest and the assumed inability of prisoners to assess the consequences of the experiment, even if informed. Accordingly prisoners were 'in a forced situation' and could not be volunteers. This allowed the defence to point out that dangerous human experiments on prisoners throughout the last hundred years had taken place, often without their consent, in countries like France, the Netherlands, Britain, and the United States. Nazi doctors, so the argument went, had only followed commonly accepted research practices. The difference between Allied and German medical science became increasingly blurred.

The most embarrassing example introduced by Servatius was evidence of large-scale malaria experiments on 800 American prisoners, many of them black, who had been selected from federal penitentiaries in Atlanta, the Illinois state penitentiary and New Jersey state reformatory.[42] In June 1945 the magazine *Life* had given the story broad publicity in an article entitled

'Prison Malaria' which revealed that the research was directed by the government-funded Office of Scientific Research and Development.[43] Human experiments had been conducted with malaria tropica, the most dangerous of malaria strands, to aid the war effort in the Asian theatre of operation. 'Enemies of society are helping to combat other enemies', the article stated because 'the experimenters ... have found prison life ideal for controlled laboratory work with humans.'[44] Servatius read out the entire article in open court and described in meticulous detail each of the images and their captions; these referred to 'violent chills' and 'fever often as high as one hundred [and] six degrees'. Some of the prison cases developed to 'a considerable extent' before being treated with drugs. Then Servatius asked Leibbrand the obvious question: 'Now, will you please express your opinion on the admissibility of these experiments?'[45] Leibbrand could not retract his answer which he had previously given. American malaria experiments, he told the court, were likewise 'excesses and outgrowths of biological thinking' because the consequences for the malaria-infected prisoner could not be foreseen. Malaria is not 'a mere cold' he said. Leibbrand also referred to Moll who had insisted that the morality of a physician is to hold back his 'natural research urge in order to maintain his basic medical attitude that is laid down in the Oath of Hippocrates and which may result in doing harm to his patient'.[46] 'In consequence', Leibbrand concluded, 'such experiments should be carried out on guinea pigs and not on human beings.'[47]

The cross-examination of Leibbrand was a powerful condemnation of American wartime research in a court of American judges. It undermined the case of the prosecution by giving the impression to the tribunal that German and Allied medical science were essentially the same. Although having anticipated this line of defence, the prosecution was caught off-guard by the sheer force of the accusations against American medicine, not least because they came from their own medical expert. Beyond that, Leibbrand had been discredited as a trial expert, because as a medical historian and psychiatrist he showed himself unfamiliar with the literature and details of human experimentation. Significantly, for the three days of Leibbrand's testimony Alexander made no diary entries. He may have just taken a rest, but he also may have wanted to conceal the dire situation of the prosecution, or, perhaps, hide his own frustration because he had been responsible for writing Leibbrand's trial brief.[48] His mind certainly seems to have been concerned with other, more personal matters, mostly related to his family. On 28 January he told his son Gustave that he had not yet been in Vienna 'and therefore have not yet seen my father's grave but I expect to get over to Vienna before I leave, preferably with Mother if she can manage to come and join me here. I also have not yet been to the Netherlands to see Helen [*sic*].'[49] For Alexander the personal and the professional became mixed up; he was the expert witness for the prosecution, yes, but he was also a Jewish neurologist from Vienna, whose family had been persecuted and scattered all over the world as a result of the actions of the Nazis. His brother Alfred now lived in England and his sister Helene in the Netherlands. He had no knowledge of the whereabouts of his sister Anne, and he and his family lived in the United States. It is quite understandable that he might have suffered from an occasional sense of sadness, perhaps even anger, about the state of his private affairs in the post-war world. The day after Leibbrand's testimony the prosecution screened a film about the Hadamar killing centre as an emotional reminder and evidence of the medical atrocities which had been committed.[50]

From the perspective of the prosecution Leibbrand's philosophical discourse had become an unwanted delay in the conviction of the defendants. Inter-Allied frictions over questions about how to tackle medical war crimes, together with mounting political tensions in the American zone of occupation about war crimes trials generally, made the prosecution aware that any success by the defence was of potentially far-reaching consequence for all subsequent Nuremberg trials. At the end of January the judges apparently invited Ivy to lunch where they indicated that 'the prosecution had not made a case since the defence was arguing that medical scientists had done to prisoners in penitentiaries and to "Conscientious objectors" in the USA the same thing and under the same conditions that the Nazi physicians had done to their prisoners'.[51] This account, written by Ivy in 1964, almost twenty years after the Doctors' Trial in a climate in which a number of scientists were claiming authorship of the Nuremberg Code, needs to be treated with great caution. It probably reveals more about Ivy's intention to place himself centre-stage in the debate on medical ethics in the 1960s, than it tells us about his close connection to the judges. In any event, it seems highly unlikely that the judges – who throughout the trial displayed the greatest degree of fairness and impartiality – would all of a sudden chat about their perception of the case to the medical expert of the US prosecution over the dinner table. Moreover, Ivy does not seem to have been in Nuremberg at the end of January. We can safely assume that Ivy added some extra colour to his otherwise important role in the trial. Whatever the sequence of events, the prosecution, and Ivy and Alexander in particular, realised at the end of January that the Doctors' Trial could seriously backfire and become a trial against American medical research practice. They needed a sophisticated medical ethics code if they wanted to stand a chance of convincing the tribunal about the ethical differences between German and Allied medicine.

The defence on the offensive

For weeks the defence team had been waiting for the introduction of evidence by the prosecution to be completed. Now the table could be turned. The twenty-three defendants were represented by nineteen defence lawyers and eight assistants, many of whom had been actively involved in the Nazi judiciary system and some of whom were known members of the Nazi party.[52] Defence attorneys like Kurt Kaufmann, Hanns Marx, Rudolf Merkel, Otto Nelte, Horst Pelckmann, Fritz Sauter, Alfred Seidl and Robert Servatius had already served, with varying degree of success, in the IMT and were thus more familiar with the Anglo-American court procedure.[53] Central to the Anglo-American legal system was the cross-examination, the questioning of the defendant or witness by both the defence lawyers and the prosecution. In general, the witness would first be questioned by the party which had produced the witness, and then by the opposite party. The first party was then permitted to question the witness again, but only on those issues which had been raised during the previous cross-examination by the opposite party. For the German defence lawyers unfamiliar with the procedure, this meant hours of homework, misunderstandings and legal disputes in the courtroom. They also had to get used to the fact that the prosecution only needed to present the incriminating evidence and no material in support of the defendant. In July 1947, the defendant Paul Rostock remarked in a letter to Hermann Friedrich Rein that 'if the American prosecutor has 999 documents in support of the defendant in his possession and only one incriminating document, he will produce only that [in court] and none of the 999 others. The German prosecutor, however, has to assess the entire incriminating and supporting evidence, and present this [in court].'[54]

The defence team devised a number of strategies to ensure that the defendants would not incriminate themselves during cross-examination. One of the golden rules was to deny knowledge of meetings and contacts unless evidence was produced to the contrary. If that happened, however, one could always explain things away through a convenient loss of memory. Another line of defence was that the defendant could not be held responsible for a certain crime because of his or her subordinate position, or, in a slightly modified form, that one was not in a position of power to stop certain experiments or unlawful acts. With regard to human experiments almost all of the defendants were adamant that the research subjects had been sentenced to death. This apparently justified the use of non-volunteers in the experiments. Most of the defendants described the experiments as a 'chance' for the prisoners to pay retribution for the alleged crimes, or as an opportunity to be pardoned. One of the most common and powerful lines of defence was the reference to the exceptional circumstances of the war which had apparently made it necessary that extraordinary measures for problem-solving be introduced, including the expeditious testing of drugs and other military-medical equipment in concentration camps. Most of the defendants were saying, in effect, that in order to save the lives of hundreds of thousands of German soldiers in a national emergency it was justifiable to sacrifice a number of condemned prisoners. In short, the number of combinations of these different lines of defence was almost infinite.

For the 'euthanasia' programme the defence followed a two-track approach by arguing that the killing of patients did not constitute a crime because the patients had been severely handicapped. The defendants had only attempted to 'deliver' the mentally ill from their unbearable suffering out of humanitarian and ethical considerations. Reference was also made to the fact that the programme had been ordered by the head of state. Independent of whether or not Hitler's decree from 1 September 1939 was legally binding, for the defendants it constituted an 'administrative order' which they believed they had to carry out. In general, defence lawyers claimed that similar, if not the same kind of experiments had been carried out by the Allies in the past, that their clients had acted under superior orders by the head of state, or that they had no knowledge of any illegal intention behind the orders.

Brandt knew that he was up for a death sentence as one of Hitler's most trusted, and, throughout the war, most powerful physicians of the Reich. Shortly after Germany's unconditional surrender he had confided to his friend Albert Speer that if the Americans found out what he had been involved with 'it'll all be over for me'.[55] British intelligence sources described him as a 'nice looking and intelligent and, to the outward eye ... pleasing personality', but the moment one touched upon issues of chemical warfare or the SS 'an almost impenetrable smoke-screen was found'.[56] As it turned out, Brandt would be one of the most hard-headed, ideologically stubborn and proud defendants the court would encounter over the next six months. Investigators, legal experts and the judges were likewise astonished about the 'remarkable ignorance' for a man in his position. Brandt himself, on the other hand, if we can trust his diary, felt completely innocent and wrongfully accused. On 17 January, at around 5.30 p.m., he reflected upon his situation:

> So, now the charge is obviously complete, apart from some minor points (and unless there are some shots being fired). If I look at the whole and relate it to the actual facts, then there is a huge mountain of guilt and offence which concerns me [although] I have nothing to do with it. If, on the other hand, the main criteria would be truth, justice and the fulfilment of duty, then one would have to open the door and let me walk out into life. That's exactly how I feel. Almost an hour ago there were heavy attacks – now I am calm. I am standing before a new beginning and counter-attack. I will use these days to work and work and work! Whereas I have felt drained in recent times, I am now beginning to gather pace again. I am happy that out there, there are the Beelitzer[57] who help. In this way I know that everything is tried, and if the Gods do not want it otherwise, then it must work! And if they want it otherwise –

then I will walk the way, unbroken, and in a straight fashion, not crawling like a louse! ... Today I am so relieved of some pressure, I cannot really tell. I feel really free. I know that it will not be possible that I will persevere in the way and the technique in which the procedure is being conducted – but I will persevere before myself. Now, do you [his family] understand what this means! These are mountains which fall from my heart. And I ask myself, was this effort necessary to put such lies into the world?[58]

Brandt, while wallowing in Nazi rhetoric of heroism and pretended ignorance, was absolutely convinced that he had not committed a crime. In his view the murder of tens of thousands of mentally and physically handicapped had been a 'medical programme', ordered and sanctioned by the head of state. He felt no responsibility, remorse or regret for organising and supervising what was effectively the Nazis' first programme of mass murder. His moral belief system had eroded to the extent that he had become unable to distinguish morally between right and wrong. The lives of human beings had lost their meaning behind undefined and diffuse concepts of blood, race and national power. As long as there was no evidence to the contrary, Brandt would deny any knowledge of any unlawful experiments.

On the day the trial had opened the *New York Times* noted that 'Karl Brandt ... will take Hermann Göring's corner seat in the dock in the same court where the international trials were held.'[59] Now, after twenty-eight trial days, on Monday, 3 February 1947, Brandt settled in the witness box as Göring had done a year earlier to give his testimony as the first of the defendants. Security precautions in and outside the court house had been stepped up for fear of rescue attempts or bombing attacks. January had seen a period of heightened tensions in the American zone of occupation after a number of bomb attacks on denazification tribunals in Frankfurt am Main and in Nuremberg had put the security forces on high alert. In February General Clay informed the German Council of States that in the future 'more and stronger subversive activity' was to be expected.[60]

The session started at 9.30 a.m. with a brief dispute over the question of why the prosecution had not been given due warning that Brandt would be called as a witness. For a moment Brandt looked slightly nervous, but then calmed down when he raised his hand to take the oath. Straightening his pitch-black hair Brandt waited for his counsel, Robert Servatius, to lead him through his carefully prepared statement for the whole of the morning and the afternoon, and the whole of the next morning.[61] His questions and Brandt's answers were concise and to the point, and despite occasional objection from the prosecution, the tribunal was satisfied with Servatius' examination.[62]

Brandt started off by establishing his expert credentials, outlining his education and specialised medical training, his professional career as a surgeon and his multiple duties as Hitler's accompanying physician. His specialised assignments given by Hitler followed naturally one into another until the point where he had been formally appointed as a kind of health minister without ministry. A vivid description of his disputes with party fanatics like Conti, Himmler or Bormann was meant to present Brandt as a conscientious personality, a man of character, who had attempted to keep high moral and scientific standards.[63] Key to Brandt's statement was the precise definition and understanding of his office and his official position, first as General Commissioner and later as Reich Commissioner for Health and Sanitation. He painted the role of his office as that of a 'differential' which had co-ordinated the demands of the various military and civilian agencies. From there everything else followed, whether he had not yet been in a position to initiate or order certain policies and crimes, or had no staff which would have enabled him to carry them out. His approach was to stress those elements which were indisputable, that is his official rank and position, play down its importance and influence, deny any knowledge of those crimes and experiments which had led to multiple deaths, and admit 'some' knowledge of those which had not caused any significant harm or had been ordered and carried out for 'a superior state of interest'.[64] He alleged that he had not been involved in any of the experiments directly, that is, in a clinical sense (which was true), and had learned of nearly all of the experiments during the interrogation, in the indictment, or in Nuremberg for the first time. 'I knew nothing about them before', was his standard reply.[65]

To speed up the proceedings the prosecution largely ignored Brandt's jibes at his adversaries and the employment of *tu quoque* arguments. Minor objections by the prosecution that Brandt was reading his statement from a prepared text were overruled by the tribunal after Servatius had pointed out that the defendants in the IMT had likewise been permitted to use notes to make a 'fluent and sensible' statement.[66] It was one of many incidents which indicated that the tribunal attempted to conduct the hearing in a fair and unbiased atmosphere.

Once Brandt had established his apparent lack of knowledge of specific experiments, he turned to his co-defendants to stress that he hardly knew any of them. Of twenty-two co-defendants, Brandt alleged that he had met nine for the first time at Nuremberg (Ruff, Romberg, Becker-Freysing, Weltz, Schäfer, Hoven, Beiglböck, Pokorny, Oberheuser), of three he allegedly knew nothing but their name (Poppendick, Fischer and Rudolf Brandt) and with another six (Mrugowsky, Schröder, Gebhardt, Blome, Rose and Sievers) he had only brief and occasional contact. Apart from Rostock, Handloser and Brack, the head of German medicine appeared to be saying that he had not known the people in the dock.[67]

Finally, on the morning of 4 February, Brandt addressed the most difficult charge against him: the 'euthanasia' programme. He was extremely careful not to give the impression that he himself had any dealings with the programme directly, and generally was quick in shifting responsibility for the execution of the operation to other departments and officials.[68] Brandt himself had allegedly never visited T-4 headquarters, nor had he ever inspected one of the killing centres. Philipp Bouhler, the head of the Chancellery of the Führer, appeared to have been solely in charge of the administrative side of the operation. He dodged the issue of consent or obvious shortcomings of the programme, for example, when relatives had received two urns; he dismissed them as 'regrettable instances', which had occurred because Hitler had ordered the programme to be carried out in secrecy, but they did 'not effect [sic] the principle'. He was convinced that 'if this Hippocrates were alive today he would formulate his oath differently'.[69]

For Brandt it was important that the head of state had given him the assignment to implement 'euthanasia' and thus, in his view, bore responsibility. He stretched credibility to the limits by arguing that he 'certainly could not expect' that he was given such a decree for any criminal action.[70] Based on what was known of the regime by 1939, such a statement was hard to believe. For Brandt and his circle 'everything was done as if everything was in order, and it was in order as far as we were concerned'.[71] The execution of the operation may not have been 'very pleasant' and overall the death of humans was horrible, 'but everything in life that is biological is not pleasant', Brandt said.[72] His defence stressed the idealistic intentions behind the programme. To understand the programme, Brandt was saying, in effect, one should not look at the reality of the operation, but to the ideal which the Nazi leadership had in mind, namely to free the handicapped and incurably ill from suffering. Hitler had apparently only been 'motivated by absolutely human feelings' and never had he wanted anything else than 'that the painful lives of these creatures were to be shortened'.[73] Only a few in the courtroom would have questioned Brandt's sincerity and strong belief in the moral righteousness of 'euthanasia'. He had managed to paint himself as a wholehearted idealist, who wanted to stand up for what he believed, a position which earned him a certain respect by the court.

On the morning of 5 February 1947 the prosecution began the cross-examination of Brandt.[74] Brandt had given more than nine hours of evidence. He spoke with few interruptions and the bench had only rarely intervened, even when his answers were becoming long-winded and cumulative. For the prosecution it was essential to pull Brandt away from his broad generalisation and pin him down towards those specific charges in the indictment. James McHaney, the prosecutor, went straight on to the offensive in his examination. He quickly discredited Brandt's expertise in the 'euthanasia' programme, and undermined his smokescreen of lofty moral and scientific ideals. For the prosecution it was essential that

Brandt's cross-examination would not descend into the kind of public relations stunt which Göring had mounted a year earlier. In the evening Alexander recorded in his diary: 'Testimony [of Brandt] continued. McHaney really shook him to his foundations when he began the cross-examination today.'[75]

Brandt had neither trained as a psychiatrist, nor had he any expert knowledge in the field of psychiatry. He had never visited any mental asylums for observation or study. He was unable to state the average time a mentally ill person spent in an asylum, but would swear that the 'insane died at an early stage in their life' and were generally unhappy and suffered from pain. Brandt and his staff did not take any precautions to ensure that proper medical examinations of patients were carried out at the killing centres. The whole programme relied on questionnaires to determine whether or not a person was 'incurably ill' after Brandt had been 'assured' that a proper questionnaire would be filled out by a specialist.[76] He believed that the approval of parents in the children's 'euthanasia' programme was 'absolutely necessary', but he did not know whether it had ever been given, nor whether it had been given in writing or orally.[77] What Brandt saw as a medical procedure full of 'safeguards' was a system open to total arbitrariness, abuse and administrative chaos.

On 6 and 7 February Brandt was faced with a flood of incriminating evidence. It showed that he not only had knowledge of human experiments in the camps, but that he had initiated a number of them. After almost three days on the stand, Brandt was beginning to show signs of mental fatigue. Brandt admitted that he had visited concentration camps more than once and that he knew of and did not prevent the Ravensbrück sulphonamide drug experiments. He had also given a group of doctors a 'carte blanche' to conduct experiments with poisonous gases and water on camp inmates.[78] When the questions became too sensitive, Brandt would avoid answering them or talk about different matters. He was certainly a skilled and stubborn witness. After another series of dodged questions, McHaney snapped: 'Herr Brandt, I am not in the least bit of a hurry. I will keep you on this stand for three days if necessary to get responses to my questions.'[79] For McHaney, summing up the case, it showed that Brandt had permanently tried to mislead the tribunal, that he had been in contact with the SS and had tried to obtain prisoners for whatever purposes, although he had vehemently denied such contacts. The cross-examination undermined Brandt's credibility in the eyes of the tribunal and left the image of the idealistic and morally sound doctor in tatters.

Despite this victory there were other defendants where the evidence was less clear-cut, or where the prosecution was anticipating strong accusations against Allied medical research practices. There were also those attorneys who used the testimony by the other defendants to exonerate their clients.[80] In most cases the witness statements by the defence cut little ice with the court.[81] However, the prosecution was facing problems with the central issue of human experimentation, which was prompted in part by the defence of Kurt Blome, the former Deputy Reich Health Leader and representative for cancer research in the Reich Research Council. Blome challenged the notion that the German experiments on humans had not been permissible.[82] He also enlisted the support of his wife Bettina. She compiled a fifteen-page dossier on the subject of human experimentation which listed examples of experiments that had been carried out in Anglo-American research facilities.[83]

Blome used his testimony to first distance himself from the camp experiments before arguing why such experiments would in fact be permissible. In a working paper from 11 March he outlined a number of key general questions which he wanted the court to consider, for example whether 'human experiments were at all permissible? Do they always constitute a crime? Are there not conditions under which the circumstances justify human experiments, or even demand them in the interest of the general public?'[84] He started by arguing that experiments on humans had always been necessary for research and would also be necessary in the future. Medical scientists all over the world, including many non-Germans, had carried out such experiments, often on themselves and at considerable risk. Scientists like the American researcher Walter Reed, for instance, had discovered the cause of yellow fever through experiments on humans, and no one would retrospectively classify him as a criminal but honour him for his contribution to humanity, Blome argued. Then he raised the issue of whether or not human experiments could only be performed on volunteers, 'or [could] a particular group be selected by compulsory means? And who is authorised to give permission in such a case?'[85] Blome agreed in principle that research on humans should be carried out on volunteers, but in times of war 'other rules applied', making it necessary, in the interest of the public, to solve certain problems fast. Criminals sentenced to death were thereby given a chance to pay retribution to their country, or receive a lowering of their sentences if the experiment was successful. According to Blome no experiments were permitted on political prisoners or prisoners of war.

Finally, and most significantly, Blome produced material which showed that doctors and scientists in other countries, including the United States, had carried out experiments on humans without their consent, for example on yellow fever, sandfly fever, typhus, trench fever, Leishmania research, breakbone fever, Hansen's disease, dysentery, pox, measles, scarlet fever, the common cold and poliomyelitis.[86] It was one of the most sensitive aspects for the prosecution and a direct challenge to the medical case. They knew that they could hardly argue that experiments on humans were not permissible under any circumstance, unless, of course, they wanted to attract an onslaught by the international medical community. This meant that they had to define the conditions under which experiments on humans were ethically and legally permissible. Blome's testimony in March had once again made it clear that the case was far from over. And there was more to come.

Preparing the rebuttal

Throughout the spring of 1947 Taylor stayed in constant contact with Washington where a machinery of legal experts worked day and night to research individual legal issues which could not be decided in Nuremberg. On 19 February OCC staff, including Taylor and Rapp, held a lengthy tele-conference with the War Department in which they covered a total of thirty-three different subjects. Most of the issues were concerned with the forthcoming trials, especially with preparations for the 'Hostage Case', but there were some items related directly to the Doctors' Trial. There was a dis-tinct difference between the legal foundation of the IMT, on the one hand, and the subsequent Nuremberg tribunals, on the other. Whereas the IMT was legally based on the London Agreement, the subsequent trials were based on Law No. 10, which had evolved from the London Agreement, but differed in some areas from it. Law No. 10, for example, did not make the connection between crimes against humanity and the planning and waging of aggressive war. Crimes against humanity, therefore, could be punishable whether or not they were committed in relation to the war. This meant that the tribunals could, at least in theory, prosecute crimes against humanity that had been committed prior to 1939. The more press-ing issue, however, was whether the tribunal as a whole was a legitimate body with the ability to sentence and punish Germans under Law No. 10. Under a narrow interpretation of the law, and considering the overall polit-ical situation, Taylor believed that the trials were on a 'sound legal footing':

> It is certainly within the legitimate powers of the occupying countries to set up special courts for the punishment of acts which clearly were crimes under German Law prior to the Nazis and were under any civilised system of law. In view of the fact that there is no central gov-ernment of Germany, the occupying powers are in many ways exercis-ing de facto sovereignty in Germany.[87]

On the basis of international law as extant at the time, the whole issue looked much more difficult and politically sensitive. The question which needed to be answered was whether the tribunal had jurisdiction for crimes against humanity 'committed within Germany against German nationals', which was particularly relevant for the murder of tens of thousands of handicapped in the 'euthanasia' programme. 'This matter raises obvious delicate questions of foreign policy as well as of law. Questions of sover-eignty and extent of permissible interference in internal affairs of other countries is suggested', Taylor told the Assistant Secretary of War.[88] His personal view was that a 'fundamental government policy aimed at persecution and extermination of political, racial and religious groups on a grand scale should be considered [a] crime at international law, even though [when] committed by a government against its own nationals'.[89] In other words, the size, intention, government sanctioning and systematic execution of a programme of mass murder was what mattered.

Apart from the diffuse and complex legal situation the prosecution was lacking sufficient evidence and witnesses who could be introduced in rebuttal of claims made by the defendants. Alexander was asked to interview a series of witnesses in Holland, who in the meantime had been located by OCC intelligence officers. In preparation for the ongoing Milch trial, and in order to formulate a viable rebuttal strategy, Alexander also began to study the American malaria experiments to which the defence had referred in the cross-examination of Leibbrand.[90] Following his witness testimony in the Milch trial on 14 February, in which he mostly discussed the Dachau freezing experiments,[91] and after becoming aware of some 'preposterous manoeuvres of the defence', Alexander travelled to Holland to talk to members of the Dutch medical resistance and to survivors of medical experiments.[92] The trip transplanted him back in time to his early post-war investigations and evoked memories of his Jewish childhood and youth. Visiting Holland in early 1947 in search of further incriminating evidence turned into a search for his own fragmented and scattered past.

Arriving in Rotterdam on 13 March he immediately visited Gerrit Hendrik Nales. Nales had been a window dresser in a clothing shop and former male nurse in the hospital at Natzweiler and Dachau concentration camp. He knew of visits to the camp by Karl Brandt, Gebhardt and Eugen Haagen, 'a really mean fellow' and one of Germany's typhus experts.[93] When Brandt came to Natzweiler in the summer of 1943 and again in the summer of 1944 nobody was permitted to leave the block. When he was about to arrive at Dachau in the winter of 1944–5, the nurses, including Nales, were ordered to clean the ward for his visit. 'Karl Brandt looked like a God. They looked like Gods. More uniform than soul. They never had souls, the Germans', he told Alexander.[94] Most importantly, though, Nales had kept a true copy of the Natzweiler death book which included detailed information about the victims' nationality and age. He had personal knowledge of dozens of gypsies who died as a result of Haagen's typhus experiments, and of his other victims whom he killed by poison gas experiments. All of them were gypsies. Nales had witnessed English and French parachutists being murdered in cold blood, and could identify the defendants Brandt, Gebhardt, Schröder and Rose. He remembered Rose visiting Haagen and saw the people from Auschwitz who were examined for the Strasbourg skeleton collection. For Alexander, writing to the OCCWC, he 'would make an excellent rebuttal witness'.[95]

Plate 26   Leo Alexander during a trial session. Nuremberg, Germany, 1946/7.

Shocking as this evidence was, Alexander was nonetheless able to travel relatively unaffected between the different spheres of reality. He enjoyed himself in Holland, not least because Phyllis had come from America for a visit on 14 March 1947.[96] He loved being paraded around as the American celebrity from Nuremberg whom people wanted to hear talking about Germany. Feelings of strong resentment and calls for long-term isolation

Plate 27 Members of the US prosecution team. Nuremberg, Germany, 1946/47.

and control of the German nation were still governing the public debate. Many of the people Alexander interviewed were vociferous in their opposition to a sovereign German state that could determine its own affairs. The end of March saw Alexander in the company of his Dutch relatives. They introduced him to the medical establishment and brought him into contact with former members of the Dutch resistance.[97] His brother-in-law, Lambert Hulst, had been active in the Dutch medical resistance and had connections to people like Brutel de la Rivière, the leader of the group. In Amsterdam he paid a visit to the Jewish district, especially to the Portuguese Jewish Synagogue which had been preserved with the help of conservation officers. Travelling to The Hague with his sister Lene he went on an extended sightseeing and shopping tour to soothe his bad conscience for not having stayed in touch with her throughout and after the war. On the way back they 'talked of old days'.[98] On 19 March Alexander was invited by the Dutch neurologist Willem Gerrit Sillevis Smit to lecture on 'The Social-Psychological Structure of the SS' at the Medical School of the Rijks University of Utrecht, a talk which he later published in the *Archives of Neurology and Psychiatry*.[99] The audience included interested Dutch doctors, members of the resistance and war crimes investigators like Franz G. Wyslicks, a sergeant in the Dutch army who was attached to the US war crimes authorities.

Among those listening to Alexander were some of the victims of the experiments. One of them was the gynaecologist Michel Steijns from Utrecht, who had miraculously survived the concentration camps of Sachsenhausen, Auschwitz and Mauthausen. As one of the doctors working in the experimental block, he was assigned to help deliver children to many women in the full knowledge that they would be gassed the next day. And the women knew too. Time and time again they begged him for an injection. It was one of Steijn's most painful memories. He never gave one.[100] Encounters with men like Steijn, who pressed Alexander to ensure that the 'medical criminals' would receive their 'righteous punishment', strengthened Alexander's sense of mission. They also made him realise the problems which lay ahead in re-establishing a belief in justice among the people of Europe. One of Steijn's most damning accusations was not directed against the Germans, but against the 'criminal indifference ' of the Dutch government-in-exile in London which, in his view, had not taken the 'slightest trouble to relieve their own prisoners in the concentration camps by sending [them] food via the International Red Cross, as every other nation did, thus turning us into pariahs in the camp'.[101] It was an accusation against the Dutch government which for decades would remain a taboo subject, and in some cases it still is today.

After completing his interviews in Utrecht Alexander headed back in his army jeep to Nuremberg. Accompanied by Phyllis and their driver Boris

Kreis, they stayed in Heidelberg for three days, from 4–7 April, in order to take part in the celebrations for the reopening of the Rhein bridge. There the unexpected happened. During a luncheon at Rüsselheim with Colonel Heath Twichel, Commanding Officer 555th Composite Group, Engineers, US Army, their luggage was stolen from the rear of the car while Kreis had dozed off. It was a large aeroplane-type of suitcase, the contents of which were worth more than 1400 US dollars, including Phyllis' valuable jewellery collection. Among the items was an antique pearl and gold brooch, made in Vienna and a heirloom from his beloved grandmother. Alexander immediately placed a stream of telephone calls and sent letters to all existing intelligence agencies in the area. As 'Consultant to the Secretary of War' he expected that the matter would be given high priority by agencies like CIC in Heidelberg. Adverts in the Rhein-Neckar newspaper and radio broadcasts were launched to ensure that he would retrieve his stolen goods. Because of their 'sentimental value', he told the intelligence authorities, he would 'like to leave no stone unturned'. The key suspect was an 'Algerian driver' from one of the French colonels attending the dinner. Then there were the 'Polish guards' patrolling the area, and 'of course', as Alexander pointed out, German civilians. The luggage was never found.

If nothing else, the incident sharpened Alexander's determination to bring the job at Nuremberg to a successful close. Some insight into his emotional state during these weeks is demonstrated in a poem by Werner Bergengruen which had intrigued Alexander. It shows that, although outwardly friendly and helpful to German observers and citizens, he was still deeply suspicious of the Germans:

> I loved this country with a burning heart
> And many were the messengers I sent
> In many shapes I used to walk among you
> But you would never know me in my many days.

> I was the trembling Jew pounding your doors at night
> The hunted victim, my shoes in hurting shreds,
> You called the hangman, set the bloodhounds on me
> And thus it was you served your highest God.

> I was the pale old woman my mind so full of madness
> Because you had no ears to hear my silent cries
> Of fear and fright, and you thought of more heroes
> Unborn as yet, and gave my ashes free.

> I was the orphan boy who on the Eastern highways
> Would grip your knees, begging for bread to eat,
> You did not see tomorrow's avenging angel,
> You gave me death, and strutted down your road.

I was your prisoner, your slave, your daily worker,
Deported, lost, cut off, whipped on to make your guns,
You turned your glance away from my unpleasing aspect,
And now I have returned your judge: You know me now.[102]

Alexander wanted to distribute Bergengruen's poem *The Last Epiphany* to 'those of the accused whose moral sense we would like to awaken'.[103] Only days after the Rüsselheim incident he sat down and completed his article on medical ethics standards. It is the last existent text written on ethics guidelines before the Nuremberg Code was actually read out as part of the judgement.

The Nuremberg Code

Since Leibbrand's testimony in January it had become central to the prosecution to broaden the remit of the trial. The prosecution was under intense pressure to clarify what it considered to be ethical and non-ethical research on humans. In order to do so, they needed a medical authority on research physiology whose scientific work corresponded to that of the defendants.[104] Taylor and his staff had to convince the court that there were distinct differences in the methods and conduct between German and Allied experiments on humans during the war. The 'Leibbrand incident' thus led to three interconnected initiatives by the prosecution: first, after his return to the United States, Ivy initiated the creation of a commission, the so-called 'Green Committee', in order to investigate the ethics of malaria experiments which had been performed in American penitentiaries during the war. The findings of the commission were to serve as evidence to repudiate the accusation of the defence that American medical research had been unethical.[105] Secondly, Alexander modified and edited his article on ethical and unethical human experimentation and probably discussed his medical ethics principles with Telford Taylor. And thirdly, to repudiate the claims made by the defence, the prosecution invited Ivy as a rebuttal witness to Nuremberg. Although active steps to recruit him as a rebuttal witness were not undertaken before April, the creation of the Green Committee stands in connection with Ivy's anticipated role to refute Leibbrand's testimony at the end of the trial. All of these steps were undertaken to ensure that the arguments put forward by the defence were repudiated. The Nuremberg Code originated in an environment of legal argument and counter-argument, pushed along, step by step, by internal and external initiatives.

On 28 March 1947 V. A. Fenger from Copenhagen, the General Secretary of the Danish Medical Association, expressed his concern about the moral aims and progress of the ISC (WC) in a letter to Taylor who passed it to McHaney for a reply. McHaney, in turn, passed the letter to Alexander's office to draft a reply on his behalf. There the letter lay unanswered for weeks while Alexander was on his fact-finding mission in Holland. Fenger had earlier proposed the creation of an International War Crimes Commission, but had encountered practical and theoretical objections until he was told that the French had already established such a commission under the presidency of Professor Legroux. For the Danish physicians it appeared that the scope of the commission was limited, that it did not deal effectively with the issue of 'euthanasia' and that it intended to report back only to physicians. This was 'absolutely impracticable', Fenger remarked.[106] He believed that the commission did not consider 'the constructive side of the problem – the *finding of means* [emphasis added] to prevent the future participation of physicians in similar crimes against humanity and against medical ethics'.[107] The French physicians appeared to favour the role of *la patrie* above the importance of medical ethics, a position which was shared neither by Scandinavian physicians nor, Fenger believed, would it be endorsed by British or American doctors. Fenger wanted to know whether 'international agreements' would suffice to prevent medical crimes from happening again, or whether the international community would need to create 'national and international rules of medical ethics, to the adherence to which all physicians should be bound by a strict professional oath'.[108]

Alexander's reply, written as if McHaney had written it, gave himself – not surprisingly – and the Americans most of the credit and authority for dealing with medical war crimes and medical ethics regulations. After the end of the Doctors' Trial Alexander would write a comprehensive report on all medical aspects, he told Fenger.[109] Like the Danes, the US prosecution felt that the ISC (WC) was 'rather slow in its functioning'. Accordingly, the commission had not carried out any meaningful investigations, but appeared to rely on evidence discovered by American and British war crimes investigators. Alexander knew that by playing down the importance of the ISC (WC), the Nuremberg tribunal and its expected ruling on medical ethics would gain in importance. But Alexander disagreed with Fenger about a new physicians' oath:

> The main means to prevent the participation of physicians in similar crimes in the future is in our opinion the upholding of human civil rights and the non-abrogation of the well-established laws concerning murder, manslaughter, assault and battery under all circumstances and for all groups of citizens and human beings everywhere. The crimes which these doctors committed were not a thing apart by themselves but contributed merely a part of the crime committed by the Nazi state ... A special oath would not have prevented these men from committing these acts.[110]

Although the AMA had adopted a specific code of ethics with regard to human experimentation in December 1946, Alexander believed that such an ethics code would 'hardly be kept by people expected to commit crimes as members of a criminal organisation'.[111] Alexander took Fenger's letter nonetheless to prompt him to revise his article on ethical and non-ethical experimentation in a ten-page memorandum. This he wrote on the same day that he drafted Fenger's reply on 15 April 1945.[112] The creation of the memorandum was triggered by two external factors. One was Fenger's initiative to put the prosecution on the spot about the 'constructive side' of the Doctors' Trial, that is the creation of laws, regulations or codes to prevent a repetition of medical crimes in the future. The other was the attempt by the defence to 'obscure the issue' by applying the *tu quoque* argument. It had by now become clear that the defence wanted to give the impression that experiments on humans were in themselves a criminal act or an act likely to involve crimes, thereby bringing the prosecution into an increasingly difficult position. The prosecution knew that if the position of the defence could be sustained, American physicians might be open to criminal charges. That might have been the reason why Alexander resorted to poignant irony at the beginning of the memorandum in order to brush off the arguments of the defence, and defend the use of human subjects in medical research. For Alexander the argument that the Nazi experiments had any similarity with experiments on human subjects in other countries was

> as preposterous as if a man accused of bank robbery which included the killing of several of the bank tellers would defend himself first with a dissertation on the moral worth or unworth of the monetary system, and then with the allegation that plenty of other people are entering banks and emerging with pockets full of money ... The abuse of such experimentation by the accused in the concentration camps can be held as little against the ethical and accepted practice of human experimentation as the practice of working people to death in concentration camps can be held as an argument against working.[113]

At the end of the memorandum Alexander listed the six principles which he had formulated in January in his article 'Ethical and Non-Ethical Experimentation on Human Beings' and in his affidavit of 25 January 1947. The article, however, has no date and addressee, and is, as the memorandum makes clear, 'a condensation of memoranda which I have written to the Prosecution authorities from time to time'.[114] It appears that in this conglomeration of articles, memoranda and affidavits Alexander made a mistake with regard to the precise dating of his medical ethics principles. For Alexander the memorandum of 15 April was the last and most authoritative document, especially because it had a date and was sent to the prosecution. It is this memorandum which he later used to corroborate his argument about his authorship of the Nuremberg Code. In his diary

Alexander recorded on 15 April: 'Worked on medical experimentation ... Answer to Danish doctor's letter.'[115]

What exactly happened? Alexander had written one article in January in which he summarised his previous memoranda, and for which he had received clearance by the military authorities in March to publish it. The article listed the six ethics principles, but contained no date or addressee.[116] He had also written an affidavit, dated 25 January, which likewise listed the six principles, but was probably not forwarded to Taylor. After his return from Holland he once again summarised his article in a ten-page memorandum which, yet again, listed the six principles and forwarded both – the memorandum and the article – to Taylor. The material was also meant to be sent to Fenger. For Alexander the memorandum and the article belonged conceptually together at the time. In retrospect he probably had confused the formulation of the memorandum on 15 April with the actual formulation of the six principles from January the same year. Alexander had quite simply lost himself in the mass of documents and memoranda, and, at the end, did not know what he had written and when he had done it.

Despite the scarcity of sources surrounding the origins of the Nuremberg Code, the reaction of the prosecution to Alexander's article and his six ethics principles has miraculously survived at Duke University, hidden away in dozens of cardboard boxes of Alexander's private papers. At the end of the ten-page memorandum is a handwritten note, one-and-a half pages long, in which the potential legal implications of a binding code of ethics standards are discussed.[117] The note is unsigned and was probably written by Taylor after receiving Alexander's paper for comment.[118] The author of the note was undoubtedly trained in legal argument. The note not only provides an insight into the different perspectives between the legal and the medical expert of the prosecution, and their communication with one another, but also shows how the individual principles of the experts were probably understood by the judges. It is also the first time that we find someone discussing a medical ethics code with ten requirements, instead of three or six. The author of the note started by asking Alexander 'who decides' under the 'code detailed in your paper' whether a certain experiment should be undertaken:

(A) Does the doctor himself make the determination that the 6 or 10 requirements are satisfied and proceed subject only to possible later legal proceedings by the subject or next of kin or the public prosecutor or (B) must he first obtain the approval of (a) local hospital, (b) local medical society, or (c) governmental body who decides that the requirements have been met? If (A), is the doctor protected from later liability if he reasonably in good faith believed he had the requisite skill etc. or does he err at his peril. If (B), scientific experimentation and progress, to the extent that without experimentation progress will not be made in the medical or other sciences, will be immersed in some sort of bureaucracy and red tape, although there may perhaps be greater safety to indigents, prisoners, defectives and other groups who are likely subjects for such work. These people are not likely to litigate afterward nor to have relatives, funds with which to obtain counsel etc. If you propose (A) aren't you fundamentally relying upon the ethical soundness, good judgement, and adherence to the Hippocratic Oath of your fellow physicians?[119]

Moreover, the author wanted Alexander to explain whether any nation since 1947, or the United Nations, had adopted this or a similar code in their respective country. The author advised Alexander that if this was not the case he should say so in order not to create the impression that these were generally accepted principles which enjoyed legitimacy within the international community. Alexander was also advised to shift 'some of this Nazi stuff' – which referred to examples of medical atrocities – into the footnotes. If the note was written by Taylor, which is likely, then Alexander's article received a rather unfavourable response from the head of the prosecution. At the end of the note the author asks: 'What is the point of the article?'[120] Unfortunately we do not know whether, and if so how, Alexander responded to these comments. Yet the note illustrates some of the ongoing discussions in the US prosecution.

During the trial the prosecution and the judges had realised that the formulation of a medical ethics code only made sense if the code was independent, at least in part, from the sphere of influence and decision-making of the medical profession. In their view a medical ethics code had to be, if at all, part of the judgement to attain the status of law. The court probably saw this as the only guarantee that the interpretation and application of medical ethics standards would not remain solely within the power of the medical profession. Those formulating the Code did not consider, however, that the passage of time and developments in medical science might challenge the legal and ethical validity of the Code. They also may not have taken into account that the Code was issued by an American tribunal, rather than by an international court of law.

The Rose testimony

Only days after Alexander had completed his memorandum the prosecution faced another major challenge to the case when Gerhard Rose, one of the intellectually most potent and medically experienced defendants, was called into the witness box. In his testimony, which lasted from 18–25 April, the former malarialologist and adviser to the chief of the medical services of the German air force, managed to present the prosecution as hypocritical in holding German doctors to account for experimental practices which American scientists had apparently followed as well.[121] It was not so much the actual quality of Rose's criticism of the trial proceedings that wrong-footed the prosecution, nor his legalistic and cunning approach to the questions by the bench, which more often than not amounted to perfect presentations of linguistic sophistry or plain denial, but his repeated and often sophisticated comparisons between German and Allied medical research. His claim that many experiments on humans by American scientists were involuntary allowed him to stress the similarities in research methods and objectives between German and Allied medical science. Rose's testimony increasingly blurred the boundaries between ethical and non-ethical research practices. For an impartial observer Rose's testimony once again raised the question of whether German medical researchers had really been that different from their Allied colleagues, an impression, once it had been propounded convincingly, that was hard to correct and could potentially undermine the medical case.

On 18 April, the first day of his testimony, Rose produced a comprehensive overview of his professional career.[122] He knew many of the American researchers and could comment in detail whether the work had been carried out on prisoners who were condemned to death, or whether they were voluntary or non-voluntary in nature. One of the most powerful examples was of the first experiment for the development of vaccination with living plague bacteria, carried out by the American scientist Richard P. Strong in 1911.[123] Strong had performed the experiment on approximately 900 prisoners after two German scholars had succeeded in immunising guinea pigs with a living plague bacilli. Not all of Strong's experimental subjects had been condemned to death, and experts assumed at the time that they had not been volunteers. No fatalities occurred. Although the experiment was successful, the medical community remained sceptical about the procedure until the mid-1920s when it was considered safe to apply to human beings. Apparently Strong's research was criticised by experts for being too dangerous. Another of Rose's examples referred to Strong's experiments on twenty-nine people to determine the cause of beriberi disease, a severe disease of the nervous system caused by a lack of vitamin B where the patient suffers from a loss of feeling or paralysis. This time the experiment was not only unsuccessful, but one person actually died of the disease. It was the perfect example, suggesting as it did that the work of German and Allied medical scientists was determined by the same underlying motives, 'a feeling of duty and responsibility' for the health of the people which in some unfortunate circumstances resulted in the death of experimental subjects.[124] Rose wanted to stress that German doctors, like their American counterparts, were driven by their duty for the greater good, the health and well-being of the national community for which certain sacrifices were apparently justified.[125]

By drawing attention to the research practices of a well-known and successful American researcher who could not easily be discredited, Rose put extra pressure on the prosecution to explain the differences between German and Allied medical science. He knew that if the prosecution failed to make a credible case, it would be difficult for the judges to condemn the German doctors for research practices which their US colleagues had been following as well. It also turned out that Alexander and his Boston colleagues had carried out an experimental study on beriberi in 1938, which directly linked Strong's research practices with those of the medical expert, and thus subtly, but not unnoticeably, undermined the moral high ground of the prosecution.[126]

Yet Rose's passionate attacks against the case of the prosecution were far from over. Sometimes he was close to losing his temper.[127] According to Rose, the central issue of the trial was whether the 'state had the right to force individuals to submit to medical experiments and to order doctors to conduct such experiments'.[128] On 23 April he remarked that other scientists, including Germans, had taken lesser risks in conducting experiments on humans than Strong; he also referred to the recent malaria experiments which had been performed on hundreds of American prison inmates. During Rose's cross-examination by the other defence lawyers it became clear that his testimony had fallen on fertile ground; Kurt Blome's attorney, for example, told the court that he was

> interested in determining whether Professor Blome can be declared a criminal for plague experiments which he did not conduct while some foreigner, who had conducted experiments, is not a criminal but is glorified.[129]

For the prosecution this was the moment to intervene if things were not to get out of hand. During Rose's testimony the prosecution frequently tried, but failed, to prohibit comparisons with American medical research. They also pointed out that the defendant was 'trying to attack the integrity of [the] Tribunal'.[130] Rose was clearly a man with considerable courtroom skills. For most of the time he denied having any knowledge of, or connection with, the camp experiments unless the prosecution placed irrefutable evidence before him. His answers to questions were circumspect, to say the least, and if pressed on a particular issue a sudden, convenient loss of memory served to stonewall any further line of enquiry. He sensed the direction of questions, evaded those he felt uncomfortable with, and refused to enter into any hypothetical discussion because he knew that the prosecution wanted him to admit that German experiments had been criminal in principle.[131] Sometimes he would question the authenticity of material evidence, at others refuse out of hand incriminating testimony of witnesses where, according to him, the prosecution had succeeded in producing a statement 'by clever questioning'.[132] After a set of hypothetical questions, Rose retorted that he 'should prefer to discuss facts. Discussions of hypothetical questions are very interesting, but not in the situation in which I find myself at the moment.'[133]

Rose's situation was indeed problematic, especially with regard to the Buchenwald experiments. During his visit to the camp in March 1942, Rose had neither questioned whether the subjects were volunteers nor whether they had legally been condemned to death for a particular offence. His entire attitude before and after the visit suggested that, despite his subsequent protestations, he had come around to the idea of using the new opportunities which had been created by the almost limitless availability of research subjects in the camps.[134] Lacking any sense of remorse or moral outrage about the experiments, Rose managed to portray himself and his profession as the unfortunate victims of brutal state oppression. Yet, on 25 April, at the end of the cross-examination, the prosecution made headway by confronting him with the correspondence he had with Joachim Mrugowsky, head of the Hygiene Institute of the Waffen-SS and co-defendant at the Doctors' Trial. It was a contact he had previously denied. In one of the letters Rose told Mrugowsky that he had a 'number of samples of a new murine virus typhus vaccine' at his disposal and that 'it would be desirable to know if this vaccine showed in your and Ding's experimental arrangement at Buchenwald an effect similar to that of the classic virus vaccine. Would you be able to have such an experimental series carried out?'[135] The evidence not only showed that Rose had obviously lied about his contacts with Mrugowsky and his assistant, but that he had himself initiated some of the fatal Buchenwald experiments. As a result of this particular set of experiments six people died.[136] Yet, on balance, Rose had proved to be a worthy match for the prosecution.

On the first day that Rose had given his testimony, the visitors' gallery had been filled by a number of high-ranking Allied military officials, including General Clay who had come to see the progress of the trial for himself.[137] Their visit heightened the tensions among the prosecution staff. Although Alexander was seconded to prepare part of the cross-examination, which McHaney began on 24 April, it soon became apparent that the prosecution had not sufficiently discredited Rose's case.[138] The judges, now seriously alerted to the complexity of the ethical issues involved, requested an 'adviser to the court' from the Office of Chief of Counsel for War Crimes.[139] Their request was an active intervention to have an international and unbiased authority explain to the court what the criteria for ethical and non-ethical experimentation on humans appeared to be. It marked the beginning of the active involvement of the judges in considering whether it might become necessary to establish a set of professional standards as part of their judicial duty. For the judges by now, it was clear that no such standards existed. To find the accused doctors guilty of crimes or acquit

230

Plate 28 Gerhard Rose, defendant in the Doctors' Trial, in his cell. Rose was a leading malarialogist and adviser to the chief of the medical services of the German air force. He was sentenced to life imprisonment. Nuremberg, Germany, 1946/7.

Plate 29   High-ranking military officials and Allied observers at the Nuremberg Doctors' Trial. Nuremberg, Germany, 1946/7.

them they not only had to specify the law on which the judgement was based but also the ethical guidelines which the accused had either violated or not violated.

In responding to the request on 29 April, Alexander proposed Ivy. He felt that there would be a conflict of interest if he 'serve[d] as advisor to the prosecution and the court at the same time'.[140] He also knew that he did not qualify as an expert in immunology and public health. Ivy, on the other hand, was well-suited as a rebuttal witness, given his international standing and expertise as a research physiologist. 'It is my opinion', Alexander noted,

> that in this matter which is of great importance in the trial, the voice of an expert should be heard who, himself, had worked in that field ... The expert should be particularly familiar with all experiments especially in the field of virus and rickets research in the United States during the war so that he would be able to point out the fundamental differences in manner of performance of these experiments from his personal acquaintance with these researches.[141]

Ivy was the obvious candidate. He had visited Nuremberg in mid-January to see how the trial was progressing and had devised strategies to counter the defence.[142] In March he had addressed the issue of medical ethics and war crimes in a lecture about the role of moral philosophy of medicine at the University of Nebraska College of Medicine.[143] At the beginning of April, Ivy had also made representations to the War Department to discuss an International Scientific Commission on medical war crimes and formulate a code of medical ethics which could be used within the framework of the Doctors' Trial. One of the officials noted: 'He [Ivy] is interested in an international code of ethics on experimentation on humans which would condemn Nazi practices and be a guide for the future.'[144] Significantly, Ivy also suggested that the commission could complete its report within six months and that Alexander could do all the necessary 'leg work'.[145] To be downgraded, even if only symbolically, will not have escaped Alexander's attention. Yet he did not mind too much as long as the outcome was the successful conviction of the defendants. He knew that Ivy was one of the most strategic and politically minded men who was fully aware of the ethical dimensions of the trial.

Rose's testimony and the call for a second medical expert alarmed the prosecution. It was far from certain whether the available evidence would suffice to convince the judges of the guilt of the defendants. A couple of days later, at the beginning of May, Alexander departed for Austria to see whether he could find further witnesses to the experiments. Although he obtained a number of affidavits from witnesses, the journey had another, more personal dimension, namely to visit the graves of his parents and grandparents in Vienna. In some sense Alexander needed these occasional intermissions from the day-to-day reality in Nuremberg. Trips to the Netherlands or Austria were part and parcel of an ongoing search for his own past, journeys back in time to find out what had happened to all the relatives and friends of his family. On 7 May he noted in his diary: 'Visited fathers' and mothers' grave. It was recently taken care of ... Took pictures.'[146] On 8 May he returned to put flowers on the grave. Later that day he received the news that his uncle had been transported to Poland, and had probably perished.[147] On 10 May he visited the former family home in the Skodagasse.[148] On 11 May he went to the central cemetery to pay his respects to his grandfather and grandmother. 'Cleared the shrubs; laid down flowers; Phyllis planted begonias. After lunch to polyclinic. Saw father's bust.'[149] Nuremberg was his chance to return home and recover some of the traces, as well as memories, that had been left and not destroyed by recent events. On 16 May it was time to go back to Nuremberg, in time to supply the prosecution with additional material and affidavits in the case against Wilhelm Beiglböck and Konrad Schäfer.

Yet a couple of weeks later Alexander was once again conspicuously absent from Nuremberg, giving a talk in Amsterdam, exactly at the time when Ivy began to testify as a rebuttal witness.[150] Alexander surely enjoyed the attention he was receiving from his Dutch peers. Always proud of himself, he told his wife that the speech had been 'a great success' and that 'there was a great deal of interest in it'.[151] On 14 June he returned to Nuremberg to hear the conclusion of Ivy's statement, not knowing that during his three-day absence the judges had extrapolated two further ethics principles from Ivy's testimony which they later incorporated in the Nuremberg Code.[152] As it turned out, Alexander was not present when parts of the Code were formulated at Nuremberg.

Andrew Ivy

Ivy's testimony lasted four days, from 12–16 June 1947.[153] His appearance in court as the prosecution's rebuttal witness sparked fierce controversy. The defence objected to the presentation of Ivy as 'an expert on everything'. Although his credentials read like a *Who's Who* of scientific organisations and medical associations, with more than 900 articles published, Ivy was less an expert on aviation medicine than he wanted the court to believe. In fact, he had written only two articles in this field. Both had been published after the war and after it had become clear that he would probably serve as a medical expert in the Doctors' Trial. It is quite possible that Ivy published the two papers in order to establish his credentials in yet another field.[154]

The suggestion that Ivy attempted to manipulate the outcome of the trial is further corroborated when we look at some of his policy initiatives in

1946 and early 1947. In his testimony, Ivy stated that the United States had specific research standards for research on humans which were laid down by the American Medical Association (AMA). He gave the impression that these rules were generally accepted research practice in America.[155] It turned out, however, that they were of a suspiciously recent origin and had been drafted by Ivy himself. Having studied the prosecution evidence in 1946, he had reported his views on permissible human experimentation to the AMA's trustees who adopted his recommendations.[156] During cross-examination Ivy admitted that the principles had been published by the AMA on 28 December 1946, nineteen days after the opening of the trial. No such published principles had existed for the American research context before this time. Moreover, the publication of the AMA principles on medical ethics in human experimentation had been made in anticipation of Ivy's testimony in the trial:

> *Ivy*: I submitted to them [AMA] some ethical principles and asked them to take action regarding, or to make a statement regarding the ethical principles of the American Medical Association in regard to the question of human beings as subjects in medical experiments on the basis of their principles of medical ethics.
> *Sauter*: This was December 1946?
> *Ivy*: Yes.
> *Sauter*: Did that take place in consideration of this trial?
> *Ivy*: Well, that took place as a result of my relation to the trial, yes.
> *Sauter*: Before December of 1946 were such instructions in printed form in existence in America?
> *Ivy*: No. They were understood only as a matter of common practice.[157]

The defence not only exposed the lack of international and published ethics standards on human experimentation, but also discredited Ivy's attempt at exonerating American medical research practice which had been criticised during Leibbrand's testimony in January. Ivy, after having returned to Chicago, had suggested to Illinois governor Dwight Green in March that a committee be set up to examine the ethics of human experimentation, especially the malaria experiments which had been carried out at Stateville Prison.[158] He offered to serve as the chairman of the so-called 'Green Committee'. When Ivy finally gave his testimony at Nuremberg, he presented the findings of a non-existent and not-yet-functioning committee to the court. As the correspondence between the six members of the committee shows, by June 1947 the committee had not yet found 'a convenient date and time' for its first session.[159] The final report of the committee exonerating American malaria experiments was not submitted before December 1947.[160] Pressed by the defence on the nature of the Green Committee, Ivy was coming close to perjury. When asked whether there had been discussions among the committee members whether coercion had been exercised in the experiments, he cautiously answered in the first-person singular: 'Yes, I was concerned about that question.' Not satisfied with the answer, the defence queried again: 'There were discussions about that?'[161] 'Not necessarily with others, but there was always consideration of that in my own mind.'[162] What Ivy was saying, in effect, was that discussions on the ethics of human experimentation had been carried out in his own mind; he, as the head of the Green Committee had come to certain conclusions as a result of discussions with himself.[163] When questioned about the origins of the Green Committee and about a potential link between the committee and the trial, Ivy appears not to have been entirely truthful. He told the court that the committee had been established 'according to the best of his recollection' in December 1946. But he must have known that the committee was just three months old since he himself had proposed its creation. To the question of whether the 'formation of this committee' had anything to do with the fact that the trial was going on, he replied: 'There is no connection between the action of this committee and this trial.'[164] This is perhaps the point where Ivy came closest to perjuring himself.

Ivy's testimony was nevertheless bad news for the defence. On the first day the defence mainly sat in silence, unsure how to respond. Not only had they not expected such a distinguished medical expert at the end of the trial, evidenced by the physical absence of some of the lawyers, but Ivy's presentation raised questions that the lawyers felt unable to answer. On the second day they went on to the attack, objecting to the attempt to 'overthrow the entire evidence' of the defence, especially at a time where the prosecution knew the 'entire case of the defence by the statements of the defendants themselves, as well as by the documents the defence has submitted'.[165] They also objected to the fact that they had only one hour after the end of the daily proceedings in which they could discuss the various issues with their clients. This was made worse by the inadequacy of the location, where communication between the lawyers and their respective clients was only possible through a window protected by barbed wire, making the conferences exhausting and ineffective for all parties. As a result of this dispute the defence requested permission to have the witness cross-examined by their clients, which, although highly unusual, was granted by the tribunal.[166] The bench also permitted the defence to consult with their clients at any time or to be excused from the tribunal upon request.[167] The tribunal thereby wanted to show that the court procedure could be adapted to the specific circumstances of the case in order to achieve the highest degree of fairness in the trial.

The most poignant part of Ivy's testimony came when Gerhard Rose cross-examined the witness. Rose quickly established Ivy's limited expertise in a number of scientific areas, for example, in the case of Reed's yellow fever experiments. 'There is no point in asking further questions ... if you are not informed about it', Rose replied.[168] In another instance Rose showed that Ivy had misrepresented a paper by Strong on beriberi by claiming that none of the experimental subjects had died. As was clear from the paper, one of the patients had died from the disease. Ivy was forced to admit this embarrassing mistake.[169] As for the malaria experiments on American prisoners, Ivy was unable to testify what the strains of malaria were and had to retract the notion that he was an expert on malaria. He also had to admit that he was not an expert in the field of typhus, that he had not checked certain references in the papers he had introduced as evidence, and could not comment on the experiments by a number of European scientists.[170] Furthermore, he had no knowledge of human experiments by his American colleagues McCalla and Brereton, who had infected two persons with Rocky Mountain spotted fever and did not know that these experiments had been criticised in a number of American medical journals. He also did not know of Adler's experiments, who had infected cancer patients with kala-azar with the result that all five patients died. Moreover, Ivy found himself on slippery ground when stating that malaria experiments on humans were scientifically and ethically justified, even to the extent where they were endangering the life of the subject if the subjects were volunteers and the hazards had been adequately explained.[171]

Despite these momentary victories for the defence, Ivy's testimony as a rebuttal witness served another, more important purpose. He helped to explain the boundaries between ethical and non-ethical human experimentation, and clarify some of the loose ends for the judges in shaping a code of medical ethics. In a series of probing questions by Judge Sebring, the bench tried to extract what criteria had to be fulfilled to make human experiments ethical, and therefore legally permissible. Sebring's questions, however, were not directed towards the most important issues of human experimentation, like voluntary consent or the importance of animal experimentation, nor did the bench interfere when Ivy read his three ethics principles into the record. We need to understand that by June 1947 the judges had, in all probability, laid down some if not most of the ethics principles as we later find them in the Nuremberg Code.

At the end of June, before the judges finalised the judgement, testimonies by a number of prosecution witnesses focused attention back on the essential nature of the trial. Above all this was a murder case as people had been killed in cold blood and used for previously unimaginable experiments. Camp inmates had been maltreated and tortured to death in the experiments. They had not enjoyed any form of protection, had been forced against their will to participate in the experiments, and had suffered the most severe injuries, disabilities and death. This was not some philosophical seminar on the ethics of human experimentation. On 27 June Karl Höllenreiner, former prisoner at Dachau concentration camp and victim of

Beiglböck's seawater experiments, shocked the court when he suddenly jumped from his seat in the witness box, ran to the dock and slapped his former tormentor Beiglböck in the face.[172] 'This bastard has ruined my life', he shouted while the guards overpowered him. Alexander's examination of the witness ten days earlier had given a clear indication that Höllenreiner was psychologically unstable. The witness had told Alexander that he developed a 'tremendous feeling of inner rage' whenever he thought of the 'humiliating experience' to which he had been subjected at Dachau.[173] Höllenreiner's arms and fingers had been shaking throughout the examination. In what he experienced as a 'powerless rage' the witness could 'see the doctor in front of him who ... had ruined his life and killed three of his comrades'.[174]

Alexander and the prosecution obviously wanted to see a man like Höllenreiner in the witness box at the end of the trial, as a poignant reminder of individual human tragedy. In the subsequent report about the incident, Alexander pointed out that Höllenreiner might even have 'benefited clinically from the accidental outburst which he experienced in the court room' and that he should be permitted to 'tell his story'.[175] Although sentenced to a ninety-day prison term for having 'dishonoured the Tribunal' Höllenreiner was released on bail after Alexander had vouched on his behalf.[176] A couple of days later he was permitted to conclude his testimony.[177] On 30 June the court was presented with further chilling testimony by two Dutch witnesses, Constantyn Johan Broers and Gerrit Hendrik Nales. In March, Alexander had secured Nales' affidavit in the Netherlands, knowing that he would make an 'excellent rebuttal witness'.[178] Nales provided the court with a detailed description of fatal typhus and poison gas experiments at Natzweiler concentration camp, identified many of the Nuremberg defendants, and could remember the names of individual victims, as well as when and where they had been murdered. His testimony was further corroborated by what became known as Exhibit 560, the 'Death Book, Natzweiler', a complete record of all people killed at Natzweiler which included their nationality and date of birth. Together with two fellow inmates, Nales had copied the book from the original death book in the camp.[179] The testimony of these witnesses served a dual purpose. Not only were they meant to refute the claims made by some of the defendants, but, more significantly, to make a strong and unambiguous impression on the court. On 1 July Alexander told his wife that the strategy had worked:

> The two Dutch witnesses, Mr. Nales and Mr. Broers went on the stand yesterday and were a great success. Many people thought they were the best witnesses of the trial. The fact that Mr. Nales knew exactly the names, dates and places of birth in regard to most of Haagen's victims added an air of definiteness which helped the judges to find themselves

on familiar ground, namely on the ground of murder cases of definite specific persons. After each name he was asked whether he saw the corpses and he said 'yes' and in most cases added specific statements that he, himself, washed the corpse before sending it to the morgue or the autopsy room. The great definiteness was impressive and a sort of relief from the horror of the nameless murdered masses which we dealt with on so many other occasions.[180]

In contrast to the emotive nature of the witnesses' testimonies, the closing argument by the prosecution concentrated all minds on the role of the law which needed to be applied. Above all it was essential to merge Hippocratic medical ethics with patient-centred human rights. The prosecution made it unequivocally clear that the principle of informed voluntary consent stood at the centre of the case. For Taylor and his team it was of central importance that the judges would accept this principle, and would give it legal standing through the judgement. This was seen as the only way to enforce, and indeed create, international as well as German law.[181]

Closing arguments

On the morning of 14 July the chief prosecutor in the Doctors' Trial, James McHaney, summed up the case for the prosecution. He started off by stressing the fairness of the trial which the defendants themselves 'in the days of their pomp and glory, never gave to any men'.[182] Considering the anticipated legal implications of the trial, fairness of the procedure was central to the case. Underlying the case were the legal principles of war crimes and crimes against humanity as laid down in the London Charter and Law No. 10. For the prosecution it was important to convince the court, and indeed the German public, that no retroactive law was going to be applied. The controversy surrounding this issue was never fully resolved and reverberates to this day in contemporary war crimes trials. McHaney quoted Taylor's description of the London Charter and Law No. 10 as 'important items in this stream of acts and declarations through which international law grows; they are way stations from which the outlook is both prospective and retrospective, but they are not retroactive'.[183] Taylor himself had referred to the lawyer Henry L. Stimson from the US War Department in clarifying the specific nature of the law which was applied at Nuremberg. According to Stimson,

> international law is not a body of authoritative codes or statutes; it is the gradual expression, case by case, of the moral judgements of the civilised world. As such, it corresponds precisely to the common law of Anglo-American tradition. We can understand the law of Nuremberg only if we

see it for what it is – a great new case in the book of international law, and not a formal enforcement of codified statutes.[184]

'A great new case in the book of international law' is what Alexander had always wanted the Doctors' Trial to be, a trial in which the judgement would be something 'really monumental, both historical and legal'.[185] For the prosecution there had never been any doubt about the far-reaching jurisdiction of the court. Crimes committed by German nationals against German nationals, as, for example, in the 'euthanasia' programme, clearly fell under the jurisdiction of the tribunal. According to Law No. 10, section 1(c), crimes against humanity constituted crimes per se, committed against *any civilian population*, and were therefore applicable where or whenever a state had commissioned systematic criminal offences against its own people.[186]

For the most part McHaney maintained that the defendants were on trial for crimes of murder, crimes which had undoubtedly been committed, and with which the defendants were inextricably connected. Under Paragraph 6 and 11 of counts II and III of the indictment (war crimes and crimes against humanity) the German doctors were charged with criminal experiments on human subjects. The criminal nature of these experiments had been established by clear and public proof so that no one, as Taylor had previously put it, can ever doubt that they were fact and not fable. But at the very core of the trial stood the fact that the experimental subjects had not been volunteers:

> That, of course, is the cornerstone of this case ... [I]t is the most funda-
> mental tenet of medical ethics and human decency that the subjects vol-
> unteer for the experiment after being informed of its nature and
> hazards. This is the clear dividing line between criminal and what may
> be non-criminal. If the experimental subjects cannot be said to have vol-
> unteered, then the inquiry need proceed no further. Such is the simplic-
> ity of this case.[187]

For the prosecution the question of what exactly constituted a volunteer was of mere academic relevance since the doctors never had the slightest intention of using volunteers.[188] There were, of course, other conditions which needed to be satisfied so that experiments on humans were ethically and legally permissible. McHaney used the opportunity to read into the record a number of Ivy's and Alexander's ethics principles to ensure that the judges could easily use this material in the judgement:

> The experiment must be based [*sic*] on the results of animal experimen-
> tation and a knowledge of the natural history of the disease under study
> and designed in such a way that the anticipated results will justify the

performance of the experiment.[189] This is to say that the experiment must be such as to yield results for the good of society unprocurable by other methods of study and must not be random and unnecessary in nature.[190] Moreover, the experiment must be conducted by scientifically qualified persons[191] in such manner as to avoid all unnecessary physical and mental suffering and injury.[192] If there is an a priori reason to believe that death or disabling injury might occur, the experimenters must serve as subjects themselves along with the non-scientific personnel[193] ... The person planning, ordering, supporting, or executing the experiment is under a duty, both moral and legal, to see to it that the experiment is properly performed. This duty cannot be delegated.[194] It is surely incumbent on the doctor performing the experiment to satisfy himself that the subjects volunteered after having been informed of the nature and hazards of the experiment. If they are not volunteers, it is his duty to report to his superiors and discontinue the experiment.[195]

McHaney's summary provided the judges with core elements of seven of the principles as they stand in the Nuremberg Code. Though the nature of human experimentation was at the heart of the trial, the conditions under which the experiments had been carried out likewise elicited a lengthy response from the prosecution. The experiments had been performed in concentration camps under the most appalling conditions and on concentration camp inmates. None of the defendants could possibly deny that they did not know that these were places of violent death and untold misery. This fact was 'known during the war to people all over the world'.[196] It was impossible that the defendant had entered these places and said

> bring forward the subjects. I see no evil; I hear no evil; I speak no evil ...
> The defendants with their own eyes open used the oppressed and persecuted victims of the Nazi regime to wring from their wretched and unwilling bodies a drop of scientific information at a cost of death, torture, mutilation, and permanent disability.[197]

For crimes such as these, justice demanded 'stern retribution'. Some of the defendants were, of course, more guilty than others, especially when they had the power to stop things. Karl Brandt, after having been appointed as General Commissioner of the Führer for the Sanitary and Health System in 1942, was not only the highest authority in the Reich for medical services, but, more importantly, could issue instructions that no experiments on concentration camp inmates would be carried out. This he had never done. Nor, so it seems, had he ever intended to do so. According to McHaney his guilt was therefore beyond any reasonable doubt. Others in the dock had likewise committed the most unimaginable crimes, but hoped that they would be pardoned because of their subordinate role in the regime. The most breathtaking of defence arguments came from Rudolf Brandt, chief of Himmler's personal staff, whom Gebhardt described as an 'extraordinarily irrelevant type-writer' but who was in fact the co-ordinating link to some of the most atrocious medical experiments. From a total of more than 160 000 letters which he had received or produced as Himmler's right-hand man, *only* 113 letters showed his direct complicity with the crimes under consideration in the trial. He therefore wanted the tribunal to declare that he was 'really not very guilty'.[198] It was this kind of utilitarian mathematics which had also been applied to sanction many of the concentration camp experiments. In June Ivy had made it clear that 'there is no justification in killing five people in order to save the lives of 300'.[199] What was needed for the future was not only a different kind of medical ethic, but a different kind of mathematics for which the life of the individual would be sacred.

> This Tribunal must solemnly reaffirm an entirely different type of mathematics; mathematics in the light of religious and humane education which teaches that the value of even one human life is infinite, which means, again mathematically expressed, that one times infinity is just as infinite as 500 times infinity.[200]

McHaney's closing argument was far-reaching in its condemnation of Nazi medical atrocities and also with regard to the general changes which were needed in re-educating German society, whether in the field of medicine or the education of children and students. With hindsight the prosecution expressed a certain wisdom in that they were perfectly aware of the relative effectiveness of medical ethics codes to prevent doctors from violating the lives of patients. For McHaney and his colleagues it appeared that the physicians' conscience and respect for the rights and dignity of individual human lives, inculcated in years of training and practice, could ultimately function as the best safeguard against human and civil rights violations in medical science. Or, as Ivy had formulated it, 'there is no state or politician under the sun who could force me to perform a medical experiment which I thought was morally unjustified'.[201] For the prosecution 'all medical men and decent people of the civilised world' held this opinion, and it was time for the judges not only to reaffirm this view but to issue a stern 'condemnation of the acts of these defendants'.[202]

The closing arguments for the defence were heard between 14 and 18 July.[203] Finally, on 19 July Brandt gave his personal statement. Each of the defendants had been allotted a maximum of ten minutes to make such a statement.[204] Standing next to the microphone in the middle of the defendants' box, his speech combined notions of idealism with a half-baked philosophical discourse about medical ethics in human experimentation. Brandt's

242 Justice at Nuremberg

defence came down to arguing that he had done nothing wrong except obey the orders of the head of state. It was a defence which the bench had to endure many more times. 'There is a word which seems so simple' he rhapsodised before pausing rhetorically, 'and that is the word order, and yet how atrocious are its implications, how immeasurable are the conflicts which hide behind the word. Both affected me, to obey and to give orders, and both are responsibilities. I am a doctor and before my conscience there is this responsibility as the responsibility towards men and towards life.'[205] Brandt believed that it was 'immaterial for the *experiment* [emphasis added]' whether it was conducted with or without the informed consent of the experimental subject. He assigned a value to the human experiment itself without considering the human subjects involved. The value of the experiment apparently was 'much deeper' than the life of the individual:

Can I, as an individual, remove myself from the community? Can I be outside and without it? Could I, as a part of this community, evade it by saying I want to thrive in this community, but I don't want to sacrifice anything for it, not bodily and not with my soul. I want to keep my conscience clear. Let them see how they get along.[206]

For Brandt such a position was clearly untenable. He believed that he and the community were 'somehow identical'. Continuing his rhetoric, he asked the court to have sympathy with both his action and inaction:

Would you believe that it was a pleasure to me to receive the order to start Euthanasia? For fifteen years I had laboured at the sick-bed and every patient was to me like a brother, every sick child I worried about as if it had been my own. And then that hard fate hit me. Is that guilt? Was it not my first thought to limit the scope of Euthanasia? Did I not, the moment I was included, try to find a limit as well as finding a cure for the incurable? Were not the professors of the Universities there? Who could there be who was more qualified?[207]

Brandt defended himself against the charge of 'inhuman conduct'. He certainly did not want to be seen as being on the same level as some of the SS murderers from the occupied Eastern territories. Against such a charge, he felt he had the 'right to human treatment'. He then repeated his deep conviction of the moral justification of the 'euthanasia' programme. His simplistic view of this complex problem must have been hard to stomach for some spectators after eight months of sustained and appalling evidence:

I am deeply conscious that when I said 'Yes' to Euthanasia I did so with the deepest conviction, just as it is my conviction today, that it was right. Death can mean relief. Death is life – just as much as birth. *It was never meant to be murder* [emphasis added]. I bear this burden but it is not the burden of crime. I bear this burden of mine, though, with a heavy heart as my responsibility. Before it, I survive and prevail, and before my conscience, as a man and as a doctor.[208]

Brandt's closing speech made it clear that he had genuinely believed in the righteousness of the killing operation. His arguments were nevertheless unconvincing; neither did he give any explanation as to why he had accepted a commission from someone who was governing a regime which was obviously barbarous and criminal, nor why he believed that it had not been necessary to supervise an unprecedented government programme which aimed at killing part of the country's population. It may not have been envisaged as murder, but for the court it was de facto murder beyond any reasonable doubt.

Communicating evidence

Before addressing the issue of authorship it is worth looking at the material evidence which was at the disposal of the judges when they were writing the Code. Ivy's testimony in June as well as the closing argument of the prosecution allow us to speculate about some of the means of communication between the prosecution and the bench. Evidence from the trial record suggests that the judges, in addition to the material supplied directly by the prosecution, made use of the trial transcript in formulating the Code. The transcript was evidence in itself, given in open court, under oath, and, most importantly, on record. The judges might have preferred to base their opinion about professional medical ethics standards on the trial transcript rather than on the memoranda of the medical experts. This may explain the conspicuous absence of any of the expert memoranda in the judges' papers. Yet we must assume that in all likelihood they had copies of, or at least access to, this material. In the end they seem to have used both.

Of central importance in formulating the Code were Ivy's three principles from the autumn of 1946, which had been adopted and published by the American Medical Association in December, and which had also been read into the trial record in June 1947. Then there were Alexander's six principles from January and April 1947 respectively, which, we must assume, were in the hands of the judges, and, of course, the summary of Ivy's and Alexander's memoranda which had been read into the record by McHaney in July. By comparing the bulk of this material with the Nuremberg Code it becomes clear that there are a total of eight principles that are almost identical to those in the actual Code.

For some of Alexander's principles this is particularly apparent. Some of them were used as they stand in the Nuremberg Code (see pp. 256f.). The first sentence of principle five of Alexander's second memorandum is an exact copy of principle six of the Code:

> The degree of risk taken should never exceed that determined by the humanitarian importance of the problem to be solved by the experiment.[209]

The first sentence of principle four of Alexander's memorandum hardly differs from principle seven in the Code. Whereas Alexander's principle four says that 'adequate preparations must be made and proper facilities be provided to aid the experimental subject against any remote chance of injury, disability, or death', principle seven of the Code says:

> Proper preparation should be made and adequate facilities provided to protect the experimental subject against even remote possibilities of injury, disability, or death.[210]

Only the words 'proper' and 'adequate' have been changed, and instead of 'must' the code speaks of 'should'. By using the word 'should' the judges wanted to highlight that this was a professional code of conduct rather than a universal law which was legally binding. In other words, by June 1947 the judges had clarified most of the ethical principles for themselves, on the basis of the existing record. This then explains the specific nature of Sebring's questions to Ivy which resulted in the formulation of principles nine and ten of the Code.

On 12 June, the first day of Ivy's testimony, Sebring questioned the witness as to the circumstances in which a volunteer should be allowed to drop out of an experiment before its conclusion, adding 'I mean be allowed to drop out of his responsibility on his own request.' Ivy made it clear that he had always permitted 'the volunteer subjects to withdraw from the experiment whenever they expressed the desire to do so, regardless of the fact that they agreed at the start to continue until they were released'.[211] Principle nine of the Nuremberg Code thus reads:

> During the course of the experiment the human subject should be at liberty to bring the experiment to an end if he had reached the physical or mental state where continuation of the experiment seems to him to be impossible.[212]

Once having clarified the rights of the experimental subject to withdraw from the experiment, Sebring wanted to clarify the duties and responsibilities of the experimenting scientists:

> *Sebring*: Let us assume that at the outset and prior to the beginning of the experiment the person who is going to conduct the experiment

advised the potential experimental subjects that he himself was going to reserve for himself the decision, the sole decision, whether an experimental subject would be allowed to drop out during the course of the experiment and let us assume that the experiment started and that, because of extreme physical or mental distress or discomfort, one of the experimental subjects expressed a desire to drop out and let us assume that the man conducting the experiment determined that they should not drop out because prior to the beginning of the experiment he had warned them that he would reserve that decision for himself, would you think that after that time that experimental subject would be in the sense of a volunteer?[213]

'No', was Ivy's response, 'because when you coerce or cause a volunteer subject to continue as a subject you can expect cheating and unreliable cooperation and, hence, that challenges the scientific nature of the complete experimental design, and at the same time you are exercising coercion.'[214] Principle ten of the Nuremberg Code thus reads:

> During the course of the experiment the scientist in charge must be prepared to terminate the experiment at any stage, if he had probable cause to believe, in the exercise of the good faith, superior skill, and careful judgement required of him, that a continuation of the experiment is likely to result in injury, disability, or death to the experimental subject.[215]

The judges now only needed to formulate all the principles in a more legalistic and general language and amend or modify minor changes which had arisen as part of Ivy's testimony. So by the time they drafted the final version of the Code they would have checked the wording of Ivy's earlier ethics principles against those he had read into the record, and amended their own principles accordingly. A case in point is principle three of the Nuremberg Code. In Ivy's 1946 memorandum, he stated that the experiment to be performed 'should be so designed and based on the results of animal experimentation that the anticipated results will justify the performance of the experiment'. In his testimony in June 1947, he stated that the experiment 'must be so designed and based on the results of animal experimentation *and a knowledge of the natural history of the disease under study* [emphasis added] that the anticipated results will justify the performance of the experiment'. Principle three of the Nuremberg Code reads:

> The experiment should be so designed and based on the results of animal experimentation and a knowledge of the natural history of the disease or other problem under study that the anticipated results will justify the performance of the experiment.[216]

The only amendment the judges made in comparison to the principle as stated in the record was the inclusion of the phrase 'or other problem' in order to lift the principle on to a more general legalistic plane and make it generally applicable. This shows that the Nuremberg Code was drafted in stages and that those who formulated it used a great variety of material in the process. The creation of individual principles was part of an ongoing process for the judges to clarify the ethical issues which had arisen during the trial. In doing so, they relied on four main channels of information. Firstly, on the material supplied by the prosecution, including the various memoranda which reflected the discourse within the prosecution and views from outside experts. Secondly, informal discussion with members of the prosecution and with expert witnesses, mostly with Taylor, Alexander and Ivy, who advised them on individual questions related to medical ethics. We know, for example, that Alexander was corresponding with Judge Sebring as late as 15 July 1947.[217] Thirdly, the actual court hearings and trial transcript provided one of the main sources that shaped their opinion about the degree of guilt of individual defendants, both from a legal and a medical ethics perspective. Finally, and most importantly, their own views and discussions on the matter which they held for most of the time in camera. Except for the so-called executive sessions during the planning period of the trial, records have yet to be discovered which would allow the reconstruction of these discussions. Another possibility is, of course, that no such minutes were ever produced.

Authorship

This raises the question of authorship. Both Ivy and Alexander claimed authorship of the Nuremberg Code in the mid-1960s. Their retrospective recollections have to be treated with considerable caution, however, especially since they were written at a time when the issue of medical ethics violations was making national headlines in the United States and elsewhere. As we have seen, both scientists were skilled operators when it came to promoting their professional image to a wider public. They knew that it could be beneficial for their own reputation to position themselves as the authors of the Code. Ivy, in particular, may have wanted to divert attention from his work into a natural cancer therapy which attracted considerable criticism at the time. In March 1964, Ivy told some of his peers in a personal correspondence that 'the foregoing is a brief review of the origin and development of the Nuernberg [*sic*] Code. The judges and I were determined that something of [a] preventive nature had to come of the "Trial of Medical Atrocities".'[218] The language itself, 'the judges and I', seems to suggest that Ivy had a certain Galenic personality; he was obviously determined to make his mark as a distinguished medical ethicist in the history of medicine.[219] Alexander, on the other hand, claimed somewhat less credit for himself, but made sure that the public knew that he had played a significant part in the formulation of the Code. In 1966 he wrote:

> In order to define conditions under which medical experimentation on human beings is ethically and legally permissible, I prepared a memorandum entitled, 'Ethical and Non-Ethical Experimentation on Human Beings', which was submitted to the United States Chief of Counsel for War Crimes and the Court on April 15, 1947. With additions derived from Dr. Andrew C. Ivy's testimony of June 12, 13, and 14, 1947, this memorandum became the basis of the so-called Nuernberg [sic] Code incorporated in the judgement.[220]

This statement is important in many respects. First, it seems to suggest that Alexander submitted his material not only to Taylor and the prosecution but also to the judges. Second, it shows that Alexander acknowledged the importance of Ivy's testimony in June in clarifying and defining medical ethics standards for the judges. However, as an explanation of who actually wrote the Code, Ivy's and Alexander's claims fall short of the historical complexity which shaped the trial at the time.[221]

The most convincing argumentation to date has been put forward by Evelyn Shuster. She argues that 'authorship was shared' between a number of persons including Ivy, Alexander and the judges, and that 'the famous 10 principles of the Code grew out of the trial itself'.[222] I fully agree with her view that the 'key to Nuremberg is to understand the actual testimony of the witnesses at the trial', except that I would extend this point to the testimony of all participants, be this the defendants, the experts, or the prosecution, who were involved at any one time during the trial.[223] As we have seen, the origin of the Code needs to be assessed in the context of a specific evolutionary process which took place during the trial. In this sense the creation of the Code was a 'joint solution' (*Gemeinschaftslösung*). Certain individuals contributed at different times important elements to the Code and drafted some of the principles which constituted the basis for the judges to write the Code. Without this material, supplied and annotated by the experts, and communicated to the judges directly or indirectly through the trial transcript, and other perhaps less formal channels, the creation of the Code in its existing form would hardly have been possible. 'He [Alexander] never told me that he wrote it alone', Cecily told me:

> He never said that. I think if he had sat down and wrote it himself, and presented it to a committee and that they approved it, he would have said so. He was not a man to hide his accomplishments whatsoever. He gave me the impression that it was a matter of hours of work and discussion, that there were many people involved.[224]

Yet the question remains as to whether authorship of the Code, in a strict sense of the term, can really be 'shared' with the judges. The purpose of the experts was to advise and inform the prosecution and the court in all questions of medical science and ethics. They undoubtedly shaped the opinion of the judges and influenced the actual wording of the Code. Yet can they really be considered joint authors of the Code? The Code is an integral part of the judgement. In that sense the author or authors of the Code have to be identical with the authors of the judgement. To write the judgement was the most important, intellectually challenging, legally and ethically complex endeavour of the entire trial. It was the sole duty of the four judges to do so. Their job was to apply the relevant legislation to the specific conditions of the trial and form an opinion on each of the defendants' guilt. No one can have a justified claim over the authorship of the judgement – and therefore the Code – other than the four judges.

That the judges considered the interpretation of the law their exclusive domain became apparent whenever the prosecution – or occasionally the defence team – transgressed into the legal and judgmental realm of the tribunal. When, during Ivy's testimony, one of the prosecutors touched on legal questions about how scientists should act under certain situations, Sebring made it clear that the question was not for the witness to answer, but for the judges. They claimed the right to issue a legal opinion on medical ethics guidelines and professional medical conduct, and it was for no one else to do so: 'Isn't it possible', Sebring told the prosecution, 'that this Tribunal will, in its opinion, answer that question in such a way [so that] scientists in the future will have some landmark to guide them.'[225] The Nuremberg Code was meant to be exactly this landmark.

So who was the most influential force among the judges in writing the judgement and the Code? Did they write the judgement and the Code in a series of joint meetings, or was it a single judge, or perhaps two, who drafted the outline of the Code, and the others later commented on it? In the absence of sufficient documentation we need to be cautious in our assessment. Neither do we have precise information as to when the Code was formulated in its existing form, nor about the actual process of its formulation. We also have little knowledge about the communication between the prosecution and the judges, and it is uncertain if and when the judges may have had access to individual reports and memoranda of the medical experts. So far no draft version of the Code from the judges seems to have survived. Most of what can be said therefore remains somewhat speculative. The most likely sequence of events is that one of the judges wrote sections of the judgement in the later part of the trial before discussing it with the members of the bench. During these discussions, the others will have made corrections, suggestions, amendments and changes to the text. They could have formulated questions for individual defendants and witnesses in order to clarify specific points, as Sebring did during

Ivy's testimony in June 1947, and ultimately will have approved the judgement as the result of their joint endeavour. The judgement was meant to be the expression of the bench rather than of one individual judge, unless, of course, there was a dissenting opinion. For the Nuremberg Doctors' Trial there is no dissenting opinion.

According to Tom Sebring, the son of Judge Sebring, who had accompanied his father to Nuremberg, the judges had a gentlemen's agreement that one of them would write the judgement.[226] Justice Beals was already quite old and suffering from arthritis – he died in 1952, five years after the trial – and Justice Crawford was apparently sick during 1947.[227] This left Swearingen and Sebring with the main task of writing the judgement. We can safely rule out Swearingen, not only because he was a junior member of the bench, but because he had not been a judge before coming to Nuremberg but a prosecuting attorney. He asked not a single question of any of the witnesses or defendants throughout the entire trial, and was excluded from reading out the judgement in court. By taking these factors into consideration, whilst being careful not to put too much weight on the oral testimony of interested parties, there is reason to believe that the judge who drafted most of the opinion, and therefore the Nuremberg Code, was probably Harold Sebring.

Since the beginning of the trial Sebring had turned out to be the most meticulous, intellectually able and legally minded of the tribunal. He would frequently point to some of the far-reaching legal and procedural problems during the planning period of the trial. Although Beals had been elected presiding judge because of his seniority, he would always consult with Sebring during the executive sessions in November 1946 before presenting a motion to the tribunal. Questions asked by the bench came for most of the time from either Beals or Sebring. Only once, on 7 May, did Judge Crawford question the defendant Georg August Weltz.[228] Otherwise he appears to have remained mostly silent, like his colleague Judge Swearingen.[229] Beals only examined a witness on eleven occasions, Sebring did so in a total of thirty-one cases, starting with Karl Brandt on 6 February and concluding with the witness Constantyn Johan Broers on 30 June 1947.[230] Sometimes Sebring would also interrogate a witness more than once.[231] Even more significantly, almost all questions relating to medical ethics and professional standards of practice were asked by Sebring, particularly during the testimonies of Brandt, Handloser, Hartleben and Rostock in February, and during those of Sievers, Hielscher, Ruff, Romberg and Weltz at the end of April and beginning of May, and also during Beiglböck's and Hoven's testimony in June 1947 and, of course, during Ivy's rebuttal testimony in the same month. In marked contrast to this, Beals rarely touched on issues of medical ethics.[232] Sebring was not only the most actively involved judge during the second half of the trial, but also the one who seems to have been in charge of matters relating to professional medical ethics.[233]

The suggestion that Sebring was the most active, if not the most potent, force among the judges in this field is further corroborated if we look at the particular examinations he carried out. A poignant example is Sebring's interrogation of Brandt in February, the first examination of a witness by one of the judges in the trial. Sebring's questions were sharp and concise and were aimed at a general, abstract level to establish the moral and legal belief system of the defendant:

> *Sebring*: Witness … let us assume that it would have been highly important to the Wehrmacht to ascertain, as a matter of fact, how long a human being could withstand exposure to cold before succumbing to the effects of it. Do you understand that? Let's assume secondly that human subjects were selected for such freezing experiments without their consent. Let's assume thirdly that such involuntary human subjects were subjected to the experiments and died as a direct or indirect result thereof. Now, would you be good enough to inform the Tribunal what your view of such an experiment is – either from the legal or from the ethical point of view?
>
> *Brandt*: In this case I am of the opinion that, when considering the circumstances of the situation of war, this state institution [government] which has laid down the importance in the interest of the state at the same time takes the responsibility away from the physician if such an experiment ends fatally and such a responsibility has to be taken by the state.
>
> *Sebring*: Now, does it take away that responsibility from the physician, in your view, or does it share that responsibility jointly with the physician?
>
> *Brandt*: This responsibility is taken away from the physician because, from that moment on, the physician is merely an instrument, maybe in the same sense as it would be in the case of an officer who receives an order at the front and leads a group of three or four soldiers into a position where they have to meet death.[234]

Now Brandt had manoeuvred himself into a corner. 'The Tribunal has one further question', Sebring asked:

> Would an order which authorised or directed a subordinate medical officer or subordinate medical group to carry out a certain medical experiment … without delineating or specifying in detail the exact course of those experiments – would you conceive that such an order would authorise the medical officer to whom the order was addressed to select subjects involuntarily and subject them to experiments, the execution of which that officer absolutely knew or should have known would likely result in death to the subject?[235]

'This question is extremely difficult to answer', Brandt said before giving a number of examples which he hoped would show him a way out. For

Brandt the 'personal feeling' and the 'ethical obligation' of the professional had to come second to the totalitarian nature of the government and, of course, the war:

This authoritarian leadership interfered with the personality and the personal feeling of the human being. At the moment as [when] a personality is dissolved in the concept of a collective body [body politic], every demand which is put to that personality [person] has to be dissolved in the concept of a collective system. Therefore, the demands of society are put above every individual human being ... and this individual ... is completely used in the interest of that society ... At that moment everything was done in the interest of humanity and so that the individual person had no meaning whatsoever.[236]

Brandt was saying, in effect, that the physician, once he became a soldier, had to subordinate any medical or ethical principles which he may have had and which may have been in conflict with a military order from a higher authority. It was a position which Sebring could not accept. 'Dr Brandt', Sebring enquired rhetorically,

is it not true that in any military organisation, even one of an authoritarian State, there comes a point beyond which the officer receiving an order subjects himself to individual responsibility, at least in the eyes of civilised society, for carrying out any military orders, particularly if the order is unlawful or transcends the limits of an extreme military necessity?[237]

This exchange shows that from the beginning Sebring took the initiative in order to establish for the international public and on record the overall Nazi moral belief system. It was a system of society in which individual responsibility and morality had been totally abandoned or corrupted. Within Nazi medical research 'the point' at which decent human beings would say 'stop' and disobey an order had almost never come. The following weeks, and indeed months, saw Sebring relentlessly querying the testimony of the witnesses, independent of whether they contradicted themselves. And each time he would address different aspects and dimensions of medical ethics and human rights in human experimentation.[238]

Sebring's line of enquiry was directed towards a certain number of basic issues. For example, he wanted to know whether or not the experimental subjects had been volunteers and had been informed about the potential risks of their assignments; whether or not some of these subjects had been killed as a result of these experiments and how; whether or not the experiments had been conducted on non-German nationals; whether or not the German armed forces had benefited from the research; how the experiments had been ordered and who had knowledge of them; and ultimately, who had been responsible for the experiments. Time and time again Sebring returned to these issues. Beals, on the other hand, seems to have been rather more concerned with the official lines of command in various military and civilian organisations in Germany. As a result of what appears to have been a kind of 'job-sharing' among the judges, Sebring managed to assert his influence over the tribunal in the field of medical ethics, and in all likelihood, it was he who drafted most, if not all, of the medical ethics principles of the Code.

Sebring's biography reveals why he was so interested in upholding professional standards. Married to the daughter of a well-known physician of the Florida region, and an active member of the Baptist Church, Sebring enjoyed a reputation for adherence to professional ethics. He strongly believed in the responsibility of the doctor to society, whilst advocating the protection of the rights of the individual.[239] Colleagues described him as plainspoken and easy to work with, but extremely hard working and with a great sense of formality and protocol.[240] He once advised one of his younger colleagues: 'When you accept the robe, remember it is like a clerical collar; don't do this unless you are willing to be a judge the rest of your professional life.'[241] Sebring was also known for formulating lucid, intellectually flawless and convincing interpretations of the law. Many of his opinions later became landmarks in American law and were used for reference purposes by law students. It might not be altogether surprising therefore that the person with the greatest sense of professional legal standards appears to have been the driving force in devising a set of professional medical ethics standards.

There is, however, no evidence to substantiate this claim. Sebring was a modest man. If he wrote something on the subject he made sure that it could not be construed in such a way that it appeared that he had written the judgement or the Code. To do so would have meant not only to betray his Nuremberg peers, but also to act against the professional code of conduct of the legal profession. When during the IMT the British requested that either the ageing Gustav Krupp should be tried *in absentia* or his son Alfried should be added to the indictment, the tribunal was shocked. One of the judges, while pacing up and down the park, told his aide: 'Cap'n, if we were to grant this motion, there wouldn't be a lawyer in North Carolina that didn't think we had permitted substitution in a criminal trial.'[242] For this judge the North Carolina Bar was the most important and trustworthy yardstick against which all principles and procedures would have to be measured. Likewise, the Florida Bar was the most important yardstick for Sebring.[243] He knew that for all Florida lawyers, and indeed for all members of the American Bar, it was an unquestioned principle that the judgement would be issued jointly, and not by any of the judges individually. If Sebring ever told someone about the origin of the Code he would probably have done so in the strictest of confidence. For him it was important to follow the professional rules, far more important than any claim to fame.

The actual formulation of the Code stands in close connection with the progression and development of the trial. The debates about, and proposals for the creation of a new international medical ethics code in the months before the start of the Doctors' Trial, both within the US prosecution and as part of the ISC (WC), were certainly important in drawing the attention of the judges to the issue of professional medical ethics. Yet it is during the trial that originally vague and broadly defined principles were being formulated into a code of legally binding, professional and moral-ethical guidelines for permissible research on humans which attained a universal status. These guidelines were preformulated in a collaborative environment between the US prosecution and the medical expert witnesses, and adopted by the judges in a partly identical or modified form in the judgement of the tribunal. Moreover, the judges used the actual testimonies that were read into the record in order to formulate specific principles for research on humans. The authorship of the Nuremberg Code thus remains inextricably linked with the role of the judges, independent of whether parts of the Code were preformulated. Educated in the case law tradition it was not unusual for American judges to go significantly beyond the case in front of them if they believed that they were dealing with a precedent which needed the formulation of new law. In this case the new law constituted a code of medical ethics that was to serve as a guide to future research on human subjects. The decision of the judges to include the Code formally into the judgement also meant that, for the first time, written guidelines for permissible research on humans were incorporated into the canon of international law. This was a substantial achievement, irrespective of the limited effect that the Code may have had in the following decades for the protection of human and patient rights.

The judgement

Secrecy was paramount in the writing, translation and final preparation of the judgement in the Doctors' Trial. The weeks leading up to the judgement were marked by heightened tension among the members of the court. Twenty-three defendants had produced voluminous closing briefs, which needed to be translated before the judgement was read out in court. Becker-Freysing's brief had a total of 203 pages, Beiglböck's made up 206 pages, Hoven's 212 pages, Handloser's 156 pages, and Brandt's consisted of three books with a total of 246 pages. Only Fischer and Oberheuser submitted a mere five pages as their closing brief. All of Brandt's material was translated and handed to the office of the Secretary General by 1 August, although Brandt later alleged that the material had not been in the hands of the judges prior to the day when judgement was handed down.[244] During the translation process Thomas Hoeges, head of the Language Division, personally carried out the original rough translations for the judges so that they would be able to read them before final mimeographed copies were produced.

The translation of the judgement into the German language was carried out in total secrecy and under the guard of the United States armed forces. It was of utmost importance that the verdict, or parts of it, would not become known before it was actually read out in court. Any leaks among the personnel of the court could lead to a serious public relations disaster. The date when the translation of the judgement was to commence was only known to the bench, the head of the Language Division, and a few clerical personnel performing the actual translation. Judge Beals personally swore to secrecy each person who might have knowledge of the contents of the document.[245] When the first portions of the judgement were received for translation by the Language Division on 15 August, the translators and clerical personnel were placed 'incommunicado' with all other persons, and they had to remain in that situation for four days. The last portion of the judgement was received on 18 August, one day before it was delivered in court.

It had taken the judges more than two weeks to draw up the judgement. It constituted a significant document of linguistic precision, objectivity and strict impartiality.[246] On Tuesday, 19 August, while the region was suffering from an oppressive heatwave, it was read out to a packed court for about eight-and-a-half hours by Beals and two of the senior judges, each taking turns. Judge Swearingen listened intently; he remained content 'where circumstances had put him'. All of the defendants had been dressed for the occasion, 'less sloppy than usual'.[247]

Beals started off by giving a brief overview of the history of Military Tribunal I and the law on which it had been established and on which it would now pass sentence. The trial had lasted 139 trial days and had been conducted in two languages. For 133 days evidence had been presented to the court. Thirty-two witnesses had given oral testimony for the prosecution and fifty-three witnesses, including twenty-three defendants, had given oral evidence for the defence. There had been 570 affidavits filed by the prosecution and a total of 901 for the defence. In total the court had been presented with 1471 documents of evidence. An enormous amount of material had been submitted, final arguments of the defence had been concluded, and the tribunal had listened to the personal statements by the defendants. All that remained was the rendition of judgement and the imposition of sentence.[248] Judge Crawford, taking over from Beals, continued to specify the law on which the judgement was based, reading out and detailing the charges of common design or conspiracy, war crimes and crimes against humanity, and membership in an organisation declared criminal by the IMT.[249]

Now it was Sebring's turn. Significantly, he read out the part of the judgement which contained the Nuremberg Code which is, perhaps, another indication that he was most strongly involved in its formulation.

255

Plate 30 The defendants in the Doctors' Trial. Nuremberg, Germany, 1946/7.

The Code was first of all part of the proof to establish whether war crimes and crimes against humanity had been committed. 'Judged by any standard of proof', Sebring began, 'the record clearly shows the commission of war crimes and crimes against humanity.' Criminal medical experiments had been performed on non-German nationals, both on prisoners of war and civilians, including Jews and 'asocial' persons, throughout Germany and the occupied territories. The evidence was conclusive that these experiments had not been individual incidents or acts by individual medical scientists, but the result of planned, large-scale and co-ordinated policies at the highest level of the government. The experiments had been 'ordered, sanctioned, permitted or approved by persons in positions of authority who under all principles of law were under the duty to know about these things and to take steps to terminate or prevent them'.[250]

Judged by the material which had been presented in court there were 'certain types' of experiments on humans which, as long they remained within 'reasonably well-defined bounds', conformed to the ethics of the medical profession in the civilised world. The tribunal acknowledged that scientists justified human experiments on the basis that they yield results for the good of human society which could not be produced by other means of study. 'All agree, however, that certain basic principles must be observed in order to satisfy moral, ethical and legal concepts.'[251] These principles were as follows:

1. The voluntary consent of the human subject is absolutely essential This means that the person involved should have legal capacity to give consent; should be so situated as to be able to exercise free power of choice, without the intervention of any element of force, fraud, deceit, duress, overreaching, or other ulterior form of constraint or coercion; and should have sufficient knowledge and comprehension of the elements of the subject matter involved as to enable him to make an understanding and enlightened decision. This latter element requires that before the acceptance of an affirmative decision by the experimental subject there should be made known to him the nature, duration, and purpose of the experiment; the method and means by which it is to be conducted; all inconveniences and hazards reasonably to be expected; and the effects upon his health or person which may possibly come from his participation in the experiment.

The duty and responsibility for ascertaining the quality of the consent rests upon each individual who initiates, directs or engages in the experiment. It is a personal duty and responsibility which may not be delegated to another with impunity.

2. The experiment should be such as to yield fruitful results for the good of society, unprocurable by other methods or means of study, and not random and unnecessary in nature.

3. The experiment should be so designed and based on the results of animal experimentation and a knowledge of the natural history of the disease or other problem under study that the anticipated results will justify the performance of the experiment.

4. The experiment should be so conducted as to avoid all unnecessary physical and mental suffering and injury.

5. No experiment should be conducted where there is an *a priori* reason to believe that death or disabling injury will occur; except, perhaps, in those experiments where the experimental physicians also serve as subjects.

6. The degree of risk to be taken should never exceed that determined by the humanitarian importance of the problem to be solved by the experiment.

7. Proper preparation should be made and adequate facilities provided to protect the experimental subject against even remote possibilities of injury, disability, or death.

8. The experiment should be conducted only by scientifically qualified persons. The highest degree of skill and care should be required through all stages of the experiment of those who conduct or engage in the experiment.

9. During the course of the experiment the human subject should be at liberty to bring the experiment to an end if he had reached the physical or mental state where continuation of the experiment seems to him to be impossible.

10. During the course of the experiment the scientist in charge must be prepared to terminate the experiment at any stage, if he had probable cause to believe, in the exercise of the good faith, superior skill, and careful judgement required of him, that a continuation of the experiment is likely to result in injury, disability, or death to the experimental subject.[252]

Sebring stressed that only those principles had influenced the judgement that were 'purely legal in nature' or 'so clearly related to matters legal that they assist us in determining criminal culpability and punishment. To go beyond that point would lead us into a field that would be beyond our sphere of competence.'[253] The judges did not further specify which of the principles they meant. What is significant, though, particularly in comparison to other existing medical ethics codes, is the detailed nature of the informed consent principle. The first principle is by far the most clearly and comprehensively defined which adds additional weight to the suggestion that the judges had created a Code that was not just applicable to the case in front of them, but was meant to guide scientists performing research on humans in the future, like a landmark, as Sebring once said during the trial proceedings.[254] It is an attempt to anticipate almost all potential future cases by qualifying precisely, or at least as closely as possible, the meaning of the words voluntary and consent in human experimentation. Though unable to foresee the complex culture of experimental research that would engulf the modern world, they spoke to the 'entire universe'; they wanted to create 'basic principles' that researchers had to observe to satisfy 'moral, ethics and legal concepts in the practice of human experimentation'.[255] Another potent explanation for the peculiar character of the first principle might be found in the way in which the voluntary consent issue had become the central issue of the entire trial, but had been inadequately defined by the prosecution and its expert witnesses. Being lawyers, the judges may well have felt that Ivy's and Alexander's ethics regulations, and in particular their consent principle, were far too vague for a medical ethics code that was to be universally applied to the medical profession in the future.[256]

Apart from the Code's prospective character, the judgement also highlights the link between the Code and the sentencing of the accused, a connection which the prosecution had been keen to establish since the beginning of the trial. Whereas the concept of Thanatology had been the attempt to secure the conviction of all of the defendants, the Code was to function as a legal instrument to determine different degrees of criminal culpability. It was a pragmatic tool, a yardstick, which they had created on the basis of both existing ethics regulations and by deducing others from the views of medical experts. The bench, in formulating the Code in a legalistic language, relied heavily on existing documentation and expert views in order to ensure that the principles would not appear to have retroactive force, that is, being created after the crimes had been committed. In a sense the ten principles on human experimentation constituted another law on which the judgement was based. That explains why they are mentioned immediately after the Allied legislation and the particular charges in the judgement', but before the individual case of the defendants.

In examining the experiments which had been proven in the trial, the judges had come to the conclusion that the ten principles had 'much more frequently [been] honoured in their breach than in their observance'.[257] The victimisation of hundreds of non-German nationals for involuntary and brutal experiments was clearly established by the record:

> In every single instance ... subjects were used who did not consent to the experiments; indeed, as to some of the experiments, it is not even contended by the defendants that the subjects occupied the status of volunteers. In no case was the experimental subject at liberty of his own free choice to withdraw from any experiment. In many cases experiments were performed by unqualified persons; were conducted at random for no adequate scientific reason, and under revolting physical conditions. All of the experiments were conducted with unnecessary suf-

fering and injury and but very little, if any, precautions were taken to protect or safeguard the human subjects from the possibilities of injury, disability, or death. In every one of the experiments the subjects experienced extreme pain or torture, and in most of them they suffered permanent injury, mutilation, or death, either as a direct result of the experiments or because of lack of adequate follow-up care.[258]

The judges based their assessment of the experiments on international rules and regulations. The experiments had been conducted in 'complete disregard' of international laws, the laws and customs of war, the general principles of criminal laws and Law No. 10. They were contrary to 'the principles of laws of nations as they result from the usages among civilised peoples, from the laws of humanity, and from the dictates of public conscience'.[259] However, whether individual defendants were guilty of the crimes was another question, Sebring said, one which needed to be determined according to the evidence available.

Throughout the judgement each case was examined at great length before the judges gave their verdict. The actual reading of the judgement was a solemn procedure, conducted in the deepest silence of the courtroom. Brandt was the first of the defendants whose case was considered. Though engaging with Brandt's idealistic intentions, the tribunal had not lost sight of the crimes which had been committed, real crimes by real people against real people. Overall they accepted the view of the prosecution that Brandt had

held a position of the highest rank directly under Hitler. He was in a position to intervene with authority on all matters; indeed, it appears that such was his positive duty. It does not appear that at any time he took any steps to check medical experiments upon human subjects.[260]

Following the completion of the case against Brandt, who had been found guilty under counts two, three and four of the indictment, the tribunal had one of four court recesses, each lasting for about ten minutes.[261] The public remained seated, mummified from what they had heard. Hardly any comments were exchanged. If people talked at all, it was about the unbearable heat. At 6.30 p.m. the reading of the judgement was terminated, followed by the announcement that sentences would be delivered the next day (see Table 7.1). Fifteen of the twenty-three defendants had been found guilty of war crimes and crimes against humanity: Brandt, Handloser, Schröder, Genzken, Gebhardt, Brandt, Mrugowsky, Sievers, Rose, Brack, Becker-Freysing, Hoven, Beiglböck, Oberheuser and Fischer. Seven were found not guilty and acquitted: Rostock, Blome, Ruff, Romberg, Weltz, Schäfer and Pokorny. One of them, Poppendick, was acquitted of the charges, but found guilty of membership in an organisation declared

Table 7.1   Sentences and commutations in the Nuremberg Doctors' Trial

Defendant	Sentences	Commutations
Karl Brandt	Death	–
Siegfried Handloser	Life	Twenty years
Paul Rostock	Acquitted	–
Oskar Schröder	Life	Fifteen years
Karl Genzken	Life	Twenty years
Karl Gebhardt	Death	–
Kurt Blome	Acquitted	–
Rudolf Brandt	Death	–
Joachim Mrugowsky	Death	–
Helmut Poppendick	Ten years	Time served
Wolfram Sievers	Death	–
Gerhard Rose	Life	Fifteen years
Siegfried Ruff	Acquitted	–
Hans Wolfgang Romberg	Acquitted	–
Victor Brack	Death	–
Hermann Becker-Freysing	Twenty years	Ten years
Georg August Weltz	Acquitted	–
Konrad Schäfer	Acquitted	–
Waldemar Hoven	Death	–
Wilhelm Beiglböck	Fifteen years	Ten years
Adolf Pokorny	Acquitted	–
Herta Oberheuser	Twenty years	Ten years
Fritz Fischer	Life	Fifteen years

Source: NARA, RG232, Entry 159, box 1, Teleconference, War Crimes Operations, 22.8.1947; also RG238, Entry 213, box 1, Nuremberg Cases.

criminal by the IMT. The next day the *New York Times* carried a brief article under the headline 'Hitler's Doctor, 14 Others Guilty in Medical Experimentation Trial'.[262]

For the pronouncement of sentences secrecy was even tighter. No one except the four judges had prior knowledge of them. They were read out and translated extemporaneously on the floor of the court on 20 August 1947.[263] Since the early hours the courtroom had been filling up with official Allied and German observers, journalists and public spectators. All hotel rooms in Nuremberg and the surrounding areas had been reserved for weeks in advance. By 9.45 a.m. all seats were occupied. Those who were late had to find a place in the adjacent corridors. For the last time the courtroom was packed in total silence, 'almost meditative', as one commentator noted. Only the smooth sound of the film cameras could be heard. The seats and the door of the dock had been removed to ensure an expeditious procedure. The session opened half an hour later than usual, at 10 a.m. sharp. At 10.04 a.m. the president ordered the guards to bring in the first defendant: Karl Brandt. The official film record shows Brandt being led by a guard to the centre of the dock where he stood motionless, to attention, between two military policemen, facing Walter Beals and the other judges. He picked up the headphones and heard:

> Karl Brandt, Military Tribunal I has found and adjudged you guilty of War Crimes, Crimes against Humanity, and membership in an organisation declared criminal by the judgement of the International Military Tribunal, as charged under the indictment heretofore filed against you. For your said crimes, on which you have been, and now stand convicted, Military Tribunal I sentences you, Karl Brandt, to death by hanging. And may God have mercy on your soul.[264]

'Not a muscle of his face moves, not a wink, not a respiratory motion more rapid than the precedent one, completely insensitive, he seems to listen to a sentence which does not concern him and which strikes a stranger', one commentator remarked.[265] Brandt remained motionless for a number of seconds, waiting for the translation to come through. 'The Officer of the Guards will remove the defendant Brandt', Judge Beals finally said. Before leaving the courtroom Brandt briefly turned to the cameras, for the last time, and smoothed out a strand of his black hair. In the shadow of the elevator the figures of the two guards who took possession of the condemned became visible. Then the automatic door closed in silence. 'It is perhaps the most poignant moment and it seems for everyone that the condemned already does not belong any longer to the world of human beings that he has disappeared definitely, for ever ... ', one observer said.[266] The event had lasted one minute and forty seconds.

In addition to Brandt, six of the accused were sentenced to death by hanging: Brack, Sievers, Gebhardt, Hoven, Mrugowski and Rudolf Brandt. Five of the defendants were sentenced to life imprisonment, later commuted to fifteen or twenty years.[267] Herta Oberheuser, the only women on trial, dressed in a black woollen dress, was sentenced to twenty years' imprisonment, but was released in the mid-1950s. At 10.33 a.m. the last of the defendants, Fritz Fischer, sentenced to life imprisonment, disappeared into the dark through the sliding door in the courtroom wall. The final drama of Nuremberg had lasted twenty-nine minutes. At 10.35 p.m. Walter Beals lifted the gavel and, with a brief rap, the session was adjourned. Military Tribunal I, Case 1, had completed its mission.

At first the prosecution was disappointed with the judgement, hoping that none of the accused would be acquitted.[268] Two weeks before the pronouncement of sentences, on 6 August, Alexander had returned to his family. After several years of military service abroad he was longing for a holiday with his children, somewhere on Cape Cod, where he first had spent his long, lonely summers after the Nazi regime had forced him to

Plate 31 Karl Brandt, Hitler's doctor, being sentenced to death for war crimes, crimes against humanity and membership of an organisation declared criminal by the International Military Tribunal. Nuremberg, Germany, 20 August 1947.

emigrate.[269] It was here that he had produced some of his most colourful, somewhat naive paintings of this particular maritime landscape, not quite like Edward Hopper's *The Long Leg* from 1935, but also not bad. His home now was Boston. For the moment he, and others, were trying to leave their memory of Germany behind and settle back into their professional lives. Besides, Germany first needed to come to terms with itself. 'Outside, no gatherings', Charles Sillevaerts reflected on his way back to Belgium after having reported for nine months from Nuremberg, 'It seems to me that the German public is not very interested by these judgements; life is hard, very hard; bread good or bad is hard to earn. One has no time to lose, everybody for himself. The past does not matter, neither does the future, provided that one can live, half decently, in the present.'[270]

8

Post-war Medical Ethics

A good code for barbarians

He told me that he had worked on the creation of the Nuremberg Code for human experimentation and ... there was still discussion to be brought up how to implement these rules in the Code, but that those were the basis ... and that people needed to really pay attention to that, that these things should never ever ever happen again, that's why he was in Nuremberg to see to it ... He felt that he had sacrificed a year of his career to help bring about these changes and that it was very important to protect that ... He felt that was, when he looked back on it, that that was the whole point, to create a new standard, not just to convict those people.[1]

This is how Cecily remembered Alexander talking about the Nuremberg Code after the war. At first, though, people paid little attention to it. The German people were not interested in the Nuremberg judgement, nor was the international medical community keen to acknowledge the existence of the Code. Western medical scientists were unwilling to relate what had been discussed in Nuremberg to their own research practice. The Code, in other words, had come into this world by default, mostly hidden away from the public eye, known to a few experts and institutions, and applied by even fewer medical innovators. The medical ethicist Jay Katz poignantly captured the attitude of post-war Western medical researchers who felt that 'it was a good code for barbarians but an unnecessary code for ordinary physician-scientists'.[2] Others, such as David J. Rothman, have observed that 'the prevailing view was that [the Nuremberg medical defendants] were Nazis first and last; by definition nothing they did, and no code drawn up in response to them, was relevant to the United States'.[3] But as evidence from Cold War Allied research laboratories is beginning to emerge in no small measure, one can wonder whether it might have been wiser, perhaps, if Western scientists had not ignored, or simply dismissed, the new professional guidelines on human experimentation which their own experts had formulated at Nuremberg. It not only might have prevented much subsequent embarrassment by the authorities and ongoing compensation claims in Anglo-American courts, but, more significantly, may in fact have prevented serious injuries, disabilities and death of hundreds of experimental subjects, not to speak of the untold human suffering of the relatives involved.

The Doctors' Trial heralded a period of great uncertainty for health professionals and national medical organisations, not just financially, but more with regard to the role that the medical profession was supposed to play in a post-war society. Nazi medical experiments had seriously undermined the reputation of medical practice and had damaged doctor–patient relationships. Doctors in Great Britain and elsewhere feared that a sweeping condemnation of the Nazi physicians could negatively affect the profession as a whole. Large-scale funding for experimental research or the foundation of research institutes was potentially at risk. Medical lobbying for the autonomy of medical scientists therefore reached new heights.[4] Any government scheme that advocated a greater degree of central or state planning of medical research was denounced as totalitarian by organisations such as the Society for Freedom in Science. The *British Medical Journal* declared that the individual conscience of the researcher would surrender to the 'mass mind of the totalitarian state'.[5] Critics of the National Health Service alleged that a greater state direction of science would apparently lead to a Nazi or Soviet system of government. Among the critics of greater state control in the health and welfare system were Alexander and Ivy.[6] Overall, it was an attempt by British and American medical lobbyists to shift the responsibility for medical war crimes away from individual scientists on to an authoritarian state, a strategy that the Nuremberg defendants had themselves tried.

The foundation of the World Medical Association (WMA) occurred in response to the revelations in the Doctors' Trial. At the end of 1946 100 delegates representing thirty-two national medical associations gathered together in London to form the first international medical organisation in the world. The objectives of the WMA were to maintain the honour of the medical profession, the promotion of world peace and the helping of all peoples to attain the highest possible level of health.[7] Behind these laudable aims stood a calculated policy, namely to protect the interests of the medical profession in the forthcoming power struggle with national governments. On Wednesday, 17 September 1947, only weeks after the Nuremberg judgement had been pronounced, the French Minister of Public Health opened the first annual meeting of the WMA in Paris.[8] Costa Rica's suggestion that the organisation call itself the World Medical Confederation was dismissed, as was the proposal by Czechoslovakia to exclude the German medical profession from membership for a period of twenty-five years.[9] The organisation was nonetheless unambiguous in its moral condemnation of Nazi crimes. Not only was the 'widespread criminal conduct of the German medical profession since 1933' acknowledged, but the delegates also expressed their 'astonishment' that 'no sign whatever had come from Germany that the doctors were ashamed of their share in the crimes, or even that they fully realised the enormity of their conduct'.[10] German medical associations were invited to make a formal declaration that would help to rehabilitate German medicine in the eyes of the world.

There were other, more material, yet less publicised, issues at stake which set the tone for the following years. For example, the WMA discussed what it called the 'principles of social security'. This meant that all doctors were to be free to choose their location and type of practice. All medical services were to be controlled by physicians. WMA delegates announced that it would 'not be in the public's interest that doctors be full-time salaried servants of government or social-security bodies' and that the 'remuneration of medical services' should not depend directly on the financial conditions of the insurance. Finally, doctors were to be given the freedom to choose their patients except in cases of emergencies or other humanitarian considerations.[11]

The stated model of medical practice stood in contrast to what almost all industrialised nations were favouring in Europe at the time: a universal, egalitarian, health care system based on social welfare, irrespective of class, gender, race or economic considerations. Issues of medical ethics now became a propaganda weapon in the increasingly hostile battles between the WMA and the respective national governments. In 1949 the WMA declared in its 'International Code of Medical Ethics' that it was 'unethical' to take part in 'any plan of medical care in which the doctor does not have complete professional independence'.[12] This had undoubtedly little to do with the welfare of patients or with the social and moral responsibilities of physicians. The WMA at this point was largely influenced by, and showed allegiance to, market interests. During the first meeting in 1947 the organisation accepted a 'gift' of 50 000 US dollars a year for five years from 'a group of American industrialists' for the 'development' of the organisation. It was an attempt by North American pharmaceuticals and other business interests to exercise considerable influence over the organisation from the moment it was created.

The Nuremberg Code hardly figured in the discussions of the WMA. Only the medical associations from Denmark and the Netherlands proposed to 'devise measures' that would prevent the participation of physicians in medical crimes in future.[13] It took another six years, until 1953, before a position paper on human experimentation was tabled and another year until the 'Resolution on Human Experimentation: Principles for those in Research and Experimentation' was adopted by the WMA during its eighth General Assembly in Rome in 1954.[14] These principles were less comprehensive and far-reaching than those of the Code and excluded a number of key provisions, for example, that the subject can withdraw from the experiment at any time.[15] Also, the 'informed, free consent' principle, which was 'absolutely essential' to the Code, was now listed almost at the end of the document. Above all, the principle indicated a shift away from the rights of patient-citizens to the duties of physicians, a shift which ten years later, in 1964, was formalised in the first Declaration of Helsinki.[16] The process of watering down the Nuremberg Code had begun.

The German patient

On the other side of the Atlantic, political scientists, historians and sociologists were trying to make sense of the Nazi phenomenon. Experts hoped that by studying Nazi Germany one could learn about the nature of Soviet Russia, the new ideological enemy of the Western hemisphere. Following Churchill's speech at Westminster College, Missouri, in 1946, it had become apparent that Communism was seen as the new threat to Western liberal democracy. In a climate of distrust and open criticism of the Soviet Union, the study of Nazi war crimes and crimes against humanity became linked with the study of totalitarianism and dictatorial regimes.[17] It was to Alexander's advantage that he had been at the forefront of investigating Nazi medical crimes and now was the time to capitalise on his unique expertise and on the international media attention that surrounded the Doctors' Trial. He wanted to study medical science under a dictatorship.[18]

Alexander believed that his knowledge of sociology as applied to psychiatry had given him an extra edge in his work as a war crimes expert.[19] In a flood of lectures and publications shortly before and after the Doctors' Trial, he attempted to explain some of the underlying psychological and sociological causes of Nazism, and offered a series of suggestions about how a country's destructive potential could be 'diagnosed' and perhaps be contained.[20] Between 1948 and 1949 Alexander published a total of eight academic papers which addressed the issue of war crimes and human experimentation.[21] As one of the first, he offered a psychological and psychoanalytical explanation as to why German doctors had committed medical war crimes. The trials of doctors and other government officials, he argued, offered a unique opportunity in history for a 'scientific post mortem of the body politic of the defeated enemy'.[22] Others, like Gitta Sereny, who in 1945 visited German concentration camps as a child welfare officer of the United Nations Relief and Rehabilitation Administration (UNRRA), were also conscious of the opportunity which the psychological study of large numbers of people from a former totalitarian state offered.[23] Many experts thought to conduct mass-psychology examinations to determine the underlying motivating and emotional factors that had turned ordinary citizens into willing collaborators, and some into willing perpetrators. Alexander, for one, wanted to interrogate people 'in the prison, the witness house, and on the streets, railroad trains and farms of Germany'.[24] Behind this stood the idea of learning more about how the social fabric of totalitarian regimes functioned, particularly in the Soviet Union.[25] Alexander believed that the moral belief system and thinking in the high echelons of the Nazi leadership was like that of a criminal organisation which he compared to the Mafia or Camorra in Italy. Concentration camps, Alexander believed, had become 'training grounds' for encouraging criminal behaviour.[26] Apparently, the group cohesion of criminal organisations like the SS was maintained through *Blutkitt* (blood cement), which meant that each crime by a member of the group reinforced the group's cohesion.[27] For those who had fallen out of favour with the leadership, a crime constituted a way to prove allegiance to the regime, and regain acceptance by those in power. In addition, it served to replace human responses such as sympathy or respect for individual persons with hardness and rigidity.[28] Although the concept of 'blood cement' was potentially far-reaching, scholars like Robert J. Lifton were less convinced that it is applicable in attempting to explain war crimes.[29]

Alexander tried to explain medical war crimes on the basis of contemporary teachings in psychology and psychoanalysis. He applied this knowledge not only to individuals and groups, but to the German people as a whole. In effect, he projected psychological and psychoanalytical expertise on to the field of international politics and international relations. He alleged that the evidence demonstrated that large numbers of Germans had shown a 'generalised eruption of aggressive, destructive activity' which had permeated the entire social sphere of society. Alexander had in fact identified one of the key characteristics of the regime: its self-perpetuating, cumulative, radical nature. It was a system of government which was bent on destruction to such an extent that it was ultimately self-destructive. The mechanisms by which destructive energy was built up had a snowball effect. Radical measures were continuously pushed forward by a totally uncontrolled, highly competitive, social-Darwinistic system, in which everyone fought against one another. Those who pursued the most ruthless of policies had the most likely chance of being rewarded. Alexander realised that the existence of destructive urges of such magnitude and depth in a society could not remain contained or limited but 'must inevitably spread and be directed against one's own group, and, ultimately, against the self'.[30] 'We must see in the destruction of the morals, the institutions, the ideals and the cities of Germany the ultimate realisation of this destructive drive', he wrote.[31] But he did not want to be misunderstood. The 'instinctual destructive drives' among the German people were not the result of some biological or racial determination, but the consequence of social, cultural and political conditioning.[32]

The combination of indoctrination with anti-rationality and anti-spirituality, group seduction and subsequent sanctioning created, according to

Alexander, a peculiar German culture in which reality was often denied or resented, and in which the acceptance of individual responsibility was virtually absent.[33] Talking to the Nuremberg defendants, as well as to ordinary citizens, Alexander concluded that there was a certain affinity for 'fanatical and even delusional thinking' among the Germans. At times, 'delusional distortions' turned into manifestations of real delusions of reality among some Germans, that is, that the country, after all, had not lost the war but that the people had been misled and were the victim of some extraordinary misunderstanding. Germans, in this view, were deeply disinterested, apolitical citizens. Their ego, especially their political ego, had been insufficiently developed or crushed by education and other forces. 'The emptiness of the ego sphere is the most striking finding which differentiates members of the German cultural group from members of other cultural groups.'[34] Germany, in other words, was a country without a political culture, a nation full of disinterested and detached individuals.

In yet another psychological twist Alexander observed that some disillusioned Nazis turned their aggressive, genocidal drive towards their own group and, as a logical consequence, advocated the geno-suicide of the German people. Since the quest for living space (*Lebensraum*) had failed and since the country had been utterly defeated, so the argument went, it was only right that Germany 'should cease to exist as a national and cultural unit'. Alexander felt that although these were individual cases, they were nonetheless deeply worrying as far as the collective German conscience was concerned:

> I would not consider it too difficult at all to sell a former SS activist the idea that the German problem should be solved within one year by shooting every German on his birthday, and to create for this purpose a *Reichsgeburtstagsabschussammelstelle* [Reich Birthday Shooting Collection Point] patterned after the various *Sammelstellen* (collection points) for annihilation purposes which the SS had established all over occupied Europe. The only reason I have not made this psychological experiment is the fear that such a preposterous suggestion, copied after the old but deadly-serious SS pattern, would be taken seriously by these people.[35]

These findings were of importance in the ongoing denazification process and what Alexander called the 'socio-psychological rehabilitation' of German society. The study of the 'German patient' led Alexander to conclude that the field of psychiatry needed to shift its perspective. The discipline had contributed to a better understanding of family relationships, to the child–parent relationship, to the teacher–pupil relationship, to the mental health of armies and the upholding of military morale.[36] Following the establishment of the United Nations, it was time that the field made a constructive contribution to national and international politics.[37]

Turning the world into one large-scale imaginary hospital, Alexander devised a system of international relations in which individual countries were either healthy and peaceful, or sick and in need of treatment. According to this scheme certain criteria had to be developed to 'diagnose' nation-states as to whether they showed early symptoms of destructive energy that could be unleashed under certain circumstances. Assuming the rather megalomaniac role of a world psychiatrist, whose assignment was to diagnose, if not to cure, other nation-states, Alexander asked rhetorically: 'What should a psychiatrist assigned to the United Nations ... be looking for in order to find out whether a destructive-aggressive outburst may be expected in any member nation?'[38] The first sign was apparently the way in which a country was dealing with its social problems, whether leading authorities advocated the destruction of life, especially of those seen as 'socially useless or socially disturbing'. Then there was the factor of fear, especially the extent to which fear governed the decision-making process of large numbers of people in a given society. According to Alexander's analysis, it was one of the key criteria that made war crimes possible: 'We found fear to be one of the most important motivations for those aggressive outbursts which constitute war crimes.'[39] A third criterion was the extent to which individuals enjoyed rights in a society. The non-existence or curtailment of basic civil rights produced fear which in turn was likely to produce aggression. Finally, the fourth area, was freedom of information. For Alexander it was apparent that 'the restriction of access to information by any nation should be regarded as a danger sign of potential aggressive-destructive behaviour.'[40] It remained to be seen whether nations that fulfilled one or all of these criteria could be 'treated', and, if necessary, in Alexander's words, could be 'certified, committed, and confined'. Here Alexander's character as a psychiatrist exhibited its full expression. Considering the above criteria, it was certainly no coincidence that all of them, in one way or another, applied to the Soviet Union. Alexander's analysis of German war crimes, in other words, was an attempt at alerting experts to the dangers of another power-seeking totalitarian state. He not only deeply resented Nazism, but he deplored Stalinism as well.

The Lisbon controversy

Alexander, as we have seen, was an outspoken, often overly self-confident personality who had little or nothing good to report about the German medical profession during the Third Reich. Although tarring all the Germans with the same brush, he was not entirely wrong to do so. Significantly, many of his allegations against members of the then ruling medical elite, especially against the neuropathologist Julius Hallervorden, turned out to be true. Despite vociferous denials from the German medical establishment at the time, and despite attempts at clearing the historical record, Hallervorden's involvement in the 'euthanasia' programme can be demonstrated.[41] Yet in 1953, during the preparations for the fifth international congress of neurologists in Lisbon, Alexander became embroiled in a heated debate over Hallervorden's Nazi past. The Lisbon controversy is emblematic of the extent to which the German medical profession, supported by international colleagues, was unwilling to accept collective responsibility in the post-war period for having violated traditional medical ethics standards.

In his article 'Science under Dictatorship', published in 1949, Alexander examined the factors that led doctors to adopt a crudely utilitarian, Hegelian perspective towards human beings. That which was considered useful to society, was also considered to be good. Once doctors had started to think in terms of valuable and invaluable members of society, and accepted the premise that 'life unworthy of life' existed, the moral fibre of the profession began to disintegrate. The 'euthanasia' programme only served as a first step in the implementation of a much larger killing programme: the extermination of the European Jewry. Alexander was clearly ahead of his time in understanding the connection between the 'euthanasia' programme and the Holocaust. He realised long before Holocaust historians did, that the 'euthanasia' programme provided vital expertise and personnel that were needed to set up the killing centres in the occupied Eastern territories. He saw the 'euthanasia' programme as the primary move towards the murder of a whole people: 'The methods used and personnel trained in the killing centres for the chronically sick became the nucleus of the much larger centres in the East.'[42]

As an example of the way in which medical scientists tried to use the programme to advance their own research, Alexander cited part of his conversation with Hallervorden from 1945. Hallervorden, who probably initiated the collaboration with the organisers of the killing programme, obtained more than 500 brains from victims. He had commented to Alexander at the time of their conversation: 'There was wonderful material among those brains, beautiful mental defectives, malformations and early infantile diseases. I accepted those brains of course. Where they came from and how they came to me was really none of my business.'[43] These and similar remarks by Hallervorden recorded by Alexander had circulated in Germany since early 1946. In February 1946 Hallervorden wrote to the president of the IMT, vividly denying allegations made by the French prosecutor that he had been involved in the 'euthanasia' programme and that he had asked for the victims' brains, particularly in his alleged use of the phrase 'the more the better'. The IMT, in its reply, conceded that the French prosecution had misrepresented the material, but refused to hear Hallervorden on the matter in person. In August 1946, Hallervorden wrote to Alexander, asking him to correct what appeared to be a 'misunderstanding'.[44] Alexander apparently never replied. More than a year later

Hallervorden approached Countess Alice von Platen, one of the trial observers of the German 'commission of doctors', in an attempt to stop the spread of rumours about his Nazi past. Although Hallervorden's letter was intended to exculpate him from any suggestion of complicity in Nazi medical crimes, it highlighted his attitude towards the use of patient material that had been obtained by criminal means. Hallervorden was of the opinion that a refusal to examine the victims' brains would only have meant that 'science would have lost valuable knowledge' (*der Wissenschaft wertvolle Erkenntnisse verloren gegangen wären*).[45] He maintained that his morality as a doctor had not been compromised since it resembled that of an anatomist 'who was trying to obtain the body of an executed person because he was particularly in need of fresh research material'.[46] Hallervorden's verbose denials were not only failing to cut much ice with the occupying authorities, but he was also considered to be one of the less important figures in the denazification process, and was, more or less, forgotten in the aftermath of the Nuremberg trials.

It took another six years for the rumours about the ethics of this scientist to develop into a full-blown international controversy. No mention was made of Hallervorden's shady past when he moved from Dillenburg to the Max Planck Institute for Brain Research in Giessen, and participated undisturbed at international conferences. During the planning of the fifth international conference of neurologists in Lisbon, however, a number of distinguished Dutch neurologists, including Rademaker (Leiden), Sillevis Smit (Utrecht), Biemond (Amsterdam) and Verbiest (Utrecht), protested against the presence of too many German scientists, and especially against the participation of Hallervorden. As a result, an international controversy threatened to engulf the field of neuropathology.[47] The accusations were mostly based on Alexander's document L-170, itself an edited version of Alexander's CIOS reports from 1945, and on his publication from 1949 on 'Science under Dictatorship'. In February 1953 an American neuropathologist from New York commented that 'if the facts are true, this would seem to be very damning evidence against Hallervordern'. Another told Oskar Vogt that 'if he [Hallervorden] had made the remark "the more the better" and this in any way has had any influence in augmenting the number of victims, than the matter is very grave indeed – and he must be asked to withdraw'.[48]

Alexander, now alerted to the controversy, endorsed his critical attitude towards Hallervorden *vis-à-vis* a number of American neuropathologists. Hallervorden was 'a man who actively collaborated with the murderers of his patients', Alexander maintained, 'one of the protagonists of the German state-enforced euthanasia program' who had initiated 'certain organisational procedures concerning the killing centres for the insane'.[49] But many of his colleagues felt that Alexander, and indeed the Dutch delegation, had overreacted and had made unsubstantiated allegations against an internationally respected scientist. Some even felt that the whole affair was an 'obvious miscarriage of justice' and that Alexander owed Hallervorden a public apology.[50] Alexander's problem with the affair, so it seems, was not what Hallervorden had said or not said to him in 1945, but his general attitude towards his involvement in Nazi crimes. He was particularly concerned that Hallervorden had 'never expressed regret or repentance or anything else that may re-establish his eligibility to a medical group founded on the common ground of ethical purposes'.[51] Thus, it appears, the decisive factor that triggered, and perhaps even prolonged, the controversy was the total lack of any kind of public apology from Hallervorden, and the refusal by the German medical profession to accept moral responsibility for the crimes that had been committed.

The affair left Alexander as a lonely and controversial voice in a sea of experts who longed for a return to normality. Yet the Lisbon controversy made one thing clear – Alexander was and remained on the side of the victims. His charitable work for the former Ravensbrück victims in the 1950s shows that his time as a war crimes investigator and medical expert at Nuremberg had left its mark on his personality. His support for the victims of Nazi persecution resulted to a large extent from the fact that he considered himself to be one of them.

The charitable imperative

In 1951 the International Rescue Office approached Alexander and Taylor to see whether it would be possible to organise medical care for some of the most severe cases of the Ravensbrück experimental subjects.[52] The Ravensbrück women meant a lot to Alexander. During the Doctors' Trial, the women had created one of the most poignant moments, when Alexander showed their mutilated legs to a shocked international public. Together with Jacob Fine, chief surgeon of the Beth Israel Hospital in Boston, Alexander arranged for three of the women to visit the United States in 1951. Their names were Janina Iwanska, Jadwiga Kaminska and Helen Piasecka. The trip was independently financed and occurred almost unnoticed by the public. All three women lived in non-Communist countries after the war which made travel arrangements relatively easy. One of the women had been examined by Alexander in Nuremberg and stayed at the house of the Alexanders in Boston.[53] She was suffering from intense leg pains which, as it turned out, were due to nerve cells that had formed in the scar left by the experiment. A surgical operation at the Beth Israel Hospital relieved her pain. Throughout the mid- and late 1950s, Fine and Alexander also monitored the women's medical and psychological rehabilitation process, and helped them to file restitution claims with the West German government.[54] By corresponding with the Polish women, they realised that a great number of the Ravensbrück victims were in need of medical care. But because most of the women lived in Poland, visa arrangements were painstakingly slow. By the end of the 1950s almost no progress had been made.

Yet in 1958 the editor of the *Saturday Review*, Norman Cousins, who a couple of years earlier had brought some of the victims of the atom bomb – the so-called 'Hiroshima Girls' – to the United States, organised a campaign to find medical treatment for the Ravensbrück victims. Cousins established a committee that travelled to Poland to examine the medical records of the experimental subjects. From a total of seventy-four victims, twenty-seven women were selected for medical treatment in the United States.[55] Four of the women, Maria Skibinska-Pietrzak from Olsztyn, Władysława Marczewska and Helena Rafalska-Hegier, both from Warsaw, and Czesława Kostecki[56] were brought to Boston where they received medical treatment at the Beth Israel Hospital.[57] All of the women had been sent to Ravensbrück in September 1941, and had been experimented upon in 1942 and 1943.[58] Whereas Alexander chaired the local committee, Sidney Lee, the Director of Clinical Services, co-ordinated the various Jewish and Polish groups that offered lodgings and hospitality for the women during their stay. Some of the women also received dental treatment and psychotherapy. The charitable efforts by Beth Israel Hospital put Alexander, once more, centre-stage with journalists from the New England press. Indeed, he became something of a Boston celebrity. Newspaper and television reporters monitored the conditions of the women in short biographical features. When in mid-1959 the women returned to Poland, the regional press praised Alexander's role and that of the other Boston physicians. Above all, the work had been a public relations coup for the Boston Jewish community.

Although Alexander was never a practising Jew in the strict sense of term, his loyalty to the Jewish community grew as the years went by. When I spoke to his daughter Cecily in May 1999 at their weekend resort in Marion, Cape Cod, she told me that Alexander had told her after returning from Nuremberg that 'he could never not be a Jew. He would never consider converting to any other religion, even though he didn't agree with all of the principles'.[59] 'Do you think that he became more Jewish', I asked her. 'As time went on', she finished my sentence,

> no question ... We always celebrated Channukah and a few Jewish holidays. On Rosh Hashanah he would go to a synagogue, a different one, often his friends would invite him, somebody that he knew ... he would say, oh, you are going to [the] services, why don't you come to my synagogue. Often I went with him when I was in High School anyway, but he and my mother evidently felt very strongly that the children should learn about religion, but not belong to a church.[60]

It became quite clear from our conversation that for Alexander the persecution of the European Jewry, and the Nuremberg Doctors' Trial, in particular, was a very personal experience; he never belonged to a particular synagogue, but his charity towards the Ravensbrück women and other people in need made him a prominent figure in the Jewish community and in a number of charitable organisations in New England.

The case of the Ravensbrück women propelled issues of human research and medical ethics into the public domain. The mutilated women not only highlighted the role that doctors had played in medical war crimes, but, more importantly, the dangers that, as Alexander noted, a 'rapid decline in standards and professional ethics' could have for society. Because of the media attention that the Ravensbrück victims received, and the growing debate on medical ethics, some experts decided to examine the existing research practices in the United States. Their findings were a massive shock. Once their results were published, it became clear that American researchers had, in a great number of cases, carried out human experiments without clear and informed consent, or without informing the subjects about the health risks involved. Medical experts like Henry K. Beecher, Dorr Professor of Research in Anaesthesia at Harvard University, who in the late 1950s and early 1960s examined unethical human experiments in the United States, realised that the Nuremberg Code had, with few exceptions, rarely been implemented by the American research community after the Second World War.

Cold War medical ethics

'What most troubled the committee was the lack of respect for the American people that seemed to permeate the conduct of research', was how Ruth Faden, Professor of Bioemedical Ethics at Johns Hopkins University summarised the findings of the Advisory Committee on Human Radiation Experiments, established by President Clinton in January 1994.[61] In the late 1940s military scientists first gathered experiences about the effects of radiation mostly by chance. A number of accidents in the laboratories to develop an atomic bomb in the Manhattan Project, the mass exposure – and documentation[62] – of tens of thousands of people in Hiroshima and Nagasaki or the fallout effects from underwater detonations made military officials realise the enormous health risks of radiation exposure and of the difficulties in controlling it. The authorities felt an increased need to study the new weapons, 'in particular, experiments involving humans'.[63] The kind of experiments that were conducted in the 1940s, 1950s and 1960s under the auspices of the Atomic Energy Commission and other government agencies varied considerably. These ranged from cases in which subjects were exposed to extensive doses of radiation, to studies involving the administration of radioiron to pregnant women in order to determine the extent to which the substance could be found in their infants, to radioactive materials that were released into the environment without informing the population about the potential risks.[64] We know that some hospital patients were being fed with 'radiation-laced breakfast cereals' and that others were being injected with plutonium. In total the US government sponsored approximately 4000 human radiation and non-therapeutic radioactive tracer experiments that involved tens of thousands of research subjects, many of whom had no knowledge that they were being experimented upon.

From 1946 until the early 1960s more than 200 000 members of the US armed forces took part in nuclear weapons tests, mostly for training purposes. Up to 3000 of the participants were used as experimental subjects to measure the psychological and physiological effects of participating in atomic bomb tests. The risks for those participating in the experiments were generally extensive, and in some cases fatal. When in 1954 the government tested its hydrogen bomb on the Marshall Islands, the inhabitants – including the crew of a Japanese fishing boat that was in the vicinity – were exposed to excessive amounts of radiation that resulted in severe burns, cases of thyroid cancer and other medical disorders such as leukaemia. The Marshallese were also exposed to the long-term effects from radiation in the food chain. In the same year US soldiers at the weather station on the Rongerik Atoll were exposed to dangerous amounts of radiation.[65] From the beginning, military planners were interested in the short-term effects of radiation exposure on the fighting capability of combat soldiers, but not in any long-term concern for the health of these men. During the discussions of these issues in the Pentagon in 1950, one of the officials remarked: 'When you start thinking militarily of this, if men are going out on these missions anyway, a high percentage is [sic] not coming back, the fact that you may get cancer twenty years later is just of no significance to us.'[66] Others felt that it was unlikely 'that any particular person would realise that any damage had been done to him by such exposure'.[67] In the climate of the Cold War the health of human beings had seemingly become a cheap commodity.

Non-therapeutic radiation experiments were also conducted on children to measure the physiological effects of radioactive tracers in healthy subjects and patients. In all probability the research subjects will have developed thyroid cancers. Additional studies were carried out on pregnant women who were given radioiron. Although a causal link is difficult to establish, the rate of cancer in the children who were exposed to radioiron in the uterus turned out to be significantly higher than the average rate of cancer in the population. Even more troubling was the fact that in a great number of cases the research subjects were selected from the economically weak, underprivileged and relatively powerless sections of society. Often they were African-Americans, prisoners or seriously ill patients who could easily be exploited and misled, and, in the case of institutionalised children, enjoyed no proper legal representation. Moreover, in hundreds of cases the government intentionally, and in secret, released radiation into the environment, mostly in or around the United States atomic testing sites. Throughout the 1950s and 1960s the government also conducted 250 intentional releases of radioactive material close to the land of the Pueblo Indians in New Mexico.[68] Apparently in thirteen cases the purpose of the experiment was to measure the effects on humans who, for security reasons, legal liability and fear of embarrassment, were not informed that they were research subjects.[69]

Britain's Cold War experiments on humans will also have to undergo a comprehensive historical assessment. So far, Great Britain has shown itself unable – and perhaps unwilling – to face up to its Cold War past, for reasons only too understandable to government officials. Any study of the experiments could lead to compensation claims by the survivors and their relatives, and, perhaps worse, to a retrospective loss of the much-publicised moral high ground of Western democracy which needed to defend itself against the Soviet threat. A closer scrutiny of the evidence reveals that the British government violated human rights and democratic values in experiments that were performed on a large number of service personnel, often without their knowledge about the risks involved.

The most recent revelations are connected with Britain's chemical and biological warfare establishment at Porton Down in Wiltshire.[70] During the 1950s and 1960s Porton Down scientists secretly carried out nerve gas and chemical warfare experiments on thousands of soldiers who were exposed to highly toxic nerve agents and chemicals such as mustard gas, sarin and LSD.[71] In most cases it appears that the soldiers had only partial, if any, knowledge about the precise nature of the experiments, and that they were not fully informed about the risks involved. The consent, if it was obtained, would not have qualified as having been 'informed' according to the standards of the time.[72] In 1953 one of the so-called volunteers, the then twenty-year-old Ronald Maddison, was exposed to sarin, one of the most poisonous nerve agents extant at the time. Maddison subsequently died and his case is currently the subject of an inquest by HM Coroner for Wiltshire and Swindon.[73] Other soldiers, who participated in the experiments, have apparently suffered respiratory problems, skin diseases, poor eyesight and heart and lung problems. It is possible that in some cases the experiments may have led to an above-average level of ill health and premature death of the research subjects. The British government also released biological and chemical agents into the atmosphere to monitor their spread.[74] In 1956, for example, bacteria were released in the London underground to measure how far the micro-organism would travel. It appears that in none of these experiments were the people exposed to the agents fully informed that they had been research subjects because of 'defence security consideration aimed obviously at restricting public knowledge'.[75]

This fragmentary overview of some of the human experiments that were carried out in the United States and Great Britain after the war raises the question about the existing rules and regulations that scientists were required to follow. Above all, it raises the question why the Nuremberg Code does not seem to have played any meaningful role in regulating experimental research on human beings. Whatever Alexander and Ivy claimed in Nuremberg to secure the conviction of the defendants, evidence seems to suggest that some US agencies required the consent of experimental subjects long before the Second World War. But investigators do not seem to have been required to inform the subjects about the potential risks involved, nor was it generally specified what consent meant, or how it should be obtained.

In February 1953 the Secretary of Defence, Charles Wilson, issued a top secret memorandum to the secretaries of the army, navy and air force in which he made it clear that the Department of Defence adopted the Nuremberg Code for the use of human volunteers in experimental research related to atomic, biological and chemical warfare.[76] During the preliminary discussions one of the legal experts of the department had insisted that the principles of the Code would be used 'in toto in the document [1953 memorandum] since ... these already had *international juridical sanction* [emphasis added], and to modify them would open us to severe criticism along the line – "see they use only that which suits them".'[77] The above passage is, as Jonathan Moreno has pointed out, of profound importance because it shows that by 1953 US government officials were fully aware of the fact that the Code constituted part of international law and that a violation of its principles, irrespective of national security requirements, could undermine the self-proclaimed moral superiority of the Western governments.

The Code was adopted almost verbatim in the memorandum, except for three additions. Specifically, the Code had not addressed the issue of how informed consent was to be obtained.[78] Researchers wanting to perform experiments on service personnel were obliged to obtain the consent of the subjects *in writing* in a letter that was affixed to a written statement containing the principles of the Code, and in the presence of at least one witness.[79] Furthermore, the memorandum added two principles to the existing ten principles of the Code, one which ruled that the number of volunteers should be kept to a minimum, and one that reiterated that the established policy of prohibiting the use of prisoners of war for human experiments would be continued. Prisoners of war were to be excluded from human experiments 'under any circumstances'.[80] Before any experiment could commence, approval needed to be obtained from the secretary from the relevant service department in which the research was to be carried out. Finally, and crucially, the memorandum stated that 'the addresses' would be responsible to ensure the proper dissemination and compliance of the regulations.[81] This appears to have never happened in a systematic and comprehensive fashion. We do know, though, that copies of the memorandum were circulated to the Joint Chiefs of Staff and to the Research and Development Board. We also know that four months later, in June 1953, the secretary of the army rewrote the memorandum as an unclassified directive which soon after was adopted by the Surgeon General of the army, but disseminated only as a 'nonmandatory guide'.[82] A number of other government agencies such as the National Institute of Health or the Atomic Energy Commission also adopted the consent principle throughout the 1950s and 1960s. Overall, the dissemination and implementation of the Nuremberg Code was haphazard, often arbitrary and largely uncoordinated.

However, this does not explain why the Nuremberg Code was officially being adopted on one level, while being ignored by those carrying out the research on another. In other words, what went wrong in the dissemination process? The Advisory Committee on Human Radiation Experiments found that there was little evidence that the 1953 memorandum had been distributed or transmitted to medical researchers who were contracted or funded by government agencies for experiments related to atomic, biological and chemical warfare research.[83] By looking at the origins of the 1953 memorandum, particularly at the controversies which preceded its promulgation, we can see that it 'grew out of the decision making of a few top officials ... rather than out of the advisory process of internal experts on military medical research'.[84] The memorandum was the brainchild of a few senior military officials and legal advisers, who had managed to persuade the incoming Secretary of Defence to adopt the Nuremberg Code as part of a new policy on human experimentation. But the Code was not widely accepted by those officials who were actually responsible for the implementation of that policy. As a result, the content of the memorandum remained practically 'stuck' at the higher echelons of the military establishment and was not implemented. At one point in November 1952, after the reading of a draft proposal of the memorandum, members of the Committee on Chemical Warfare of the US Department of Defence descended into general laughter, prompting one of them to remark: 'If they can get any volunteers after that I'm all in favour of it.'[85] Such was the general atmosphere and 'culture of resistance' in the military medical establishment that an effective introduction of the Nuremberg Code was practically impossible under the existing conditions of the time.

Central to the explanation of the failure to communicate the Nuremberg Code effectively was the almost paranoid level of secrecy that characterised the US military and other government agencies during the Cold War. Important discussions about ethical standards in human experimentation almost always took place in secret. The classification of the 1953 memorandum as 'top secret' and its gradual and slow downgrading also adversely affected the dissemination process.[86] Information about specific programmes was strictly classified to protect the government from embarrassing public inquiries which, it was believed, could potentially jeopardise research enterprises. In some cases agencies intentionally used deception. Another reason for the lack of communication of medical ethics regulations was the inherent tension between the protection and respect for the rights and lives of patients on the one hand, and the objective to further medical and military knowledge on the other. During the Cold War most government agencies were unwilling to address this issue.

Finally, since many of the experiments were closely related to the training of service personnel, it is easy to see why many government agencies felt that their programmes should be exempt from the provisions of the Code. US Army Regulation No. 70-25 from 1962, for example, stated that 'research and non-research programs, tasks, and tests which may involve inherent occupational hazards to health or exposure of personnel to potentially hazardous situations encountered as part of training or other normal duties, e.g., flight training, jump training, fire drills, gas drills, and handling of explosives' were exempt from the provisions of the Nuremberg Code-based regulations.[87] Accordingly, a pilot who was flying through an atomic cloud was officially considered to be conducting 'flight training'. Investigators were also not required to obtain consent from subjects if the experiment was 'part of training or other normal duties'.[88] This applied, for example, to experiments measuring the physiological and psychological effects of servicemen who participated in atomic, biological and chemical warfare tests. Research conducted by the Army Medical Service which involved the 'basic disease process or new treatment procedures' was likewise exempt from the existing medical ethics regulations. This evidence supports the view that government and military agencies allowed for a waiver of the consent principle, not necessarily out of national security considerations as some have suggested, but more pragmatically in the context of military training.[89] Exposure to radiation and other agents could conveniently be classified as part of ongoing training programmes.

It appears that within the climate of the Cold War the concern for human rights and the inviolability of the experimental subjects, be they patients or service personnel, came second to the strategic considerations of most Western governments. According to Jay Katz, government officials and their advisers at best paid lip service to the principle of informed voluntary consent.[90] One former scientist remarked that in the 1940s and 1950s 'the doctor was king or queen. It never occurred to a doctor to ask for consent for anything.'[91] On the contrary, some investigators felt that they had a right to exploit patients for their own research and career: 'We were taking care of them and felt we had a right to get some return from them, since it wouldn't be in professional fees and since our taxes were paying their hospital bills.'[92] Another US researcher commented: 'I am

aware of no investigator (myself included) who was actively involved in
research involving human subjects in the years before 1964 who recalls
any attempts to secure "voluntary" and informed consent according to
Nuremberg's standards.'[93]
The Nuremberg Code was not shelved nor were its legal and ethical
implications completely ignored. For example, studies conducted in the
1950s by the sociologist Renee Fox showed that some laboratory
researchers knew of the ethical dilemmas inherent in their work and that
they used the Code as the guiding principle in their use of human subjects.[94] But such critical investigators were rare. In general, the Code was
not assigned any meaningful degree of priority in the complex power struggle between two opposing political ideologies.[95] It first needed a significant
shift in the domestic climate of the United States, and indeed elsewhere,
towards greater liberalisation and democratisation of society in the early
1960s. The growing public awareness of civil rights and democratic values
called for a revaluation of doctor–patient relationships, and for a reassess-
ment of the duties that experimenters had towards their patient-citizens.

The twisted road to Helsinki

What becomes apparent is that the political climate of the time is central
not only to the efficiency with which medical ethics regulations are being
introduced and disseminated, but, more importantly, to the extent to
which the rules are actually being followed by medical professionals,
funding and state agencies. But the history of post-war medical ethics also
tells another story, namely that the public perception of government-spon-
sored research, and of the medical profession more generally, increasingly
began to play a central role in shaping Western medicine. The first indication that criticism against the prevailing medical ethics standards might be
mounting from within the medical profession came during the 1950s,
when a few experts started to question the existing research culture. A crisis
of trust in the social relations of doctors and patients that was a part of a
long and twisted history of estrangement was further amplified by growing
tensions between hospitals and communities, and by the arrival of new
and costly biomedical technologies. Controversies over the allocation of
resources for, and beneficiaries of, medical research propelled the issue
of morals into the public and academic domain.

Medical professionals, lawyers, philosophers and sociologists increasingly
incorporated the issue of morals, however vaguely and randomly defined, in
their professional debate. Quite often a debate on morals was motivated by
deeper political and ideological objectives. In Alexander's 1952 publication on
'Morale and Leadership', a continuation of his work on medical science under
dictatorship, he attempted to claim the moral high ground for 'democratic
leadership' as opposed to the 'totalitarian leadership' under Stalinism.[96]

Others showed awareness for the shortcomings in the profession itself. In 1954 Joseph F. Fletcher contested the traditional doctor–patient relationship in his book on *Morals and Medicine: the Moral Problem of the Patient's Right to Know the Truth*.[97] The image of the paternalistic doctor who was acting in the best interests of the patient, whether as a healer or as a researcher, was increasingly challenged by minority and other interest groups. By the late 1950s the call for greater transparency and accountability in medicine and experimental research grew significantly louder. This resulted in a situation where the medical profession was nervously following sensitive disclosures about its practices, most notoriously in the Thalidomide scandal from 1962.[98]

What today's bioethics community, in the attempt to construct its own, often greatly biased historical narrative, likes to see as a number of courageous whistleblowers like Henry Beecher was in fact a largely opportunistic and measured response by some of the leaders of the profession to a significant change in the political, social and cultural climate that challenged the status quo and power of medical science.[99] The 1964 Helsinki Declaration must likewise be seen in the context of a largely successful project by the international medical community to supplant the Nuremberg Code with research regulations that were in line with the 'realities of medical research', and which reaffirmed and protected the position of the researcher. To see the early 1960s as a time of medical whistleblowers who, intentionally or not, gave 'birth' to modern bioethics would retrospectively turn professionals under pressure into subsequent heroes. Just to be clear. These men were surely not heroes as such but experts who knew how to secure their professional status and, above all, their financial interests. Change, if at all, was gradual and slow.

Yet the response by the medical establishment deserves attention as an indicator of new pressures in the profession, particularly in all areas related to research involving human participants. Changes in both research culture and medical ethics regulations were driven by the realisation among scientists that further resistance against human and civil rights issues in experimental medicine could only be counter-productive. The best strategy in order to remain in control over the issues was to take the lead. This insight was not the result of an acceptance or even admiration for the Nuremberg Code. On the contrary, since the late 1950s American medical scientists tried to water down the Code's 'rigid rules' which, it was argued, would stifle medical progress. Ironically, those resisting the effective implementation of the Code in the late 1950s were, in many cases, the same people who in the mid-1960s became known as the 'whistleblowers'. Foremost among them was Beecher himself. In an act of 'moral transformation', those attacking the Code's impracticability changed tack to become the most outspoken advocates for the inviolability of patient-citizens. Looking at it retrospectively, it was not just a master stroke in image management, but in the calculated preservation of professional power.[100]

In 1961 the Medical Ethics Committee of the WMA, chaired by Hugh Clegg, editor of the *British Medical Journal*, produced a draft 'Code on Ethics on Human Experimentation' which, after some discussion, was published in the autumn of 1962.[101] Two years later the World Medical Association officially adopted parts of the draft code during its General Assembly in June 1964. The document became known as the Helsinki Declaration. Important provisions of the draft code, however, such as the prohibition on using prisoners of war, whether military or civilian, or persons confined to prisons and mental institutions in human experiments, were deleted from the Helsinki Declaration.[102] In 1964 a crucial shift was initiated in the Helsinki Declaration about the quality of international medical ethics codes, from the rights of patients and the protection of human subjects in experimental research to the protection of patient welfare through physicians' responsibility. It was a move away from the essential requirement of informed consent as stated in the Nuremberg Code, beginning a watering-down process of the Code that continues to this day.

In the Helsinki Declaration the doctor 'should, if at all possible, consistent with the patient's psychology' obtain the patient's consent. At the same time the personal, non-transferable, legal responsibility of the physician for his research subjects was deleted from the Declaration, as was the right of the subject to terminate the experiment at any time. Compared to the Nuremberg Code, the Helsinki Declaration is a researchers' paradise, full of legal loopholes. Words like 'should' or 'if at all possible' or 'consistent with the patient's psychology' meant that the medical community had gained substantial leverage in shaping experimental research practice. From its early conception, the Helsinki Declaration was trying to adapt to the current research culture.[103] But it thereby undermined the central importance of the informed consent principle of the Code and reintroduced it with a paternalistic value system of the traditional doctor–patient relationship.

Constructing bioethics

Despite the apparent success of the international medical community in softening the impact of the Code on research practice, human and civil rights issues continued to be high on the political and international agenda. This included attention to the consent principle. In article seven of the Draft Covenant on Civil and Political Rights from 1958, the General Assembly of the United Nations adopted the principle that 'no-one shall be subjected to torture or to cruel, inhuman or degrading treatment or punishment. In particular, no-one shall be subjected without his free consent to medical or scientific experimentation.'[104] Such declarations of moral intent flew in the face of research being carried out at the time in the United States.

The Tuskegee Syphilis Study which started in 1932, and continued through the war and the Doctors' Trial, was still being carried out while the international medical community was watering down medical ethics regulations in the 1960s. It was not until 1972 that the gross violation of patient rights and lives was exposed.[105] For four decades medical treatment had been withheld from 399 black males who were suffering from tertiary syphilis in order to study the natural progression and the serious complications in the final stages of the disease. The men from Macon County, Alabama, close to the county seat of Tuskegee, had never been informed that they were subjects in a large-scale and long-term study, nor had they been told that they were suffering from syphilis. Instead they were told that they had 'bad blood' and were made to believe that they were being treated. Civil rights lawyers called it 'a programme of controlled genocide'.[106] It truly was one of the greatest medical ethics scandals in American history and initiated the creation of the Federal Regulations for the Protection of Subjects of Research.[107]

Few people in the 1960s knew that this kind of work was being carried out in the United States. Yet leading researchers sensed that their current research practice was likely to bring them sooner rather than later into conflict with the law. Attempts by the medical community to 'soften' the 'rigid rules' of the Code by formulating 'improved' medical ethics standards therefore have to be understood as part of an initiative to reduce the risk of legal liability for medical investigators. The objective was to move towards a situation where the profession would incur as little damage as possible once the anticipated exposures of unethical experiments occurred, both in terms of its reputation and financial compensation. That this was a realistic assessment became clear in 1963, when it turned out that twenty-two chronically ill patients had been injected without their consent with 'live cancer cells' at the Chronic Disease Hospital in Brooklyn, New York. The objective of the experiment had been to examine the reaction of the body's immune system to live cancer cells. Patients had apparently been told that they would receive 'some cells' to which they had given their 'oral consent'. The ensuing public debate led the journal *Science* to detect an 'ethical wilderness', with a myriad of questions that needed to be addressed. The most pressing issue that suddenly made newspaper headlines was whether there were 'adequate ethical guideposts for medical research on human subjects'. The journalist Elinor Langer noted that although the American research community adhered in principle to the Nuremberg Code, it did not provide researchers with sufficient guidance for particular situations, nor did the Code offer the researcher 'a secure legal backstop for his actions'.[108]

Beecher realised that such revelations were only the tip of the iceberg. In 1966 he published some of his findings in the *New England Journal of Medicine* so that the situation would remain under control. As he put it, by exposing cases of unethical medical practice the 'disservice to medicine' would not be as great as 'a continuation of the practices to be cited'.[109] At the same time he ensured that the identities of the investigators, who were guilty of serious professional misconduct, were not exposed. Beecher's 1966 survey of the existing literature on non-therapeutic human experimentation revealed that the American medical research community had been, and still was, continuously violating medical ethics standards since the end of the Second World War. Beecher's material was based on examples from medical schools, university hospitals, governmental and military research institutions. It showed that

many of the patients [who were used in the experiments] never had the risk satisfactorily explained to them, and it seems obvious that further hundreds have not known that they were the subject of an experiment although grave consequences have been suffered as a direct result.[110]

The article was a serious indictment of the US medical research culture, particularly because it came from one of the leading figures in the field who could not easily be silenced or discredited. According to Beecher the majority of patients 'would not have been available if they had been truly aware of the uses that would be made of them'.[111] Such 'troubling charges' as he called them, could only have resulted from 'troubling practices'. He alleged that the research culture in the United States had largely become unethical because of the enormous transformation which medical science underwent in the 1960s. Whereas funding for research at government institutions such as the National Institute of Health had increased 624-fold, from some $701 000 in 1945 to $36 000 000 in 1955 to $436 000 000 in 1965, medical schools had not been able to catch up with the training of a sufficiently large number of informed, conscientious and responsible researchers; in other words, the resources appeared to be greater 'than the supply of responsible investigators'.[112] With millions of dollars readily available for research, young and ambitious doctors knew that they had to become investigators to advance their career. Publish or perish, as the saying goes, meant that a 'culture of shortcuts' came to be accepted in the field of non-therapeutic human experimentation, particularly when it concerned the issue of informed, voluntary consent. In addition to new technologies and operations, Beecher detected an 'awakening of social conscience' in society that put further pressure on medical experts for greater accountability.

The evidence that Beecher presented was worrying. Dozens of published studies showed that investigators had acted, beyond any reasonable doubt, unethically and in some cases negligently. Studies that had endangered the health of the subjects turned out to be unnecessary. In many cases existing and efficient treatment was withheld from the patients. Researchers readily used groups of the mentally ill, children and juvenile prisoners in their research without informing their legal guardians about the hazards involved. In one case, twenty-six healthy babies, who were less that forty-eight hours old, were exposed to high doses of X-rays to monitor on film the filling and emptying of their bladder. 'What the result to the extensive X-ray exposure may be, no-one can yet say', Beecher remarked diplomatically. The United States was not alone in this kind of cavalier attitude in experimental research practice. In Britain Maurice H. Pappworth collected more than 500 unethical research papers which he reviewed in his book on *Human Guinea Pigs* in 1967.[113] Beecher and others had obviously addressed a widespread and in many ways embarrassing phenomenon in medicine which could no longer be ignored.

Yet unethical research continued despite these voices of dissent. It was as if the Code had not entered in the minds of those for whom it had been formulated. At some institutions mentally ill children were exposed to radioactive isotopes or hepatitis. At others, such as the Holmesburg Prison, hundreds, if not thousands of prisoners were used as readily available research subjects to test such essential cultural products as facial and skin moisturising creams and perfumes. The temptation to experiment under such ideal laboratory conditions was often too great for young and ambitious researchers. When the investigating dermatologist, Albert M. Kligman, first visited Holmesburg Prison in 1966 he was overcome with joy: 'All I saw before me were acres of skin. It was like a farmer seeing a fertile field for the first time.'[114]

For a man like Kligman neither the Nuremberg Code nor the Helsinki Declaration nor any other ethics code mattered. What mattered to him were the enormous profits which his company Ivy Research Laboratories, Inc., was making at Holmesburg Prison. But the Code did matter to Alexander. In early 1966, even before Beecher had published his findings in the same year, Alexander claimed authorship of at least part of the Code in his paper on the 'Limitations of Experimentation on Human Beings'.[115] Whether coincidence or not, Alexander, like Beecher, had clearly read the writing on the wall. As one of those who believed that he had brought the Nazi doctors to justice, he wanted to be at the forefront of the debate. What better way to boost his image than by claiming to be the author of the Code, even if this meant being slightly economical with the truth? Alexander was clearly seeking public and academic attention. In 1966 he published eleven papers.[116] In a sense Beecher and Alexander were both competing for publicity. Whereas the former proclaimed himself as a whistleblower, which, considering the historical facts, he was not, the latter announced himself as the author of the Code, which he could not claim either. Both, along with many others, were vying for a place in the history of medical ethics.

Alexander and Beecher were in agreement over a number of issues; both were opposed to the introduction of greater legal accountability of the medical profession. According to Alexander the interference in medical research by government agencies which were not bound by the Code and by the 'mutual approval-dependence of the scientific fraternity' created a conflict of interest. Alexander, like many of his peers, was deeply distrustful of allowing the state to regulate medical research. But Beecher and Alexander differed profoundly in their evaluation of the Code. Alexander saw the Code as a 'useful guide' which helped to define the limits of experimental research.[117] The 'advantage of the Code' was that it offered medical scientists a landmark against which they could measure the ethical quality of their own experiments. He was adamant that the 'strict adherence to this Code is not only in the interest of the experimental subjects, but also in the interest of the investigator'.[118]

Alexander, unlike many of his American peers, seems to have been more open-minded towards the democratisation process that shaped the formulation of civil and human rights issues in the 1960s. He welcomed the fact that patients had gained greater knowledge of medicine through health magazines, radio broadcasts and films. Far from fearing the intrusion of patient groups into the work of doctors, he believed that their 'cooperative research attitude' facilitated medical progress. Since the Doctors' Trial Alexander had been particularly concerned for the welfare of prisoners who were used as experimental subjects. Although research with prisoners could be considered ethical under certain circumstances, it remained doubtful 'whether any consent given by a prisoner, who by definition is restricted in his choices, could ever be regarded as truly voluntary'.[119]

Yet when it came to his own research Alexander showed little regard for proposed changes in the research culture or with people intruding on what he considered his academic territory. Then it was he, and he alone, who wanted to decide what was considered to be ethical and unethical human experimentation. Since the 1950s, Alexander had been conducting a great number of human experiments in the field of mental illness and multiple sclerosis. According to Alexander the 'strict adherence to the spirit and letter of the Nuremberg Code at no time hindered nor hampered our research'.[120] It was not the Code, but other colleagues, who 'hindered' his work. In 1974 the thirty-eight-year-old Peter Breggin, a former Harvard graduate and director of the non-profit Centre for the Study of Psychiatry in Washington DC, filed a $6 million slander suit against Alexander. Breggin's institute opposed the uncontrolled practice of psychosurgery and called for the reform in the application of methods like electric convulsive treatment (ECT) and insulin coma treatment (ICT). It was an area of research in which Alexander had been working since the early 1940s and in which he had published extensively, particularly during the 1950s.[121] Breggin had touched a raw nerve. During the annual meeting of the American Psychiatric Association, Alexander allegedly told participants that Breggin was 'an enemy of mankind' and a 'danger to medicine'.[122] At one point he supposedly called Breggin 'a paranoid kook'.

The case received considerable publicity. In May 1974 Breggin used a Boston conference that was financed by the Church of Scientology and the Citizens Committee on Human Rights to boost the work of his institute and position himself as the young, liberal investigator, who respected human rights but was being attacked by the older, established researcher. For Alexander the whole affair was a major blow to his reputation, even though the law suit was eventually settled out of court. He must have felt that it was time to retire. 'He felt unfairly [done by] because of this', Cecily remembered, 'and it cost him a lot, a lot of energy and a lot of money and a lot of time, which he felt took him away from things that were much more important to do, and he really felt persecuted ... he ran out of energy and he was depressed at that time'.[123] More important than fighting one's professional corner was to wait for the right moment to construct one's own role in history. When in the late 1970s Robert J. Lifton, Professor of Psychiatry at Yale University, contacted Alexander in order to write a major study on the Nazi doctors, that moment had arrived.

Reflections

The man who approached Alexander in February 1978 was not just any scholar.[124] Robert J. Lifton was an academic who had won international acclaim after the publication of his book on the survivors of Hiroshima in 1967, *Death in Life*.[125] This was followed by a major edition on *Crimes in War* in 1971.[126] Lifton was interested in studying the psychological mechanisms which motivated perpetrators to commit war crimes, how they had developed strategies to keep uncomfortable knowledge at bay, in short, their psychological blocking and survival mechanisms. He also wanted to examine similarities and differences in feelings of guilt, experienced by both the perpetrators and their children, and by the victims and their children. Like the London-based émigré journalist Gitta Sereny, who at around the same time explored the psychology of men like Franz Stangl, the former commandant of the Treblinka concentration camp, and later exposed Albert Speer's battle with truth, Lifton wanted to offer a psychological explanation as to why German doctors had turned into murderers. His study was based on dozens of interviews, not just with the perpetrators and the victims, but with psychiatrists, sociologists, prison chaplains and war crimes investigators.[127] These experts had studied the people for whom the Nazi period meant an irrevocable turning point in their lives. From the perspective of a psychologist, Nazism constituted an ideal case to study the nature of extreme human behaviour, and the effects of extreme trauma resulting from such behaviour. Lifton knew that he had one major advantage because many of the people were still alive. Some were more willing to talk than others. Alexander was one of the former.

When Lifton discovered copies of Alexander's CIOS reports on German war crimes, he contacted Alexander in Boston. What started off as an academic enquiry became a scholarly and in many ways passionate historical and philosophical discourse between two men, both of whom wanted to understand the origins of the Holocaust. Alexander readily supplied Lifton with a wealth of historical material, including his notebooks and personal recollections, and invited him over to spend time discussing the issues at his favourite weekend resort at Cape Cod. In his first letter, written in February 1978, Lifton told Alexander that he was in the early stages of a 'study of medical behaviour in Auschwitz', and hoped to learn more from Alexander about his time at Nuremberg. Two months later he met with Alexander and the historian Erich Goldhagen, author of a book on ethnic, especially Jewish minorities in the Soviet Union and the father of the controversial Holocaust historian Daniel J. Goldhagen, for an evening in Boston.[128] Reflecting on their first meeting, Lifton told Alexander that

> it takes time to explore these complicated issues, and I would like very much to continue the dialogue we have begun. Would there be a possibility of my seeing more of your materials – even very casual, handwritten notes – concerning your observations on Nazi doctors at Nuremberg? Those early impressions would be very valuable for me.[129]

Alexander did as he was asked and unearthed many scattered notes which he had produced during his tour of duty in Europe. Many of them were 'illegible' because of his terrible handwriting and his habit of oscillating between the English and German languages.[130] In July 1978 Alexander told Lifton that he had changed his vacation plans; he had decided to stay in New England and book himself a room at the Harbour Lights Inn in Provincetown. Here he would be happy to meet Lifton for further discussions about Nazi medicine.[131] Instead the Liftons invited Alexander – and his then girlfriend Lois – over for dinner at their summer house. It was, as Alexander remarked, 'perfect enjoyment intellectually, aesthetically and gastronomically!'[132]

Two weeks later, on 29 August, Alexander returned with the material Lifton was interested in.[133] Of this meeting Lifton produced a comprehensive summary of what was discussed. It provides rare insight into how Alexander dealt with his own role in bringing Nazi doctors to justice in the Doctors' Trial. Both started off by talking about Alexander's experience with the Ravensbrück victims, some of whom, as Lifton knew, had recently been visiting the United States. One of the women, who had resisted the camp commander at the time, had since then stuck in Alexander's mind as a reminder that 'these bastards could be defeated'.[134] More than thirty years after the war Alexander was still full of pent-up emotions about Nazism.

Lifton and Alexander also came to realise that work in the field somehow affected one's own life. For Lifton it was a feeling that one became somehow 'stained' by the constant reading and digesting of immoral and criminal material. As a historian, and even more so as a psychiatrist, this process is, of course, alleviated by the existing professional defence mechanisms. Yet probably few Holocaust historians would deny that their work has left them affected. For Lifton it was an important insight at the beginning of his research:

> We talked about the extent to which anyone getting involved in the work felt tainted – I told him how survivors I had interviewed had immersed themselves in the issue immediately after the war in order to tell the tale, sometimes working with the Americans or with other[s] at Nuremberg, and had the need to leave the whole subject – to start their lives in a way that was free of it … We agreed that this affects those of us who study the problem also – we feel tainted by it – as though the filth of the Nazis rubs off on us in some way – I told him how I had promised myself that, once this study is over, I will leave it and them forever – and I have hardly begun.[135]

Alexander was clearly one of those who had 'immersed' themselves after the war in order to understand the rationale behind one of the greatest crimes in modern history. His meticulous and, in many ways, obsessive investigation into the nature of medical war crimes was his way of rationalising what remained so extraordinarily difficult to comprehend. Others, like Primo Levi, had felt the same, a desire to 'tell the tale', to bear witness, albeit knowing that they were not the 'true witnesses', those who had touched bottom in full possession of the truth. The true witnesses were the *sommersi* for Levi, the drowned and submerged, those 'blotted out of existence'. They, the survivors, were the *salvati*, the saved.[136] And when he felt that he had said what he had to say, Levi committed suicide. In this he was not alone among the survivors. It was as if the meaning of life after Auschwitz had been reduced for him to 'performing a task', a mission to tell his story so that it would not be forgotten by future generations. At times Levi felt that it had been the only task clearly defined for him.[137]

In a sense Alexander's psychological response was not dissimilar to that of Levi, even if the extent of suffering and feelings of guilt were probably less profound. Above all, the memory of the offence had been less severe. To write, to take notes, to produce dozens of letters and hundreds of pages of diary entries, all this was Alexander's way of coming to terms with the Holocaust, mostly on an intellectual and rational level, as the response of a reasonable man. Emotionally, however, he never recovered from the painful experience. At one point, like Levi, he felt unable, perhaps unwilling, to examine for the rest of his life a world that was so full of criminal and amoral human behaviour. He 'needed to put it all aside' and re-establish his professional work as a psychiatrist, to start his life in a way, as Lifton put it, 'that was free of this whole subject'.[138] It is quite possible that the severe illness and then death of his wife Phyllis in February 1956 may also have contributed to Alexander's decision to leave the subject. He needed to return to an area of work where he felt he was helping people and saving lives, something that had given him the greatest sense of satisfaction since following his father on his medical rounds as a young man. The romantic notion of saving human lives had been the reason why Alexander had become a doctor in the first place.[139] His calling was that of a doctor, not that of a historian or a political scientist. 'I didn't want to become famous from studying those bastards', he told Lifton.[140] Yet on another level Alexander had become famous for exactly that.[141]

But what exactly was it that made Alexander, and indeed Lifton, feel so uneasy about examining the subject in greater depth? Both were professional psychiatrists. Their focus of analysis was first of all the psychology of human behaviour, not the history of how political and philosophical ideas had shaped human society, nor how processes of modernisation and industrialisation had affected the structure and functioning of government. In some sense their focus on Nazism was narrow because they did not attempt to locate the behaviour of human beings in the context of a highly industrialised, economically powerful, modern nation-state of the twentieth century. Their self-analysis nevertheless shows a great deal of insight into why the study of Nazi Germany, and indeed of many other periods of history, can be a particularly difficult undertaking. When they talked about the reason why one 'felt this taint', Alexander brought up the role of empathy, the ability and readiness to feel oneself into the thinking of other people. It was this process of identification with the perpetrators, which in part is necessary if one wants to understand them, which turned the work for Alexander and Lifton into an uncomfortable journey. 'It has to do, I think, with the problem I feel with Münch',[142] Lifton said:

> the very act of probing the humanity of one of these people – their conflicts – their mental function, especially around maintaining something like humanity as opposed to pure evil – all this is threatening ... in the very act of probing conflicts around humanity of one who has been so deep into evil, one feels all the more threatened by that evil. It brings it closer to the investigator. It is partly a matter of 'maybe I could have done such things myself!' – but also, I believe, partly of being absorbed into the world in which all restraints are down, everything is possible – requirements of structure and morality that are taken for granted, never talked about (for instance, that one does not do fatal experiments upon young women) are suddenly not functional – and one is forced into an imaginative realm that one never wished to touch – a realm one is ordinarily protected against. In any case, the taint is there, and it does pain.[143]

292 *Justice at Nuremberg*

The conversation revealed that Alexander had obviously entered into that world and, as a result, had lost his distance from the subject matter. Alexander told Lifton that during the war he had been trained as a 'forensic specialist' who would 'condemn the crime but not the criminal'. He wanted to be seen as an objective observer, reasonable and fair in his approach, without a personal grudge or hatred which might affect his sound judgement:

> What anguish I did not feel was probably prevented by the satisfaction of having been victorious over so much evil. Therefore, I was able to view this evil no longer as a threat, but just as an awful example of the degrading inhumanity of man viewed as not only hopefully ended, but also with the hope of even preventing it in the future. I am sure my psychiatric training in the habit of disapproving of a crime, but not necessarily of the criminal, contributed to this objective attribute.[144]

Yet Alexander's use of language about the Nazis revealed that he felt a great deal of contempt for them. His obsessive study of individual Nazi personalities had led to what Lifton called an 'imaginative connection' between the investigator and the perpetrator. Whereas Alexander showed contempt for men like Karl Wolff, chief of Himmler's personal staff, who possessed an ability to cover his tracks, he showed compassion for Rudolf Brandt, Himmler's subsequent adjutant: 'So poor Rudy Brandt, who is just an adjutant of Himmler, got hanged because he and Himmler signed all the death certificates.'[145] Alexander showed even more understanding for Karl Brandt, Hitler's doctor. Throughout the Third Reich and during the Doctors' Trial Brandt had remained consistent in his ideological fanaticism, something that earned him a certain amount of respect from the tribunal. 'At least [Brandt] held on to his convictions', Alexander remarked.[146] This kind of identification and empathic understanding with the perpetrators showed the extent to which Alexander, despite his feelings of contempt for some individuals, had 'entered into the Nazis' mental realm' and, as a result, came out with what he experienced as being tainted.

For Alexander the discussions with Lifton were a way to 're-experience his own work' after more than thirty years. On 10 October 1978 he told Lifton that he was still 'astonished at the equanimity' with which he had responded to his discoveries. Only once had he felt raging anger, upon visiting the crematorium at the Dachau concentration camp which he had apparently visited 'two days after its liberation'. According to Alexander:

> there still hovered the smell of the blood of the 90 French officers who had been shot on this sandy plot near the crematorium, perhaps mixed with some of the smell of the remnant of cyanide gas from the adjacent gas chamber. As I stood on this freshly blooded sand plot, my hands

became pale, with vaso-constriction similar to an attack of Reynand's disease. They became white and insensitive, and remained so for about 10 minutes. I never had another attack of Reynand's disease either before or after.[147]

Considering that the Dachau camp was liberated by the US army at the end of 1945, and that Alexander did not arrive in Germany before 23 May, this account seems highly unlikely. In his first letter to his wife Phyllis in May 1945 Alexander had written that they had flown 'low over Dachau, smoke still rising from some of the ... buildings which were being burned down. Surviving inmates were waving and cheering at the plane and you could see that two American field hospitals were set up near the camp grounds.'[148] What he experienced at the time as 'smoke still rising from the buildings' turned into 'the smell of the blood' and into 'the smell of the remnants of cyanide gas' some thirty years later. Even taking into account that the smell of cyanide gas and the burning of human flesh takes a considerable time to evaporate in the atmosphere, it is unlikely that Alexander could smell it more than three weeks after his arrival.

What becomes evident from these passages is that Alexander, like many other survivors and witnesses, had begun to construct his own memory of the event. Sensitised through the intensity of the offence which was often existential and life threatening, survivors experienced a heightened sense of receptivity in which every detail was believed to be carved in their memory, in which smells and colours predominated the recollection of facts. The same appears to be true for those who, like Alexander, witnessed the effects of the crime first-hand or shortly after it had been committed. Human memory now needed to construct a narrative from what a person had smelled, seen or felt that was compelling and powerful enough to correspond to the level of the crime. Not surprisingly, many of those who survived or witnessed the most unbearable events were mostly silent. They lost the ability to express themselves and repressed their memory of the past. Others showed significant creativity in re-evoking their experience. Writers like Levi were surely aware that human memory is a 'marvellous but fallacious instrument'. Whereas the memory of the offence was exposed to slow processes of degradation, to 'an obfuscation of outlines, a, so-to-speak, physiological oblivion', memory could also be cultivated and perfected. 'It is certain', Levi remarked,

that practice (in this case, frequent re-evocation) keeps memories fresh and alive in the same manner in which a muscle that is often used remains efficient; but it is also true that a memory evoked too often, and expressed in the form of a story, tends to become fixed in a stereotype, in a form tested by experience, crystallised, perfected, adorned, which installs itself in the place of the raw memory and grows at its expense.[149]

For Alexander the time for story-telling had begun, not necessarily in a misleading or falsifying way, but with the intention of constructing a narrative that was vivid and powerful enough to match his own emotions which his memory evoked. In Levi's words, he showed a 'tendency to round out the facts or heighten the colours', perhaps because the raw feelings of the event had long since been repressed in some unknown part of his mind.[150] Alexander appears to have been genuinely happy to provide Lifton with material and knowledge on the subject. It gave him a sense that they both would 'make a contribution to the future'. Despite Lifton's suggestion, Alexander never followed up on the idea of writing an autobiography. When leaving Lifton's house, Alexander had explained why he had been chosen to investigate German medical war crimes in the spring of 1945 and not someone else:

> At the very end, somewhat modestly, he told that, rather than the Air Force showing such marvellous wisdom in appointing a man like him, it was total chance because there was a young lieutenant who had been in the Air Force two weeks who had been his student at Duke University and when he saw Alexander's name as one of those scientifically qualified, more or less at the top of the list because ... it started with an A, he settled on that name – which is how Alexander got the appointment.[151]

For Lifton the meeting with Alexander was one of many personal encounters which had a significant impact for his work on Nazi Germany. Alexander certainly made him conscious of the problems inherent in this kind of research. By November Lifton had read through most of Alexander's material. He thought it was 'fascinating – extremely valuable ... and moving as well'. Shortly before Christmas 1978 Lifton thanked Alexander for the valuable discussions they both had on the topic: 'Your notebooks have been very important to me in this work – indeed *you* have been very important to me in this work!'[152] Lifton's thanks was genuine. Alexander appears to have influenced Lifton's work more than the latter may have realised. In particular, Alexander's concept of *Blutkitt*, that is the creation of group cohesion by implicating each member of the group in criminal behaviour, thus making them susceptible to blackmail, or his idea of Thanatology, the 'idolatrous delight' in producing death, seem to have entered into Lifton's scholarly analysis of the *The Nazi Doctors: Medical Killings and the Psychology of Genocide*, first published in 1986.[153] In it, Lifton developed the psychological principle of 'doubling' which he described as 'the division of the self into two functioning wholes, so that a part-self acts as an entire self'.[154] He sees 'doubling' as an essential part in explaining the 'healing–killing paradox' which led doctors to abandon their duty to heal

Plate 32   Leo Alexander in his later years.

patients in exchange for a 'science of killing. Nazi medicine was not just corrupted, it was inverted.'[155] It was this insight into the 'destructive perversion of medicine' which Alexander had realised as early as November 1946, 'this preoccupation with methods of producing death [which ran] through many of the other investigations like a red thread', and which constituted an essential part of the nature of Nazi medicine.[156] Lifton's book became a milestone in the historiography on Nazi medicine. For Alexander the publication came too late to appreciate it. He died of cancer in July 1985 in Boston.[157]

At the end of our long conversation, I asked Cecily what kind of man Alexander really was. There was a moment of silence. Outside a canoe was ploughing through the water towards the harbour of Marion. I knew that it was a difficult question to ask, and I had thought for some time whether or not I should really put it to her, especially because although she had been close to her father, she had also suffered under his strictness and unreasonable expectations. It took her some time to find the right words, but when she finally described him, I knew that she had managed to capture his complex personality:

> Intellectual, brilliant, sophisticated, fascinating, he had very little time for introspection, he had a great deal of insight into the problems of other people, but not into those that he was close to. When people that were close to him were ill or in trouble, it took a long time for him to realise it. It's not that he was cruel, I don't mean that, but concerned mostly for himself, for his research, for his schedule, rather than fitting with anybody else. Didn't require much sleep. He loved. He lived a good life, he loved to travel, he loved to dance, he loved art, he loved parties, he loved women. He wasn't concerned too much with money. On occasion he didn't quite have enough, but he managed to carry on and he felt that it would always come, there is always another day.[158]

Alexander was a man who was difficult and ambiguous in many ways, but also warm and loving. Nuremberg had surely given him a sense of purpose. In a paper from 1954 he remarked: 'I have rambled on not only about why I became a doctor, but also why I am the sort of doctor I am – perhaps, in my delusion of potential creative omnipotence I have tried my brain and my hands at too many different things – but I was ever mindful of never becoming a one-treatment doctor or a one-answer philosopher.'[159] That he certainly was not. To have always remained an optimist and full of hope in the good nature of human beings I find one of the most striking features in Alexander's life. In a way Alexander's life serves as a powerful reminder that life is rich and colourful and that behind the many things that appear to be black or white there is the colour of grey. To have fought for the rights of those whose lives were violated I find equally important.

His was a life dedicated to a future in which human and patient rights would be universally accepted and indeed protected in the world. We are still far away from this goal and need to redouble our efforts. Alexander's contribution to modern biomedical research ethics may have been small and insignificant in the stream of suffering which has engulfed our human society since the days of Nuremberg. But it was a worthy contribution nonetheless.

Notes

1. Prologue

1 BAK, ZSg 154, box 63,˙ Leo Alexander, 'An Un-Numbered Document', 12 July 1947. The two characters Archie the Cockroach and Mehitabel the Cat originated from a visit to friends in Cambridgeshire in 1945 when Alexander flicked through a children's book called 'Archie and Mehitabel'; AP, Leo Alexander to Phyllis Alexander, 27 January 1945.

2 *Ibid.*

3 *Ibid.*

4 Alexander borrowed these characters from one of Britain's wartime humour-columnists. 'Scar Face' referred to the historical figure Al Capone, one of the most notorious gang leaders during the prohibition period in the United States.

5 BAK, ZSg 154, box 63, Leo Alexander, 'An Un-Numbered Document', 12 July 1947.

6 For the literature on the Nuremberg Doctors' Trial and its impact on modern biomedical ethics see, for example, Alexander 1966; Alexander [1946] 1976; Alexander 1976; Ambroselli 1988; Ambroselli 1997; Annas and Grodin 1992; Annas and Grodin 1999; Barondess 1996; Beecher 1966; Beecher 1970; Benzenhöfer 1996; Biddiss 1997; Bleker 1996; Burleigh 1997; Caplan 1992; Cooter 2002; Dörner 2000; Dörner 2001; Dörner and Ebbinghaus 1999; Dörner and Ebbinghaus 2001b; Ebbinghaus 2001; Elkeles 1996; Ernst and Weindling 1998; Faden *et al.* 1986; Faden *et al.* 1996; Frewer and Eickhoff 2000; Frewer and Wiesemann 1999; Glover 1999; Grimley Evans and Beck 2002; Grodin 1992; Harkness 1996; Harkness and Shuster 1998; Helmchen and Winau 1986; Horner 1999; Howard-Jones 1982; Katz 1966; Katz 1972; Katz 1997; Katz 1998; Kolb and Seithe 1998; Loewy 1995; Maio 1996; Maio 2001; Maio 2002; Marrus 1999; Mausback 1998; McFarland-Icke 1999; Michalczyk 1994; Mitscherlich and Mielke 1960; Moreno 1999; Pappworth 1967; Peiffer 1992; Pernick 1991; Peter 1994; Peter 2001; Popper and McCloskey 1995; Roth *et al.* 1999; Schmidt 1997; Schmidt 1999; Schmidt 2001a; Schmidt 2001b; Schmidt 2002a; Schmidt 2002b; Schmidt 2003; Seidel 2001; Seidelmann 1998; Shuster 1997; Taylor 1949a; Taylor 1949b; Taylor 1976; Taylor 1992; Toellner 1998; Tröhler and Reiter-Theil 1997; Vollman and Winau 1996; Weindling 1996a; Weindling 1996b; Weindling 2000; Weindling 2001a; Weindling 2001c; Weindling 2001d; Wiesemann and Frewer 1996; Winau 1996; Wunder 1998.

7 See also Marrus 1999.

8 For some of the literature on the Nuremberg Code see, for example, Alexander [1946] 1976; Annas 1992a; Arnold and Sprumont 1997; Bonah *et al.* 2003; Deutsch 1997; Drinan 1992; Gerst 1996; Glantz 1992; Grodin 1992; Harkness and Shuster 1998; Herranz 1997; Katz 1992; Katz 1996; Krause and Winslade 1997; Macklin 1992; Maio 1996; Mathieu 1997; Mathieu 1998; Moreno 1996; Moreno 1997; Perley *et al.* 1992; Rothman 1997; Schmidt 2001a; Seidler 1998; Shevell 1996; Shevell 1998; Shuster 1997; Shuster 1998; Taylor 1976; Tröhler and Reiter-Theil 1997; Vollmann and Winau 1996; Weindling 2001c; Wiesing 1997; Winau 1996; Winau 2001; Wiesemann and Frewer 1996; Wunder 2001.

9 Wunder 2001, 476–88.

10 *Ibid.*, 479.
11 Katz 1996, 1665.
12 See pp. 256–7 below.
13 Wunder 2001, 477.
14 Arnold and Sprumont 1997.
15 See also Warren 1998, 7–9.
16 Mathieu 1998, 551f.
17 Proctor 2000, 15–16; also Robert Proctor, Statement and Response to M. Susan Lindee (unpublished typescript, 23 August 1997).
18 Schmidt 1997; Schmidt 1999a; Schmidt 1999b; Roth *et al.* 1999; Schmidt 2000a; Schmidt 2000b; Schmidt 2000c; Schmidt 2001a, Schmidt 2001b, Schmidt 2001c, Schmidt 2001d, Schmidt 2001e; Schmidt 2002b; Schmidt 2003.
19 Schmidt 2002a.
20 *Ibid.*, 182ff., 246, 268f.
21 See Peiffer 1997.
22 See Schmidt 2001b, note 2.
23 See Schmidt 2001d.
24 Mitscherlich and Mielke 1947; Mitscherlich and Mielke 1949a and 1949b; Mitscherlich and Mielke 1960; Platen-Hallermund 1948.
25 Peter 1994.
26 Bayle 1950.
27 Burman 1985.
28 Annas and Grodin 1992.
29 See note 8.
30 Dörner and Ebbinghaus 1999. The microfiche edition contains the trial transcripts of the Nuremberg Doctors' Trial (in the following referred to as NDT Records) as well as background material (in the following referred to as NDT Documents and Material); see also Dörner and Ebbinghaus 2001b. The University of Harvard has recently begun to digitalise the documents and transcripts of all twelve Nuremberg war crimes trials and is making the material publicly available on the internet. A significant proportion of documents from the Nuremberg Doctors' Trial are now accessible through the internet; see www.nuremberg.law.harvard.edu.
31 See Gerst 1996; also Matheiu 1998; Schmidt 2001a.
32 Menkin 1968, 189; I am grateful to Sandra Marlow for drawing my attention to the article.
33 Beecher 1970, Appendix A, 215.
34 *Ibid.*, 219.
35 See Katz 1984, Appendix A, 230–6.
36 Beecher 1970, Appendix A, 234.
37 Grodin 1992, 130f.; for details about the Neisser case see Moll 1902, 560f.
38 Moll 1902.
39 *Ibid.*, 557f.
40 *Ibid.*, 560f.
41 See also Katz 1997, 407f.
42 Vollman and Winau 1996, 1446.
43 Moll 1902, 566ff.
44 Maehle 1999, 309–38; also Maehle 1998, Maehle 2000; Moll 1902, 357–404.
45 Frewer 2000, 139–45; also Maio 2002; Winau 1996, 25f.
46 Sass 1983; Grodin 1992; Katz 1997, 410; see especially Bonah *et al.* 2003.
47 For Lieck see Proctor 1999, 22ff.; for Abderhalden see Frewer 2000.

48 Thüringer Landeshauptarchiv Weimar, Thüringer Ministerium des Innern, E 663; (1) Niederschrift über die Sonderberatung des Reichsgesundheitsrats, 14 March 1930; (2) Reichsminister des Innern an die Landesregierungen, 28 February 1931; (3) Endgültiger Entwurf von Richtlinien für neuartige Heilbehandlung und für die Vornahme wissenschaftlicher Versuche am Menschen; (4) Thüringisches Ministerium des Innern an den Reichsminister des Innern, 17 March 1931. I am grateful to Michael Grodin, Boston, for providing me with a copy of the manuscript.

49 Thüringer Landeshauptarchiv Weimar, Thüringer Ministerium des Innern, E 663, Reichsminister des Innern an die Landesregierungen, 28 February 1931; Thüringisches Ministerium des Innern an den Reichsminister des Innern, 17 March 1931.

50 Proctor 1999, 7.

51 Uexküll 1947.

52 Katz 1992, 228; also Katz 1996, 1663; Katz 1997, 412; Final Report 1996, 151.

53 'Wir brauchen ein zentrales Strafgericht', *Der Spiegel*, 27 (2001), 147–50, 150; also Schmidt-Häuer 2001, 9–11.

54 Hill 1963; also Beecher 1970, Appendix A, 269–71.

55 Katz 1996, 417; see also Katz 1984.

2. The Austrian Jew

1 Hamann 1999, 325–59.

2 *Ibid.*, 326.

3 *Ibid.*, 326f.

4 *Ibid.*, 327.

5 See also Mahler 1984; Mahler 1998.

6 Hamann 1999, 329.

7 *Ibid.*, 339.

8 *Ibid.*, 331.

9 *Ibid.*, 330.

10 This account is based on material compiled by Leo Alexander's grandmother; AP, Family Memories, by Caecily Alexander, Vienna, 16.7.1930.

11 *Ibid.*

12 *Ibid.*

13 Interview with Cecily Alexander-Grable, Marion, Cape Cod, May 1999.

14 The name of Alexander's daughter Cecily is spelled without an 'a'; see also AP, Alfred Alexander to Leo Alexander, 30 August 1936.

15 AP, Family Memories, by Robert Alexander, no date.

16 *Ibid.*; also Interview with Irene Hulst, Loenen a/d Veht, March 1998.

17 UAV, file Gustav Alexander.

18 *Ibid.*

19 UAV, Rigorosum file, PN 1550; DUMC, Alexander papers, Application for Federal Employment; Interview with Irene Hulst, Loenen a/d Veht, March 1998.

20 UAV, Rigorosum file, PN 1550.

21 Rubel-Schaefer 1902/03. The University record states that she passed the exam only 'per vota maiore'; UAV, Rigorosum file, PN 1550; also Rubel-Schaefer 1905.

22 Anne (*24 January 1908–†10 August 1990), Alfred (*30 April 1909–†13 June 1983), Helene (*9 April 1914–†13 August 1965), Theodore (*1 August 1919–†19 August 1994); personal correspondence with Cecily Alexander-Grable, 23 October 2002.

23 Bodleian Library, Oxford, SPSL papers, folder 402, Alfred Alexander.
24 UAV, file Gustav Alexander; AP, curriculum vitae of Gustav Alexander.
25 AP, curriculum vitae of Gustav Alexander.
26 Doslak *et al.* 1982; Doslak *et al.* 1979.
27 See also Hochenegg 1907; Alexander 1912; Alexander 1914; Alexander/Marburg 1926.
28 See also Gustav Alexander, *Zur Anatomie der kongenitalen Taubheit* (Vienna, 1905); *ibid.*, *Das Gehörorgan der Kretinen* (no date); *ibid.*, *Die Histologie der Typischen Hereditär Degenerativen Taubstummheit* (Wien, 1919); *ibid.*, *Kongenitale Syphilis* (Berlin, 1927).
29 UAV, file Gustav Alexander.
30 Alexander 1954c, 76.
31 AP, curriculum vitae of Gustav Alexander (includes a list of publications).
32 See bibliography of Leo Alexander; also DUMC, Alexander papers, box 1, folder 21, Leo Alexander, Index of Publications.
33 Alexander 1954c, 75.
34 Interview with Irene Hulst, Loenen a/d Veht, March 1998.
35 Photographic collection Cecily Alexander-Grable, Waban, MA.
36 Interview with Irene Hulst, Loenen a/d Veht, March 1998; see also Mahler 1983.
37 Interview with Cecily Alexander-Grable, Marion, Cape Cod, May 1999.
38 Interview with Irene Hulst, Loenen a/d Veht, March 1998.
39 Interview with Cecily Alexander-Grable, Marion, Cape Cod, May 1999.
40 *Ibid.*
41 AP, Siegfried Jung to Leo Alexander, no date.
42 Interview with Cecily Alexander-Grable, Marion, Cape Cod, May 1999.
43 Alexander 1954c, 76.
44 *Ibid.*, 76.
45 *Ibid.*, 77.
46 Interview with Irene Hulst, Loenen a/d Veht, March 1998.
47 *Ibid.*
48 Brunner 1932, 569; also interview with Irene Hulst, Loenen a/d Veht, March 1998.
49 Alexander 1954c, 77.
50 *Ibid.*, 77.
51 For some of Alexander's early publications see Alexander 1926; 1927a; 1927b; 1928a; 1928b; 1928c; 1928d; 1929.
52 Alexander 1926, 479–87.
53 *Ibid.*, 486.
54 RAC, CMB, Inc., box 96, folder 691, curriculum vitae Leo Alexander; also Alexander 1927a, 11; Alexander 1927b, 213–35.
55 ZfA, personal file Leo Alexander, curriculum vitae; RAC, CMB, Inc., box 96, folder 691, curriculum vitae Leo Alexander; also Hubenstorf 1987, 376.
56 BAK, ZSg 154, box 75, Alexander diary (1945), 170–78, 14.6.1945 (in the following referred to as: BAK, Alexander diary (1945)).
57 Kleist has only recently become the focus of historical debate; see Kaendler 1993, 141–4; Burleigh 1994, 50; Schmidt 2002a, 26, 94, 97f, 171f., 183–197, 200, 203–211, 286f.
58 Alexander did not even have time to attend his graduation ceremony on 5 July 1929; AP, Leo Alexander to Gustav Alexander, 30 June 1929.
59 *Ibid.*, 22 July 1929.
60 *Ibid.*, 25 March 1930.
61 *Ibid.*, 22 July 1929.

62 Schmidt 2002a, 183ff.

63 Alexander 1932b, 1932c and 1932d; Herz 1934; also National Library of Medicine, Bethesda, Nichtenhauser papers, MS C277, box 9; for the history and ethics of medical film making during Weimar and Nazi Germany see Schmidt 2002a.

64 Tape-recorded interview with Eleonore Strümpel and Adelheid Kleist, Frankfurt am Main, December 1996.

65 It is interesting to note that Alexander's fiancée 'Gisela' Preitz had the same Christian name as his mother 'Gisela'.

66 IfSt, personal file Karl Albert Kleist, 42.966; Siemen 1993, 103ff.

67 Weindling 1985, 303–18.

68 Schmidt 2002a, 37–58.

69 Peiffer Archive, Report on the Collaboration between Regional Asylums and the Frankfurt Clinic, 1 February 1932–1 July 1932 and 1 July 1932–20 January 1933. I am grateful to Professor Jürgen Peiffer, Tübingen, for providing me with a copy of Alexander's reports.

70 Weber 1993.

71 Peiffer Archive, Report on the Collaboration between Regional Asylums and the Frankfurt Clinic, 1 February 1932–1 July 1932.

72 Peiffer Archive, Report on the Collaboration between Regional Asylums and the Frankfurt Clinic, 1 July 1932–20 January 1933.

3. The Émigré

1 AP, photographic collection Cecily Alexander-Grable, Waban, MA.

2 For Lyman's biography see RAC, CMB, Inc., box 97, folder 696, biographical data on Richard S. Lyman.

3 AP, Lyman to Alexander, 30 August 1932.

4 AP, Alexander to Schaltenbrand, 6 September 1932; Schaltenbrand to Alexander, 8 September 1932; Alexander to Lyman, 10 September 1932; Lyman to Alexander, 29 October 1932; also Schaltenbrand 1931, 168ff.

5 AP, Lyman to Alexander, 29 October 1932; Greene to Alexander, 29 October 1932; Alexander to Greene, 31 December 1932.

6 Brunner 1932, 569; 'Der Mord an Professor Gustav Alexander. Racheakt eines Patienten nach 27 Jahren', *Neue Freie Presse*, 13 April 1932; also interview with Irene Hulst, Loenen a/d Veht, March 1998.

7 AP, Alfred Alexander to Leo Alexander, 28 February 1933.

8 Interview with Cecily Alexander-Grable, Marion, Cape Cod, May 1999.

9 Bullock 1980, 1.

10 *Ibid.*, 21.

11 *Ibid.*, 42.

12 RAC, CMB, Inc., box 96, folder 689, Dieuaide to Greene, 30 January 1932.

13 RAC, CMB, Inc., box 97, folder 696, biographical data on Richard S. Lyman; also note by Green, 20 January 1932.

14 RAC, CMB, Inc., box 96, folder 691, Greene to Committee of Professors, 27 October 1932.

15 *Ibid.*, Greene to Lambert, 2 November 1932.

16 *Ibid.*, Greene to Gregg, 26 July 1933.

17 At the end of 1932 Dr Suh T. H. from the National Medical School in Shanghai joined Lyman, followed shortly thereafter by Alexander and a Dr Wu T. T. from Shanghai. RAC, CMB, Inc., box 165, folder B, Report of Neuropsychiatry in Peiping, by R. S. Lyman, October 1932 to October 1935.

18 See also Lyman 1937, 771.
19 AP, Alexander to Kleist, 28 March 1933.
20 AP, Leo Alexander to Alfred Alexander, 20 April 1933.
21 Lyman 1937, 765–71; also Schaltenbrand 1931, 168ff.
22 Lyman 1937, 765.
23 AP, Alexander to Kleist, 28 March 1933; AP, PUMC, Weekly Calendar.
24 AP, Alexander to Kleist, 28 March 1933.
25 *Ibid.*
26 *Ibid.*
27 AP, Leo Alexander to Alfred Alexander, 20 April 1933.
28 Alexander quickly established contacts with Chinese, European and American colleagues; AP, PUMC, Dr Alexander: Neuropathology for advanced postgraduate and students.
29 AP, Leo Alexander to Alfred Alexander, 20 April 1933; also Alexander to Kleist, 26 May 1933.
30 AP, Alexander to Miss Hayes (art collector), 29 August 1934.
31 AP, Alexander to Gitta, 26 August 1934.
32 AP, Arnold Merzbach to Leo Alexander, 12 May 1933.
33 IfSt, personal file on Eduard Beck, 42.972; also AP, Alice Rosenstein to Alexander, 20 June 1933.
34 AP, Beck to Alexander, 6 July 1933; also Alexander to Beck, 9 October 1933; Alexander to Beck 12 October 1933. Alexander's letter to Beck from 9 October 1933 was never sent.
35 AP, Leo Alexander to Alfred Alexander, 2 August 1933.
36 Ash and Söllner 1996, 6ff.
37 'Zentrum deutsch-jüdischer Medizin', *Frankfurter Stadt-Rundschau*, 1997.
38 AP, Burchard to Alexander, 2 April 1933.
39 AP, Friedmann to Alexander, 3 May 1933.
40 *Ibid.*
41 AP, Alfred Alexander to Leo Alexander, 9 June 1933.
42 AP, Caecily Alexander and Robert Alexander to Leo Alexander, 14 July 1933.
43 *Wiener Sonn- und Montags-Zeitung*, 9 October 1933.
44 AP, Marburg to Alexander, 14 September 1933.
45 AP, Alfred Alexander to Leo Alexander, 9 June 1933.
46 AP, Kleist to Alexander, 10 July 1933.
47 Interview with Cecily Alexander-Grable, Marion, Cape Cod, May 1999.
48 *Ibid.*
49 AP, Strauss to Alexander, 19 July 1933.
50 AP, Kleist to Alexander, 15 July 1933.
51 *Ibid.*
52 See also AP, Yen to Alexander, 15 July 1933.
53 AP, Alexander to Rosenstein, 27 July 1933.
54 *Ibid.*; also Alexander to Merzbach, 5 October 1933.
55 AP, Leo Alexander to Alfred Alexander, 2 August 1933.
56 AP, Alexander to Schaltenbrand, 2 August 1933.
57 AP, Alexander to Rosenstein, 4 October 1933.
58 *Ibid.*
59 AP, Alexander to Spiegel, 11 October 1933. At this point Alexander had received about ten negative responses to applications that he had sent to places such as Denver, New York and Washington DC.
60 AP, Alexander to Spiegel, 11 October 1933.

61 AP, Alexander to von Randow, 26 October 1933.
62 Interview with Ivan Brown, Lakeland, Florida, March 1998; interview with
    Nicolas Camera-Peon, Washington DC, May 1999; interview with Cecily
    Alexander-Grable, Marion, Cape Cod, May 1999; interview with Irene Hulst,
    Loenen a/d Veht, March 1998. Alexander's personal correspondence and
    photographic collection also contain a good amount of material about his
    romantic affairs. However, this aspect of Alexander's biography has not been
    given extensive treatment, for it is not of central importance to the present
    study.
63 AP, Alexander to Schütz, 5 October 1933.
64 *Ibid.*
65 AP, Alexander to Kleist, 11 November 1933.
66 AP, Leo Alexander to Alfred Alexander, 2 August 1933.
67 Interview with Cecily Alexander-Grable, Marion, Cape Cod, May 1999.
68 Alexander 1934a, 1934b; 1934c; 1934d and 1935a.
69 Alexander 1954c, 79.
70 AP, Lyman to US Commissioner of Immigration, 4 December1933.
71 For the emigration of doctors and medical scientists from Austria and Germany to
    America see Hubenstorf 1984, 85–107; Hubenstorf, 1987, 359–415; also Kröner
    1989, 1–37. The literature on the history of medical emigration only rarely covers
    the next generation of physicians and medical scientists such as Alexander. For an
    excellent account about some of the methodological problems see Hubenstorf
    1987, 361f.
72 Kröner 1989, 1–37, here 3.
73 *Ibid.*
74 *Ibid.*, 16ff.
75 Pearle 1984, 112–37, 113; also Pearle 1981; for the proportion between Austrian
    and German émigré doctors see Kröner 1989, 18.
76 Kröner 1989, 15ff.
77 Ash and Söllner 1996, 9ff.
78 RAC, RG 12.1., box 22, 1933, diary entry by Gregg, 20 July 1933.
79 AP, Alexander to Henschel, 12 June 1934.
80 RAC, CMB Inc., box 96, folder 691, Memorandum for RSG, 20 September 1933.
81 AP, Hoskins to Lyman, 28 September 1933; also in RAC, CMB Inc., box 96,
    folder 691, Dieuaide to Eggleston, 3 November 1933, Enclosure.
82 AP, Hoskins to Lyman, 28 September 1933.
83 *Ibid.*
84 AP, Leo Alexander to Alfred Alexander, 10 November 1933.
85 AP, Leo Alexander to Alfred Alexander, 16 February 1934.
86 AP, Black to Lockhart (American Consul General), 31 October 1933; also RAC,
    CMB Inc., box 96, folder 691, Lyman to Dieuaide, 1 November 1933; Dieuaide
    to Lockhart, 2 November 1933; also Dieuaide to Eggleston, 3 November 1933.
87 AP, Warner (American Vice-Consul) to Alexander, 6 November 1933.
88 AP, Alexander to Preitz, 18 November 1933; also Preitz to Alexander, April
    1933.
89 *Ibid.*
90 AP, Mr Preitz to Alexander, 9 November 1934.
91 AP, Leo Alexander to Theodore Alexander, 21 January 1934.
92 Ash and Söllner 1996, 3ff.
93 AP, Alexander to Black, 19 February 1934.
94 RAC, RG 12.1., box 22, 1934, diary entry by Gregg, 11 January 1934.

95 AP, Leo Alexander to Alfred Alexander, 16 February 1934.
96 Greenberg 1996, 273–89.
97 AP, Alexander to Henschel, 12 June 1934.
98 See AP, Alexander to Kleist, 19 January 1934; Alexander to Joshua, 23 January 1934; Alexander to Schaltenbrand, 23 January 1934; Alexander to Gitta, 27 April 1934.
99 See AP, Alexander to Lyman, 1 February 1934; Alexander to Black, 19 February 1934; Alexander to Lyman, 20 February 1934; Alexander to Lyman, 24 April 1934; Alexander to Ms Lyman, 15 May 1934; Alexander to Doris, 27 May 1934.
100 For the re-migration of physicians and medical scientists see Hubenstorf 1984, 100f.; Hubenstorf 1987, 389ff.
101 AP, Leo Alexander to Alfred Alexander, 25 April 1934.
102 Ibid.
103 AP, Alexander to Schüller, 1 May 1934.
104 AP, Alexander to Henschel, 4 May 1934.
105 AP, Alfred Alexander to Leo Alexander, 9 May 1934.
106 Ibid.
107 AP, Leo Alexander to Alfred Alexander, no date (about early June 1934).
108 AP, Leo Alexander to Alfred Alexander, 16 February 1934; also Alexander to Gitta, 27 April 1934, 25 May 1934; Gitta to Alexander, mid-April 1934, mid-May 1934.
109 AP, Alexander to Henschel, 12 June 1934; Alexander to Necheles, 23 August 1934.
110 RAC, RG 12.1., box 22, 1933, diary entry by Gregg, 26 January 1933.
111 AP, Leo Alexander to Alfred Alexander, 1 June 1934.
112 Interview with Cecily Alexander-Grable, Marion, Cape Cod, May 1999.
113 AP, Leo Alexander to Alfred Alexander, 1 June 1934; for Helene's Palestine plans see Alfred Alexander to Leo Alexander, 22 April 1934.
114 AP, Alexander to Edwin, 17 August 1934.
115 AP, Alexander to Necheles, 24 May 1934.
116 AP, Leo Alexander to Helene Alexander, 24 August 1934.
117 AP, Alexander to 'Hansl', 1 February 1934; see also 'Hansl' to Alexander, end of January 1934.
118 AP, Alexander to Rose, 21 August 1934.
119 AP, Alexander to Myerson, 30 July 1934; see also RAC, RF 1.1., 200, box 117, folder 1446, Greene to Dieuaide, 7 August 1934.
120 Myerson 1935a, 453–66.
121 Ibid., 462.
122 Ibid., 463.
123 Kühl 1994; also Alexander 1935c, 7.
124 Alexander 1935c; Alexander 1936b; also Myerson 1935a, 453–63; Myerson 1935b, 615–25.
125 Alexander 1935c, 20.
126 Alexander 1935c, 110; see also RAC, RG 1.1., 200, box 72, folder 872, Report of the Research Division of the Boston State Hospital, 17 March 1936.
127 Alexander 1935c, 26.
128 Alexander 1935c, 115.
129 AP, Kleist to Alexander, 20 February 1934.
130 AP, Alexander to Kleist, 19 August 1934.
131 AP, Alexander to Rosenstein, 23 August 1934.
132 AP, Mr Preitz to Alexander, 9 November 1934.

133 *Ibid.*
134 AP, Kleist to Alexander, 5 June 1936; also Leo Alexander to Phyllis Alexander, 19 September 1944. Phyllis Elora Alexander (*18 August 1908; †7 February 1956). Personal correspondence with Cecily Alexander-Grable, 16 October 2002.
135 AP, Leo Alexander to Phyllis Alexander, 23 January 1944.
136 Alexander's son Gustave is spelled with an 'e' at the end of his name.
137 Gustave Osgood Alexander (*15 March 1937); Cecily Kate Alexander (*23 November 1938) and Jonathan Harrington Alexander (*11 April 1940). Personal correspondence with Cecily Alexander-Grable, 30 November 2002.
138 Greenberg 1996, 282ff.
139 RAC, RF 1.1., 200, box 117, folder 1446, Greene to Dieuaide, 7 August 1934; Hoskins to Gregg, 12 September 1934; Gregg to Hoskins, 14 September 1934; Putnam to Gregg, 14 September 1934; see also Alexander's excitement about his job prospects in AP, Leo Alexander to Alfred Alexander, 19 August 1934; Alexander to Necheles, 23 August 1934.
140 For lectures and seminars see AP, documents relating to Harvard Medical School, the Boston Society of Psychiatry and Neurology, American Association of Neuropathologists and the American Psychiatric Association.
141 Alexander 1934d, 1935a, 1935b, 1935c, 1935e, 1936a, 1937a, 1937b, 1937c, 1937d, 1938a, 1938b, 1938c, 1938d, 1938e, 1938f, 1938g, 1938h, 1938i, 1938j, 1938k, 1937e, 1937f, 1938l, 1938m, 1938n, 1939a, 1939b, 1939c, 1939d, 1939e, 1939f, 1939g, 1939h, 1939i, 1939j, 1939k, 1939l, 1939m, 1939n, 1939o, 1940a, 1940b, 1940c, 1940d, 1941a, 1941b, 1941c, 1941d, 1941e, 1941f, 1941g, 1941h.
142 Alexander 1940a, 1940b.
143 'Dr. Leo Alexander, Miss Sarah Evarrs Address Vocational Conference', *The Radcliffe News*, 22 November 1935.
144 Bodleian Library, SPSL papers, folder 402, Alfred Alexander; also General Medical Council to the author, 24 February 1999. Alfred Alexander later established a private practice as a Harley Street physician.
145 AP, Leo Alexander to Phyllis Alexander, 18 August 1939.
146 AP, Leo Alexander to Phyllis Alexander, 18 August 1939; 4 February 1944.
147 AP, E. Roth (HQ First Corps Area), 11 October 1938.
148 One of his fellow soldiers from the 65th General Hospital, Ivan Brown, recalled that Alexander 'was different. He was the butt of all jokes ... in the Unit. It was because he was sloppy, he was clumsy, and at the same time he could be annoying. He had a talent for rubbing people the wrong way – completely innocent on his part – made people dislike him amongst all the other officers ... even the nurses would kid about him'; Interview with Ivan Brown, Lakeland, Florida, March 1998.
149 On Allied military neuropsychiatry see Shephard 2000; for American military neuropsychiatry see Ingraham and Manning 1986, 38–46; Jones *et al.* 1995; also Hale 1995; for British military psychiatry in the Second World War see Binneveld 1997 and Shephard 1999, 491–524.
150 See also the film 'The Treatment of War Neurosis' in which Eliot Slater and William Sargant from the Maudsley Hospital, London, demonstrate some of the abreactive drug treatments that they applied to wartime casualties at the Belmond Emergency Medical Services Hospital between 1940 and 1943; Audio-Visual Collection, The Wellcome Trust, London, Shelfmark: 1270V, b & w, 17 minutes; for German neuropsychiatric films see Schmidt 2002a.
151 Ingraham and Manning 1986, 38–46; Shephard 1999, 521.
152 Shephard 1999, 511.

153 Heller 1988, 62f.
154 For Alexander's colleagues at Fort Bragg see DUMC, Alexander papers, box 1, file 20; box 5, file 9.
155 AP, Leo Alexander to Phyllis Alexander, 5 August 1943; also DUMC, Lyman papers, Alexander to Lyman, 2 March 1943; Alexander to Lyman, 15 March 1943; Alexander to Lyman, 28 April 1943; Lyman to Alexander 30 April 1943; Lyman to Alexander, 13 August 1943.
156 AP, Leo Alexander to Phyllis Alexander, 20 October 1943; Leo Alexander to Gustave Alexander, 21 October 1943.
157 AP, Leo Alexander to Phyllis Alexander, 31 October 1943.
158 AP, Leo Alexander to Phyllis Alexander, 16 December 1943.
159 AP, Leo Alexander to Phyllis Alexander, 27 January 1945; also Leo Alexander to Phyllis Alexander, 12 February 1945.
160 AP, Leo Alexander to Phyllis Alexander, 23 January 1944.
161 For example, to Hans Strauss, Merill Moore and Abraham Myerson; AP, Leo Alexander to Phyllis Alexander, 15 March 1944; 10 April 1944.
162 AP, Leo Alexander to Phyllis Alexander, 12 February 1945.
163 AP, Leo Alexander to Phyllis Alexander, 13 January 1944.
164 AP, Leo Alexander to Phyllis Alexander, 30 September 1943; 12 December 1943; 4 January 1944.
165 Interview with Cecily Alexander-Grable, Marion, Cape Cod, May 1999.
166 AP, Leo Alexander to Phyllis Alexander, 18 October 1943.
167 AP, Leo Alexander to Phyllis Alexander, 23 January 1944.
168 AP, Leo Alexander to Phyllis Alexander, 2 February 1944.
169 AP, Leo Alexander to Phyllis Alexander, 4 January 1943; 4 February 1944.
170 Interview with Ivan Brown, Lakeland, Florida, March 1998; see also Cosmas and Cowdrey 1992.
171 AP, Everts (War Department) to Alexander, 18 April 1944.
172 AP, Leo Alexander to Phyllis Alexander, 27 April 1944.
173 AP, Leo Alexander to Phyllis Alexander, 19 June 1944.
174 *Ibid.*
175 DUMC, Alexander papers, box 4, file 1 (24), NP Report for January 1944, 6 February 1944.
176 AP, Leo Alexander to Phyllis Alexander, 10 July 1944; also Leo Alexander to Phyllis Alexander, 19 July 1944.
177 Interview with Nicolas Camera-Peon, Washington DC, May 1999.
178 AP, Leo Alexander to Phyllis Alexander, 27 September 1944 and 28 September 1944.
179 AP, Leo Alexander to Phyllis Alexander, 10 April 1945 and 12 September 1945.
180 Alexander 1947a; 1952a.
181 Alexander 1947a, 112.
182 Alexander 1952c, 113.
183 United Nations War Crimes Commission 1948, 87f.
184 *Ibid.*, 88.
185 *Ibid.*
186 Lemkin 1944.
187 *Ibid.*, vii.
188 *Ibid.*, xi, 79–95.
189 See also AP, Leo Alexander to Phyllis Alexander, 27 November 1946.
190 AP, Leo Alexander to Gustave Alexander, 24 February 1944. See also Leo Alexander to Phyllis Alexander, 6 April 1944.
191 Interview with Nicolas Camera-Peon, Washington DC, May 1999.

192 AP, Leo Alexander to Phyllis Alexander, 10 April 1944.
193 AP, Leo Alexander to Phyllis Alexander, 21 July 1944; Lord Haw-Haw is the synonym for the radio broadcaster William Joice who functioned as Goebbels' mouthpiece to communicate Nazi propaganda to Anglo-America.
194 AP, Leo Alexander to Phyllis Alexander, 18 September 1944.
195 AP, Leo Alexander to Phyllis Alexander, 19 September 1944.
196 Merrit 1995, 50.
197 Of the 901 men charged with war crimes in the notorious Leipzig trials after the First World War, 888 were acquitted or summarily dismissed, and only 13 convicted. Those convicted were either released after brief sentences or allowed to escape; United Nations War Crimes Commission 1948, 48–52; also Tusa and Tusa 1995, 17–20.
198 For the machinery to trace and apprehend war criminals see also United Nations War Crimes Commission 1948, 344–91.
199 For the history of the International Criminal Court, which had been proposed as early as 1926 by the Vienna Conference of the International Law Association, see United Nations War Crimes Commission 1948, 84ff., 102ff.
200 *Ibid.*, 103.
201 *Ibid.*
202 Breitman 1998, 119f.
203 Browning 1998, 149–59, here 158f.
204 United Nations War Crimes Commission 1948, 109–34.
205 *Ibid.*, 107; also Breitman 1998, 215.
206 See, for example, Abzug 1985, 89–103; see also AP, Alexander calendar (1945), note on Dachau concentration camp; see also Barer 1998.
207 Davidson 1997, 7ff.
208 Frei 1996, 141f.; also United Nations War Crimes Commission 1948, 365f.
209 'The German Atrocities', *Life*, 18 (1945), No. 19, 32–7; also Klier 1994, 216ff.

4. The War Crimes Investigator

1 AP, Leo Alexander to Phyllis Alexander, 4 May 1945.
2 *Ibid.*
3 AP, Phyllis Alexander to Leo Alexander, 7 May 1945.
4 AP, Leo Alexander to Phyllis Alexander, 22 May 1945.
5 AP, Leo Alexander to Phyllis Alexander, 30 May 1945.
6 See also Bower 1987.
7 See, for example, Bower 1982; Bower 1995; Marrus 1999.
8 See Marrus 1999.
9 Bower 1982, 111.
10 Nicolas Camera-Peon, Alexander's former assistant from the 65th General Hospital, recalled: 'I don't think he would have been deliberately unjust. But I doubt if he could have separated his own feelings entirely from that ... because I remember while we were still in the 65th, when he would talk about his friends and so on, thinking, musing, "[it's] awful to think that people I know may be in an abattoir", and those were his words. So, that so far as his own feelings are concerned, I am sure that he thought all of them deserved to be hanged. Period.' Interview with Nicolas Camera-Peon, Washington DC, May 1999. See also Kemp 1988, 14f.
11 See also United Nations War Crimes Commission 1948, 362ff.

12 Ziemke 1975, 219.
13 United Nations War Crimes Commission 1948, 142.
14 RG 338 HQ USAREURJAG War Crimes Case Files 14.2.45; Bower 1995, 125f.
15 AP, Alexander calendar (1945), 23.5.1945; for the establishment of the British war crimes programme see United Nations War Crimes Commission 1948, 366–74; Bower 1995, 127–39; Glees 1992, 171–97; Ulf Schmidt, 'The Scars of Ravensbrück: Medical Experiments and British War Crimes Policy, 1945–1950', *German History* (forthcoming).
16 AP, Leo Alexander to Phyllis Alexander, 26 May 1945.
17 *Ibid.*
18 Abzug 1985, 100f.
19 Interview with Ivan Brown, Lakeland, Florida, March 1998; DUMC, Alexander papers, box, 1, folder 2, Diary by Dr Ali Kuçi, The Last Days of Dachau, 23 May 1945.
20 AP, Leo Alexander to Phyllis Alexander, 26 May 1945.
21 *Ibid.*
22 CIOS report, Neuropathology and Neurophysiology, 42f.
23 Weber 1993, 282ff.
24 Klee 1997, 203.
25 CIOS report, Neuropathology and Neurophysiology, 41f.
26 *Ibid.*, 42.
27 *Ibid.*, 46–54.
28 Cocks 1985, 6ff.; also Lohmann 1993, 116–27, 121.
29 CIOS report, German Neuropsychiatry, 76; also 47.
30 Article 2 of the Nuremberg Race Laws from 1935 prohibited 'mixed marriages' and sexual relations between Jews and non-Jews. The violation or attempted violation of this law constituted a case of *Rassenschande* (racial disgrace). CIOS report, German Neuropsychiatry, 97–108; BAK, Alexander diary (1945), 18–35; 29 May 1945; also BA-BDC, personal file Wilhelm Tönnis; see also Geiger 1981; Tönnis 1984 and Arnold 1996.
31 CIOS report, Mental Health Practices, 28.
32 CIOS report, German Neuropsychiatry, 97–108; BAK, Alexander diary (1945), 18–35; 29 May 1945; also BA-BDC, personal file Wilhelm Tönnis; see also Geiger 1981; Tönnis 1984 and Arnold 1996.
33 BAK, ZSg 154, box 72, Dennis Williams, Report on CIOS Trip No. 277, 25 May–4 June, 1945. Neuropsychiatric Organisations in the German Air Force.
34 BAK, Alexander diary (1945), 18, 29 May 1945.
35 AP, Leo Alexander to Phyllis Alexander, 30 May 1945.
36 *Ibid.*; BAK, Alexander diary (1945), 22f., 29 May 1945.
37 BAK, Alexander diary (1945), 19–23, 29 May 1945.
38 AP, Leo Alexander to Phyllis Alexander, 30 May 1945.
39 CIOS report, German Neuropsychiatry, 108–116; also BAK, Alexander diary (1945), 35–55, 29 May 1945–31 May 1945; some of Tönnis' neurosurgical films can be found in the BAFA; for army medical film see Schmidt 2002a.
40 CIOS report, German Neuropsychiatry, 104f.
41 AP, Leo Alexander to Phyllis Alexander, 30 May 1945.
42 BA-BDC, personal file Hans Pittrich.
43 CIOS report, German Neuropsychiatry, 98 and 106; BA-BA-BDC, personal file Hans Pittrich.
44 See especially the detailed account by Freund 1991.
45 Abzug 1985, 121; also Freund 1991.

46 FCLM, Beecher papers, Arthur R. Truner, SHAEF, G-5 Division, Displaced Persons Branch, Displaced Persons Report No. 34, 18 June 1945.
47 *Ibid.*
48 AP, Phyllis Alexander to Leo Alexander, 2 June 1945.
49 BAK, Alexander diary (1945), 55–9, 31 May 1945; see also Abzug 1985, 122.
50 AP, Leo Alexander to Phyllis Alexander, 7 June 1945.
51 *Ibid.*
52 CIOS report, German Neuropsychiatry, 83–9; BAK, Alexander diary (1945), 61–73, 2.6.1945.
53 *Ibid.*, also BAK, BAK, ZSg 154, file 72, Dennis Williams, Report on CIOS Trip No. 277, 25 May–4th June, 1945. Neuropsychiatric Organisations in the German Air Force, 4.
54 CIOS report, German Neuropsychiatry, 86.
55 CIOS report, German Neuropsychiatry, 89.
56 CIOS report, Mental Health Practices, 7–29; BAK, Alexander diary (1945), 75–9, 3 June 1945.
57 CIOS report, Mental Health Practices, 10.
58 BAK, Alexander diary (1945), 75, 3 June 1945.
59 CIOS report, Mental Health Practices, 9.
60 CIOS report, German Neuropsychiatry, 54–60; BAK, Alexander diary (1945), 82–7, 4 June 1945.
61 BAK, Alexander diary (1945), 87, 4 June 1945.
62 See Alexander 1948a, 1948b, 1948e, 1948f, 1949a, 1949c, 1949d, 1950k, 1966a, 1976c; also DUMC, Memorandum to McHaney, 26 March 1947.
63 CIOS report, Exposure to Cold, 3–68; BAK, Alexander diary (1945), 88–100, 5 June 1945–6 June 1945.
64 For Werz see Klee 1997, 214, 237, 240; for Seelkopf see Klee 1997, 214; for Lutz see Klee 1997, 214, 237.
65 CIOS report, Exposure to Cold, 4f. and BAK, Alexander diary (1945), 96f.; 5 June 1945–6 June 1945.
66 CIOS report, Exposure to Cold, 8.
67 *Ibid.*, 12.
68 BAK, Alexander diary (1945), 101f., 7 June 1945.
69 CIOS report, Mental Health Practices, 4, 29f.; see also CIOS report, German Neuropsychiatry, 60f.
70 CIOS report, Mental Health Practices, 30.
71 *Ibid.*, 30–8; also Friedlander 1995, 130.
72 Friedlander 1995, 52.
73 For Carl Schneider see Schmidt 2002a, 238, 265–7, 270.
74 CIOS report, Mental Health Practices, 35f.
75 *Ibid.*, 36.
76 *Ibid.*, 38.
77 BAK, Alexander diary (1945), 139, 10 June 1945.
78 A local pub which serves cider.
79 BAK, Alexander diary (1945), 140, 10 June 1945.
80 BAK, Alexander diary (1945), 149f., 11 June 1945. On 12 June Alexander reflected about what he did the previous day. This explains the inconsistency in the page numbers in the diary when compared to the entries on 11 June 1945.
81 BAK, Alexander diary (1945), 141ff., 11 June 1945; also DUMC, Alexander papers, box 4, folder 27, Leo Alexander, Target Evaluation Report, 11 and 12 June 1945.

82 For the history of the Reich Institute for Film and Picture in Science and Education see Schmidt 2002a.
83 CIOS report, Mental Health Practices, 67.
84 *Ibid.*
85 CIOS report, Mental Health Practices, 166–73.
86 CIOS report, German Neuropsychiatry, 82f.
87 *Ibid.*, 73.
88 IfSt, personal file Karl Albert Kleist, 42.966, 39.261, 17.339.
89 BAK, Alexander diary (1945), 150f., 12 June 1945.
90 CIOS report, German Neuropsychiatry, 89–93; see also BAK, Alexander diary (1945), 151f., 13 June 1945.
91 CIOS report, Mental Health Practices, 40–3; BAK, Alexander diary (1945), 161–6, 14 June 1945.
92 CIOS report, Mental Health Practices, 40.
93 CIOS report, Neuropathology and Neurophysiology, 14–22.
94 For Noetzel and Welte see Klee 1997, 214.
95 Peiffer 1999, 339–56, 345f.; BAK, Alexander diary (1945), 171, 14 June 1945.
96 According to Alexander, Hallervorden had obtained 500 victims' brains. This figure corresponds to research conducted by Peiffer, who has established that there were at least 593 cases from a total of 824 in Hallervorden's department, which derived with certainty or with high probability from the victims of the 'euthanasia' programme; Peiffer 1999, 345; also BAK, Alexander diary (1945), 174, 14 June 1945.
97 On 14 June 1945 Alexander stated in his diary: 'Die Gemeinnützige Krankentransport Gesellschaft hat ihm die Gehirne gebracht, in batches of 50–150 at a time'. This is another example of Alexander oscillating between German and English. Why he exaggerated the figures a month later is not clear. Perhaps he wanted to highlight the seriousness of the crime which had been committed and emphasise that the victims' brains had been exploited for spurious scientific reasons. It seems that this inconsistency does not devalue the overall gist of the conversation which Alexander noted verbatim; see BAK, Alexander diary (1945), 177, 14 June 1945.
98 CIOS report, Neuropathology and Neurophysiology, 20; also BAK, Alexander diary (1945), 177f., 14 June 1945.
99 CIOS report, Neuropathology and Neurophysiology, 21.
100 See also Peiffer 1999.
101 BAK, Alexander diary (1945), 173, 14 June 1945; for the Jewish neuropathologist Karl Neubürger see Weber 1993, 193ff.
102 CIOS report, Exposure to Cold, 13; also AP, Alexander calendar (1945), entry of meeting with Biegelow on 14 June 1945; see also DUMC, Alexander papers, box 4, folder 27, Secret Cable from Alexander to UK Base for SHAEF for CIOS Secretariat [no date; approx. mid-June 1945].
103 See also CIOS report, Exposure to Cold, Appendix 5, 161 for the use of radio broadcasts by the 'International Investigation-Office for Medical SS-Crimes in the German Concentration-Camps'. Lieutenant Biegelow will probably have heard one of the broadcasts of the office about the Dachau freezing experiments.
104 CIOS report, Exposure to Cold, 13.
105 For Strughold's role during the Second World War see the TV programme 'The Wrong Stuff', Part 3 in the Channel 4 series 'Science and the Swastika' (2001).
106 CIOS report, Exposure to Cold, 13f.

107 Bower 1987.
108 CIOS report, Exposure to Cold, 16.
109 *Ibid.*, 15f.
110 *Ibid.*, 16f.
111 BAK, Alexander diary (1945), 200f., 17 June 1945; CIOS report, Exposure to Cold, 17f.
112 Enloe 1947, 801–5, 804.
113 Rascher's wife was described as a 'typical overdressed, ageing ex-actress'; CIOS report, Exposure to Cold, 41.
114 *Ibid.*, 18–37.
115 *Ibid.*, 17.
116 BAK, Alexander diary (1945), 202f., 19 June 1945.
117 AP, Alexander calendar (1945), verbatim record of conversation with Lutz, 20 June 1945; also CIOS report, Exposure to Cold, 37–42.
118 CIOS report, Exposure to Cold, 40; AP, Alexander calendar (1945), verbatim record of conversation with Lutz, 20 June 1945.
119 Klee 1997, 252.
120 DUMC, Alexander papers, box 4, folder 41, Interrogation by Major Alexander MC USA at Dachau, 21 June 1945. Among the names Alexander was given by the former camp inmates was that of August Weltz. It is probably no coincidence that Weltz was arrested on the same day that Alexander was passing on this information to the Allied authorities; NARA, RG 238, Entry 200, prison file August Weltz.
121 CIOS report, Exposure to Cold, 42 and Appendix 5, 160–3; also NDT Documents and Material, frames 105–8.
122 CIOS report, Exposure to Cold, 42–6; DUMC, Alexander papers, box 4, folder 41, Interrogation by Major Alexander MC USA at Dachau, 21 June 1945.
123 DUMC, Alexander papers, box 4, folder 33, Alexander diary (1946/47), 149–52, 21 December 1946. This is the original Alexander diary which chronicles his time in Nuremberg in 1946/47 (in the following referred to as: DUMC, Alexander diary (1946/47)); see also Schmidt 2001b, note 2.
124 NDT Records, testimony Leo Michalowski, 21 December 1946.
125 *Ibid.*
126 See CIOS report, Exposure to Cold, Appendix.
127 CIOS report, Exposure to Cold, 52.

5. The Road to Nuremberg

1 AP, Leo Alexander to Phyllis Alexander, 26 June 1945.
2 *Ibid.*
3 Interview with Nicolas Camera-Peon, Washington DC, May 1999.
4 AP, CIOS reports; see also Shevell 1996.
5 AP, Leo Alexander to Phyllis Alexander, 26 June 1945.
6 CIOS report, German Neuropsychiatry, 128.
7 CIOS report, Neuropathology and Neurophysiology, 43f.
8 *Ibid.*, 35–36.
9 DUMC, Alexander papers, box 4, file 41.
10 Peiffer 1999, 340f.
11 CIOS report, Neuropathology and Neurophysiology, 43; CIOS report, German Neuropsychiatry, 128.

12 CIOS report, Mental Health Practices; also Weindling 2001b, 311–33.
13 CIOS report, Exposure to Cold.
14 CIOS report, Aviation Medicine.
15 AP, Leo Alexander to Phyllis Alexander, 8 July 1945.
16 See also the TV programme 'The Wrong Stuff', Part 3 in the Channel 4 series 'Science and the Swastika' (2001).
17 CIOS report, Exposure to Cold, 67.
18 *Ibid.*
19 *Ibid.*
20 Proctor 1999, 273.
21 See especially BAK, Kl. Erw. 441–3, Karl Brandt on 'Luftfahrtmedizin', 20.7.1945.
22 This report was discovered by the author in 1998 at the Harvard Medical Library, Boston, Massachusetts; see FCLM, Beecher papers, Technical Report No. 331–45, German Aviation Medical Research at the Dachau Concentration Camp. The summary states: 'This report presents the research done on prisoners involving studies on altitude physiology, exposure to cold water and air, and studies on drugs with blood coagulating properties. October 1945 US Naval Technical Mission in Europe.'
23 *Ibid.*
24 *Ibid.*
25 *Ibid.*
26 The annotations to the report indicate Beecher's comments on the scientific validity of the data; *ibid.*
27 *Ibid.*
28 CIOS report, Exposure to Cold, 13f.
29 See AP, correspondence and witness testimonies taken by the Office of Special Investigations concerning the involvement of Hubertus Strughold in medical experiments, 1979.
30 United States Department of Justice, Office of Special Investigation, Washington DC, Investigations on Hubertus Stughold; minutes of the conference 7/43. I am grateful to Eli Rosenbaum, director of the Office of Special Investigation, for providing me with the material.
31 Mitscherlich and Mielke 1960, 76.
32 AP, Alexander to J. Mausner (Office of Special Investigation), 16 August 1979, 31 August 1979. To a former colleague from Nuremberg, Alexander confided: 'I have been working with Mr. Mausner on the investigation of one suspect, Dr. Hubertus Strughold, whom I interviewed in Göttingen on June 16, 1945, who is probably innocent, at least I considered him that way at the time of my interview and had recommended him for assignment to the action "paper clip"'; Alexander to Maryann Jessup MacConochie, 20 September 1979; also interview with Cecily Alexander-Grable, Marion, Cape Cod, May 1999.
33 Tusa and Tusa, 68.
34 *Ibid.*, 69.
35 See also United Nations War Crimes Commission 1948, 191ff.
36 The term 'crimes against humanity and civilisation' was first used by the governments of France, Great Britain and Russia in 1915 in response to the wholesale murder of the Armenian people and as a warning to the Turkish government that those responsible would be held to account. After the First World War, the Allies concluded that the Central Empires and their allies had conducted the war by illegitimate means and in violation of the 'laws

and customs of war' and the 'laws of humanity'. In 1919 these two types of offences were, for the first time, listed separately, but were not as yet clearly defined. For the history of the two categories see United Nations War Crimes Commission 1948, 35ff.; for the definition and development of the concepts of 'war crimes', 'crimes against humanity', and 'crimes against peace' see 169–261.

37 For the Nuremberg legacy see also Wolfe 1998.
38 NARA, RG 153/84–1, box 1, folder 2, Taylor to Petersen, 22 May 1946.
39 Tusa and Tusa 1995, 94.
40 *Ibid.*, 138.
41 Lemkin 1944, 75–95.
42 AP, Leo Alexander to Phyllis Alexander, 24 August 1945; for his apologies see letters on 1 September 1945; 5 September 1945 and 6 September 1945.
43 AP, Phyllis Alexander to Leo Alexander, 25 May 1945.
44 AP, Leo Alexander to Phyllis Alexander, 24 August 1945.
45 AP, CIOS reports.
46 AP, Leo Alexander to Phyllis Alexander, 25 August 1945.
47 AP, Leo Alexander to Phyllis Alexander, 1 September 1945.
48 See also the subsequent correspondence between Alexander and Lyman between October 1945 and April 1946; DUMC, Lyman papers.
49 DUMC, Lyman papers, Alexander to Lyman, 17 October 1945.
50 RAC, RG 1.2., 200A, box 126, folder 1114. Report on Grant for Psychiatry at Duke University, by Richard Lyman, 11 October 1947.
51 RAC, RG 1.2., 200A, box 126, folder 1114, Alexander to Gregg, 1 November 1945.
52 *Ibid.*
53 RAC, RG 1.2., 200A, box 126, folder 1114, diary entry by Lambert, 5 November 1945.
54 AP, Alexander calendar (1945), 9 November 1945.
55 Schafft and Zeidler 1996, 92.
56 Connery 1945.
57 AP, Alexander calendar (1945), 9 November 1945.
58 AP, Alexander calendar (1945), 13 November 1945.
59 *Ibid.*
60 RAC, RG 2–1946, 200.
61 *Ibid.*
62 RAC, RG 1.2., 200A, box 126, folder 1114, diary entry by Morrison, 13.11.45.
63 Ratcliff 1946.
64 NDT Records, London Charter, 8 August 1945.
65 NARA, RG 153/84–1, box 1, folder 2, Jackson to Patterson, 7 February 1946.
66 Tusa and Tusa 1995, 93, 138; for the position of the French and the Russians see NARA, RG 153/84–1, box 1, folder 2, Taylor to Petersen, 22 May 1946. The French were permitted to send trial observers to Nuremberg, but no French attorneys were allowed on the prosecution team; Weindling 2000b, 381.
67 Trials of War Criminals, vol. I, XVI–XX; also Annas and Grodin 1992, 317–21.
68 See also Weindling 2001b, 311–33.
69 NDT Records, fiche 289 and 290, frames 460–560.
70 Tusa and Tusa 1995, 279–90.
71 NARA, RG 238, Entry 159, box 2, Organisation for Subsequent Proceedings, 29 March 1946.
72 PRO, FO371, file 57576, Special Release No. 50.

73 NARA, RG 232, Entry 159, box 1, communication to Maj. Gen. C. B. Magruder, 19 July 1946; see also RG 153/85–1, box 2, folder 1, Taylor to Petersen, 29 June 1946.
74 NARA, RG 232, Entry 159, box 1, communication to Maj. Gen. C. B. Magruder, 19 July 1946.
75 NARA, RG 153/84–1, box 1, folder 2, Jackson to Patterson, 7 February 1946; also Taylor to Petersen, 22 May 1946; Taylor 1992, 287.
76 Weindling 2000b, 368; see also NARA, RG 232, Entry 159, box 1, Investigation of War Crimes in the Industrial and Financial Fields, 20 June 1946.
77 Tusa and Tusa 1995, 343ff.
78 NARA, RG 153/84–1, box 1, folder 2, Taylor to Petersen, 22 May 1946.
79 NARA, RG 153/84–1, box 1, folder 2, Petersen to Taylor, 17 June 1946.
80 NARA, RG 153/84–1, box 1, folder 2, Taylor to Patterson, 29 July 1946.
81 PRO, FO1049, file 428, Jackson to Truman, 7 October 1946.
82 NARA, RG 153/84–1, box 1, folder 3, Taylor to Jackson, 30 October 1946.
83 Buscher 1989, 31; see also NARA, RG 153/84–1, box 1, folder 3, Taylor to Petersen, 30 September 1946.
84 Taylor 1976, 4–7.
85 Taylor 1976, 4; Klee 1997, 356–60.
86 PRO, WO309, file 1652.
87 *Ibid.*
88 NDT Documents and Material, frames 460–525; also BAK, ZSg 154, box 73, International Scientific Commission (War Crimes), 15 January 1947.
89 Weindling 1997, 33; see also Weindling 2001c, 45f.; 70.
90 NDT Documents and Material, frame 475.
91 *Ibid.*, frames 466–7.
92 *Ibid.*, frame 469, frame 475.
93 *Ibid.*, frames 468–83; frame 468.
94 *Ibid.*, frame 473 and frame 479; for Mant's medical war crimes investigations see NDT Documents and Material, frames 253–88; also Mant 1949; Weindling 2000b, 377f.
95 *Ibid.*, frame 474.
96 BAK, ZSg 154, box 72, Conference of International Commission on Investigation of War Crimes of a Medical Nature, Hardy to McHaney, 26 October 1946.
97 *Ibid.*
98 NARA, RG 153/85–1, box 2, folder 1, Jackson to Taylor, 16 August 1946.
99 NARA, RG 153/85–1, box 2, folder 1, Taylor to War Department, 17 August 1946.
100 PRO, WO309, file 468. On 6 September 1946 the British War Office informed the UNWCC about the plan by the United States to mount a trial against German doctors. The United States proposed that the trial should either be held by Anglo-American Military Government Courts under Law No. 10, or by American Military Courts in the American zone.
101 Annas and Grodin 1992; Taylor 1993, 611.
102 Quoted from Weindling 2000b, 383.
103 PRO, 'Operation Fleacomb', WO309, files 476–7, 1458, 1460, WO311, file 650; 'Operation Haystack', WO309, file 1606; United Nations War Crimes Commission 1948, 366f.; Weindling 2000b, 368.
104 For Mengele see, for example, Aziz 1976; Cefrey 2001; Lifton 1985 and Lifton 1986; Müller-Hill 1988; 1992; Posner 2000.

105 For Rascher see Benz 1988, 190–214.
106 For Conti's suicide on 6 October 1945 see NARA, RG 238, Entry 200, box 5, prison file Leonardo Conti; see also Kater 1985, 299–325; for de Crinis see Jasper 1991; for Grawitz see BA-BDC, personal file Ernst Robert Grawitz; also Markus Wicke, 'Arzt und Mörder', *Berliner Zeitung*, 16/17 January 1999.
107 NARA, RG 238, Entry 28, box 3, War Crimes News Digest, 22 January 1947. The Nuremberg defendants, including Brandt, later attempted to shift responsibility to the 'missing defendants' who could no longer defend themselves or be produced in court.
108 Schmidt 2001b, 381–9.
109 NARA, RG 238, Entry 200, box 8, prison file Dr. Fritz Fischer (*5 October 1912).
110 *Ibid.*
111 *Ibid.*
112 NARA, RG 238, NM-70, Entry 200, box 3, Detention Report Viktor Brack.
113 NARA, RG 238, NM-70, Entry 200, box 4, Detention Report Rudolf Emil Hermann Brandt.
114 Padfield 1995, 609–11.
115 NARA, RG 238, NM-70, Entry 200, box 2, Detention Report Wilhelm Beiglböck.
116 NARA, RG 238, NM-70, Entry 200, box 2, Detention Report Becker-Freysing.
117 See also 'The Germans Sign the Surrenders', *Life*, 18 (1945), No. 21, 25–31.
118 PRO, WO171, file 8017.
119 PRO, FO371, file 46914.
120 Annas and Grodin 1992; also BAK, Kl. Erw. 441-3, Bl. 54–59; StaNü, KV-Anklage, Dokumente, No. 332; also KV-Anklage, Interrogations, B154, Karl Brandt, 9 October 1946.
121 NARA, RG 238, NM-70, Entry 200, box 4, Detention Report Karl Brandt.
122 NARA, RG 238, NM-70, Entry 200, Detention Report Paul Rostock. Blome was arrested on 16 May by members of the American Counter-Intelligence Corps in Munich; NARA, RG 238, NM-70, Entry 200, box 3, Detention Report Kurt Blome.
123 NARA, RG 238, NM-70, Entry 200, box 4, Detention Report Karl Brandt.
124 Sereny 1995, 558.
125 StaNü, KV-Anklage, Dokumente, No. 333.
126 CIOS report, Mental Health Practices.
127 PRO, FO371, file 57576.
128 StaNü, KV-Anklage, Interrogations, B154, Karl Brandt, 3 September 1947.
129 CIOS report, Exposure to Cold.
130 BIOS, Final Report No. 542, Interrogation of Certain German Personalities Connected with Chemical Warfare, 1946.
131 PRO, FO371, file 57576; also WO309, file 468.
132 *Ibid.*
133 PRO, FO371, file 57596/U4040.
134 NARA, RG 238, Entry 188/190/191, box 2, Individual Responsibility of Prof. Dr. Karl Brandt, May 1946.
135 *Ibid.*
136 *Ibid.*
137 NARA, RG 238, Entry 186, box 1, Attention Interrogation Branch, 19 August 1946.
138 For Ivy's appointment as the Special Consultant to the Secretary of War on 3 July 1946 see Weindling 2000b, 376.
139 I am grateful to Michael Grodin, Boston University, for supplying me with the most complete copy of Ivy's reports as a Consultant to the Secretary of War. It

consists of three parts: Part One: A Report on War Crimes of a Medical Nature Committed in Germany and Elsewhere on German Nationals and the Nationals of Occupied Countries by the Nazi Regime During World War II, 26 Bl. + Appendix A on Rules for Animal Experimentation; Part Two: A Report on the Paris Meeting (31 July 1946) of the Representatives of the American, British and French Governments to Consider the War Crimes of a Medical Nature; Part Three: An Outline of the Itinerary. All three parts can also be found in NARA, RG 153/86-3-1, box 11, folder 4, book 3.

140 Moreno 1999, 65ff.; for Ivy's colourful biography see also UWAHC, Andrew C. Ivy Papers (#8768), box 101, folder 12, Andrew Ivy, 'An Oral History', The American Gastroenterological Association, Los Angeles, California, 1969; also box 6, folder 13, Albert H. Stroupe, 'The Nuremberg Code – An Ivy Contribution. The Operation of Conscience in the Nuremberg Trials and the Krebiozen Controversy' [no date].

141 'Prison Malaria: Convicts Expose Themselves to Disease so Doctors can Study it', *Life*, 18 (1945), No. 23, 43–6.

142 Quoted from Moreno 1999, 67.

143 Taylor 1976, 6; see also Moreno 1997, 348.

144 UWAHC, Andrew C. Ivy Papers (#8768), box 6, folder 12, Andrew Ivy, 'Nazi War Crimes of a Medical Nature', talk presented to the Federation of State Medical Boards, Chicago, 10 February 1947; see also Ivy 1947 and Ivy 1948a, 5ff.

145 Taylor 1976, 6.

146 Grodin papers, Ivy's Itinerary.

147 Grodin papers, A Report on the Paris Meeting (31 July 1946).

148 NARA, RG 238, Entry 159, box 3, Operation of the Interrogation Service Unit, 17 June 1946.

149 Grodin papers, A Report on the Paris Meeting (31 July 1946), Appendix D.

150 *Ibid.*, 4.

151 *Ibid.*, Appendix C, 4.

152 *Ibid.*

153 *Ibid.*

154 *Ibid.*, Appendix B.

155 'Report of Reference Committee on Miscellaneous Business', *Journal of the American Medical Association*, 133 (1946), 33. The AMA guidelines stated: 'In order to conform to the ethics of the AMA three requirements must be satisfied: (1) the voluntary consent of the person on whom the experiment is to be performed must be obtained; (2) the danger of each experiment must be previously investigated by animal experimentation; and (3) the experiment must be performed under proper medical protection and management'; see Katz 1996, 1663f.; for the discussion on medical ethics in the *Journal of the American Medical Association* see JAMA, 13 July 1946, 920; 12 November 1946, 714–15; 30 November 1946, 783–5; 28 December 1946, 1090, 1104; 1 March 1947, 645; 10 May 1947, 178–9; 14 February 1948, 457–8; also Weindling 2001c, 53.

156 Katz 1996, 1663f.

157 Grodin papers, A Report on War Crimes of a Medical Nature, 9.

158 *Ibid.*, 11.

159 *Ibid.*, 12.

160 *Ibid.*, 12.

161 See also Ebbinghaus 2001, 405–35.

162 Grodin papers, A Report on War Crimes of a Medical Nature, 11.
163 *Ibid.*, 14; see also the testimony by Leibbrand, NDT Records, frame 2060.
164 *Ibid.*, 18–23.
165 Grodin 1992, 131; see also Bonah *et al.* 2003.
166 Grodin papers, A Report on War Crimes of a Medical Nature, 23.
167 *Ibid.*
168 'It is recommended that a person with medical and scientific training and a fluent speaking knowledge of German be assigned immediately to the agency which will try these cases, since some of the experiments are medically quite technical and such a person will render valuable assistance to the attorneys in collecting evidence, in interrogating witnesses, and in the preparation and conduct of the trials, as a medical expert serves in all cases of a medico-legal nature'; Grodin papers, A Report on War Crimes of a Medical Nature, 23.
169 Grodin papers, Ivy's Itinerary, 3.
170 Grodin papers, A Report on War Crimes of a Medical Nature, 23f.
171 *Ibid.*, 24.
172 *Ibid.*, 1.
173 BAK, ZSg 154, box 72, Conference of International Commission on Investigation of War Crimes of a Medical Nature, Hardy to McHaney, 26 October 1946.
174 PRO, WO235, file 316; Russel of Liverpool 1954, 191–225; for the handover of defendants and material by the British see also PRO, WO309, file 418, file 468 and file 471; FO371, file 57645; also Weindling 2000b, 378–81.
175 NARA, RG153/84-1, box 1, folder 2, Taylor to Petersen, 30 September 1946.
176 NARA, RG 153/87-2, book 2, box 14, Beals to Gunn, 21 November 1946.
177 United Nations War Crimes Commission 1948, 333.
178 NARA, RG 153/87-2, book 3, box 14, Memorandum for Petersen, 5 August 1946; also book 1, box 13, Memorandum for Gunn, 7 August 1946.
179 NARA, RG 153/87-2, book 1, box 13, Memorandum for Gunn, 7 August 1946.
180 NARA, RG 153/87-2, book 1, box 13, Memorandum for Mr Petersen, Assistant Secretary of War, 21 August 1946.
181 See also NARA, RG 153/84-1, box 1, folder 3, Taylor to Petersen, 30 September 1946.
182 NARA, RG 153/84-0, box 1, correspondence of judges and legal experts to the War Department. E. Riggs McConnell from North Carolina told the War Department that he did not feel qualified 'because of the lack of any strong moral conviction with respect to certain aspects of the prosecutions ... To try a man for cruelty seems to be one thing, but my general reaction to the aspects of the trial as related to people who in one way or another participated in the national movement was not at all certain.' McConnell to Gunn, 3 December 1946.
183 NARA, RG 153/87-2, book 1, box 13, Petersen to McNarney, 21 September 1946.
184 NARA, RG 153/87-2, book 1, box 13, Gunn to Secretary of War, 27 September 1946.
185 *Ibid.*
186 NARA, RG 153, 87-2, book 2, box 14, Moynihan to Swearingen, 27 September 1946.
187 NARA, RG 153, 87-2, book 4, box 14, folder 2.
188 *Ibid.*
189 NARA, RG 153, 87-2, book 1, box 13. Marian Elizabeth Blair was Beals' secretary; Edith Elizabeth Martin was Sebring's secretary and Nora Agnes Healy was Crawford's secretary.

190 NARA, RG 153, 87-2, book 3, box 14, Denman to War Department, 27 September 1946.
191 *Ibid.*
192 NARA, RG 153, 87-2, book 2, box 14, Denman to Patterson, 3 October 1946; also Patterson to Denman, 7 October 1946.
193 NARA, RG 153, 87-2, book 2, box 14, Vinson to Patterson, 19 November 1946; also Gunn to Beals, 3 December 1946.
194 SCHST, Sebring papers, Clay to Sebring, 25 October 1946, Patterson to Sebring, 28 November 1946; Executive Order No. 9813, signed by President Harry S. Truman, 20 December 1946.
195 NARA, RG 153, 87-2, book 6, box 14, 'Military Tribunals: Appointment of Judges at Nuremberg', *American Bar Association Journal*, 33 (1947), 896ff.
196 PRO, FO371, file 57576.
197 *Ibid.*
198 SCHST, Sebring papers.
199 Interview with H. L. (Tom) Sebring, Tallahassee, March 1998.
200 NARA, UD 25, box 1-12; RG 238-NT, box IV; executive session of Tribunal I, 13 November 1946; see also Brackman 1987.
201 NARA, RG 238, Entry 145, box 1, minutes of first and organisation meeting of Military Tribunal I held at the Palace of Justice, Nurnberg, Germany, 26 October 1946.
202 PRO, FO371, file 57576.
203 Davidson 1997, 21; Tusa and Tusa 1995, 109f.; PRO, FO371, file 57576.
204 NARA, UD 25, box 1-12; RG 238-NT, box IV; executive session of Tribunal I, 8 November 1946.
205 PRO, FO371, file 57576.
206 Ferencz 1948/9, 151.
207 NARA, RG 238, NM-70, box 1, Entry 213, list of defence lawyers of subsequent Nuremberg proceedings and their political affiliation, 31 January 1949; see also Ferencz 1948/9, 146.
208 Taylor 1993, 230; also Andrus 1969, 22ff.
209 NARA, UD 25, box 1-12; RG 238-NT, box IV; executive session of Tribunal I, 15 November 1946.
210 NARA, UD 25, box 1-12; RG 238-NT, box IV; executive session of Tribunal I, 20 November 1946. Bayle was later permitted to conduct his studies which he published in 1950 under the title *Croix Gammée Contre Caducée*; see Bayle 1950.
211 *Ibid.*
212 Taylor 1976, 6; see also Marrus 1999, 110.
213 NARA, RG 153/84-1, box 1, folder 3, Taylor to Petersen, 30 September 1946.
214 *Ibid.*
215 *Ibid.*
216 For some of the staff see NARA, RG 238, Entry 159, box 2.
217 NARA, RG 153/84-1, box 1, folder 3, Taylor to Jackson, 30 October 1946.
218 DUMC, Alexander diary (1946/47), 1, 13 November 1946.
219 NARA, RG 153/86-3-1, book 2, box 10, Taylor to War Department, 1 November 1946.
220 For the selection of experts for the defence see NDT Documents and Material, fiche 296, frames 1045-7.
221 NARA, UD 25, box 1-12; RG 238-NT, box IV; executive session of Tribunal I, 20 November 1946.
222 Taylor 1976, 6.

223 DUMC, Alexander papers, box 4, folder 9, Alexander travel orders, 8 November 1946.
224 Grodin papers, A Report on War Crimes of a Medical Nature, 25.
225 NARA, RG 153/86-3-1, book 2, box 10, Taylor to War Department, 7 November 1946.
226 Interview with Cecily Alexander-Grable, Marion, Cape Cod, May 1999.
227 DUMC, Alexander diary (1946/47), 5, 15 November 1946.
228 DUMC, Alexander papers, box 4, folder 9, Alexander travel orders, 8 November 1946.
229 DUMC, Alexander diary (1946/47), 1, 12 November 1946; see also Raphaël Lemkin, 'The Importance of the Genocide Concept for the Doctors Case. Memorandum for Colonel David Marcus, Chief, War Crimes Branch', 10 January 1947, in: NDT Documents and Material, fiche 303, frames 1802–4.
230 DUMC, Alexander diary (1946/47), 1, 13 November 1946.
231 *Ibid.*
232 *Ibid.*
233 AP, Leo Alexander to Phyllis Alexander, 13 November 1946.
234 DUMC, Alexander diary (1946/47), 5, 14 November 1946–15 November 1946.
235 DUMC, Alexander diary (1946/47), 5, 15 November 1946–18 November 1946.
236 DUMC, Alexander diary (1946/47), 6, 19 November 1946.
237 AP, Leo Alexander to Phyllis Alexander, 27 November 1946.
238 *Ibid.*
239 *Ibid.*
240 *Ibid.*
241 NARA, RG 238, Entry 159, box 3, Operation of the Interrogation Service Unit, 17 June 1946, 18 June 1946, 26 June 1946, 8 July 1946, 19 July 1946, 8 November 1946, 21 November 1946.
242 NARA, RG 238, Entry 159, box 3, Operation of the Interrogation Service Unit, 17 June 1946.
243 Grodin papers, A Report on War Crimes of a Medical Nature, 26.
244 NARA, RG 238, Entry 159, box 3, Operation of the Interrogation Service Unit, 17 June 1946.
245 NARA, RG 238, Entry 159, box 3, Interrogation of Major War Criminals, 8 November 1946.
246 StaNü, KV-Anklage, Interrogations, B49, Wilhelm Beiglböck, 28 February 1947.
247 AP, Leo Alexander to Phyllis Alexander, 27 November 1946.
248 For Robert Kempner see Frei 1996, 86, 103f., 149ff., 177, 202, 221.
249 StaNü, KV-Anklage, Interrogations, R128, Hans Wolfgang Romberg, 26 November 1946.
250 StaNü, KV-Anklage, Interrogations, R128, Hans Wolfgang Romberg, 27 February 1947.
251 StaNü, KV-Anklage, Interrogations, R128, Hans Wolfgang Romberg, 26 November 1946.
252 StaNü, KV-Anklage, Interrogations, F36, Fritz Fischer, 3 December 1946.
253 *Ibid.*
254 StaNü, KV-Anklage, Interrogations, F36, Fritz Fischer, 24 December 1946.
255 NARA, RG 238, Entry 200, box 8, prison file Dr Fritz Fischer (*5 October 1912); Fritz Fischer to Magdalene Fischer, 20 September 1945.
256 StaNü, KV-Anklage, Interrogations, O1, Herta Oberheuser, 28 December 1946.
257 BA-BDC, personal file Herta Oberheuser; Mergenthal 1997, 191–6; also Ebbinghaus 1987, 250–73.

258 BAK, ZSg 154, box 73, Interrogation of Herta Oberheuser, 4 December 1946.
259 PRO, WO309, file 469 and file 420; also BAK, ZSg 154, box 73, Interrogation of Herta Oberheuser, 4 December 1946.
260 StaNü, KV-Anklage, Interrogations, B154, Karl Brandt, 26 November 1946.

6. Constructing the Doctors' Trial

1 NDT Documents and Material, fiche 303, frame 1803.
2 *Ibid.*, frames 1802–4.
3 *Ibid.*, frame 1802; see also Levi 1996, p. x.
4 *Ibid.*, frame 1803.
5 DUMC, Alexander diary (1946/47), 79, 3 December 1946.
6 Katz 1996, 1662.
7 Alexander Paper 1: The Fundamental Purpose and Meaning of the Experiments of the Experiments in Human Beings of which the Accused (Military Tribunal No. 1, Case No. 1) have been Indicted: Thanatology as a Scientific Technique of Genocide, 30 November 1946; Alexander Paper 2: Suggestions for a Discussion of the Thanatology Genocide Angle, 5 December 1946; Alexander Paper 3: Ethical and Non-Ethical Experimentation on Human Beings, 7 December 1946; Alexander Paper 4: One Major Aim of the German Vivisectionists: Ktenology as a Scientific Technique of Genocide, 15 January 1947; Alexander Paper 5: Ethical and Non-Ethical Experimentation on Human Beings, 15 April 1947 (10 pages); Alexander Paper 6: Ethical and Non-Ethical Experimentation on Human Beings, General Ethical, Medico-Legal and Scientific Considerations in Connection with the Vivisectionists Trial Before the Military Tribunal in Germany, no date (29 pages); for the whereabouts of these papers see DUMC, Alexander papers, box 1, folder 9 and 12; box 4, folder 34; see also Alexander 1976c. The author discovered and consulted these papers for the first time in March 1998; see Schmidt 2001b, note 2. Others have in the meantime also used these papers.
8 See also Shuster 1998.
9 Tröhler and Reiter-Theil 1997, 14.
10 Rothman 1997, 75–87, 87.
11 Weindling 1996, see also Weindling 2000 and Weindling 2001a.
12 See also Ebbinghaus 2001, 406.
13 Alexander Paper 1, 30 November 1946.
14 Alexander Paper 2, 5 December 1946.
15 Alexander Paper 1, 30 November 1946.
16 Alexander Paper 4, 15 January 1947.
17 DUMC, Alexander diary (1946/47), 1f., 13 November 1946; also Alexander Paper 4, 15 January 1947.
18 DUMC, Alexander diary (1946/47), 1f., 13 November 1946.
19 NARA, RG 153/86-3-1, book 2, box 10, Alexander to Perkins, 13 November 1946.
20 NARA, RG 153/86-3-1, book 2, box 10, Alexander to Cramer, 14 November 1946; Alexander to Overholser, 14 November 1946; Alexander to Taliaferro, 14 November 1946; Alexander to Rappleye, 14 November 1946; Alexander to Chesney, 14 November 1946; Alexander to Chairman, Board of Scientific Directors, Rockefeller Institute of Medical Research, 15 November 1946.
21 DUMC, Alexander diary (1946/47), 11f., 21 November 1946.

22 DUMC, Alexander diary (1946/47), 18, 22 November 1946; 19, 24 November
    1946; 19, 25 November 1946; 34, 28 November 1946; 49, 29 November 1946;
    78, 3 December 1946; 79, 3 December 1946; 107, 10 December 1946, 199,
    1 March 1947, 199, 10 March 1947; 199, 11 March 1947.
23 AP, Leo Alexander to Phyllis Alexander, 27 November 1946.
24 Alexander Paper 1, 30.11.1946; see also Alexander Paper 4, 15 January 1947.
25 DUMC, Alexander diary (1946/47), 78f., 3 December 1946; also Alexander
    Paper 2, 5 December 1946; see also Schmidt 2001b, 374f.
26 Alexander Paper 1, 30 November 1946.
27 BAK, ZSg 154, box 65, Andrew Ivy; Report on War Crimes of a Medical Nature
    Committed in Germany and Elsewhere on German Nationals and the
    Nationals of Occupied Countries by the Nazi Regime During World War II,
    22 Bl., o.D. (1946); also Andrew Ivy, Medical Aspects of Nazi War Crimes.
    Speech delivered to the University of Illinois Colleges of Medicine, Dentistry
    and Pharmacy on 9 October 1946.
28 Alexander Paper 1, 30 November 1946.
29 AP, Leo Alexander to Phyllis Alexander, 7 December 1946.
30 Alexander Paper 2, 5 December 1946.
31 DUMC, Alexander diary (1946/47), 105, 7 December 1946.
32 DUMC, Alexander diary (1946/47), 105, 8 December 1946.
33 AP, Leo Alexander to Phyllis Alexander, 7 December 1946; DUMC, Alexander
    diary (1946/47), 105, 8 December 1946; also Tusa and Tusa 1995, 150ff.
34 The rational for the 'euthanasia' programme lay as much in economic factors
    as in a peculiar interpretation of racial hygiene, that is, to balance the loss of
    'valuable' life in times of war with the killing of 'useless eaters'; see Burleigh
    1994; Friedlander 1995; also Schmidt 2002a.
35 DUMC, Alexander diary (1946/47), 4, 13 November 1946.
36 In the Doctors' Trial the legal concept of a 'common design' was adopted
    instead of the concept of a 'common plan' after it had become apparent that
    the latter was difficult to prove in open court during the IMT; for the debate
    within the prosecution see NARA, RG 238, Entry 159, box 4, Memorandum,
    Subject: The Concept of 'Common design', Ferencz to Heath, 17 July 1946.
37 DUMC, Alexander diary (1946/47), 4, 13 November 1946.
38 For an interesting, although largely ahistorical discussion about the shortcom-
    ing of the Doctors' Trial see Marrus 1999.
39 Alexander Paper 4, 15 January 1947.
40 DUMC, Alexander papers, box 4, file 34, Memorandum, 'Countering the
    Defense that Germans were Experimenting on Prisoners Condemned to Death',
    23 November 1946.
41 DUMC, Alexander diary (1946/47), 79, 3 December 1946.
42 *Ibid.*
43 DUMC, Alexander diary (1946/47), 105, 6 December 1946.
44 DUMC, Alexander diary (1946/47), 105; 7 December 1946; NDT Documents
    and Material, fiche 303, frames 1714–24; also Alexander 1976c.
45 DUMC, Alexander papers, box 1, folder 9, Alexander Paper 6 (see bibliography),
    22f.
46 Alexander 1976c, 40f.
47 *Ibid.*, 41.
48 *Ibid.*
49 *Ibid.*
50 *Ibid.*

51 *Ibid.*; also Ebermayer 1930.
52 NDT Documents and Material, fiche 303, frames 1783–1801.
53 *Ibid.*, frame 1790.
54 Alexander 1976c, 41.
55 *Ibid.*
56 NDT Records, frame 50.
57 *Ibid.*, frames 61–124.
58 Annas and Grodin 1992, 68.
59 *Ibid.*
60 *Ibid.*
61 *Ibid.*, 71.
62 NDT Records, frames 64f.
63 Annas and Grodin 1992, 71–86.
64 *Ibid.*, 87.
65 *Ibid.*
66 *Ibid.*, 89.
67 *Ibid.*
68 *New York Times*, 10.12.1946.
69 NDT Records, frame 119.
70 Annas and Grodin 1992, 70ff.
71 *Ibid.*, 70.
72 *Ibid.*
73 *Ibid.*
74 *Ibid.*, 70f.
75 For newspaper responses about the opening of the trial see NARA, RG 238, Entry 28, box 3, Daily Press Review; *Philadelphia Record*; *Baltimore News Post*; *Philadelphia Bulletin*, 9 December 1946; *Minneapolis Times Dispatch*; *Dallas Morning News*; *Baltimore Sun*; *Philadelphia Record*, *Washington Post*; *Chicago Sun*, *New York Harald Tribune*, 10 December 1946; *Frankenpost*; *Fränkischer Tag*; *Badische Neuste Nachrichten*, 11 December 1946; *Darmstädter Echo*; *Fränkische Nachrichten*, *Mittelbayrische Zeitung*; *Frankfurter Rundschau*, 12 December 1946; *Die Neue Zeitung*; *Main Post*; *Frankenpost*, 13 December 1946; *Fränkische Landeszeitung*; *Weser Kurier*; *Stuttgarter Nachrichten*; *Fränkischer Tag*, 14 December 1946; *Liberation*, *Le figaro*, *L'Époque*, *La Dépeche de Paris*, *L'Humanité*, *Paris Matin*, *L'Aurore*, *L'Aube*, 17 December 1946; see also the reporting about the trial in *Die Welt*, in: NDT Documents and Material, fiche 308, frames 2250–7.
76 NARA, RG 238, Entry 28, box 3, Daily Press Review; *Philadelphia Record*, 9 December 1946.
77 NARA, RG 238, Entry 28, box 3, Daily Press Review, *L'Ordre*; *L'Époque*, 11 December 1946.
78 NARA, RG 238, Entry 28, box 3, Daily Press Review.
79 FCLM, Beecher papers, box 11, folder 79.
80 NARA, RG 238, Entry 28, box 3, Daily Press Review.
81 *New York Times*, 12 December 1946.
82 Von Platen 1947a, 29–31, 29.
83 *Ibid.*, 29; also Von Platen 1947b, 199–202.
84 *New York Times*, 10 December 1946.
85 StaNü, KV-Prozesse, Generalia, P318, DANA papers, 9 December 1946; NARA, RG 238, Entry 28, box 3 Daily Press Review, 11 December 1946 and 13 December 1946.

86 DUMC, Alexander diary (1946/47), 105, 9 December 1946.
87 *Ibid.*
88 DUMC, Alexander diary (1946/47), 112, 10 December 1946.
89 AP, Leo Alexander to Phyllis Alexander, 10 December 1946.
90 AP, Leo Alexander to Phyllis Alexander, 18 December 1946.
91 For the full list of names of the experimental victims see PRO, WO235, file 531; WO309, file 420; also Martin 1994a, Appendix.
92 Martin 1994c, 113–22, 116; see also Martin 1994b.
93 See especially Michejda 1947, 123–75; also RA IV, No. 16 ('Collection Warsaw'), Protokoll der Hauptkommission zur Untersuchung von hitlerschen Verbrechen (27 April 1957–25 May 1957); Mitcherlich 1960, 131–59.
94 Porter 1959.
95 NARA, RG 238, Case History of Polish Witnesses – Broel-Plater, Karołewska, Dzido and Kuśmierczuk by Dr Leo Alexander, 17 December 1946.
96 *Ibid.*
97 *Ibid.*
98 *Ibid.*
99 *Ibid.*
100 *Ibid.*
101 DUMC, Alexander diary (1946/47), 146, 18 December 1946–20 December 1946.
102 NARA, RG 238, Alexander to McHaney, 18 December 1946.
103 *Ibid.*
104 *Ibid.*
105 *Ibid.*
106 NDT Records, frames 863–928; also DUMC, Alexander diary (1946/47), 146, 20 December 1946.
107 NDT Records, frame 868.
108 *Ibid.*, frame 895.
109 *Ibid.*, frame 924.
110 StaNü, KV-Anklage, Interrogations, F36, Fritz Fischer and Karl Gebhardt, 24 December 1946.
111 AP, Leo Alexander to Phyllis Alexander, 21 December 1946.
112 *Ibid.*
113 'Human Laboratory Animals', *Life* (1947), 26–7.
114 *Ibid.*
115 *Newsweek*, 23 December 1946.
116 IWM, Film and Video Archive, *Welt im Film*, 17 January 1947.
117 'Experimente ...', *Heute* (1947), 6; see also BAK, ZSg 154, box 73.
118 *Ibid.*
119 DUMC, Alexander diary (1946/47), 153, 26 December 1946.
120 DUMC, Alexander diary (1946/47), 155, 29 December 1946.
121 AP, Leo Alexander to Phyllis Alexander, 31 December 1946; as to the role of Otmar von Verschuer and Karin Magnussen see Müller-Hill, 1988; also Weindling 2000c, 635–52.
122 For the Milch trial see Frewer and Wiesemann 1999, 99–105; NDT Documents and Material, frames 1653–70.
123 AP, Leo Alexander to Phyllis Alexander, 31 December 1946 and 8 January 1947.
124 AP, Leo Alexander to Gustave Alexander, 31 December 1946.
125 FCLM, Beecher papers, box 11, folder 79.
126 *Ibid.*

127 Mielke 1948, 29–31; also Platen-Hallermund 1998, 1; for the controversy in the *Göttinger Zeitung* between Alexander Mitscherlich and Friedrich Hermann Rein about Nazi medicine see NDT Documents and Material, fiche 307/8, frames 2272–84.

128 Peters 2001, 455ff.; see also Peters 1994, 39.

129 Countess Alice von Platen, today Contess Alice von Platen-Hallermund, was born on 28 April 1910 in Weißenhaus (Holstein). She lives in Cortona and in Rome.

130 Alice von Platen Hallermund to the author, 12 January 1998.

131 StUF, AMA, II2/115; von Platen to Mitscherlich, 10 January 1947.

132 *Ibid.*

133 Kogon 1946.

134 DUMC, Alexander papers, box 4, folder 40, Wolfe H. Frank, 10 January 1947; also box 4, folder 34, Memorandum to Taylor, Appraisal of the Accused by Dr A. Wiskott, 30 November 1946; see also box 4, folder 40, Broadcast, 27 January 1947.

135 DUMC, Alexander papers, box 4, file 40, Wolfe H. Frank, 10 January 1947.

136 See Schmidt 2001b, 381–9.

137 DUMC, Alexander papers, box 4, file 40, Wolfe H. Frank, 10 January 1947.

138 NDT Documents and Material, fiche 296, frames 1048–51.

7. The Nuremberg Code

1 Anonymous author (editor), 'A Moral Problem', *The Lancet*, 30 November 1946; K. Mellanby, 'A Moral Problem', *The Lancet*, 7 December 1946, 850; T. B. Layton; A. Nelson-Jones, 'A Moral Problem', *The Lancet*, 14 December 1946, 882; S. H. Hilton, 'A Moral Problem', *The Lancet*, 4 January 1947, 43; D. Herbert, 'A Moral Problem', *The Lancet*, 11 January 1947, 84f.

2 DUMC, Alexander papers, box 1, folder 20, Office of Chief of Counsel for War Crimes, Public Relations Office, Special Release No. 99, 11 January 1947.

3 'Doctors on Trial', *British Medical Journal*, 1 (1947), 25 January 1947, 143, Kenneth Mellanby, 'Medical Experiments on Human Beings in Concentration Camps in Nazi Germany', *British Medical Journal*, 1 (1947), 25 January 1947, 148–50; also Mellanby 1947; Rißmann 1947.

4 DUMC, Alexander papers, box 1, file 20.

5 The phrase 'Snafu' refers to an acronym which soldiers used to make a mocking comment about the military. It stands for 'Situation Normal, All Fouled Up'. Soldiers would also use an expletive instead of the word 'Fouled'. I am grateful to Jonathan D. Moreno for pointing this out.

6 AP, Leo Alexander to Phyllis Alexander, 16 December 1946.

7 AP, Leo Alexander to Phyllis Alexander, 8 January 1947.

8 *Ibid.*

9 Interview with Cecily Alexander-Grable, Marion, Cape Cod, May 1999.

10 DUMC, Alexander papers, box 4, file 35.

11 United Nations War Crimes Commission 1948, 147.

12 BAK, ZSg 154, box 73, International Scientific Commission (War Crimes), 15 January 1947.

13 For the make-up of the British commission see NARA, RG 153/86-3-1, book 3, box 11.

14 PRO, FO371, file 57576, Attlee to Moran, 28 October 1946. The chairman of
    the UNWCC, Lord Wright, recommended to Attlee to appoint 'a British com-
    mittee of outstanding British medical men ... "on a high level" to sit with the
    French medical committee'; NARA, RG 153/86-3-1, book 1, box 9.
15 Weindling 1996, 1468; Blacker 1952a and Blacker 1952b. For talks between the
    British members of the ISC (WC) and German scientists see Weindling 2001c, 41f.
16 For the make-up of the French commission see NARA, RG 153/86-3-1, book 3,
    box 11.
17 BAK, ZSg 154, box 73, International Scientific Commission (War Crimes),
    15 January 1947.
18 *Ibid.*; also Weindling 2001c, 63.
19 DUMC, Alexander papers, box 4, file 35.
20 In addition to recommending himself, Alexander proposed the appointment of
    the following experts to the Commission: Andrew Ivy (University of Illinois),
    George Minot (Harvard Medical School), Professor Bazett (University of
    Pennsylvania), Frank Lahey (Lahey Clinic, Boston), Abraham Myerson (State
    Research Committee, Boston) and General Kirk (Surgeon General of the US
    Army); NARA, RG 153/86-3-1, book 1, box 9, Alexander to Gunn, 15 February
    1947.
21 Buscher 1989, 31.
22 NARA, RG 153/86-3-1, book 1, box 9, Springer to Secretary of State, 31 January
    1947.
23 NARA, RG 153/86-3-1, book 1, box 9, Springer to Secretary of State, 31 January
    1947. Ivy made similar proposals; RG 153/86-3-1, book 3, box 11.
24 NARA, RG 232, Entry 159, box 1.
25 NARA, RG 153/86-3-1, box 11, folder 4, book 3, Memorandum on Investigation
    of War Crimes of a Medical Nature, 25 February 1947.
26 Foreign Office 1949, 3; see also United Nations War Crimes Commission 1949;
    also Weindling 2001c, 69.
27 Alexander Paper 4, 15 January 1947; also BAK, Zsg 154, No. 73.
28 DUMC, Alexander diary (1946/47), 168, 21 January 1947.
29 DUMC, Alexander diary (1946/47), 168, 22 January 1947.
30 Quoted from Weindling 2001c, 64.
31 DUMC, Alexander diary (1946/47), 174, 24 January 1947.
32 DUMC, Alexander diary (1946/47), 174, 25 January 1947.
33 For a draft of the six ethics principles which Alexander drew up in January
    1947 see DUMC, box 4, folder 33.
34 Schmidt 2001a.
35 StUF, Alexander-Mitscherlich-Archiv, II 2, 106.7, Affidavit of Leo Alexander,
    25 January 1947; also NDT Documents and Material, fiche 303, frames 1725–8.
36 NARA, RG 153/86-3-1, box 10, book 3, Leo Alexander, 'Ethical and Non-ethical
    Experimentation on Human Beings. General Ethical, Medico-Legal and
    Scientific Considerations in Connection with the Vivisectionists'.
37 NDT Records, frames 2033–2100; see also NDT Documents and Material, fiche
    304, frame 1830; for the biography of Werner Leibbrand see Seidel 2001, 358f.
38 Grodin papers, A Report on War Crimes of a Medical Nature, 25; DUMC,
    Alexander diary (1946/47), 49, 29 November 1946.
39 NDT Records, frames 2033f.
40 *Ibid.*, frame 2045.
41 Moll 1902.
42 Also NDT Documents and Material, fiche 307/8, frame 2252.

43 'Prison Malaria: Convicts Expose Themselves to Disease so Doctors can Study it', *Life*, 18 (1945), No. 23, 43–6.

44 *Ibid.*, 43.

45 NDT Records, frame 2070.

46 *Ibid.*, frame 2091; also Shuster 1997, 1438.

47 *Ibid.*, frame 2071.

48 DUMC, Alexander papers, box 4, folder 35, 'Memorandum for Mr. McHaney. Subject: Questions for interrogation of Dr Leibbrand. From: Dr. Alexander', 14 January 1947; also DUMC, Alexander diary (1946/47), 163, 13 January 1947; Weindling 2001c, 57.

49 AP, Leo Alexander to Gustave Alexander, 28 January 1947.

50 NDT Documents and Material, fiche 304, frame 1831.

51 UWAHC, Andrew C. Ivy Papers (#8768), box 89, folder 5, Andrew Ivy to Irving Ladimer, Roger W. Newman and W. J. Curran, 23 March 1964; also Weindling 2001c, 67.

52 NARA, RG 238, NM-70, Entry 213, box 1, Defense Counsel, Military Tribunals, Nurnberg, 31 January 1949.

53 Ebbinghaus 2001, 405–35.

54 StaNü, Rep. 502A, KV-Verteidigung, Handakten Rostock, file 8, Rostock to Rein, 9.7.1947; also Ebbinghaus 2001, 407.

55 Sereny 1995, 558.

56 PRO, WO208, file 2178.

57 The 'Beelitzer' refers to his former colleagues from Beelitz, located on the outskirts of Berlin, which was Brandt's headquarters as Reich Commissioner for Health and Sanitation in the later part of the war.

58 Brandt papers, diary entry, 17 January 1946; for the preparation of Brandt's defence see PRO, WO309, file 420.

59 *New York Times*, 9 December 1947.

60 *New York Times*, 5 February 1947, 8 February 1947.

61 NDT Records, frames 2377–2517.

62 *Ibid.*, frames 2447f.

63 *Ibid.*, frames 2382ff., frames 2389ff.

64 *Ibid.*, frame 2459.

65 *Ibid.*, frames 2444f.

66 *Ibid.*, frame 2395.

67 *Ibid.*, frame 2466.

68 *Ibid.*, frames 2501f.

69 *Ibid.*, frames 2511f.

70 *Ibid.*, frame 2503.

71 *Ibid.*, frame 2503.

72 *Ibid.*, frame 2514.

73 *Ibid.*, frame 2516.

74 *Ibid.*, frames 2548–2730.

75 DUMC, Alexander diary (1946/47), 187, 5 February 1947.

76 NDT Records, frame 2598.

77 *Ibid.*, frame 2621.

78 *Ibid.*, frames 2716–20.

79 *Ibid.*, frame 2576.

80 See, for example, the defence strategy by Hans Pribilla, defence attorney for Paul Rostock; StaNü, Rep. 502 A, KV-Verteidigung, Handakten Rostock, file 3 and file 5, also Ebbinghaus and Dörner 2001b, 640f.

81 For the defence strategy by Gebhardt and Fischer see Schmidt 2001b; also Ebbinghaus 2001.
82 Ebbinghaus 2001, 431–5; for a summery of Blome's testimony see NDT Documents and Material, fiche 304, frames 1865–74; also fiche 307/8, frames 2190–6.
83 StaNü, Rep. 502 A, KV-Verteidigung, Handakten Sauter, file 6; also in NDT Documents and Material, fiche 296, frames 1061–75.
84 StaNü, Rep. 502 A, KV-Verteidigung, Handakten Sauter, file 3, working paper by Blome on the subject of human experimentation, 11 March 1947.
85 *Ibid.*
86 NDT Documents and Material, fiche 296, frames 1061–75.
87 NARA, RG 232, Entry 159, box 1, War Crimes Operations, 19 February 1947.
88 *Ibid.*
89 *Ibid.*
90 NDT Documents and Material, frames 1653–70, frames 1665f.
91 *Ibid.*, frames 1653–70; also DUMC, Alexander diary (1946/47), 195, 14 February 1947.
92 DUMC, Alexander diary (1946/47), 197f., 26 February 1947.
93 See also DUMC, Alexander papers, box 4, folder 35, Interrogation of Haagen, 9 July 1947.
94 DUMC, Alexander diary (1946/47), 201, 13 March 1947.
95 DUMC, Alexander papers, box 4, file 36. For Nales' witness testimony in the Doctor's Trial see NDT Records, frames 10593–10655; also DUMC, Alexander diary (1946/47), 200–21, 13 March 1947–21 March 1947.
96 DUMC, Alexander diary (1946/47), 203, 14 March 1947.
97 On 14 March he met with Bert and Helene Hulst, née Alexander, and their two children Steffen and Irene; DUMC, Alexander diary (1946/47), 203, 14 March 1947.
98 DUMC, Alexander diary (1946/47), 204, 16 March 1947–19 March 1947.
99 Alexander 1948b; in July 1947 Alexander returned the hospitality of his Dutch colleagues by playing host to Hulst, Sillevis-Smit and Boellard who interviewed a number of the Nuremberg defendants; see Irene Julst (Loenen a/d Veht), Lambert Hulst Papers (Diary by Dr Boellaard, De Nuerenbergsche Processen in de Zomer van 1947).
100 DUMC, Alexander diary (1946/47), 219, 21 March 1947.
101 DUMC, Alexander papers, box 1 file 11, Steijns to Alexander, 21 March 1947.
102 DUMC, Alexander papers, box 4, folder 35, Alexander to Kurtz, 4 March 1947.
103 *Ibid.*
104 Shuster 1997, 1438.
105 See Harkness 1996.
106 DUMC, Alexander papers, box 4, folder 35, Fenger to Taylor, 28 March 1947.
107 *Ibid.*
108 *Ibid.*
109 DUMC, Alexander papers, box 4, folder 35, Alexander/McHaney to Fenger, 16 April 1947.
110 *Ibid.*
111 *Ibid.*
112 DUMC, Alexander diary (1946/47), 222, 15 April 1947; also Alexander Paper 5 and Alexander Paper 6.
113 Alexander Paper 5, 2f.
114 *Ibid.*, 7.
115 DUMC, Alexander diary (1946/47), 222, 15 April 1947.

116 Alexander Paper 6.
117 DUMC, Alexander papers, box 1, folder 9, attached, handwritten note to Alexander Paper 6, no date and signature, which discusses Alexander's paper on ethical and non-ethical experimentation in human beings from 15 April 1947.
118 *Ibid.*
119 *Ibid.*
120 *Ibid.*
121 NDT Records, frames 6211–6618.
122 *Ibid.*, frames 6213f.
123 *Ibid.*, frames 6313ff. and frame 6406.
124 *Ibid.*, frame 6316.
125 *Ibid.*, frame 6316.
126 Alexander 1938n.
127 NDT Documents and Material, fiche 307/8, frames 2200ff.
128 NDT Records, frame 6323.
129 *Ibid.*, frame 6515; also NDT Documents and Material, fiche 307/8, frame 2203.
130 *Ibid.*, frame 6418.
131 *Ibid.*, frames 6538ff.
132 *Ibid.*, frame 6540.
133 *Ibid.*, frame 6542.
134 See also Ebbinghaus 2001, 430.
135 NDT Records, frame 6598.
136 *Ibid.*, frame 6601; see also NDT Documents and Material, fiche 307/8, frame 2208.
137 DUMC, Alexander diary (1946/47), 223, 18 April 1947.
138 DUMC, Alexander diary (1946/47), 223, 24 April 1947; NDT Records, frames 6522–6618.
139 DUMC, Alexander papers, box 4, folder 35, Alexander to McHaney, 29 April 1947.
140 *Ibid.*
141 *Ibid.*
142 DUMC, Alexander diary (1946/47), 163, 13 January 1947.
143 UWAHC, Andrew C. Ivy Papers (#8768), box 6, folder 8, Andrew C. Ivy, 'The Significance of the Moral Philosophy of Medicine', talk at the University of Nebraska College of Medicine, 22 March 1947; also box 7, folder 8, Andrew C. Ivy, 'Some Ethical Implications of Science', talk presented to the Central Association of Science and Mathematics Teachers, 28 November 1947.
144 NARA, RG 153/86-3-1, box 11, book 3, International Scientific Commission (on medical war crimes). Note of a meeting in the War Department on 9 April 1947; see also War Department to Ivy, 25 March 1947.
145 *Ibid.*
146 DUMC, Alexander diary (1946/47), 226, 7 May 1947.
147 DUMC, Alexander diary (1946/47), 229, 8 May 1947.
148 DUMC, Alexander diary (1946/47), 231, 10 May 1947.
149 DUMC, Alexander diary (1946/47), 232, 11 May 1947.
150 DUMC, Alexander papers, box 4, folder 37, Leo Alexander, 'The Socio-Psychological Structure of the SS', talk presented to the Nederlandsche Vereeniging voor Psychiatrie en Neurologie, Amsterdam, Netherlands, 12 June 1947 [original manuscript].
151 AP, Leo Alexander to Phyllis Alexander, 1 July 1947.

152 AP, Leny Alexander-Hulst to Phyllis Alexander, 5 August 1947.
153 NDT Records, frames 9196–9494; for a summary of Ivy's rebuttal testimony see NDT Documents and Material, fiche 304, frames 1952–7; also fiche 307/8, frames 2224–6; also NARA, RG 238, Entry 159, box 5, Daily Trial Report, Report No. 69, Tribunal No. I – SS Medical Case, 12 June 1947; see also Moreno's groundbreaking analysis of Ivy's trial testimony; Moreno 1999, 74–9.
154 *Ibid.*, frames 9323ff.
155 Moreno 1999, 74.
156 NDT Records, frames 9141ff.
157 *Ibid.*, frames 9337f.; also Moreno 1999, 75f.
158 Harkness 1996, 1673.
159 *Ibid.*, 1674.
160 NDT Documents and Material, fiche 303, frames 1756–62.
161 NDT Records, frame 9382.
162 *Ibid.*
163 Harkness 1996, 1674.
164 NDT Records, frame 9389; Harkness 1996, 1674.
165 NDT Records, frame 9254.
166 *Ibid.*, frames 9260ff.
167 *Ibid.*, frame 9275.
168 *Ibid.*, frame 9424.
169 *Ibid.*, frame 9426.
170 *Ibid.*, frames 9433ff.
171 *Ibid.*, frame 9435.
172 *Ibid.*, frames 10412–16; also NDT Documents and Material, fiche 304, frame 1962; also fiche 307/8, frame 2228.
173 DUMC, Alexander papers, box 4, folder 35, Alexander to McHaney, 28 June 1947.
174 *Ibid.*
175 *Ibid.*
176 NDT Documents and Material, fiche 304, frame 1962.
177 NDT Records, frames 10693–10729.
178 DUMC, Alexander papers, box 4, folder 36; also Alexander diary (1946/47), 201, 13 March 1947; for Nales' testimony see NDT Records, frames 10593–10655.
179 NDT Records, frames 10593–10624.
180 AP, Leo Alexander to Phyllis Alexander, 1 July 1947.
181 NDT Records, frames 10908ff.
182 *Ibid.*, frame 10907; also Alexander's preparation of the closing argument in DUMC, Alexander papers, box 4, folder 35, Memo to McHaney, Subject: Closing Statements, 12 July 1947.
183 *Ibid.*, frame 10908.
184 *Ibid.*, frames 10908f.
185 AP, Leo Alexander to Phyllis Alexander, 16 December 1946.
186 NDT Records, frame 10914.
187 *Ibid.*, frames 10920ff.; see also Shuster 1998, 974.
188 *Ibid.*
189 *Ibid.*, frames 11568–9; see principle three of the Nuremberg Code.
190 *Ibid.*; see principle two of the Nuremberg Code.
191 *Ibid.*; see principle eight of the Nuremberg Code.
192 *Ibid.*; see principle four of the Nuremberg Code.

193 *Ibid.*; see principle five of the Nuremberg Code.
194 *Ibid.*; see principle one of the Nuremberg Code.
195 *Ibid.*, frames 10921–4; also NDT Records, frames 11568–9; see principle ten of the Nuremberg Code.
196 *Ibid.*, frame 10925.
197 *Ibid.*
198 *Ibid.*, frame 10976.
199 *Ibid.*, frame 10982.
200 *Ibid.*, frame 10983.
201 *Ibid.*, frame 10983.
202 *Ibid.*, frame 10984.
203 For a summary of the closing arguments see NDT Documents and Material, fiche 304, frames 1969–75; also fiche 307/8, frames 2230–2.
204 *Ibid.*, frame 1976.
205 NDT Records, frames 11504–7.
206 *Ibid.*, frame 11505.
207 *Ibid.*
208 *Ibid.*, frame 11507.
209 *Ibid.*, frames 11568–9.
210 *Ibid.*
211 *Ibid.*, frame 9243.
212 *Ibid.*, frames 11568–9.
213 *Ibid.*, frame 9244.
214 *Ibid.*, frame 9244.
215 *Ibid.*, frames 11568–9.
216 *Ibid.*, frames 11568–9.
217 DUMC, Alexander papers, box 4, folder 35, Alexander to Sebring, 15 July 1947.
218 UWAHC, Andrew C. Ivy Papers (#8768), box 89, folder 5, Andrew Ivy to Irving Ladimer, Roger W. Newman and W. J. Curran, 23 March 1964; also box 6, folder 13, Albert H. Stroupe, 'The Nuremberg Code – An Ivy Contribution. The Operation of Conscience in the Nuremberg Trials and the Krebiozen Controversy'.
219 Ivy believed in the heroic achievements of great medical scientists like Galen and Pasteur and probably saw himself as one of them; UWAHC, Andrew C. Ivy Papers (#8768), box 88, folder 2, Andrew C. Ivy, Correspondence Jan.–Dec. 1954, 'The Message of Pasteur', 30 September 1954.
220 Alexander 1966h, 62; see also Alexander 1966a.
221 In 1982 Alexander credited himself retrospectively with the formulation of the Nuremberg Code; see Leo Alexander, 'The Physician and the State, Ethical Implications of the Nuremberg War Crimes Trials & More Recent Events', Talk held at the St Elizabeth's Hospital, Boston, 23 March 1982; see also Blomquist 1978.
222 Shuster 1997, 1436f.; see also Michael Grodin's groundbreaking work on the historical origins of the Nuremberg Code. He was the first to examine the various personalities who shaped the formulation of the Code; Grodin 1992. My interpretation of the origins of the Nuremberg Code and of its author-ship stands in marked contrast to that of Paul Weindling who offers a set of sometimes contradictory explanations of how the Code originated. In one article Weindling argues that 'Judge Beals' outlined 'a set of ethics and moral principles', that 'it may well be that Sebring recognized the value of creating such a code', that the origins of the Code 'lie beyond the courtroom', that is

in inter-Allied discussions, that the Code 'arose from the concerns of Allied medical war crimes investigators' and, finally, that it was 'generated' by 'judicial procedures'. I agree that the origins of the Code are complex, yet we need to understand that the Code was effectively the work of the judges of which we know relatively little. This is unfortunate, but we need to concentrate our attention where the actual power for writing the Code was located, rather than assigning credit to some bilateral and overall less relevant International Commission for the Investigation of War Crimes; see Weindling 2001c.

223 Shuster 1998b, 995f.

224 Interview with Cecily Alexander-Grable, Marion, Cape Cod, May 1999.

225 NDT Records, frame 9277.

226 Interview with H. L. (Tom) Sebring, Tallahassee, March 1998; Tom accompanied his father to Nuremberg as an adolescent. According to Tom Sebring, Nuremberg was one of the most stressful experiences in his father's life.

227 NARA, RG 153, 87–2, book 5, box 14.

228 NDT Records, frames 7284–5.

229 The trial transcript does not seem to record that Swearingen ever questioned any of the witnesses or defendants individually throughout the trial. Those instances where the tribunal questioned a witness jointly were not taken into consideration.

230 Sebring examined the following witnesses: Brandt, 6 February 1947, NDT Records, frames 2646–55; Gutzeit 10 February 1947, frames 2808–10; Handloser, 12 February 1947, frames 2963–70; Hartleben, 20 February 1947, frames 3315–19; Rostock, 21 February 1947, frames 3461–7; Rostock, 24 February 1947, frames 3517–20; Schröder, 26 February 1947, frames 3657–72; Jentsch, 26 February 1947, frames 3691–3; Schröder, 27 February 1947, frame 3792; Pieck, 20 March 1947, frames 4863–4; Sievers, 11 April 1947, frames 5934–8; Borkenau, 15 April 1947, frames 6032–5; Topf, 15 April 1947, frames 6049–50; Hielscher, 15 April 1947, frames 6087–95; Hielscher, 16 April 1947, frames 6107–8; Ruff, 29 April 1947, frames 6775–87; Romberg, 2 May 1947, frames 7076–8; Romberg, 5 May 1947, frames 7096–7159; Romberg, 6 May 1947, frames 7170–2; Weltz, 6 May 1947, frames 7238–44; Weltz, 7 May 1947, frames 7277–84, Weltz, 7 May 1947, frames 7286–9; Pfannmüller, 9 May 1947, frames 7479–80; Volhard, 3 June 1947, frames 8637–8; Beiglböck, 10 June 1947, frames 8981–90; Beiglböck, 11 June 1947, frames 9120–1; Ivy, 12 June 1947, frames 9236–44; Ivy, 13 June 1947, frames 9279–80; Hoven, 21 and 23 June 1947, frames 9980–10002; Hoven, 24 June 1947, frames 10160–8; Broers, 30 June 1947, frames 10584–7. Beals examined the following witnesses: Hartleben, 19 February 1947, frames 3295–3300; Hartleben, 20 February 1947, frames 3319–20; Schröder, 26 February 1947, frames 3655–7; Schröder, 27 February 1947, frames 3792–3; Genzken, 3 March 1947, frames 3978–80; Gebhardt, 7 March 1947, frames 4352–3; Hielscher, 15 April 1947, frames 6095–6; Hielscher, 16 April 1947, frames 6115–20; Block, 17 April 1947, frames 6151–2; Volhard, 3 June 1947, frames 8639–42; Beiglböck, 10 June 1947, frames 8990–1.

231 For example, Sebring examined Rostock on 21 and 24 February, Schröder on 26 and 27 February, Hielscher on 15 and 16 April, Romberg on 2, 5 and 6 May, Weltz on 6 and 7 May, Beiglböck on 10 and 11 June, Ivy on 12 and 13 June, and Hoven on 21, 23 and 24 June. Guide to the Microfiche Edition (2001), 189–99.

232 See Gebhardt, 7.3.1947, NDT Records, frames 4352–3; Volhard, 3 June 1947, NDT Records, frames 8639–42.

233 Weindling seems to be on the wrong track with regard to the role of individual judges in formulating the Nuremberg Code, particularly by assigning undue importance to the presiding judge Walter Beals. He also does not seem to have studied the trial transcript and the executive sessions sufficiently; Weindling 2001c.

234 NDT Records, frames 2646f.

235 *Ibid.*, frame 2648.

236 *Ibid.*, frames 2651f.

237 *Ibid.*, frame 2653.

238 *Ibid.*, frames 3466f.; frame 3519; frame 5935; frame 6092; frame 6783; frame 7110f.; frame 7280; frame 8985.

239 SCHST, Sebring papers, Honorable Justice Harold L. Sebring; Fla.Cas. 86–9, So.2d, XLV.

240 SCHST, Sebring papers, Transcript of interview with Justice Roberts, 21 April 1980.

241 SCHST, Sebring papers, 'Remarks' by Overton about Sebring, 2 November 1990.

242 Tusa and Tusa 1995, 139.

243 See also NARA, RG 153, 89–1, book 2, box 5, folder 2, Sebring to Young, 20 September 1948.

244 NARA, RG238, Entry 146, box 1, Affidavit Thomas K. Hodges, Director, Language Division, and Chief of Translation Branch, 3 November 1947.

245 *Ibid.*

246 Sillevaerts 1947.

247 *Ibid.*

248 NDT Records, frames 11553–7.

249 *Ibid.*, frames 11557–67.

250 *Ibid.*, frame 11567.

251 *Ibid.*, frame 11568.

252 *Ibid.*, frames 11568–9.

253 *Ibid.*, frame 11569; see also Katz 1997, 413.

254 Jay Katz is one of the strongest proponents of this argument; Katz 1996.

255 NDT Records, frame 11568.

256 Katz 1996, 1664.

257 NDT Records, frame 11570.

258 *Ibid.*

259 *Ibid.*

260 *Ibid.*, frame 11583.

261 *Ibid.*, frames 11589f.; see also StaNü, Dokumente, No. 5294.

262 FCLM, Beecher papers, box 11, folder 79.

263 NARA, RG238, Entry 146, box 1, Affidavit Thomas K. Hodges, Director, Language Division, and Chief of Translation Branch, 3 November 1947; also Petitions to Military Governor filed by Defendants in Case 1, Tribunal I, Karl Brandt *et al.*, September–November 1947; also RG232, Entry 159, box 1, Teleconference, War Crimes Operations, 22 August 1947; also RG238, Entry 213, box 1, Nueremberg Cases.

264 NDT Records, frame 11728.

265 Sillevaerts 1947.

266 *Ibid.*

267 Annas and Grodin 1992, 105ff.

268 DUMC, Alexander papers, box 4, folder 35, McHaney to Alexander, 23 April 1948.
269 AP, Leo Alexander to Phyllis Alexander, 1 July 1947. Alexander later decided to spend his holiday with his family in Southold on Long Island; NARA, RG 153/86-3-1, book 1, box 9, Alexander to Young, 9 August 1947.
270 Sillevaerts 1947.

8. Post-war Medical Ethics

1 Interview with Cecily Alexander-Grable, Marion, Cape Cod, May 1999.
2 Katz 1992, 228; also Katz 1996, 1663.
3 Rothman 1991, 62f.
4 See also Ivy 1948c.
5 Weindling 1996, 1469.
6 Ivy 1948a, 5–12; also UWAHC, Andrew C. Ivy Papers (#8768), box 6, folder 10, Andrew C. Ivy, 'The Meaning of Medical Ethics Learned and Emphasised at the Nurnberg Trials', 18 August 1949; also box 7, folder 8, Andrew C. Ivy, 'Does Science have an Ethics?', talk presented to Roosevelt College, 20 November 1951.
7 BAK, ZSg 154, box 70.
8 World Medical Association, Minutes of the First Annual Meeting of the General Assembly, Paris, 17–20 September 1947, 4. I am grateful to Sev Fluss, policy adviser to the WMA, for supplying this material to me.
9 *Ibid.*, 11.
10 BAK, ZSg 154, box 70.
11 Annas and Grodin 1998, 303f.
12 Beecher 1970, Appendix A, 236.
13 World Medical Association. Minutes of the First Annual Meeting of the General Assembly, Paris, 17–20 September 1947, 10.
14 Fluss 1999, 19f.
15 *Ibid.*
16 For the history of the Declaration of Helsinki see Schaupp 1993; Fluss 1999.
17 See also Arendt 1951.
18 Alexander 1949d.
19 Alexander 1954c, 79.
20 For Alexander's lectures between 1947 and 1950 see 1947a–f; 1948 a, f, h, i, j, l; 1949c, d, g, j, k, l, q, t, u, x, z; 1950c, e, f, i, j, k, q, s, ii, kk; DUMC, Alexander papers, box 1, folder 21, Index of Lectures; see also BUL, Notes taken during Dr Alexander's talk 23 May 1947, before the Utrecht Society of Physicians, Utrecht, Holland.
21 Alexander 1948a, b, e, f and 1949a, b, c, d.
22 Alexander 1948f., 298.
23 Sereny 2000; Interview with Gitta Sereny, London, April 2002.
24 Alexander 1948f., 298.
25 *Ibid.*, 299.
26 DUMC, Alexander papers, box 1, folder 3, Memorandum to McHaney, 26 March 1947.
27 Alexander 1948f., 300.
28 Glover 1999, 317–97.
29 NYPL, Robert J. Lifton papers, correspondence with Leo Alexander. 'August 29 – Talk with Leo Alexander'.

30 Alexander 1948b, 626.
31 Alexander 1949a, 563.
32 Alexander 1948e, 174; also Alexander 1949c, 16.
33 Alexander 1948b, 630f.; Alexander 1948e, 175.
34 *Ibid.*, 632f.; Alexander 1948e, 175.
35 Alexander 1949c, 13f.
36 See also Cooter *et al.* 1998 and Cooter *et al.* 1999.
37 Alexander 1949c, 27.
38 Alexander 1948e, 176.
39 *Ibid.*
40 *Ibid.*
41 Peiffer 1997, 45–55; see also Shevell 1992.
42 Alexander 1949d, 4.
43 *Ibid.*
44 AzGdMPG, Hauptabteilung II, Rep. 1 A, Personalia Hallervorden, Heft 5, Bl. 4.
45 AzGdMPG, Hauptabteilung II, Rep. 1 A, Personalia Hallervorden, Heft 7, Bl. 22c.
46 *Ibid.*
47 Peiffer 1997, 48f.
48 AzGdMPG, Hauptabteilung II, Rep. 1 A, Personalia Hallervorden, Heft 5, Bl. 34.
49 AzGdMPG, Hauptabteilung II, Rep. 1 A, Personalia Hallervorden, Heft 7, Alexander to Wartenberg, 17 March 1953; Alexander to Munch-Peterson, 27 March 1953; Alexander to Jeanty, 10 April 1953; Alexander to Fulton, 13 April 1953; Wartenberg to Lima, 29 April 1953.
50 AzGdMPG, Hauptabteilung II, Rep. 1 A, Personalia Hallervorden, Heft 7, Wartenberg to Lima, 29 April 1953.
51 AzGdMPG, Hauptabteilung II, Rep. 1 A, Personalia Hallervorden, Heft 5, Bl. 43; also Peiffer 1997, 53.
52 Porter 1959.
53 Interview with Cecily Alexander-Grable, Marion, Cape Cod, May 1999.
54 BAK, B126, folder 27579.
55 Porter 1959; also Cousins 1958.
56 BAK, B126, folder 27579; for Wladyslawa Marczewska see Waltz 2001.
57 Porter 1959; also BAK, B126, folder 27579.
58 PRO, WO235, file 531; WO309, file 420.
59 Interview with Cecily Alexander-Grable, Marion, Cape Cod, May 1999.
60 *Ibid.*
61 Lee 1995.
62 See, for example, United States Strategic Bombing Survey, Summary Report (Pacific War), Washington, DC, 1 July 1946, 22ff.
63 Moreno 1996, 11f.
64 Final Report 1996, 497–511.
65 *Ibid.*, 506ff.
66 Moreno 1996, 14.
67 *Ibid.*, 13.
68 Final Report 1996, 508.
69 *Ibid.*, 505.
70 A critical assessment of the history of Porton Down has yet to be conducted. For the existing literature on Porton see, for example, Carter 1992; Carter and Pearson 1996, 59–68; Hammond and Carter 2002. The author is currently conducting a comprehensive research project to examine the ethical and legal

history of Porton Down during the Cold War. Talitha Bolton from the University of Kent is currently writing her MA dissertation on 'Film, Ethics and Politics – Porton Down, 1939–1964'.

71 Carrell 2001; Evans 2002.

72 Ulf Schmidt, 'Report on Informed Consent', unpublished manuscript written for HM Coroner for Wiltshire and Swindon in the Maddison Inquest, November 2003.

73 Gilligan 1997; Stuttaford 1997; Barnett 2002; also Hammond and Carter 2002, 19–55.

74 Barnett 2002.

75 For some of the internal debates that led to the promulgation of the memorandum see Moreno 1996, 11–19; Moreno 1997, 351–7.

76 Moreno 1996, 16.

77 As early as November 1947, only months after the promulgation of the Nuremberg Code, the general manager of the Atomic Energy Commission ruled that scientists had to obtain 'informed consent in writing' from patients who were subjected to 'substances known to be or suspected of being poisonous or harmful'; Final Report 1996, 499.

78 Annas and Grodin 1992, 343–5.

79 *Ibid.*, 344f.; see also Moreno 1996, 15; Moreno 1997, 355.

80 Annas and Grodin 1992, 345.

81 Final Report 1996, 500.

82 See Moreno 1997, 347–60, 354.

83 Moreno 1996, 18.

84 *Ibid.*, 16.

85 *Ibid.*, 17.

86 Beecher 1970, Appendix A, 252.

87 *Ibid.*

88 See, for example, Annas and Grodin 1992, 201–22.

89 Final Report 1996, 544.

90 Katz 1996, 1665.

91 *Ibid.*

92 *Ibid.*; see also Katz 1997, 416.

93 Moreno 1997, 350.

94 Final Report 1996, 544.

95 Alexander 1952c.

96 Fletcher 1954.

97 See, for example, Kirk 1999 and Stephens 2001.

98 See Katz 1993, 31–9; also Moreno 1997, 347–60.

99 Final Report 1996, 88–92; Moreno 1997, 357f.; Beecher 1970, Appendix A, 214–44.

100 Fluss 1999, 19; also 'Draft Code of Ethics on Human Experimentation', *British Medical Journal*, 2 (1962), 1119.

101 Katz 1992, 233.

102 See also Young's ahistorical and greatly biased analysis of previous medical ethics codes; Young 1998.

103 Beecher 1970, Appendix A, 247–51, 251.

104 Jones 1981, 188–205; see also Reverby 2000.

105 *Ibid.*, 216.

106 See also Glantz 1992, 183–200.

107 Langer 1964; also Guttentag 1964.

108 Beecher 1966, 1354.

109 *Ibid.*
110 *Ibid.*
111 *Ibid.*, 1355.
112 Pappworth 1967; see also Mellanby's criticism of Pappworth's work in the preface to his 1973 edition of his book *Human Guinea Pigs*, first published in 1945; Mellanby 1973, Preface to the 2nd edition, 11–17, 17.
113 Hornblum 1998, xx.
114 Alexander 1966a; see also Alexander 1966h.
115 Alexander 1966a–k.
116 Alexander 1966h, 62.
117 *Ibid.*, 62.
118 *Ibid.*, 63. This position stood in marked contrast to the one which the prosecution, especially Ivy, had maintained in Nuremberg. It seems that Alexander had come closer to accepting Leibbrand's position from January 1947.
119 Alexander 1966h, 63.
120 See, for example, Alexander 1942j, 1944a, 1950a, 1950f, 1950j, 1952d, 1953b, 1953e, 1953f, 1954f, 1956a, 1956c, 1958j, 1958l, 1958n, 1958r, 1962a.
121 Dietz 1974.
122 Interview with Cecily Alexander-Grable, Marion, Cape Cod, May 1999.
123 AP, Lifton to Alexander, 14 February 1978.
124 Lifton 1967.
125 Lifton 1971.
126 NYPL, Robert J. Lifton papers.
127 See Goldhagen 1968; Goldhagen 1996.
128 AP, Lifton to Alexander, 1 May 1978.
129 BAK, Alexander diary (1945) and DUMC, Alexander diary (1946/47).
130 AP, Alexander to Lifton, 28 July 1978.
131 AP, Alexander to Mrs Lifton, 17 August 1978.
132 NYPL, Robert J. Lifton papers, correspondence with Leo Alexander. 'August 29 – Talk with Leo Alexander'.
133 *Ibid.*
134 *Ibid.*
135 Levi 1988.
136 Levi 1986, 9.
137 NYPL, Robert J. Lifton papers, correspondence with Leo Alexander, 'August 29 – Talk with Leo Alexander'.
138 Alexander 1954c, 75–9.
139 NYPL, Robert J. Lifton papers, correspondence with Leo Alexander, 'August 29 – Talk with Leo Alexander'.
140 Interview with Cecily Alexander-Grable, Marion, Cape Cod, May 1999.
141 For Münch see Lifton 1986.
142 NYPL, Robert J. Lifton papers, correspondence with Leo Alexander, 'August 29 – Talk with Leo Alexander'.
143 NYPL, Robert J. Lifton papers, correspondence with Leo Alexander, Alexander to Lifton, 10 October 1978.
144 NYPL, Robert J. Lifton papers, correspondence with Leo Alexander, 'August 29 – Talk with Leo Alexander'.
145 *Ibid.*
146 NYPL, Robert J. Lifton papers, correspondence with Leo Alexander, Alexander to Lifton, 10 October 1978.
147 AP, Leo Alexander to Phyllis Alexander, 26.5.1945.

148 Levi 1988, 11f.
149 Levi 1986, 11.
150 NYPL, Robert J. Lifton papers, correspondence with Leo Alexander, 'August 29 – Talk with Leo Alexander'.
151 NYPL, Robert J. Lifton papers, correspondence with Leo Alexander, Lifton to Alexander, 22 December 1978.
152 Lifton 1986, 432.
153 *Ibid.*, 418.
154 Lifton 1998, 430; also Katz 1997, 405.
155 AP, Leo Alexander to Phyllis Alexander, 27 November 1946; DUMC, Alexander diary (1946/47), 78f., 3 December 1946; see also Alexander Paper 2, 5 December 1946.
156 Coughlin 1985.
157 Interview with Cecily Alexander-Grable, Marion, Cape Cod, May 1999.
158 Alexander 1954c, 79.

Bibliography

Archival sources

Alexander Papers, Boston (in possession of Cecily Alexander-Grable)
    Alexander calendar
    Personal correspondence, 1929–47
    Photographic collection
    Offprints of Alexander's publications, 1926–82
Archivzentrum der Stadt- und Universitätsbibliothek Frankfurt am Main
    Mitscherlich papers
Archiv zur Geschichte der Max-Planck-Gesellschaft, Berlin
    Hauptabteilung II, Rep. 1 A, Personalia Hallervorden
Bodleian Library, Oxford
    SPSL papers, folder 402, Alfred Alexander
Boston University, Mugar Memorial Library
    Alexander Papers, #242
Bundesarchiv Abteilung III, Berlin (former Berlin Document Center)
    Personal files
Bundesarchiv, Koblenz
    Sammlung Christian Pross, ZSg 154, box 62–76
    Bundesministerium der Finanzen, B126
    Kl. Erw. 441-3, Brandt papers
Duke University Medical Center, Durham
    Alexander papers (HC, Collected Papers and Documents 65th General Hospital)
    Lyman Papers
Francis A. Countway Library of Medicine, Boston, Mass.
    Beecher Papers
Imperial War Museum, London
    CIOS reports
Institut für Stadtgeschichte, Stadtarchiv, Frankfurt am Main Magistratsakten V,
    230/VI (1917–27), personal files
National Archives and Record Administration, Washington DC
    Microfilms, M-887, Roll 1–46, United States of America v. Karl Brandt et al. (Case
    I), 21 November 1946–20 August 1947
    RG 153; RG 232; RG 238; RG 239; RG 331; UD 25, box 1–12
New York Public Library
    Robert J. Lifton Papers, Nazi Doctors Series, boxes 1–39
National Library of Medicine, Bethesda
    Adolf Nichtenhauser, A History of Motion Pictures in Medicine, a multi-volume
    unpublished typescript book (ca. 1950)
    Film: 'The N.P. Patient' (1944)
    Nichtenhauser papers (MS C277 and MS C380)
Public Record Office
    FO371; WO 309; WO 311; WO171; WO 235; WO 208
Private archives
    Cecily Alexander-Grable (Boston, Massachusetts)

Leo Alexander Papers [see Alexander Papers, Boston]
Irene Julst (Loenen a/d Veht)
Lambert Hulst Papers
Jürgen Peiffer, Tübingen
Alexander papers
Michael Grodin, Boston University
Andrew C. Ivy Papers
Rockefeller Archive Center, North Terrytown, New York
CMB, Inc.; RG 1.1., 200; RG 1.2, 200A; RG 12.1.; RG 2-1946, 200
Staatsarchiv Nürnberg
KV-Anklage, Interrogations and Dokumente
Supreme Court Historical Society Tallahassee, Florida
Sebring papers
Tape recorded interviews with:
Cecily Alexander-Grable, Marion, Cape Cod
Ivan Brown, Lakeland, Florida
Nicolas Camera-Peon, Washington DC
Irene Hulst, Loenen a/d Veht
H. L. (Tom) Sebring, Tallahassee
Gitta Sereny, London
Eleonore Strümpel and Adelheid Kleist, Frankfurt am Main
Thüringer Landeshauptarchiv, Weimar
Thüringer Ministerium des Innern
University of Wyoming, Laramie, Wyo, American Heritage Center
Andrew C. Ivy Papers (#8768)
Zentrum für Antisemitismusforschung, Berlin
Personal file Leo Alexander

CIOS reports by Leo Alexander, M.D.

German Military Neuropsychiatry and Neurosurgery, CIOS Item 24, 2 August 1945.
Methods of Influencing International Scientific Meetings as Laid Down by German
    Scientific Organisations, CIOS, Item 24, File no. XXVIII-8.
Miscellaneous Aviation Medical Matters, CIOS Item 24, File no. XXIX-21.
Neuropathology and Neurophysiology, including Electro-Encephalography, in
    Wartime Germany, CIOS Item 24, 20 July 1945.
Public Mental Health Practices in Germany: Sterilisation and Execution of Patients
    Suffering from Nervous or Mental Diseases, CIOS, Item 24, 19 August 1945.
The Medical School Curriculum in War-Time Germany, CIOS Item 24, 3 August 1945.
The Treatment of Shock from Prolonged Exposure to Cold, especially in Water, CIOS
    Target No. 24, Medical, Combined Intelligence Objectives Sub-Committee, G-2
    Division, SHAEF (Rear), APO 413, 10 July 1945.

Publications by Leo Alexander, M.D.*

* The publications have been listed in the same order in which Alexander listed
them in his Index of Publications; see DUMC, Alexander papers, box 1, folder 21,
Leo Alexander, Index of Publications.

(1926) 'Hyperplasien des Recessus lateralis ventriculi IV. Ein Beitrag zur Morphologie
    des Kleinhirnbrückenwinkels', *Anatomischer Anzeiger*, 61 (1926) 479–87.

(1927a) 'Zur Entwicklungsgeschichte der sogenannten Rautenlippe bei Selachiern', *Verhandlungen der Zoologisch-Botanischen Gesellschaft in Wien*, 77 (1927) 11.

(1927b) 'Zur Anatomie der Hypophyse und des Infundibulum Diencephali der Selachier', *Anatomischer Anzeiger*, 64 (1927) 213–35.

(1928a) 'Zur Anatomie des Kleinhirnbrückenwinkels', *Deutsche Zeitschrift für Nervenheilkunde*, 102 (1928).

(1928b) 'Zur Phylogenese der Oliva Inferior', *Deutsche Zeitschrift für Nervenheilkunde*, 102 (1928).

(1928c) 'Die Kernfreie Zone an der Eintrittsstelle der Kopfnerven in das Gehirn bei Wirbeltierembryonen. Ein Beitrag zur vergleichenden Histogenese der Kopfnervenstämme und der Obersteiner – Redlich'schen Stelle', *Journal für Psychologie und Neurologie*, 36 (1928) 350–417.

(1928d) 'Zur Frage der Farbtonunterschiede zwischen zentralem und peripherem Abschnitt eintretender Nervenwurzeln bei der Weigert'schen Markscheidenfärbung', *Arbeiten an dem Neurologischen Institut der Wiener Universtät*, 30 (1928) 185.

(1929) 'Experimentelle und pathologisch-anatomische Untersuchugen über Verbindungen der Vestibulariskerne mit dem Mittel- und Zwischenhenhirn und deren klinische Bedeutung', *Archiv für Psychiatrie*, 90 (1929) 872.

(1931) 'Die Anatomie der Seitentaschen der vierten Hirnkammer', *Zeitschrift für Anatomie und Entwicklungsgeschichte*, 95 (1931), 531–707.

(1932a) 'Doppelwirkung der belladonnaexclud – Zäpfchen in der Geburtshilfe (spasmenlösend und wehenanregend)', *Zent. f. Gyn. Apr.*, 55 (1932) 1417–20.

(1932b) 'Über gleichsinnige und symmetrische, durch passive Bewegungen und electrische Reize auslösbare Kontralaterale Mitbewegungen (Symmetrisches Mitbewegtwerden). Mit Filmvorführung und einer Krankenvorstellung', *Allgemeine Zeitschrift für Psychiatrie*, 98 (1932) 452.

(1932c) 'Über gleichsinnige und symmetrische, durch passive Bewegungen und electrische Reizung auslösbare kontralaterale Mitbewegungen (Symmetrisches Mitbewegtwerden)', *Klinische Wochenschrift*, 11 (1932) 412–14.

(1932d) 'Über symmetrische und gleichsinnige Mitbewegungen einer Extremität bei passiven Bewegungen und bei elektrischer Reizung der anderen gleichnamigen (Symmetrisches Mitbewegtwerden)', *Journal für Psychologie und Neurologie*, 44 (1932), 177–252.

(1932e) 'Die Verbinduggen der Vestibulariskerne mit dem Mittel- und Zwischenhirn. Studien auf Grund experimenteller Verletzungen', *Journal für Psychologie und Neurologie*, 44 (1932), 253–76 (with J. G. Whitaker)

(1932f) 'Über eine chronische paranoisch-halluzinatorische Psychose mit post-enzepohalitisähnlichen neurologischen Erscheinungen, hervorgerufen durch Starkstromschädigung des Gehirns. Zugleich ein Beitrag zur Symptomatologie der Aufmerksamkeitsstörungen', *Monatsschrift für Psychiatrie und Neurologie*, 83 (1932) 144–80.

(1934a) 'Symptomatic Involvement of the Nervous System in Different Forms of Dysentery', *Chinese Medical Journal*, 48 (1934) 1–19 (with T. T. Wu).

(1934b) 'Note on the Occurrence and Significance of Deficiency of the Septum Pellucidum', *Chinese Medical Journal*, 48 (1934) 138–41 (with T. H. Suh).

(1934c) 'Colloidal Thorium Dioxide. Its Use in Intracranial Diagnosis and its Fate on Direct Injection into the Brain and the Ventricles', *Archives of Neurology and Psychiatry*, 32 (1934) 1143–58 (with T. S. Jung and R. S. Lyman).

(1934d) 'The Neurofibrils in Systemic Disease and in Supravital Experiments, with Remarks on Pseudo-Atrophy of the Brain', *Archives of Neurology and Psychiatry*, 32 (1934) 933–62.

(1935a) 'Cerebral Changes in Gastrointestinal Infections with Terminal Cachexia-Histopathologic Studies on Dysentery with Comments on Similar Observation in Intestinal Tuberculosis', *Archives of Neurology and Psychiatry*, 33 (1935) 72–122 (with T. T. Wu).

(1935b) 'Cerebral Changes in Gastrointestinal Infections with Terminal Cachexia and Their Relation to Physiochemical Properties of the Brain', *The Journal of Nervous and Mental Disease*, 81 (1935) 558–60.

(1935c) 'Report of the Committee for the Investigation of Sterilisation', American Neurological Association, Boston (1935) (with A. Myerson, J. B. Ayer, T. J. Putnam and C. E. Keeler).

(1935d) 'Tumours and Cysts of the Cerebellopontine Angle and Their Relation to the Lateral Recesses of the Fourth Ventricle', *The Proceedings of the Association for Research in Nervous and Mental Disease*, 16 (1935) 266–314.

(1936a) 'Mineral Content in Cerebral Lesions', *Journal of Nervous and Mental Disease*, 84 (1936) 313 (with A. Myerson).

(1936b) *Eugenical Sterilisation, a Reorientation of the Problem* (New York, 1936) (with A. Myerson, J. B. Ayer, T. J. Putnam and C. E. Keeler).

(1937a) 'Local Anaphylactic Lesions of the Brain in Guinea Pigs', *American Journal of Pathology*, 13 (1937) 229–48 (with A. C. P. Campbell).

(1937b) 'The Mineral Content of Various Cerebral Lesions as Demonstrated by the Microincineration Method', *American Journal of Pathology*, 13 (1937) 305–440 (with A. Myerson).

(1937c) 'The Neurone as Studied by Microincineration', *Anatomical Record*, 67 (1937) 3.

(1937d) 'Arterial Supply or Lateral Parolivary Area of the Medulla oblongata in Man', *Archives of Neurology and Psychiatry*, 38 (1937) 1243–60 (with T. H. Suh).

(1937e) 'Pathological Alterations of Cerebral Vascular Patterns', *Proceedings of the Association for Research in Nervous and Mental Disease*, 18 (1937) 471–543 (with T. J. Putnam).

(1937f) 'Tissue Damage Resulting from Disease of Cerebral Blood Vessels', *Proceedings of the Association for Research in Nervous and Mental Disease*, 18 (1937) 544–67 (with T. J. Putnam).

(1938a) 'The Vascular Pattern in Various Lesions of the Human Central Nervous System', *Journal of Nervous and Mental Disease*, 87 (1938) 216–18 (with A. C. P. Campbell and T. J. Putnam).

(1938b) 'Minerals in Normal and in Pathologic Brain Tissue, Studied by Microincineration and Spectroscopy', *Archives of Neurology and Psychiatry*, 39 (1938) 131–49 (with A. Myerson).

(1938c) 'Ascorbic Acid in Cerebrospinal Fluid', *Journal of Clinical Investigation*, 17 (1938) 169–74 (with M. Pijoan and A. Wilson).

(1938d) 'Clinical and Neuropathological Aspects of Electrical Injuries', *Journal of Industrial Hygiene and Toxicology*, 20 (1938) 191–243.

(1938e) 'The Neurone as Studied in Microincineration', *Brain*, 61 (1938) 52–61.

(1938f) 'Accidental Electrical Injuries – Pathologic Aspects, Clinical Manifestations and Treatment', *International Surveys of Recent Advances in Medicine*, 2 (1938) 169–79.

(1938g) 'Electrical Injuries to the Central Nervous System', *Medical Clinics of North America*, 22 (1938) 663–88.

(1938h) 'Vascular Pattern in Various Lesions of the Human Central Nervous System, Studies with the Benzidine Stain', *Archives of Neurology and Psychiatry*, 39 (1938) 1150–1202 (with A. C. P. Campbell and T. J. Putnam).

(1938i) 'Cevitamic Acid Content of Blood Plasma in Alcoholic Psychoses', *Archives of Neurology and Psychiatry*, 40 (1938) 58–65 (with M. Pijoan, P. G. Schube and M. Moore).

(1938j) 'New Modifications of the Benzidine Stain for Study of the Vascular Pattern of the Central Nervous System', *Archives of Neurology and Psychiatry*, 40 (1938) 158–62 (with M. M. Doherty and T. H. Suh).

(1938k) 'Direct Pathological Evidence of Circulatory Disturbances in the Brain. Studies with the Benzidine Stain', *American Journal of Pathology*, 14 (1938) 677–80 (with T. J. Putnam).

(1938l) 'Physiochemical Properties of Brain, Especially in Senile Dementia and Cerebral Edema, Differential Ratio of Skull Capacity to Volume, Specific Weight, Water Content, Water-Binding Capacity, and pH of the Brain', *Archives of Neurology and Psychiatry*, 40 (1938) 877–902 (with J. M. Looney).

(1938m) 'Histologic Changes in Senile Dementia and Related Conditions, Studied by Silver Impregnation and Microincineration', *Archives of Neurology and Psychiatry*, 40 (1938) 1075–1110 (with J. M. Looney).

(1938n) 'Beri-Beri and Scurvy, an Experimental Study', *Transactions of the American Neurological Association, Sixty-Fourth Annual Meeting* (1938) 135–9 (with M. Pijoan, A. Myerson and H. N. Keane).

(1939a) 'Vascular System of the Human Spinal Cord', *Archives of Neurology and Psychiatry*, 41 (1939) 659–77 (with T. H. Suh).

(1939b) 'Suical and Intrinsic Blood Vessels of Human Spinal Cord', *Archives of Neurology and Psychiatry*, 41 (1939) 678–87 (with R. Y. Herren).

(1939c) 'Disseminated Encephalomyelitis, a Histologic Syndrome Associated with Thrombosis of Small Cerebral Vessels', *Archives of Neurology and Psychiatry*, 41 (1939) 1087–1110 (with T. J. Putnam).

(1939d) 'Cell Minerals in Amaurotic Idiocy, Tuberous Sclerosis and Related Conditions, Studied by Microincineration and Spectroscopy – Examples of Degenerative and of Neoplastic Cell Disease', *American Journal of Psychiatry*, 96 (1939) 77–85.

(1939e) 'Vascular Pattern of Certain Intracranial Neoplasms, Studies with the Benzidine Stain', *Archives of Neurology and Psychiatry*, 42 (1939) 44–66 (with A. L. Sahs).

(1939f) 'The Neurologic Aspects of Alcoholism', *Archives of Neurology and Psychiatry*, 42 (1939) 179–83.

(1939g) 'Fatal Hypoglycaemia, a Clinicopathologic Study', *Archives of Neurology and Psychiatry*, 42 (1939) 286–97 (with A. L. Sahs).

(1939h) 'The Reaction of the Cerebral Vessels to Intracartoid Injection of Horse Serum in Sensitised and Non-Sensitised Guinea Pigs', *Continia Neurologica*, 2 (1939) 215–19 (with A. Buermann).

(1939i) 'Alcoholism and Mental Disease, Mental Health', *Publication of the American Association for the Advancement of Science*, 9 (1939) 83–93.

(1939j) 'A Classroom Outline for the Pathologic Diagnosis of Primary Intracranial Neoplasms. Six Differential Characteristics', *Archives of Neurology and Psychiatry*, 42 (1939) 912–14.

(1939k) 'A Note of the Differential Diagnosis of Experimentally Reduced Brain Tumors and their Relation to Brain Tumors in Man', *American Journal of Cancer*, 37 (1939) 395–9.

(1939l) 'The Distribution of Electric Current in the Animal Body: an Experimental Investigation of 60 Cycle Alternating Current', *Journals of Industrial Hygiene and Toxicology*, 21 (1939) 517–25 (with A. W. Weeks).

(1939m) 'Deaths from Poisoning, Incidence in Massachusetts', *American Journal of Medical Jurisprudence* (1939) (with M. Moore and R. Leary).

(1939n) 'Topographic and Histologic Identity of the Experimental (Acitaminotic) Lesions of Wernicks with Lesions of Hemorrhagic Polioencephalitis Occurring in Chronic Alcoholism in Men', *Archives of Neurology and Psychiatry*, 42 (1939) 1172–3.

(1939o) 'Beri-Beri and Wenicke's Hemorrhagic Polioencephalitis, an Experimental Study', *IIIe Congrès Neurologique International*. *Comptes Rendus des Séances, Copenhague, 21–25 Août 1939* (Copenhagen, 1939) 913–16.

(1940a) 'Wernicke's Disease, Identity of Lesions Produced Experimentally by B$_1$ Avitaminosis in Pigeons with Hemorrhagic Polioencephalitis Occurring in Chronic Alcoholism in Man', *American Journal of Pathology* (1940) 61–70.

(1940b) 'The Experimental Reproduction of Wernicke's Hemorrhagic Alcoholic Encephalitis by B$_1$ Avitaminosis without Alcoholism', *American Journal of Pathology*, 18 (1940) 668–70.

(1940c) 'Elements of Optical illusion in Appearance of Preservation of Axis-Cylinders in Certain Lesions of the Central Nervous System', *Archives of Neurology and Psychiatry*, 44 (1940) 1312–18 (with T. J. Putnam).

(1940d) 'Bromide Intoxication – A Review', *Continia Neurologica*, 3 (1940) 1–52 (with M. Moore and T. Sohier).

(1941a) 'Observations on the Blood Vessels of the Spinal Ganglia', *Anatomical Record*, 79 (1941) 8 (with L. Bergmann).

(1941b) 'Electric Shock. Importance of Path, Distribution and Density of Current in Determining Symptoms and Pathology', *American Journal of Pathology*, 17 (1941) 601–2 (with A. W. Weeks).

(1941c) 'Deaths from Poisoning: Incidents in Massachusetts', *Journal of Criminal Psychopathology*, 3 (1941) 100–11 (with M. Moore and T. Leary).

(1941d) 'Neuropathological Findings in the Brain and Spinal Cord of Chronic Alcoholic Patients', *Quarterly Journal of Studies of Alcohol*, 2 (1941) 260–2.

(1941e) 'Vascular Supply of Strio-pallidum and Hypothalamus in Man', *Archives of Neurology and Psychiatry*, 46 (1941) 551–3 (with J. M. Foley).

(1941f) 'Vascular Supply of the Spinal Ganglia', *Archives of Neurology and Psychiatry*, 46 (1941) 761–82 (with L. Bergmann).

(1941g) 'Alcoholic Encephalopathy in Man and Fish-Diet-Disease in Foxes and Fishes – A Study in Comparative Neuropathology', *Transactions of the American Neurological Association, Sixty-Seventh Annual Meeting* (Richmond, Va, 1941) 119–22 (with R. G. Green, C. A. Evans and L. E. Wolf).

(1941h) 'A Proposal for Changes in Present Methods of Sale of Alcoholic Beverages to Conform with the Federal Foods, Drug and Cosmetic Act', *Transactions of the American Neurological Association, Sixty-Seventh Annual Meeting* (Richmond, Va, 1941) 203–32 (with M. Moore and A. Myerson).

(1942a) 'The Vascular Supply of the Strio-Pallidum', *Research Publications of the Association for Research in Nervous and Mental Disease*, 21 (1942) 77–132.

(1942b) 'The Fundamental Types of Histopathologic Changes Encountered in Cases of Athetosis and Paralysis Agitans', *Research Publications of the Association for Research in Nervous and Mental Disease*, 21 (1942) 334–492.

(1942c) 'Electrical Injuries of the Nervous System', *Journal of Nervous and Mental Disease*, 94 (1941) 622–32; and *Archives of Neurology and Psychiatry*, 47 (1942) 179–86.

(1942d) 'Correlation of Vital Observations with Post-Mortem Study of the Cerebral Circulation', *Journal of Neuropathology and Experimental Neurology*, 1 (1942) 118–19 (with M. M. Korb and T. Sohler).

(1942e) 'Alcoholic Avitaminosis', *Diseases of the Nervous System*, 3 (1942) 2–8 (with A. Myerson and M. Moore).

(1942f) 'The Sale of Alcoholic Beverages: a Proposal for Changes in the Present Methods to Conform with the Federal Food, Drug and Cosmetic Act and to Promote Public Health', *Mental Hygiene*, 28 (1942) 235–42 (with M. Moore and A. Myerson).

(1942g) 'The Vascular Supply of the Hypothalamus in Man', *Journal of Neuropathology and Experimental Neurology*, 1 (1942) 265–96 (with J. M. Foley and T. D. Kinney).

(1942h) 'Hypnosis', *North Carolina Medical Journal*, 3 (1942) 562.

(1942i) 'Calcified Epileptogenic Lesions as Caused by Incomplete Interference with the Blood Supply of the Diseased Areas', *Transactions of the American Neurological Association, Sixty-Eighth Annual Meeting, 1942* (Richmond, Va, 1942), 175–6 (with Barnes Woodhall).

(1942j) 'Experimental Studies on Electroshock Treatment: 1. The Intracerebral Vascular Reaction as an Indicator of the Path of the Current', *Journal of Neuropathology and Experimental Neurology*, 1 (1942) 444–6 (with H. Lowenbach).

(1943) 'Calcified Epileptogenic Lesions as Caused by Incomplete Interference with the Blood Supply of the Diseased Areas', *Journal of Neuropathology and Experimental Neurology*, 2 (1943) 1–33 (with B. Woodhall).

(1944a) 'Experimental Studies on Electroshock Treatment: the Intracerebral Vascular Reaction as an Indicator of the Path of the Current and the Threshold of Early Changes Within the Brain Tissue', *Journal of Neuropathology and Experimental Neurology*, 33 (1944) 139–71 (with H. Lowenbach).

(1944b) 'The Neurologic Examination', in R. L. Pullen (ed.), *Medical Diagnosis: Applied Physical Diagnosis* (Philadelphia and London, 1944), 773–820.

(1945a) 'The Treatment of Shock from Prolonged Exposure to Cold, Especially in Water', *Combined Intelligence Objectives Sub-committee*, Item No. 24 (July) 1945, File no. XXVI-37, 1–228.

(1945b) 'German Military Neuropsychiatry and Neurosurgery', *Combined Intelligence Objectives Sub-Committee*, Item No. 24 (August) 1945, File no. XXVIII-49, 1–138.

(1945c) 'Neuropathology and Neurophysiology, Including Electro-Encephalography in Wartime Germany', *Combined Intelligence Objectives Sub-committee*, Item No. 24 (July) 1945, File no. XXVII-1, 1–65.

(1945d) 'Public Mental Health Practices in Germany, Sterilization and Execution of Patients Suffering from Nervous or Mental Disease', *Combined Intelligence Objectives Sub-committee*, Item No. 24 (August) 1945, File no. XXVIII-50, 1–173.

(1945e) 'The Medical School Curriculum in Wartime Germany', *Combined Intelligence Objectives Sub-Committee*, Item No. 24 (August) 1945, File no. XXVII–71, pp. 1–21.

(1945f) 'Methods of Influencing International Scientific Meetings as Laid Down by German Scientific Organisations', *Combined Intelligence Objectives Sub-committee*, Item No. 24 (August) 1945, File no. XXVIII-8, 1–32.

(1945g) 'Miscellaneous Aviation Medical Matters', *Combined Intelligence Objectives Sub-Committee*, Item No. 24 (August) 1945, File no. XXIX–21, pp. 1–165.

(1947a) 'Aggressive Behaviour – Its Psychiatric and Physiologic Aspects, Especially in Combat Veterans', *Bulletin of the New England Medical Centre*, 9 (1947) 112–22.

(1947b) 'Loss of Axis-Cylinders in Sclerotic Plaques and Similar Lesions', *Archives of Neurology and Psychiatry*, 57 (1947) 661–72.

(1947c) *Multiple Sclerosis: Diagnosis and Treatment*, 1st edn (1947) 1–16 (with T. J. Putnam *et al.*).

(1947d) 'Report of Combined Intelligence Objectives Sub-committee, 10 July 1945, by Major Alexander, M. C., Hdqtrs., ETOUSA, on Experiments in Severe Chilling and Resuscitation by "Animal Heat", Carried out on Human Beings in the Concentration Camp of Dachau by the Luftwaffe and the SS', *Trial of the Major War Criminals Before the International Military Tribunal in Nuremberg*, 25 (1947), Doc. 400 PS, 536–607.

(1948a) 'The Socio-Psychological Structure of the SS', *Folia Psychiatrica, Neurologica et Neurochirirgica Neerlandica*, 1, 2 (1948) 2–14.

(1948b) 'Sociopsychologic Structure of the SS', *Archives of Neurology and Psychiatry*, 59 (1948) 622–34.

(1948c) 'Photopsia Algera (Painful Light Vision) as an Early Symptom of Pressure Atrophy of the Optic Nerve', *Transactions of the American Neurological Association, Seventy-Third Annual Meeting, 1948* (Richmond, Va, 1948) 183–7 (with B. Sachs).

(1948d) 'Aggressive Behaviour – its Psychiatric and Physiologic Aspects, Especially in Combat Veterans', *New England Journal of Medicine*, 239 (1948) 10–14.

(1948e) 'War Crimes: Their Social-Psychological Aspects', *American Journal of Psychiatry*, 105 (1948) 170–7.

(1948f) 'War Crimes and Their Motivation, the Socio-Psychological Structure of the SS and the Criminalisation of a Society', *Journal of Criminal Law and Criminology*, 39 (1948) 298–326.

(1949a) 'Destructive and Self-Destructive Trends in Criminalized Society: a Study of Totalitarianism', *Journal of Criminal Law and Criminology*, 39 (1949) 553–64.

(1949b) 'Introductory Statement', in A. Mitscherlich and F. Mielke (eds), *Doctors of Infamy: the Story of the Nazi Medical Crimes* (New York, 1949), xxix–xxxiv.

(1949c) 'The Molding of Personality Under Dictatorship: the Importance of the Destructive Drives in the Socio-Psychological Structure of Nazism', *Journal of Criminal Law and Criminology*, 40 (1949) 3–27.

(1949d) 'Medical Science under Dictatorship', *New England Journal of Medicine*, 241 (1949) 39–47.

(1949e) 'The Electroencephalogram During Sodium Amytal and Sodium Pentothal Narcosis and During Resuscitation with Benzedrine Sulfate in Normal and Schizophrenic Subjects', *Electroencephalography and Clinical Neurophysiology*, 1 (1949) 255–6 (with M. R. Winston and H. Berman).

(1949f) 'The Use of Psychotherapy in General Practice', *New England Journal of Medicine*, 241 (1949) 519–24.

(1950a) 'Biochemical Changes in Electric Shock Therapy', *Archives of Neurology and Psychiatry*, 63 (1950) 336–7 (with R. Neustadt, A. Myerson, L. C. Howard and R. Kaldeck).

(1950b) 'The Element of Psychotherapy in the Treatment of Organic Neurologic Disorders', *Journal of Nervous and Mental Diseases*, 111 (1950) 336–43.

(1950c) 'General Principles of Psychotherapy', *American Journal of Psychiatry*, 106 (1950) 721–31.

(1950d) 'Blood and Plasma Transfusions in Multiple Sclerosis. Multiple Sclerosis and the Demyelinating Diseases, Vol. XXVILLL', *Published for the Association for Research in Nervous and Mental Diseases* (1950) 178–200 (with J. Loman, M. Lesses and I. Green).

(1950e) 'The Neurologic Examination', in R. L. Pullen (ed.), *Medical Diagnosis* (Philadelphia, London, 1950) 870–918.

(1950f) 'Nonconvulsive Electric Stimulation Therapy. Its Place in the Treatment of Affective Disorders, with Notes on the Reciprocal Relationship of Anxiety and Depression', *American Journal of Psychiatry*, 107 (1950) 241–50.

(1950g) 'Capillary Resistance Studies in Multiple Sclerosis', *Journal of Neuropathology and Experimental Neurology*, 9 (1950) 420–9 (with M. H. Shulman, O. F. Ehrentheil and R. Gross).

(1950h) 'Problem of Multiple Sclerosis', *Editorial, New England Journal of Medicine*, 243 (1950) 935–6.

(1950i) 'The Urinary Bladder in Multiple Sclerosis', *Transactions of the American Neurological Association, Seventy-fifth Annual Meeting, 1950* (1950) 210–13 (with S. R. Muellner and J. Loman).

(1950j) 'The Suppression of the Clonic Phase in Electrically Induced Convulsions in Man', *Transactions of the American Neurological Association, Seventy-fifth Annual Meeting, 1950* (1950) 244–7.

(1950k) 'Science Under Dictatorship. The One Hundredth Anniversary Discourse of the New York Academy of Medicine', in *The Future in Medicine* (New York) (1950) 51–106.

(1951a) 'New Concept of Critical Steps in Course of Chronic Debilitating Neurological Disease in Evaluation of Therapeutic Response', *Archives of Neurology and Psychiatry*, 66 (1951) 253–71.

(1951b) 'The Element of Psychotherapy in the Treatment of Organic Neurologic Disorders', *Journal of Nervous and Mental Disease*, 114 (1951) 283–306.

(1952a) 'Rorschach Studies in Combat Flying Personnel', in P. H. Hoch and J. Zubin (eds), *Relation of Psychological Tests to Psychiatry* (New York, 1952) 219–43 (with A. Ax).

(1952b) 'Deaths from Poisoning', *New England Journal of Medicine*, 246 (1952) 46–52 (with M. Moore and J. Ipsen, Jr).

(1952c) 'Morale and Leadership', 'Transactions of the Conference on Morale – and the Prevention and Control of Panic', held in New York City on 2 February 1951, New York (Academy of Medicine and Josiah Macy, Jr, Foundation, 1952) 59–71.

(1952d) 'The Suppression of the Clonic Phase in Electrically Induced Convulsions in Man', *Journal of Neuropathology and Experimental Neurology*, 9 (1952) 169–83.

(1952e) 'Quantitative Aspects of the Neurological Examination as a Means of Evaluating Improvement in Chronic Disease of the Nervous System', *Quarterly Review of Pediatrics*, 7 (1952) 82–4.

(1952f) 'Prevalence of Alcoholism in the Population and Among Suicides and Accidents from Poisoning, Massachusetts 1938–1948', *Quarterly Journal of Studies on Alcohol*, 13 (1952) 204–14 (with J. Ipsen, Jr, and M. Moore).

(1952g) 'The Urinary Bladder in Multiple Sclerosis', *Journal of Urology*, 68 (1952) 230–6 (with S. R. Muellner and J. Loman).

(1952h) 'The Role of Food Allergy in Multiple Sclerosis', *Neurology*, 2 (1952) 412–26 (with O. F. Ehrentheil and M. H. Shulman).

(1952i) 'Neurobiologic Research in Psychiatry', *Diseases of the Nervous System*, 13 (1952) 333–6.

(1952j) 'Psychic and Neural Dynamics in the Treatment of Mental Disease', *Continia Neurologica*, 12 (1952) 292–7.

(1953a) *Treatment of Mental Disorder* (Philadelphia, London, 1953) (with W. B. Saunders).

(1953b) 'The Effect of Electroshock on a "Normal" Person under Recent Stress. An Experiment Elucidating the Influence of Electroshock on the Defensive Mechanisms of the Ego', *American Journal of Psychiatry*, 109 (1953) 696–8.

(1953c) 'A Simple Aid to Locomotion for Patients with Spinal or Cerebellar Ataxia', *Transactions of the American Neurological Association, Seventy-seventh Annual Meeting* (1953) 224–5 (with A. Mills).

(1953d) 'Histochemical Studies of Active Carbonyl Groups (Proteolipids) in Brains with Multiple Sclerosis', *Journal of Neuropathology and Experimental Neurology*, 12 (1953) 293–301 (with R. Ashbel and N. Raskin).

(1953e) 'Effects of Electroshock on the Cortical and Intracerebral Electro-activity of the Brain in Schizophrenic Patients', *Confinia Neurologica*, 13 (1953) 287–294 (with J. M. R. Delgado and H. Hamlin).

(1953f) 'Unidirectional Electroshock Relaxed by Succinylcholine Chloride', *Continia Neurologica*, 13 (1953) 324–32 (with I. E. Gilbert and S. E. White).

(1953g) 'Predictability of Exacerbation and Remission in Multiple Sclerosis', *Transactions of the American Neurological Association, Seventy-eighth Annual Meeting* (1953) 220–1 (with W. Paxton Parker).

(1953h) 'Supportive Psychotherapy in the Practice of Neurology', *Transactions of the American Neurological Association, Seventy-eighth Annual Meeting* (1953) 253–4 (with M. Moore).

(1954a) 'Treatment of Multiple Sclerosis', in H. F. Conn (ed.), *Current Therapy* (Philadelphia, London, 1954) 693–6.

(1954b) 'The Influence of Physical Treatment Methods in Mental Disease Upon the Defensive Operations of the Ego', in P. Hoch and J. Zubin (eds), *Depression* (New York, 1954) 210–24.

(1954c) 'Why I Became a Doctor and Why I Became the Sort of Doctor I Am', in D. N. Fabricant (ed.), *Why We Became Doctors* (New York, 1954) 75–9.

(1954d) 'The Commitment and Suicide of King Ludwig II of Bavaria', *American Journal of Psychiatry*, 111 (1954) 100–7.

(1954e) 'Predictability of Exacerbation and Remission in Multiple Sclerosis', *Annals of the New York Academy of Sciences*, 58 (1954) 673–81.

(1954f) 'Outpatient Electroshock Therapy in Psychoses', *The Medical Clinics of North America*, 38 (1954) 1363–76.

(1954g) 'An Anti-Epinephrine Factor in Treatment-Resistant Schizophrenia and in Intractable Psychalgia', *Archives of Neurology and Psychiatry*, 72 (1954) 639–41.

(1954h) 'An Anti-Epinephrine Factor in Treatment-Resistant Schizophrenic Patients', *Society Transactions, Archives of Neurology and Psychiatry*, 72 (1954) 652–3.

(1954i) 'Carbohydrate Metabolism in Brain Disease. 1. Glucose Metabolism in Multiple Sclerosis', *Archives of Neurology and Psychiatry*, 72 (1954) 688–95 (with D. H. Henneman, M. D. Altschule and R. M. Goncz).

(1955a) 'Psychiatric Diagnosis and Management of the Great and Near-Great in Public Life', *American Journal of Psychiatry*, 111 (1955) 552–3.

(1955b) 'Multiple Sclerosis', in H. F. Conn (ed.), *Current Therapy* (Philadelphia, London, 1955) 501–4.

(1955c) 'Alcoholism', in A. B. Baker (ed.), *Clinical Neurology* (New York, 1955) 966–86.

(1955d) 'Epinephrine-Mecholyl Test (Funkenstein Test). Its Value in Determining the Recovery Potential of Patient with Mental Disease', *Archives of Neurology and Psychiatry*, 73 (1955) 496–514.

(1955e) 'Management of Psychological Issues in Conjunction with Physical Treatment', *Diseases of the Nervous System*, 16 (1955) 232–6 (with I. M. Rosen).

(1955f) 'Moralisms and Morality from the Viewpoint of the Psychiatrist', in I. Galdston (ed.), *Ministry and Medicine in Human Relations* (New York, 1955) 81–99.

(1956a) 'Electroshock Therapy', *JAMA*, 160 (1956) 339–40.

(1956b) *Tratamiento de las Enfermedades Mentales* (Buenos Aires, 1956).

(1956c) 'Therapeutic Process in Electroshock and the Newer Drug Therapies. Psychopathological Considerations', *JAMA*, 162 (1956) 966–9.

(1957a) 'Multiple Therapy in Private Practice', *American Journal of Psychiatry*, 113 (1957) 815–23 (with M. Moore).

(1957b) 'Discussions of Chapters 10–11', in P. H. Hoch and J. Zubin (eds), *Experimental Psychopathology* (New York, London, 1957) 187–93.

(1957c) 'The Sedac Machine in the Treatment of Mental Disorders', *Discussions of the Nervous System*, 18 (1957) 151 (with M. Moore).

(1957d) 'Objective Approaches to Treatment in Psychiatry', *Canadian Psychiatric Association Journal*, 2 (1957) 77–94.

(1957e) 'Differential Effects of the New "Psychtropic" Drugs', *Annals of the New York Academy of Sciences*, 67 (1957) 758–65.

(1957f) 'In Memoriam, Merrill Moore, M.D., 1903–1957', *New England Journal of Medicine*, 256 (1957) 893–4.

(1957g) 'Book Review – *Battle for the Mind* – by William Sargant', *Diseases of the Nervous System*, 28 (1957) 487.

(1957h) 'A Nosometric Study of Multiple Sclerosis. Its Application to Prognosis and Evaluation of Treatment', *Acta Neurologica et Psychiatrica Belgica*, 57 (1957) 685–702 (with A. Berkeley and A. M. Alexander).

(1958a) 'Multiple Approaches to Treatment in Schizophrenia and Discussion of Indications', *American Journal of Psychiatry*, 114 (1958) 577–82.

(1958b) 'Chemotherapy of Depression. Use of Meprobamate with Beactyzine (Z-Diethylaminoethyl Benxilate) Hydrochloride', *JAMA*, 166 (1958) 1019–23.

(1958c) 'Prognosis and Treatment of Multiple Sclerosis – Quantitative Nosometric Study', *JAMA*, 166 (1958) 1943–9 (with A. W. Berkeley and A. M. Alexander).

(1958d) *Objective Approaches to Treatment in Psychiatry* (Springfield, Illinois, 1958).

(1958e) 'Morale and Leadership', in I. Galdston and H. H. Zetterberg (eds), *Panic and Morale* (New York, 1958) 105–17.

(1958f) 'Depression. Recognition and Treatment', Descriptive Leaflet to accompany exhibit presented at the One Hundred and Fourteenth Annual Meeting of the American Psychiatric Association in San Francisco, California, 12–16 May 1958, and at the One Hundred and Seventh Annual Meeting of the American Medical Association in San Francisco, California, 23–27 June 1958.

(1958g) 'Polygraphic Measurement Technique of Conditioning Sequences in Mentally Disturbed and Normal Control Subjects', *EEG Clinical Neurophysiology*, 10 (1958) 363–4 (with C. Kris).

(1958h) 'Polygraphic Study of Conditional Reflexes in Man: Diagnostic Aspects of Differentiation and Generalisation', *Transactions of the American Neurological Association, Eighty-Third Annual Meeting* (1958) 147–9 (with C. Kris).

(1958i) 'Foreword. Reports of Papers Read at the Second Annual Meeting of the Eastern Psychiatric Research Association, New York, October, 1957', *Diseases of the Nervous System*, 18 (1958) 3.

(1958j) 'Function of the Anesthetist in Electroshock Therapy', *Diseases of the Nervous System*, 19 (1958) 41–3 (with I. E. Gilbert and S. E. White).

(1958k) 'Chemotherapy of Depression. Meprobamate Combined with 2-Diethylaminoethyl Benzilate Hydrocholorise (Benactyzine)', *Diseases of the Nervous System*, 19 (1958) 52–3.

(1958l) 'Succinycholine Chloride and Thiopental Preparatory to Electroconvulsive Therapy', *Diseases of the Nervous System*, 19 (1958) 42–73 (with I. E. Gilbert and S. E. White).

(1958m) 'In Memoriam, Merrill Moore, M.D., 1903–1957', *American Journal of Psychiatry*, 115 (1958) 191–2.

(1958n) 'Chemotherapy, Electrotherapy and Psychotherapy of Depression', *Transactions of the Fifth Annual Meeting of the Academy of Psychosomatic Medicine* (1958) 215–16.

(1958o) 'Panel Discussion. The New Psychotherapeutic Drugs – Their Use and Misuse', *Transactions of the Fifth Annual Meeting of the Academy of Psychosomatic Medicine* (1958) 226–8.

(1958p) 'Apparatus and Method for the Study of Conditional Reflexes in Man. Preliminary Results in Normal Control Subjects, in Mental Disorders and as a Result of Drug Action', *A.M.A. Archives of Neurology and Psychiatry*, 80 (1958) 629–49.

(1958q) 'Apparatus and Method for the Study of Conditional Reflexes in Man', *Diseases of the Nervous System*, 19 (1958) 495–6.

(1958r) 'Discussion of: A Comparison of Effect of Two Different Types of Electroconvulsive Treatment on Conditional Reflex in Dogs by Peters, J. E.', in W. H. Gantt (ed.), *Physiological Bases of Psychiatry* (Springfield, Illinois, 1958) 71–3.

(1959a) 'Depressive Psychoses', in H. F. Conn (ed.), *Current Therapy* (Philadelphia, London, 1959) 539–41.

(1959b) 'Objective Approach to Psychiatric Diagnosis and Evaluation of Drug Effects by Means of the Conditional Reflex Technique', in J. H. Masserman (ed.), *Biological Psychiatry* (New York, 1959) 154–83.

(1959c) 'The Psychiatric Armamentarium (Available Forms of Psychiatric Treatment and Their Indications)', *Diseases of the Nervous* System, 20 (1959) 75–8.

(1959d) 'Book Review – The Roots of Psychoanalysis and Psychotherapy: a Search for Principles of General Psychotherapeutics – by S. A. Szurek', *JAMA*, 170 (1959) 1133–4.

(1959e) 'Effect of Amine Oxidase Inhibitors on the Conditional Psychogalvanic Reflex in Man', *Diseases of the Nervous System*, 20 (1959) 26–33 (with S. R. Lipsett).

(1959f) 'Multiple Sclerosis in a Small New England Community', *New England Journal of Medicine*, 261 (1959) 1059–61 (with W. E. Deacon, H. D. Siedler and L. T. Kurland).

(1959g) 'The Inert Psychasthenic Reaction (Anhedonia) as Differentiated from Classic Depression and its Response to Iproniazid', *Annals of the N.Y. Academy of Sciences*, 80 (1959) 669–79 (with A. W. Berkeley).

(1959h) 'Preface' to M. A. Tudbury, *The Psychiatric Nurse in the General Hospital* (Springfield, Illinois, 1959), v–ix.

(1960) 'New Diagnostic and Therapeutic Aspects of Depression', in D. M. Rogers (ed.), *Depression and Anti-Depressant* Drugs (Wadham, Mass., 1960) 23–33.

(1961a) *Multiple Sclerosis. Prognosis and Treatment* (Springfield, Illinois, 1961).

(1961b) 'Swimming for Schizophrenia', *JAMA*, 176 (1961) 560.

(1961c) 'Effects of Psychotrophic Drugs on Conditional Responses in Man', in E. Rothlin (ed.) *Neuro-psychopharmacology* (Amsterdam, 1961) 93–123.

(1961d) 'Objective Evaluation of Anti-depressant Therapy by Conditional Reflex Technique', *Diseases of the Nervous System*, 22 (1961) 14–23.

(1961e) 'The Effect of Drugs on the Conditional Psychogalvanic Reflex in Man', *Journal of Neuropsychiatry*, 2 (1961) 246–61 (with S. R. Horner).

(1961f) 'The Effect of Hydroxyphanamate on the Conditional Psychogalvanic Reflex in Man', *Diseases of the Nervous System*, 22 (1961) 17–24.

(1961g) 'Book Review – Parkinsonism: Its Medical and Surgical Therapy – by I. S. Cooper', *JAMA*, 177 (1961) 732.

(1961h) 'The Present Status of ACTH Therapy in Multiple Sclerosis', *Transactions of the American Neurological Association* (New York, 1961) 188–90 (with L. J. Cass).

(1961i) 'Differential Diagnosis Between Psychogenic and Physical Pain – the Conditional Psychogalvanic Reflex as an Aid', *Proceedings of the Third World Conference of Psychiatry, Canadian Psychiatric Association and McGill University, Montreal, Canada*, 2 (1961) 1001–4.

(1962a) 'Electroshock Therapy', *Practitioner's Questions Box, Factor*, 3 (1962) 5.

(1962b) 'The Conditional Psychogalvanic Reflex: Its Contribution to Psychiatric Diagnosis', in J. Wortis (ed.), *Recent Advances in Biological Psychiatry* (New York, 1962) 38.

(1962c) 'Walter E. Barton, Ninetieth President, 1961–1962, a Biographical Sketch', *American Journal of Psychiatry*, 119 (1962) 16–19.

(1962d) 'The Conditional Psychogalvanic Reflex in the Measurement of Psychopharmacologic Response', in J. H. Nodine and J. H. Moyer (eds), *Psychosomatic Medicine* (Philadelphia, 1962) 399–410.

(1962e) 'Differential Diagnosis Between Psychogenic and Physical Pain. The Conditional Psychogalvanic Reflex as an Aid', *JAMA*, 181 (1962) 855–61.

(1962f) 'A Conditional Automic Response (The Conditional Psychogalvanic Reflex) as a Parameter of Psychiatric Diagnosis', *Diseases of the Nervous* System, 23 (1962) 597.

(1963a) 'The Experimental Production of Addisonian Melanoderma in Man Due to ACTH Therapy', in E. Wollheim and B. Schlegel (eds), *Transactions of the VIIth International Congress of Internal Medicine, 5–8 Sept. 1962 in Munich, Germany* (Stuttgart, 1963) 713–14 (with L. J. Cass).

(1963b) 'The Present Status of ACTH Therapy in Multiple Sclerosis', *Annals of Internal Medicine*, 58 (1963) 454–71 (with L. J. Cass).

(1963c) 'Profiling as an Aspect of Psychiatric Diagnosis with Reference to the Matching of Control Groups for the Study of Drug Effects', *American Journal of Psychiatry*, 120 (1963) 387–9.

(1963d) 'Significance of Dosage in ACTH Therapy of Multiple Sclerosis', *Transactions of the American Neurological Association, 88th Annual Meeting*, 88 (1963), 184–5 (with Leo J. Cass).

(1964a) 'ACTH-Induced Psychoses in the Light of Daily Determination of 17-Hydroxycorticoid Excretion Levels under High ACTH Dosage', in J. Wortis (ed.), *Recent Advances in Biological Psychiatry*, 6 (1964) 242–55 (with L. J. Cass, W. S. Frederik and P. Ireland).

(1964b) 'Pregnancy in Multiple Sclerosis Patients', *Obs-Gyn Collected Papers, International Correspondence Society of Obstetricians and Gynecologists, Series V* (1964) 95–6.

(1964c) 'Report of the Task Force on Occupational Mental Health to Advisory Council, Mass.', Mental Health Planning Project (Boston, 1964) (with L. Blaney *et al.*).

(1964d) 'Differential Diagnosis Between Psychogenic and Physical Pain. The Conditional Psychogalvanic Reflex as an Aid', in C. M. Franks (ed.), *Conditional Techniques in Clinical Practice and Research* (New York, 1964) 44–5.

(1964e) 'Objective Evaluation of Antidepressant Therapy by Conditional Reflex Technique', in C. M. Franks (ed.), *Conditioning Techniques in Clinical Practice and Research* (New York, 1964) 71–85.

(1964f) 'Task Force on Occupational Mental Health', in H. W. Damone (ed.), *Massachusetts Mental Health Planning Project Progress Report, April 1, 1963 to June 30, 1964, Document DMH-1, 700-6-64-938507* (1964) 19–21.

(1964g) 'ACTH-Induced Addisonian-Like Melanoderma in Man', *Current Therapeutic Research*, 6 (1964) 601–7 (with L. J. Cass, W. S. Frederik and P. Ireland).

(1965a) 'Clinical Experiences with Hypnosis in Psychiatric Therapy', *The American Journal of Clinical Hypnosis*, 7 (1965) 190–206.

(1965b) 'Contributo Del Trattamento Biologico Ai Processi E Scopi Della Psicoterapica', *Sistema Nervoso*, 27 (1965) 45–9.

(1965c) 'Desmenthylimipramine in Depressions. Study of a New Drug with the Aid of Profiling. Conditional Reflex Testing and Performance Testing', *International Journal of Neuropsychiatry*, 1 (1965) 275–93 (with L. J. Cass and W. S. Frederik).

(1965d) 'Incidence and Control of Complications of ACTH Therapy in Multiple Sclerosis', *Proceedings of the Eighth International Congress of Neurology*, 4 (1965) 87–100 (with L. J. Cass and M. Enders).

(1965e) 'Adrenocortical Response to High Dosage ACTH Therapy in Patients with Multiple Sclerosis', *Transactions of the American Neurological Association* (New York, 1965) 219–21 (with L. J. Cass, M. Enders and K. Sarai).

(1966a) 'Limitations in Experimental Research on Human Beings', *Lex et Scientia, International Journal of Law and Science*, 3 (1966) 8–24.

(1966b) 'Hypnosis in Primarily Organic Illness', *The American Journal of Clinical Hypnosis*, 8 (1966) 250–3.

(1966c) 'Conditional Reflexes as Related to Hypnosis and Hypnotic Techniques', *Journal of the American Society of Psychosomatic Dentistry and Medicine*, 13 (1966) 35–53.

(1966d) 'Effects of Physical Treatment of Mental Disease Upon the Life Instinct and the Death Instinct', in J. Wortis (ed.), *Recent Advances in Biological Psychiatry*, 8 (1966) 36.

(1966e) 'Adrenocortical Response to High Dosage ACTH Therapy in Patients with Multiple Sclerosis', *Confinia Neurologica*, 28 (1966) 1–17 (with L. J. Cass, M. Enders and K. Sarai).

(1966f) 'Contribution of Physical Treatment to the Processes and Goals of Psychotherapy', *The American Journal of Psychiatry*, 123 (1966) 87–91.

(1966g) 'Complications of Corticotropin Therapy in Multiple Sclerosis', *JAMA*, 197 (1966) 173–8 (with L. J. Cass and M. Enders).

(1966h) 'Limitations of Experimentation on Human Beings with Special Reference to Psychiatric Patients', *Diseases of the Nervous System*, 27 (1966) 61–5.

(1966i) 'General Principles of Psychotherapy', in R. D. Savage (ed.), *Clinical Psychology* (Oxford, 1966) 293–307.

(1966j) 'Conditional Reflexes as Related to Hypnosis and Hypnotic Techniques', *Conditional Reflex*, 1 (1966) 199–204.

(1966k) 'The Effect of Drug Therapy on Conditional Reflexes and Behaviour', *Journal of the American Society of Psychosomatic Dentistry and Medicine*, 13 (1966) 145–62.

(1967a) 'Recommendations on Bridgwater State Hospital', *New England Journal of Medicine*, 276 (1967) 183–4 (with W. Chasen, R. Mezer, R. Arnot and J. A. Whitney).

(1967b) 'Psychotherapy of Sexual Deviation with the Aid of Hypnosis', *The American Journal of Clinical Hypnosis*, 9 (1967) 181–3.

(1967c) 'I Riflessi Condizionati in Rapporto All'ipnosi E Alle Tecniche Ipnotiche Rassegna Di Ipnosi E Medicina Psicosomatica', *Supplemento a Minerva Medica*, 5 (1967) 345–6.

(1967d) 'Protection of Privacy in Behavioural Research', *Lex et Scientia*, 4 (1967) 34–8.

(1967e) ' "On the Couch". Book Review of *Psychoanalysis, Psychiatry and the Law*', *Trial*, 3 (1967) 54.

(1967f) 'Differences in Psychiatric and Legal Judgement', *Diseases of the Nervous System*, 28 (1967) 396–7.

(1967g) 'Clinical Experiences with Hypnosis in Psychiatric Treatment', *International Journal of Neuropsychiatry*, 3 (1967) 118–24.

(1967h) 'Book Review: *Psychoanalysis, Psychiatry and the Law*, by J. Katz, J. Goldstein and A. M. Dershowitz', *Portia Law Journal*, 3 (1967) 110–13.

(1967i) 'Conditioning and Anti-depressant Therapy', *Proceedings of the Fifth International Congress of Neuropsychopharmacology, Washington, DC, 28–31 March 1966. Excerpta Medica, International Congress Series*, 129 (1967) 882–4.

(1968a) 'Conditional Reflexes as Related to Hypnosis and Hypnotic Techniques', *American Journal of Clinical Hypnosis*, 10 (1968) 157–9.

(1968b) 'Military Psychiatry, Occupation and Refugee Problems in Israel', *Military Medicine*, 133 (1968) 265–74.

(1968c) 'Discussion of Dr Brody's Paper – "Culture, Symbol and Value in the Social Etiology of Behavioural Deviance"', in J. Zubin and F. A. Freyhan (eds), *Social Psychiatry* (1968) 34–8.

(1968d) 'Psychotherapy of Sexual Deviation with the Aid of Hypnosis', *Proceedings of the IVth World Congress of Psychiatry, Madrid. Excerpta Medica Foundation (Amsterdam), International Congress Series*, 150 (1968) 3070–2.

(1968e) 'Committee on Mental Health. Report to the Council of the Massachusetts Medical Society', *New England Journal of Medicine*, 279 (1968) 37–41.

(1968f) 'Ophthalmodynia and Steroid-Induced Somnolence in Multiple Sclerosis', *JAMA*, 206 (1968) 1801.

(1968g) 'Deaths from Poisoning – Massachusetts – 1955 to 1964', *Lex et Scientia*, 5 (1968) 176–93 (with S. Liberman).

(1969a) 'Somatic Therapies Other Than Psychotropic Drugs', *The Schizophrenic Syndrome* (1969) 569–93.

(1969b) 'Problems of Youth: Teenage Alienation and Drug Taking. A Report by the Committee on Mental Health, Massachusetts Medical Society', *New England Journal of Medicine*, 281 (1969) 388–9.

(1969c) 'ACTH-Induced Adrenocortical Response Patterns in Multiple Sclerosis and their Relation to Clinical Effectiveness of ACTH Therapy', Abstract of paper presented at the Fourth International Congress of Neurological Surgery and the Ninth International Congress of Neurology, New York, 20–27 Sept. 1969. Reprinted from *Excerpta Medica International Congress Series*, No. 193.

(1970a) 'Psychiatry: Methods and Processes for Investigation of Drugs', *Annals of the New York Academy of Sciences*, 169 (1970) 344–50.

(1970b) 'Biography of Dr H. Thomas Ballantine', *Massachusetts Physician*, 29 (1970) 18–19.

(1970c) 'Discussion to: Clinical and Experimental Trance. What's the Difference?' *American Journal of Clinical Hypnosis*, 13 (1970) 11–13, 14.

(1970d) 'Which Anti-depressant for Which Patient?', *Psychosomatics*, 11 (1970) 532.

(1970e) 'Hypnotically Induced Hallucinations: Their Diagnostic and Therapeutic Utilization', *Origins and Mechanisms of Hallucinations* (1970) 155–65.

(1971a) 'ACTH-Induced Adrenocortical Response Patterns in Multiple Sclerosis and their Relation to the Clinical Effectiveness of ACTH Therapy', *Confinia Neurologica*, 33 (1971) 1–24 (with L. J. Cass.).

(1971b) 'Hypnotically Induced Hallucinations: their Diagnostic and Therapeutic Utilization', *Diseases of the Nervous System*, 32 (1971) 89–94.

(1971c) 'The Prehypnotic Suggestion', *Comprehensive Psychiatry*, 12 (1971) 414–22.

(1971d) 'Medical Science Under Dictatorship', Reprinted from *New England Journal of Medicine*, 241 (1949) 39–47; also *Child and Family*, 10 (1971) 40–58.

(1972a) 'Which Anti-depressant for Which Patient?', *Psychosomatics*, 13 (1972) 49–56 (with A. W. Berkley and S. L. Cohen).

(1972b) 'Which Anti-depressant for Which Patient?', *Medical Insight*, 4 (1972) 12–19 (with A. W. Berkeley and S. L. Cohen).

(1972c) 'Homage to Nurnberger', *Biological Psychiatry*, 4 (1972) 261–2.

(1972d) 'Marijuana, Depression, and Drug Dependency', *Medical Counterpoint*, 4 (1972) 12–31 (with L. Moloney).

(1972e) 'Mind and Body in Biological Psychiatry', *Biological Psychiatry*, 5 (1972) 225–38.

(1972f) 'Gold Medal Award of the Society of Biological Psychiatry, Robert G. Heath, May, 1972; Remarks of President Leo Alexander', *Biological Psychiatry*, 5 (1972) 319–21.

(1973a) 'Temporal Laws and Medical Ethics in Conflict. Letter to the Editor', *New England Journal of Medicine*, 289 (1973) 324–5.

(1973b) 'Comments on Presidential Address', *Biological Psychiatry*, 7 (1973) 193–6.

(1974a) 'Treatment of Impotency and Anorgasmia by Psychotherapy Aided by Hypnosis', *American Journal of Clinical Hypnosis*, 17 (1974) 33–43.

(1974b) 'Medical Science under Dictatorship', *The Catholic Digest*, 38 (1974) 45–7.

(1974c) 'Medical Science Under Dictatorship', in *"Readings" Packet #600* – *Experimentation and Informed Consent, Institute of Society, Ethics and the Life Sciences* (1974).

(1974d) 'Felicitation', in H. Mitsuda and T. Fukuda (eds), *Biological Mechanisms of Schizophrenia and Schizophrenia-like Psychoses* (Tokyo, 1974) ix–x.

(1975a) 'Tratmiento Hipnologica en Impotencia y Anorgasmia', *Revisita Ibero Americana De Sofrologia y Medicina Psicosomatica*, 6 (1975) 113–20.

(1975b) 'Medicine Under the Nazis', *Private Practice*, 7 (1975) 36–9.

(1976a) 'How Euthanasia Worked', *Our Family*, 28 (1976) 12–13.

(1976b) 'Conditional Reflexes as Related to Hypnosis and Hypnotic Techniques', in E. Dengrove (ed.), *Hypnosis and Behaviour Therapy* (Springfield, Illinois, 1976) 39–43.

(1976c) 'Ethics of Human Experimentation', *Psychiatric Journal of the University of Ottawa*, 1 (1976) 40–6.

(1980) 'Treatment of Impotency and Anorgasmia by Psychotherapy Aided by Hypnosis', in G. Hugo and W. R. Johnson (eds), *Application of Hypnosis in Sex Therapy by Beigel* (Springfield, Illinois, 1980) 202–15.

(1981) 'Boston City Hospital Grand Rounds: a Case of Intractable Rage', *Behavioural Medicine*, 8 (1981) 32–41.

(1982a) 'Erickson's Approach to Hypnotic Psychotherapy of Depression', in J. K. Zeig (ed.), *Ericksonian Approaches to Hypnosis and Psychotherapy* (New York, 1982).

(1982b) 'Lithium in Aggressive Behaviour', *American Journal of Psychiatry*, 139 (1982) 10.

Secondary Sources

Abzug, R. H. 1985. *Inside the Vicious Heart. Americans and the Liberation of Nazi Concentration Camps* (Oxford, 1985).

Ahrendfeldt, R. H. 1958. *Psychiatry in the British Army in the Second World War* (London, 1958).

Alexander, G. 1912. *Die Ohrenkrankheiten im Kindesalter* (Leipzig, 1912).

Alexander, G. 1914. *Die Syphilis des Gehörorgans* (Vienna, 1914).

Alexander, G. and O. Marburg (eds) 1926. *Handbuch der Neurologie des Ohres* (Berlin, 1926).

Ambroselli, C. 1988. *L'Éthique Médicale* (Paris, 1988).

Ambroselli, C. 1997. 'Procès des médecins a Nuremberg 1946–1997', *Journal de l' Association des médecins Israelites de France*, 45 (1997) 1–51.

Angell, M. 1992. 'Editorial Responsibility: Protecting Human Rights by Restricting Publication of Unethical Research', in G. J. Annas and M. A. Grodin (eds), *The Nazi Doctors and the Nuremberg Code. Human Rights in Human Experimentation* (New York, Oxford, 1992) 276–85.

Annas, G. J. 1992. 'The Nuremberg Code in US Courts: Ethics versus Expediency', in G. J. Annas and M. A. Grodin (eds), *The Nazi Doctors and the Nuremberg Code. Human Rights in Human Experimentation* (New York, Oxford, 1992) 201–22.

Annas, G. J. and M. A. Grodin (eds) 1992. *The Nazi Doctors and the Nuremberg Code. Human Rights in Human Experimentation* (New York, Oxford, 1992).

Annas, G. J. and M. A. Grodin. 1998. 'Medizinische Ethik und Menschenrechte: Das Vermächtnis von Nürnberg', in S. Kolb and H. Seithe (eds), *Medizin und Gewissen: 50 Jahre nach dem Nürnberger Ärzteprozeß* (Frankfurt a.M., 1998) 244–59.

Annas, G. J. and M. A. Grodin. 1999. 'Medicine and Human Rights: Reflections on the Fiftieth Anniversary of the Doctors' Trial', in J. M. Mann *et al.* (eds), *Health and Human Rights* (New York, 1999) 301–11.

Arendt, H. 1951. *The Origins of Totalitarianism* (New York, 1951).

Arnold, H. 1996. 'Deutsche Neurochirurgen zwischen den beiden Weltkriegen und ihre internationalen Beziehungen', *Schriftenreihe der Deutschen Gesellschaft für Geschichte der Nervenheilkunde*, 1 (1996) 7–19.

Arnold, P. and D. Sprumont. 1997. 'Der Nürnberger Kodex: Regeln des Völkerrechts', in U. Tröhler and S. Reiter-Theil (eds), *Ethik und Medizin: 1947–1997* (Göttingen, 1997) 115–30.

Ash, M. G. and A. Söllner (eds) 1996. *Forced Migration and Scientific Change: Emigré German-Speaking Scientists and Scholars after 1933* (Cambridge, New York, 1996).

Aziz, P. 1976. *Doctors of Death* (Geneva, 1976).

Baker, R. 1997. 'Transkulturelle Medizinethik und Menschenrechte', in U. Tröhler and S. Reiter-Theil (eds), *Ethik und Medizin: 1947–1997* (Göttingen, 1997) 433–60.

Bankowski, Z. and N. Howard-Jones (eds) 1982. *Human Experimentation and Medical Ethics* (Geneva, 1982).

Barer, R. 1998. *One Young Man and Total War. From Normandy to Concentration Camp: A Doctor's Letters Home* (Edinburgh and Durham, 1998).

Barnett, A. 2002. 'Germ War Tests Used on Millions. Large Areas of Britain Exposed to Bacteria Sprayed in Secret Trials', *The Observer*, 21 April 2002.

Barondess, J. A. 1996. 'Medicine against Society. Lessons from the Third Reich', *JAMA*, 276 (1996) 1657–61.

Bayle, F. 1950. *Croix Gammée Contre Caducée. Les Expériences Humaines en Allemagne pendant la Deuxième Guerre Mondiale* (Berlin, 1950).

Beecher, H. K. 1966. 'Ethics in Clinical Research', *New England Journal of Medicine*, 274 (1966) 1354–60.

Beecher, H. K. 1970. *Research and the Individual. Human Studies* (Boston, 1970).

Benz, W. 1988. 'Dr. med. Sigmund Rascher. Eine Karriere', in W. Benz and B Diestel (eds), *Medizin im NS-Staat. Täter, Opfer, Handlanger* (Dachau, 1988) 190–214.

Benz, W. and B. Diestel (eds) 1988. *Medizin im NS-Staat. Täter, Opfer, Handlanger* (Dachau, 1988).

Benzenhöfer, U. 1996. 'Die Auswahl der Angeklagten. Nürnberger Ärzteprozeß', *Deutsches Ärzteblatt*, 93 (1996) 2057–9.

Berger, R. L. 1992. 'Nazi Science: Comments on the Validation of the Dachau Human Hypothermia Experiments', in A. L. Caplan (ed.), *When Medicine Went Mad. Bioethics and the Holocaust* (Totowa, New Jersey, 1992) 109–33.

Biddiss, M. 1997. 'Disease and Dictatorship: the Case of Hitler's Reich', *Journal of the Royal Society of Medicine*, 90 (1997) 342–6.

Binneveld, J. M. W. 1997. *From Shellshock to Combat Stress: a Comparative History of Military Psychiatry* (Amsterdam, 1997).

Blacker, C. P. 1952a. '"Eugenic" Experiments Conducted by the Nazis on Human Subjects', *Eugenics Review*, 44 (1952) 9–19.

Blacker, C. P. 1952b. *Eugenics. Galton and After* (London, 1952).

Bleker, J. 1996. '50 Jahre Nürnberger Ärzteprozeß. Medizin, Wissenschaft und Menschenwürde', *Berliner Ärzte*, 33 (1996) 11–14.

Blomquist, C. D. D. 1978. 'What is Psychiatry and What is Ethics?', *Psychiatric Annals*, 8 (1978) 15–20.

Bonah, C. 2002. '"Experimental Rage": the Development of Medical Ethics and the Genesis of Scientific Facts. Ludwik Fleck: an Answer to the Crisis of Modern Medicine in Interwar Germany?', *Social History of Medicine*, 15 (2002) 187–207.

Bonah, C. et al. (eds) 2003. *La Médecine Expérimentale au tribunal: Implications éthiques de quelques procès médicaux du XXe siècle européen* (Paris, 2003).

Boue, A. 1997. 'Prädikative Medizin, Gentests und die Ethik', in U. Tröhler and S. Reiter-Theil (eds), *Ethik und Medizin: 1947–1997* (Göttingen, 1997) 379–94.

Bower, T. 1982. *The Pledge Betrayed: America and Britain and the Denazification of Post-War Germany* (New York, 1982).

Bower, T. 1987. *The Paperclip Conspiracy: the Battle for the Spoils and Secrets of Nazi Germany* (London, 1987).

Bower, T. 1995. *Blind Eye to Murder. Britain, America and the Purging of Nazi Germany: a Pledge Betrayed* (London, 1995).

Brackman, A. C. 1987. *The Other Nuremberg: the Untold Story of the Tokyo War Crimes Trials* (New York, 1987).

Brennan, T. A. 'Proposed Revision to the Declaration of Helsinki – Will They Weaken the Ethical Principles Underlying the Human Research?', *The New England Journal of Medicine*, 341 (1999) 527–30.

British Foreign Office. 1949. *Scientific Results of German Medical War Crimes* (London, 1949).

Browning, C. 1998. *Der Weg zur 'Endlösung'. Entscheidungen und Täter* (Bonn, 1998).

Brunner, H. 1932. 'Prof. Gustav Alexander', *Wiener klinische Wochenschrift*, 18 (1932) 569.

Bullock, M. B. 1980. *An American Transplant: the Rockefeller Foundation and Peking Union Medical College* (Oxford, 1980).

Burkeman, O. and R. Norton-Taylor. 2002. 'Newborn World Court Fights for Survival', *The Guardian*, 1 July 2002.

Burleigh, M. 1994. *Death and Deliverance: 'Euthanasia' in Germany, 1900–1945* (Cambridge, New York, 1994).

Burleigh, M. 1997. *Ethics and Extermination: Reflections on Nazi Genocide* (Cambridge, New York, 1997).

Burman, W. P. (ed.) 1985. *The First German War Crimes Trial. Chief Judge Walter B. Beals' Desk Notebook of the Doctors' Trial* (Chapel Hill, 1985).

Buscher, F. 1989. *The US War Crimes Program in Germany, 1946–1955* (Westport, Conn., 1989).

Caplan, A. L. (ed.) 1992. *When Medicine Went Mad. Bioethics and the Holocaust* (Totowa, New Jersey, 1992).

Carrell, S. 2001. 'Porton Down Scientists Face Prosecution', *The Independant*, 18 July 2001.

Carter, G. B. 1992. *Porton Down. 75 Years of Chemical and Biological Research* (London, 1992).

Carter, G. B. and G. S. Pearson. 1996. 'Past British Chemical Warfare Capabilities', *RUSI Journal* (1996) 59–68.

Cefrey, H. 2001. *Dr Josef Mengele: the Angel of Death* (New York, 2001).

Charatan, F. B. 1996. 'Anatomy Textbook has Nazi Origin', *British Medical Journal*, 313 (1996) 1422.

Cocks, G. 1985. *Psychotherapy in the Third Reich: the Göring Institute* (New York, Oxford, 1985).

Cooter, R. 2002. 'The Resistable Rise of Medical Ethics. Review Article', *Social History of Medicine, Social History of Medicine*, 8 (2002) 257–70.

Cooter, R., Harrison, M. and S. Sturdy (eds) 1998. *War, Medicine and Modernity* (Stroud, 1998).

Cooter, R., Harrison, M. and S. Sturdy (eds) 1999. *Medicine and Modern Warfare* (Atlanta, 1999).

Connery, G. 1945. 'Buried Nazi "Science" of Freezing Man', *The Washington Post*, 4 November 1945.

Cosmas, G. A. and A. E. Cowdrey. 1992. *The Medical Department: Medical Service in the European Theatre of Operations* (Washington, DC, 1992).

Coughlin, W. P. 1985. 'Dr. Leo Alexander, 79; Psychiatrist Studied Psychology of War Crimes', *The Boston Globe*, 23 July 1985.

Cousins, N. 1958. 'Dialogue in Warsaw. Report on the Ravensbrueck Lapins', *The Saturday Review*, 28 June 1958.

Daum, M. and H.-U. Deppe (eds) 1991. *Zwangssterilisation in Frankfurt am Main, 1933–1945* (Frankfurt a.M., New York, 1991).

Deutsch, E. 1997. 'Der Nürnberger Kodex. Das Strafverfahren gegen Mediziner, die zehn Prinzipien von Nürnberg und die bleibende Bedeutung des Nürnberger Kodex', in U. Tröhler and S. Reiter-Theil (eds), *Ethik und Medizin: 1947–1997* (Göttingen, 1997) 103–14.

Dietz, J. 1974. 'Doctor is Sued for $6m in Brain Experimentation Controversy', *The Boston Globe*, 4 May 1974.

'Doctors on Trial', *British Medical Journal*, 1 (1947) 143.

Dörner, K. 2000. 'Nationalsozialismus und Medizin – Wurden die Lehren gezogen?', in E. Gabriel and W. Neugebauer (eds), *NS-Euthanasie in Wien* (Vienna, Cologne, Weimar, 2000) 131–6.

Dörner, K. 2001. '"Ich darf nicht denken". Das medizinische Selbstverständnis der Angeklagten', in K. Dörner and A. Ebbinghaus (eds) 2001. *Vernichten und Heilen: Der Nürnberger Ärzteprozeß und seine Folgen* (Berlin, 2001) 331–57.

Dörner, K. and A. Ebbinghaus (eds) 1999. *The Nuremberg Medical Trial 1946/47. Transcripts, Material of the Prosecution and Defense, Related Documents* (Munich, 1999), Microfiche.

Dörner, K. and A. Ebbinghaus (eds) 2001a. *The Nuremberg Medical Trial 1946/47. Transcripts, Material of the Prosecution and Defense, Related Documents. Guide to the Microfiche-Edition* (Munich, 2001).

Dörner, K. and A. Ebbinghaus (eds) 2001b. *Vernichten und Heilen: Der Nürnberger Ärzteprozeß und seine Folgen* (Berlin, 2001).

Doslak, M. J., L. F. Dell'Osso and R. B. Daroff. 1979. 'A Model of Alexander's Law of Vestibual Nystagmus', *Biol Cybern*, 34 (1979) 181–6.

Doslak, M. J., L. F. Dell'Osso and R. B. Daroff. 1982. 'Alexander Law: A Model and Resulting Study', *Ann Otol Rhinol Laryngol*, 91 (1982) 316–22.

Douraki, T. 1997. 'Die Anerkennung der Patientenrechte, insbesondere der psychisch Kranken. Internationale Organisation und die Europäische Menschenrecht skonvention', in U. Tröhler and S. Reiter-Theil (eds), *Ethik und Medizin: 1947–1997* (Göttingen, 1997) 309–20.

Doyal, L. and J. S. Tobias. 2000. *Informed Consent in Medical Research* (London, 2000).

'Draft Code of Ethics on Human Experimentation', *British Medical Journal*, 2 (1962) 1119.

'Dr. Leo Alexander, Miss Sarah Evarrs Address Vocational Conference', *The Radcliffe News*, 22 November 1935.

Drinan, R. 1992. 'The Nuremberg Principles in International Law', in G. J. Annas and M. A. Grodin (eds), *The Nazi Doctors and the Nuremberg Code. Human Rights in Human Experimentation* (New York, Oxford, 1992) 174–82.

Ebbinghaus, A. (ed.) 1987. *Opfer und Täterinnen* (Nordlingen, 1987).

Ebbinghaus, A. 2001. 'Strategien der Verteidigung', in K. Dörner and A. Ebbinghaus (eds), *Vernichten und Heilen: Der Nürnberger Ärzteprozeß und seine Folgen* (Berlin, 2001) 405–35.

Ebermayer, L. 1930. *Der Arzt im Recht* (Leipzig, 1930).

Edsall, D. L. and T. J. Putnam. 1941. 'The Emigré Physician in America, 1941', *JAMA*, 117 (1941) 1882.

Elkeles, B. 1985. 'Medizinische Menschenversuche gegen Ende des 19. Jahrhunderts und der Fall Neisser. Rechtfertigung und Kritik einer wissenschaftlichen Methode', *Medizinhistorisches Journal*, 20 (1985) 135–48.

Elkeles, B. 1996. *Der Moralische Diskurs über das medizinische Menschenexperiment im 19. Jahrhundert* (Stuttgart, 1996).

Engelhardt, D. V. 1997. 'Wissenschaftlicher Fortschritt im soziokulturellen Kontext. Naturwissenschaft, Medizin und Mythos nach Nürnberg', in U. Tröhler and S. Reiter-Theil (eds), *Ethik und Medizin: 1947–1997* (Göttingen, 1997) 147–60.

Enloe, C. F. 1947. 'The German Medical War Crimes – Their Nature and Significance', *Rhode Island Medical Journal*, 30 (1947) 801–5.

Ernst, E. and P. J. Weindling. 1998. 'The Nuremberg Medical Trial: Have We Learned the Lessons?', *The Journal of Laboratory and Clinical Medicine*, 131 (1998) 130–5.

Evans, R. 2002. 'Drugged and Duped', *The Guardian*, 14 March 2002.

'Experimente', *Heute* (1947) 6.

Faden, R. R. and T. L. Beauchamp. 1986. *A History and Theory of Informed Consent* (New York, 1986).

Faden, R. R., S. E. Lederer and J. D. Moreno. 1996. 'US Medical Researchers, the Nuremberg Doctors' Trial, and the Nuremberg Code: Findings of the Advisory Committee on Human Radiation Experiments', *JAMA*, 276 (1996) 1667–71.

Ferencz, B. B. 1948–49. 'Nurnberg Trial Procedure and the Rights of the Accused', *Journal of Criminal Law and Criminology*, 39 (1948–49) 144–51.

Fletcher, J. F. 1954. *Morals and Medicine. The Moral Problem of the Patient's Right to Know the Truth, Contraception, Artificial Insemination, Sterilisation, Euthanasia* (Princeton, NJ, 1954).

Fluss, S. 1999. 'How the Declaration of Helsinki Developed', *Good Clinical Practice Journal*, 6 (1999) 18–22.

Fluss, S. 2000. *International Guidelines on Bioethics. European Forum of Good Clinical Practice* (Geneva, 2000).

Foreign Office. 1949. *Scientific Results of German Medical War Crimes* (London, 1949).

Freund, F. 1991. *Arbeitslager Zement. Das Konzentrationslager Ebensee und Raketenrüstung* (Vienna, 1991).

Frewer, A. 2000. *Medizin und Moral in Weimarer Republik und Nationalsozialismus. Die Zeitschrift 'Ethik' unter Emil Abderhalden* (Frankfurt a.M., New York, 2000).

Frewer, A. and C. Eickhoff (eds) 2000. *'Euthanasie' und die aktuelle Sterbehilfe-Debatte. Die historischen Hintergründe medizinischer Ethik* (Göttingen, 2000).

Frewer, A. and C. Wiesemann (eds) 1999. *Medizinverbrechen vor Gericht. Das Urteil im Nürnberger Ärzteprozeß gegen Karl Brandt und andere sowie aus dem Prozeß gegen Generalfeldmarschall Milch* (Erlangen, Jena, 1999).

Friedlander, H. 1995. *The Origins of Nazi Genocide. From Euthanasia to the Final Solution* (Chapel Hill, London, 1995).

Friedman, T. 1997. 'Lessons from Nuremberg: Ethical and Social Responsibilities for Health Care Professionals, Health Care Organisations, and Medical Journals', *JAMA*, 277 (1997) 710–12.

Füllberg-Stolberg, C. *et al.* (eds) 1994. *Frauen in Konzentrationslagern: Bergen-Belsen, Ravensbrück* (Bremen, 1994).

Gabriel, E. and W. Neugebauer (eds) 2000. *NS-Euthanasie in Wien* (Vienna, Collogne, Weimar, 2000).

Gabriel, R. A. (ed.) 1986. *Military Psychiatry. A Comparative Perspective* (Westport, 1986).

Geiger, I. 1981. *Das Leben und Werk von Wilhelm Tönnis unter besonderer Berücksichtigung seiner Würzburger Zeit* (Pattensen, 1981).

Genizi, H. 1976. 'American Non-Sectarian Refugee Relief Organisations (1933–1945)', *Yad Vashem Studies in the European Jewish Catastrophe*, 11 (1976) 164–219.

Gerst, T. 1996. '50 Jahre Nürnberger Kodex. Entwicklung, Wirksamkeit und künftige Bedeutung ethischer Kodizes in der Medizin', *Deutsches Ärzteblatt*, 93 (1996) 1020–1.

Gilligan, A. 1997. 'MOD's Germ Warfare Tests on London', *Sunday Telegraph*, 2 February 1997.

Glantz, L. H. 1992. 'The Influence of the Nuremberg Code on US Statutes and Regulations', in G. J. Annas and M. A. Grodin (eds), *The Nazi Doctors and the Nuremberg Code. Human Rights in Human Experimentation* (New York, Oxford, 1992) 183–200.

Glass, A. J. and R. R. Bernucci (eds) 1966/1974. *Neuropsychiatry in World War*, 2 vols (Washington, DC, 1966/1974).

Glees, A. 1992. 'The Making of British Policy on War Crimes: History as Politics in the UK', *Contemporary European History*, 1 (1992) 171–97.

Glover, J. 1999. *Humanity. A Moral History of the Twentieth Century* (London, 1999).

Goldhagen, D. J. 1996. *Hitler's Willing Executioners. Ordinary Germans and the Holocaust* (London, 1996).

Goldhagen, E. 1968. *Ethnic Minorities in the Soviet Union* (New York, 1968).

Goodchild, S. 2002. 'Hundreds of Patients Given Shock Treatment Wihout their Consent', *The Independent on Sunday*, 13 October 2002.

Greenberg, K. J. 1996. 'The Refugee Scholar in America: the Case of Paul Tillich', in M. G. Ash and A. Söllner (eds), *Forced Migration and Scientific Change: Emigré German-Speaking Scientists and Scholars after 1933* (Cambridge, New York, 1996) 273–89.

Greene, V. W. 1992. 'Can Scientists Use Information Derived from the Concentration Camps?', in A. L. Caplan (ed.) 1992. *When Medicine Went Mad. Bioethics and the Holocaust* (Totowa, New Jersey, 1992) 155–70.

Grimley Evans, J. and P. Beck. 2002. 'Informed Consent in Medical Research', *Clinical Medicine*, 2 (2002) 267–72.

Grodin, M. A. 1992. 'Historical Origins of the Nuremberg Code', in G. J. Annas and M. A. Grodin (eds), *The Nazi Doctors and the Nuremberg Code. Human Rights in Human Experimentation* (New York, Oxford, 1992) 121–44.

Grodin, M. A., G. J. Annas and L. H. Glantz. 1993. 'Medicine and Human Rights: a Proposal for International Action, *Hastings Center Report*, 23 (1993) 8–12.

Guttentag, O. E. 1964. 'Human Experimentation', *Science*, 145 (1964) 768.

Hale, N. G. Jr. 1995. *Freud and the Americans. The Rise and Crisis of Psychoanalysis in the United States* (New York, 1995).

Hamann, B. 1999. *Hitler's Vienna: a Dictator's Apprenticeship* (New York, Oxford, 1999).

Hammond, P. and G. B. Carter. 2002. *From Biological Warfare to Healthcare* (Basingstoke, 2002).

Harkness, J. M. 1996. 'Nuremberg and the Issue of Wartime Experiments on US Prisoners. The Green Committee', *JAMA*, 276 (1996) 1672–5.

Harkness, J. M. 1998. 'The Significance of the Nuremberg Code: Letter to the Editor', *New England Journal of Medicine*, 338 (1998) 995–6.

Hastedt, H. 1998. *Der Wert des Einzelnen. Eine Verteidigung des Individualismus* (Frankfurt a.M., 1998).

Hazelgrove, J. 2002. 'The Old Faith and the New Science: the Nuremberg Code and Human Experimentation Ethics in Britain, 1946–73', *Social History of Medicine*, 15 (2002) 109–35.

Heller, J. 1988. *Catch-22* (London, 1988).

Helmchen, H. 1994. 'Ärztliche Aufklärung bei aufgehobender oder eingeschränkter Einwilligungsfähigkeit', *Zeitschrift für ärztliche Fortbildung*, 88 (1994) 994–1001.

Helmchen, H. and R. Winau (eds) 1986. *Versuche mit Menschen in Medizin, Humanwissenschaft und Politik* (Berlin, New York, 1986).

Herranz, G. 1997. 'Der Eingang der zehn Nürnberger Postulate in berufsständische Ethik-Kodizes. Ein internationaler Vergleich', in U. Tröhler and S. Reiter-Theil (eds), *Ethik und Medizin: 1947–1997* (Göttingen, 1997) 171–88.

Herz, E. 1934. 'Scientific Cinematography in Medicine', *International Review of Educational Cinematography*, 6 (1934) 80–3.

Hill, A. B. 1952. 'The Clinical Trial', *New England Journal of Medicine*, 247 (1952) 113–19.

Hill, A. B. 1963. 'Medical Ethics and Controlled Trials', *British Medical Journal*, 1 (1963) 1043–49.

Hochenegg, J. von (ed.) 1907. *Lehrbuch der Speziellen Chirurgie fur Studierende und Ärzte* (Berlin, Vienna 1907).

Hoedeman, P. 1991. *Hitler or Hippocrates: Medical Experiments and Euthanasia in the Third Reich* (Sussex, 1991).

Honigmann, P. 1997. 'Zur Legitimität medizinischer Ethik-Kodizes aus britischer Sicht', in U. Tröhler and S. Reiter-Theil (eds), *Ethik und Medizin: 1947–1997* (Göttingen, 1997) 249–56.

Hornblum, A. M. 1998. *Acres of Skin. Human Experimentation at Holmesburg Prison* (New York, London, 1998).

Horner, J. S. 1999. 'Retreat from Nuremberg: Can We Prevent Unethical Medical Research?', *Public-Health*, 113 (1999) 205–10.

Howard-Jones, N. 1982. 'Human Experimentation in Historical and Ethical Perspective', in Z. Bankowski and N. Howard-Jones (eds), *Human Experimentation and Medical Ethics* (Geneva, 1982) 453–95.

Hubenstorf, M. 1984. 'Österreichische Ärzteemigration 1934–1945 – Zwischen neuem Tätigkeitsgebiet und organisierten Rückkehrplänen', *Berichte zur Wissenschaftsgeschichte*, 7 (1984) 85–107.

Hubenstorf, M. 1987. 'Österreichische Ärzte-Emigration', in F. Stadler (ed.), *Vertriebene Vernunft I. Emigration und Exil österreichischer Wissenschaft, 1930–1940* (Vienna, Munich, 1987) 359–415.

'Human Laboratory Animals', *Life* (1947) 26–7.

'Immigration of Alien Physicians', *JAMA*, 112 (1939) 737.

Ingraham, L. and F. Manning. 1986. 'American Military Psychiatry', in R. A. Gabriel (ed.), *Military Psychiatry. A Comparative Perspective* (Westport, 1986) 38–46.

Ivy, A. C. 1947. 'Nazi War Crimes of a Medical Nature', *Federation Bulletin*, 33 (1947) 133–46.

Ivy, A. C. 1948a. 'Nazi War Crimes of a Medical Nature', *Phi Lambda Kappa Quart*, 22 (1948) 5–12.

Ivy, A. C. 1948b. 'The History and Ethics of the Use of Human Subjects in Medical Experiments', *Science*, 108 (1948) 1–5.

Ivy, A. C. 1948c. 'The Moral of the Nazi Medical War Crimes', *The Medical Alumni Association Bulletin*, 7 (1948) 1–2.

Jacobeit, S. and S. Erpel (eds) 1995. '*Ich grüsse Euch als freier Mensch': Quellenedition zur Befreiung des Frauen-Konzentrationslagers Ravensbrück im April 1945* (Berlin, 1995).

Jones, J. J. 1981. *Bad Blood: the Tuskegee Syphilis Experiments* (London, 1981).

Jones, F. D. et al. (eds) 1995. *War Psychiatry* (Fall's Church, 1995).

Kahlke, W. and S. Reiter-Theil (eds) 1995. *Ethik in der Medizin* (Stuttgart, 1995).

Kater, M. H. 1985. 'Medizinsche Fakultäten und Medizinstudenten: Eine Skizze', in F. Kudlien, *Ärzte im Nationalsozialismus* (Cologne, 1985) 82–104.

Kater, M. H. 1989. *Doctors under Hitler* (Chapel Hill, London, 1989).

Katz, J. 1966. *Experimentation with Human Beings: Materials & Cases* (New Haven, 1966).

Katz, J. 1972. *Experimentation with Human Beings. The Authority of the Investigator, Subject, Profession, and State in the Human Experimentation Process* (New York, 1972).

Katz, J. 1984. *The Silent World of Doctors and Patient* (London, 1984)

Katz, J. 1992. 'The Consent Principle of the Nuremberg Code: its Significance Then and Now', in G. J. Annas and M. A. Grodin (eds), *The Nazi Doctors and the Nuremberg Code. Human Rights in Human Experimentation* (New York, Oxford, 1992) 227–39.

Katz, J. 1993. 'Ethics and Clinical Research Revisited – A Tribute to Henry K. Beecher', *Hastings Center Report*, 23 (1993) 31–9.

Katz, J. 1996. 'The Nuremberg Code and the Nuremberg Trial: a Reappraisal', *JAMA*, 276 (1996) 1662–6.

Katz, J. 1997. 'Human Sacrifice and Human Experimentation: Reflections at Nuremberg', *Yale Journal of International Law*, 22 (1997) 401–18.

Katz, J. 1998. 'Menschenopfer und Menschenversuche. Nachdenken in Nürnberg', in S. Kolb and H. Seithe (eds), *Medizin und Gewissen: 50 Jahre nach dem Nürnberger Ärzteprozeß* (Frankfurt A. M., 1998) 225–43.

Kaufmann, D. (ed.) 2000. *Geschichte der Kaiser-Wilhelm-Gesellschaft im Nationalsozialismus. Bestandsaufnahme und Perspektiven der Forschung*, 2 vols (Göttingen, 2000).

Kaufmann, D. and H.-W. Schmuhl (eds) 2001. *Rassenforschung im Nationalsozialismus: Konzepte und wissenschaftliche Praxis unter dem Dach der Kaiser-Wilhelm-Gesellschaft* (Göttingen, 2001).

Kemp, A. 1988. *The Secret Hunter* (London, 1988).

Kershaw, I. 1998. *Hitler. 1889–1936: Hubris* (London, 1998).

Kershaw, I. 2000. *Hitler. 1936–45: Nemesis* (London, 2000).

Kersting, F.-W., K. Teppe and B. Walter (eds), *Nach Hadamar. Zum Verhältnis von Psychiatrie und Gesellschaft im 20. Jahrhundert* (Paderborn, 1993).

Kirk, B. 1999. *Der Contergan-Fall. Eine unvermeidbare Arnzeimittelkatastrophe? Zur Geschichte des Arzneistoffs* (Stuttgart, 1999).

Klee, E. 1997. *Auschwitz. Die NS-Medizin und ihre Opfer* (Frankfurt a.M., 1997).

Klier, F. 1994. *Die Kaninchen von Ravensbrück: Medizinische Versuche an Frauen in der NS-Zeit* (Munich, 1994).

Kogon, E. 1946. *Der SS-Staat: Das System der deutschen Konzentrationslager* (Munich, 1946).

Kogon, E. 1995. *Ideologie und Praxis der Unmenschlichkeit. Erfahrungen mit dem Nationalsozialismus* (Berlin, 1995).

Kolb, S. and H. Seithe (eds) 1998. *Medizin und Gewissen: 50 Jahre nach dem Nürnberger Ärzteprozeß* (Frankfurt a.M., 1998).

Krause, T. L. and W. Winslade. 1997. 'Fünfzig Jahre Nürnberger Kodex', in U. Tröhler and S. Reiter-Theil (eds), *Ethik und Medizin: 1947–1997* (Göttingen, 1997) 189–220.

Kröner, H.-P. 1989. 'Die Emigration deutschsprachiger Mediziner im Nationalsozialismus', *Berichte zur Wissenschaftsgeschichte*, 12 (1989) 1–37.

Kühl, S. 1994. *The Nazi Connection. Eugenics, American Racism, and German National Socialism* (New York, 1994).

Kudlien, F. (ed.) 1985. *Ärzte im Nationalsozialismus* (Cologne, 1985).

Langer, E. 1964. 'Human Experimentation: Cancer Studies at Sloan-Kettering Stir Public Debate on Medical Ethics', *Science*, 143 (1964) 551–3.

Lederer, S. E. 1995. *Subjected to Science: Human Experimentation in America before the Second World War* (Baltimore, 1995).

Lee, G. 1995. 'Clinton Apologizes for US Radiation Tests, Praises Panel Report', *The Washington Post*, 4 October 1995.

Lemkin, R. 1944. *Axis Rule in Occupied Europe. Laws of Occupation, Analysis of Government, Proposals for Redress* (Washington, DC, 1944).

Levine, R. J. 1996. 'The Need to Revise the Declaration of Helsinki', *The New England Journal of Medicine*, 341 (1999) 531–4.

Lifton, R. J. 1985. *Mengele: What Made this Man* (New York, 1985).

Lifton, R. J. 1986. *The Nazi Doctors. Medical Killing and the Psychology of Genocide* (New York, 1986).

Loewy, E. H. 1995. *Ethische Fragen in der Medizin* (Wien, New York, 1995).

Loewy, E. 1998. 'Brauchen Wir Eine Neue Medizinische Ethik', in S. Kolb and H. Seithe (eds), *Medizin und Gewissen: 50 Jahre nach dem Nürnberger Ärzteprozeß* (Frankfurt a.M., 1998) 399–415.

Lyman, R. S. 1937. 'Psychiatrie in China', *Archives of Neurology and Psychiatry*, 37 (1937) 765–71.

Macklin, R. 1992. 'Universality of the Nuremberg Code', in G. J. Annas and M. A. Grodin (eds), *The Nazi Doctors and the Nuremberg Code. Human Rights in Human Experimentation* (New York, Oxford, 1992) 240–57.

Maehle, A.-H. 1998. 'Werte und Normen: Ethik in der Medizingeschichte', in N. Paul and T. Schlich (eds), *Medizingeschichte: Aufgaben, Probleme, Perspektiven* (Frankfurt/M., 1998) 335–54.

Maehle, A.-H. 1999. 'Professional Ethics and Discipline: the Prussian Medical Courts of Honour, 1899–1920', *Medizinhistorisches Journal*, 34 (1999) 309–38.

Maehle, A.-H. 2000. 'Assault and Battery, or Legitimate Treatment? German Legal Debates on the Status of Medical Interventions without Consent, c.1890–1914', *Gesnerus*, 57 (2000) 206–21.

Maio, G. 1996. 'Das Humanexperiment vor und nach Nürnberg: Überlegungen zum Menschenversuch und zum Einwilligungsbegriff in der französischen Diskussion des 19. und 20. Jahrhunderts', in C. Wiesemann and A. Frewer (eds), *Medizin und Ethik im Zeichen von Auschwitz. 50 Jahre Nürnberger Ärzteprozeß* (Erlangen, Jena, 1996) 45–78.

Maio, G. 2002. *Ethik der Forschung am Menschen: Zur Begründung der Moral in ihrer historischen Bedingtheit* (Stuttgart-Bad Cannstatt, 2002)

Mann, J. M. *et al.* (eds) 1999. *Health and Human Rights* (New York, London, 1999).

Mant, K. 1949. 'The Medical Services in the Concentration Camp of Ravensbrück', *The Medico Legal Journal*, 17 (1949) 99–118.

Marrus, M. M. 1999. 'The Nuremberg Doctors' Trial in Historical Context', *Bulletin for the History of Medicine*, 73 (1999) 106–23.

Martin, D. 1994a. 'Die Funktion des Krankenreviers in NS-Konzentrationslagern am Beispiel des Frauenkonzentrationslager Ravensbrück', MA dissertation (Hannover, 1994).

Martin, D. 1994b, 'Menschenversuche im Krankenrevier des KZ Ravensbrück', in C. Füllberg-Stolberg. *et al.* (eds), *Frauen in Konzentrationslagern: Bergen-Belsen, Ravensbrück* (Bremen, 1994) 99–112.

Martin, D. 1994c. 'Versuchkaninchen – Opfer medizinischer Experimente', in C. Füllberg-Stolberg. *et al.* (eds), *Frauen in Konzentrationslagern: Bergen-Belsen, Ravensbrück* (Bremen, 1994) 113–22.

Matheiu, B. 1997. 'Die ethischen Normen und das Recht: Legitimation durch die "Weisen" und demokratische Legitimation', in U. Tröhler and S. Reiter-Theil (eds), *Ethik und Medizin: 1947–1997* (Göttingen, 1997) 221–48.

Matheiu, B. 1998. 'From the Nuremberg Code to Bioethics: Follow-Ups to a Founder Text', *International Digest of Health Legislation*, 49 (1998) 549–54.

Mattei, J. F., J. P. Moatti and C. Rauch. 1997. 'Zur Ethik in der Politik der gerechten Verteilung knapper Ressourcen', in U. Tröhler and S. Reiter-Theil (eds), *Ethik und Medizin: 1947–1997* (Göttingen, 1997) 423–32.

Mausbach, H. 1998 'Thesen zum Nürnberger Ärzteprozeß. Charakter des Prozesses, Nachwirkungen und seine Bedeutung für die Zukunft', in S. Kolb and H. Seithe (eds), *Medizin und Gewissen: 50 Jahre nach dem Nürnberger Ärzteprozeß* (Frankfurt a.M., 1998) 260–8.

McFarland-Icke, B. R. 1999. *Nurses in Nazi Germany. Moral Choice in History* (Princeton, New Jersey, 1999).

Mellanby K. 1945. *Human Guinea Pigs* (London, 1945).

Mellanby, K. 1947. 'Medical Experiments on Human Beings in Concentration Camps in Nazi Germany', *British Medical Journal*, 4490 (1947) 148–50.

Mellanby, K. 1973. *Human Guinea Pigs*, 2nd edn (London, 1973).

Menkin, A. 1968. 'Historical Basis of Medical Crimes in Nazi Germany', *North Carolina Medical Journal*, 29 (1968) 189–201.

Mergenthal, F. 1997. 'Die Klinik für Haut- und Geschlechtskrankheiten – und ein merkwürdiger Entnazifizierungsfall', in M. G. Esch. *et al.* (eds), *Die Medizinische Akademie Düsseldorf im Nationalsozialismus* (Essen, 1997) 191–6.

Meyer, K. 2003, *Die Entnazifizierung von Frauen. Die Internierungslager der US-Zone Deustchlands 1945–1952* (Berlin, 2003).

Michalczyk, J. J. (ed.) 1994. *Medicine, Ethics, and the Third Reich: Historical and Contemporary Issues* (Kansas City, MO, 1994).

Michejda, K. 1947. 'Operacje Doswiadczalne w obozie koncentracyjnym Ravensbrück', *Biuletyn Glownej Komisji Badania Zbrodni Hitlerowskich w Polsce*, 2 (1947) 123–75.

Mielke, F. 1948. 'Der Nürnberger Prozeß gegen SS-Ärzte und Wissenschaftler und der deutsche Arzt', *Niedersächsisches Ärzteblatt*, 2 (1948) 29–31.

'Military Tribunals: Appointment of Judges at Nuremberg', *American Bar Association Journal*, 33 (1947) 896ff.

Mitscherlich, A. and F. Mielke (eds) 1947. *Das Diktat der Menschenverachtung. Der Nürnberger Ärzteprozeß und seine Quellen* (Heidelberg, 1947).

Mitscherlich, A. and F. Mielke (eds) 1949a. *Doctors of Infamy. The Story of the Nazi Medical Crimes* (New York, 1949).

Mitscherlich, A. and F. Mielke (eds) 1949b. *Wissenschaft ohne Menschlichkeit. Medizinische und eugenische Irrwege unter Diktatur, Bürokratie und Krieg. Mit einem Vorwort der Arbeitsgemeinschaft der westdeutschen Ärztekammern* (Heidelberg, 1949).

Mitscherlich, A. and F. Mielke (eds) 1960. *Medizin ohne Menschlichkeit* (Frankfurt a.M., 1960).

Moll, A. 1902. *Ärztliche Ethik. Die Pflichten des Arztes in allen Beziehungen seiner Thätigkeit* (Stuttgart, 1902).

Moreno, J. D. 1996. '"The Only Feasible Means": the Pentagon's Ambivalent Relationship with the Nuremberg Code', *Hastings Center Report*, 26 (1996) 11–19.

Moreno, J. D. 1997. 'Reassessing the Influence of the Nuremberg Code on American Medical Ethics', *Journal of Contemporary Health Law and Policy*, 13 (1997) 347–60.

Moreno, J. D. 1999. *Undue Risk. Secret State Experiments on Humans* (New York, 1999).

Müller-Hill, B. 1988. *Murderous Science. Elimination by Scientific Selection of Jews, Gypsies, and Others, Germany 1933–1945* (Oxford, 1988).

Myerson, A. 1935a. 'A Critique of Proposed "Ideal" Sterilisation Legislation', *Archives of Neurology and Psychiatry*, 33 (1935) 453–66.

Myerson, A. 1935b. 'Summary of the Report of the American Neurological Association Committee for the Investigation of Sterilisation', *American Journal of Psychiatry*, 92 (1935) 615–25.

Padfield, P. 1995. *Himmler: Reichsführer SS* (London, 1995).

Pappworth, M. H. 1967. *Human Guinea Pigs. Experimentation on Man* (London, 1967).

Paul, N. and T. Schlich (eds) 1998. *Medizingeschichte: Aufgaben, Probleme, Perspektiven* (Frankfurt/M., 1998).

Pearle, K. M. 1981. *Preventive Medicine. The Refugee Physician and the New York Medical Community 1933–1945* (Bremen, 1981).

Pearle, K. M. 1984. 'Ärzteemigration nach 1933 in die USA: Der Fall New York', *Medizinhistorisches Journal*, 19 (1984) 112–37.

Peiffer, J. 1991. 'Neuropathologie in the Third Reich. Memorial to those Victims of National-Socialist Atrocities in Germany who were Used by Medical Science', *Brain Pathology*, 1 (1991) 125–31.

Peiffer, J. (ed.) 1992. *Menschenverachtung und Opportunismus. Zur Medizin im Dritten Reich* (Tübingen, 1992).

Peiffer, J. 1997. *Hirnforschung im Zwielicht: Beispiele verführbarer Wissenschaft aus der Zeit des Nationalsozialismus. Julius Hallervorden – H. J. Scherer – Berthold Ostertag* (Husum, 1997).

Peiffer, J. 1999. 'Assessing Neuropathological Research Carried Out on Victims of the "Euthanasia" Programme', *Medizinhistorisches Journal*, 34 (1999) 339–56.

Perley, S. *et al.* 1992. 'The Nuremberg Code: an International Overview', in G. J. Annas and M. A. Grodin (eds), *The Nazi Doctors and the Nuremberg Code. Human Rights in Human Experimentation* (New York, Oxford, 1992) 149–73.

Pernick, M. 1991. 'The Patient's Role in Medical Decision Making: a Social History of Informed Consent in Medical Therapy', in President's Commission for the Study of Ethical Problems in Medicine and Biomedical and Behavioural Research (ed.), *Making Health Care Decisions. The Ethical and Legal Implications of Informed Consent in the Patient-Practioner Relationship* (Washington, DC, 1991) 1–35.

Peter, J. 1994. *Der Nürnberger Ärzteprozeß im Spiegel seiner Aufarbeitung anhand der drei Dokumentensammlungen von Alexander Mitscherlich und Fred Mielke* (Münster, Hamburg, 1994).

Peter, J. 2001. 'Unmittelbare Reaktionen auf den Prozeß', in K. Dörner and A. Ebbinghaus (eds), *Vernichten und Heilen: Der Nürnberger Ärzteprozeß und seine Folgen* (Berlin, 2001) 452–75.

Platen, A. von. 1947a. 'Ärzteprozeß Nürnberg', *Hippokrates*, 1 (1947) 29–31.

Platen, A. von. 1947b. 'Der Nürnburger Ärzteprozeß II', *Hippokrates*, 17 (1947) 199–202.

Platen-Hallermund, A. [1948] 1998. *Die Tötung Geisteskranker in Deutschland* (Frankfurt a.M., [1948] 1998), reprint.

Popper, S. E. and K. McCloskey 1995. 'Ethics in Human Experimentation: Historical Perspectives', *Military Medicine*, 160 (1995) 7–11.

Porter, P. 1959. 'Nazis' Guinea Pigs at Beth Israel. Tortured Women Repaired', *Boston Sunday Advertiser*, 11 January 1959.

Posner, G. L. and J. Ware. 2000. *Mengele: the Complete Story* (New York, 2000).

'Prison Malaria: Convicts Expose Themselves to Disease so Doctors can Study it', *Life*, 18 (1945), 43–6.

Proctor, R. N. 1988. *Racial Hygiene. Medicine under the Nazis* (Cambridge, Mass., 1988).

Proctor, R. N. 1992. 'Nazi Doctors, Racial Medicine, and Human Experimentation', in G. J. Annas and M. A. Grodin (eds), *The Nazi Doctors and the Nuremberg Code. Human Rights in Human Experimentation* (New York, Oxford, 1992) 17–31.

Bibliography 365

Proctor, R. N. 1999. *The Nazi War on Cancer* (Princeton, 1999).
Proctor, R. N. 2000. 'Expert Witnesses Take the Stand. Historians of Science Can Play an Important Role in US Public Health Litigation', *Nature*, 407 (2000) 15–16.
Pross, C. 1992. 'Nazi Doctors, German Medicine, and Historical Truth', in G. J. Annas and M. A. Grodin (eds), *The Nazi Doctors and the Nuremberg Code. Human Rights in Human Experimentation* (New York, Oxford, 1992) 32–52.
Ratcliff, J. D. 1946. 'Murder for Research', *Coronet* (1946) 10–14.
Records of the United States Nürnberg War Crimes Trials. 1946/47. United States of America v. Karl Brandt *et al.* (Case 1). November 21, 1946–August 20, 1947. National Archives Washington. Microfilm Publication M887 (47 reels).
Rees, J. R. 1943. 'Three Years of Military Psychiatry in the United Kingdom', *British Medical Journal* (1943) 1–6.
Rees, J. R. 1945. *The Shaping of Psychiatry by War* (New York, 1945).
Reich, W. T. 1998. 'Betrayal of Care: Medicine and the Long Shadow of Nuremberg', *Biomedical Ethics*, 3 (1998) 7–9.
Reiter-Theil, S. 1997. 'Antworten auf Wandel: Das Problem des Paradigmenwechsels in der Medizinethik. Überlegungen aus deutscher Sicht', in U. Tröhler and S. Reiter-Theil (eds), *Ethik und Medizin: 1947–1997* (Göttingen, 1997) 343–62.
'Report of Reference Committee on Miscellaneous Business', *Journal of the American Medical Association*, 133 (1946) 33.
Reverby, S. M. (ed.) 2000. *Tuskegee's Truths: Rethinking the Tuskegee Syphilis Study* (Chapel Hill, 2000).
Rißmann, B. 1947. 'Begriffsverwirrung', *Die Gegenwart*, 2 (1947) 12–14.
Roth, K. H., U. Schmidt and P. Weindling. 1999. 'Origins and Consequences of the Nuremberg Doctors' Trial: Documents and Materials,' in K. Dörner and A. Ebbinghaus (eds), *The Nuremberg Doctors' Trial 1946/47* (Munich, 1999), Fiche 285–320.
Rothman, D. J. 1991. *Strangers at the Bedside: a History of How Law and Bioethics Transformed Medical Decision Making* (New York, 1991).
Rothman, D. J. 1997. 'Der Nürnberger Kodex im Licht früherer Prinzipien und Praktiken im Bereich der Humanexperimente', in U. Tröhler and S. Reiter-Theil (eds), *Ethik und Medizin: 1947–1997* (Göttingen, 1997) 75–88.
Rubel-Schaefer, G. 1902/3. 'Versuch einer kritischen Darstellung neuerer Theorien über das Wesen der Affekte' (PhD, Vienna, 1902/3).
Rubel-Schaefer, G. 1905. *Zur Frage über den zeitlichen Verlauf des Gedächtnisbildes für verschiedene Sinnesreize* (Vienna, 1905).
Russell of Liverpool, L. 1954. *The Scourge of the Swastika: a Short History of Nazi War Crimes* (London, 1954).
Rüter, C. F. and D. W. Mild 1998. *Die Westdeutschen Strafverfahren wegen Nationalsozialistischer Tötungsverbrechen, 1945–1997* (Amsterdam, Munich, 1998).
Sass, H.-M. 1983. 'Reichsrundschreiben 1931: Pre-Nuremberg German Regulations Concerning New Therapy and Human Experimentation', *The Journal of Medicine and Philosophy*, 8 (1983) 99–111.
Schafft, G. E. and G. Zeidler 1996. *Die KZ-Mahn- und Gedenkstätten in Deutschland* (Berlin, 1996).
Schaltenbrand, G. 1931. 'Psychiatrie in Peking', *Zeitschrift für die gesamte Neurologie und Psychiatrie*, 137 (1931) 168ff.
Schaupp, W. 1993. *Der ethische Gehalt der Helsinki Deklaration. Eine historisch-systematische Untersuchung der Richtlinien des Weltärztebunds über biomedizinische Forschung am Menschen* (Frankfurt a.M., New York, 1993).
Schmidt, U. 1997. 'German Medical War Crimes, Medical Ethics and Post-War Justice: a Symposium held at the University of Oxford to Mark the 50th

Anniversary of the Nuremberg Medical Trial, 14 March 1997', *German History*, 15 (1997) 385–91.

Schmidt, U. 1998. 'Reform Psychiatry and Society between Imperial and Nazi Germany. Review of Anstaltsärzte zwischen Kaiserreich und Bundesrepublik (Kersting) and Psychiatrie und Gesellschaft in der Moderne (Walter)', *Social History of Medicine*, 11 (1998) 336–7.

Schmidt, U. 1999a. 'Reassessing the Beginning of the "Euthanasia" Programme', *German History*, 17 (1999) 541–8.

Schmidt, U. 1999b. 'The History of the Kaiser-Wilhelm-Society During National Socialism. Observations on a Three-Day Working Conference organised by the Max-Planck-Society in Berlin, 10–13 March 1999', *German History*, 17 (1999) 549–55.

Schmidt, U. 2000a. '"Der Blick auf den Körper": Sozialhygienische Filme, Sexualaufklärung und Propaganda in der Weimarer Republik', in M. Hagener (ed.), *Geschlecht in Fesseln. Sexualität zwischen Aufklärung und Ausbeutung im Weimarer Kino 1918–1933* (Munich, 2000) 23–46.

Schmidt, U. 2000b. 'Kriegsausbruch und "Euthanasie": Neue Forschungsergebnisse zum "Knauer Kind" im Jahre 1939', in A. Frewer and C. Eickhoff (eds), *Euthanasie und die Aktualität der historischen Diskussion – Zur Interaktion von Geschichte und Ethik in der Medizin* (Göttingen, 2000) 113–29.

Schmidt, U. 2000c. 'Sozialhygienische Filme und Propaganda in der Weimarer Republik', in D. Jasbinski (ed.), *Gesundheitskommunikation. Medieninhalte und Mediennutzung aus Sicht der Public Health-Forschung* (Wiesbaden, 2000) 53–82.

Schmidt, U. 2001a. 'Der Ärzteprozeß als moralische Instanz? – Der Nürnberger Kodex und das Problem "zeitloser Medizinethik", 1946/47', in A. Frewer and J. N. Neumann (eds), *Medizingeschichte und Medizinethik 1900–1950* (Göttingen, 2001) 334–73.

Schmidt, U. 2001b. 'Die Angeklagten Fritz Fischer, Hans W. Romberg und Karl Brandt aus der Sicht des medizinischen Sachverständigen Leo Alexander', in K. Dörner and A. Ebbinghaus (eds), *Vernichten und Heilen: Der Nürnberger Ärzteprozeß und seine Folgen* (Berlin, 2001) 374–404.

Schmidt, U. 2001c. 'Discussing Slave Labourers in Nazi Germany: Topography of Research or Politics of Memory?', *German History*, 19 (2001) 408–17.

Schmidt, U. (with A Frewer *et al.*). 2001d. 'Zwangsarbeit und Medizin im "Dritten Reich": Ein Desiderat historischer Forschung, *Deutsches Ärzteblatt*, (2001) A-2866-2870.

Schmidt, U. 2002a. *Medical Films, Ethics and Euthanasia in Nazi Germany* (Husum, 2002).

Schmidt, U. 2002b. 'Medicina e Nazismo', *Sistema Salute*, 5 (2002) 9–18.

Schmidt, U. 2003. 'Medicine and Nazism', in L. B. McCullough and B. Baker (eds), *A History of Medical Ethics* (Cambridge, in press).

Schubert-Lenhardt, V. 1996. 'Ärztliche Verantwortung heute – 50 Jahre nach dem Nürnberger Ärzteprozeß', *Ethik in der Medizin*, 8 (1996) 236–8.

Seidel, R. 2001. 'Die Sachverständigen Werner Leibbrand und Andrew C. Ivy', in K. Dörner and A. Ebbinghaus (eds), *Vernichten und Heilen: Der Nürnberger Ärzteprozeß und seine Folgen* (Berlin, 2001) 358–73.

Seidelmann, W. 1998. 'Mit Nürnberg Abgetan. Gewissen und Erinnerung in der Medizin', in S. Kolb and H. Seithe (eds), *Medizin und Gewissen: 50 Jahre nach dem Nürnberger Ärzteprozeß* (Frankfurt a.M., 1998) 269–79.

Seidler, E. 1998. 'Vom Nürnberger Ärztekodex zur Bioethikkonvention. Geschichte der Ethik der Menschenversuche', in S. Kolb and H. Seithe (eds), *Medizin und Gewissen: 50 Jahre nach dem Nürnberger Ärzteprozeß* (Frankfurt a.M., 1998) 307–12.

Sereny, G. 1995. *Albert Speer: His Battle with Truth* (London, 1995).

Sereny, G. 2000. *The German Trauma: Experiences and Reflections, 1938–2000* (London, 2000).

Shephard, B. 1999. 'Pitiless Psychology: the Role of Prevention in British Military Psychiatry in the Second World War', *History of Psychiatry*, 10 (1999) 491–524.

Shephard, B. 2000. *The War of Nerves* (London, 2000).

Sherman, A. J. 1997. *Mandate Days. British Lives in Palistine. 1918–1948* (London, 1997).

Shevell, M. 1992. 'Racial Hygiene, Active Euthanasia, and Julius Hallervorden', *Neurology*, 42 (1992) 2214–19.

Shevell, M. 1996. 'Neurology's Witness to History: the Combined Intelligence Operative Sub-Committee Reports of Leo Alexander', *Neurology*, 47 (1996) 1096–1103.

Shevell, M. 1998. 'Neurology's Witness to History (Part II): Leo Alexander's Contribution to the Nuremberg Code', *Neurology*, 50 (1998) 274–8.

Shuster, E. 1997. 'Fifty Years Later: the Significance of the Nuremberg Code', *The New England Journal of Medicine*, 337 (1997) 1436–40.

Shuster, E. 1998a. 'The Nuremberg Code: Hippocratic Ethics and Human Rights', *Lancet*, 351 (1998) 974–77.

Shuster, E. 1998b. 'The Significance of the Nuremberg Code: Letter to the Editor', *New England Journal of Medicine*, 338 (1998) 995–6.

Siemen, H.-L. 1993. 'Die Reformpsychiatrie der Weimarer Republik: Subjektive Ansprüche und die Macht des Faktischen', in F.-W. Kersting, K. Teppe, and B. Walter (eds), *Nach Hadamar. Zum Verhältnis von Psychiatrie und Gesellschaft im 20. Jahrhundert* (Paderborn, 1993) 98–108.

Sillevaerts, C. 1947. 'The Nurnberg Trial', *Bruxelles Medical*, 31 August 1947.

Steinbauer, G. 1949. *Die Euthanasie im Lichte des Nürnberger Ärzteprozesses* (Wien, 1949).

Stephens, T. D. 2001. *Dark Remedy: the Impact of Thalidomide and its Revival as a Vital Medicine* (Cambridge, Mass., 2001).

Stevens, T. 2000. *Bioethics in America. Origins and Cultural Politics* (Baltimore, London, 2000).

Stuttaford, T. 1997. 'Germ Warfare Trials Met With Stout Resistance', *The Times*, 3 February 1997.

Süskind, W. E. 1947. 'Hippokrates als Warner. Betrachtung zum Nürnberger Ärzteprozeß', *Süddeutsche Zeitung*, 5 April 1947.

Tashiro, E. 1991. *Die Waage der Venus. Venerologische Versuche am Menschen zwischen Fortschritt und Moral* (Husum, 1991).

Taylor, T. 1949a. *Final Report to the Secretary of the Army on the Nuremberg War Crimes Trials Under Control Council Law No. 10* (Washington, DC, 1949).

Taylor, T. 1949b. 'Nuremberg Trials – Synthesis and Projection', *Information Bulletin*, 162 (1949), 31 May 1949.

Taylor, T. 1976. 'Biomedical Ethics and the Shadow of Nazism', *Hastings Center Report*, Special Suplememt, 6 (1976) 4–7.

Taylor, T. 1992. *The Anatomy of the Nuremberg Trials: a Personal Memoir* (New York, 1992).

'The German Atrocities', *Life*, 18 (1945) 32–37.

Toellner, R. 1998. 'Der Blinde Spiegel. Über das Verhältnis der deutschen Ärzteschaft zum Nürnberger Ärzteprozeß in seiner epochalen Bedeutung', in S. Kolb and H. Seithe (eds), *Medizin und Gewissen: 50 Jahre nach dem Nürnberger Ärzteprozeß* (Frankfurt a.M., 1998) 288–304.

Tönnis, W. 1984. *Jahre der Entwicklung der Neurochirurgie in Deutschland: Erinnerungen* (Berlin, 1984).

Tröhler, U. and S. Reiter-Theil (eds) 1997. *Ethik und Medizin: 1947–1997. Was leistet die Kodifizierung von Ethik* (Göttingen, 1997).

Tusa, T. and J. Tusa. 1995. *The Nuremberg Trial* (London, 1995).

Uexküll, T. von. 1947. 'Krise der Humanität. Gedanken zum Nürnberger Ärzteprozeß', *Die Zeit*, 13 February 1947.

United Nations War Crimes Commission. 1948. *History of the United Nations War Crimes Commission and the Development of the Laws of War* (London, 1948).

United Nations War Crimes Commission. 1949. *German Medical War Crimes. A Summary of Information* (London, 1949).

United States Advisory Committee on Human Radiation Experiments. 1995. *Advisory Committee on Human Radiation Experiments Final Report* (Washington, DC, 1995).

Vanderpool, H. Y. (ed.) 1996. *The Ethics of Research Involving Human Subjects: Facing the 21st Century* (Frederick, Md, 1996).

Vollmann, J. and R. Winau. 1996. 'Informed Consent in Human Experimentation before the Nuremberg Code', *British Medical Journal*, 313 (1996) 1445–7.

Waltz, L. 2001. 'Gespräche mit Stanisława Bafia, Władysława Marczewska und Maria Plater über die medizinischen Versuche in Ravensbrück', in K. Dörner and A. Ebbinghaus (eds), *Vernichten und Heilen: Der Nürnberger Ärzteprozeß und seine Folgen* (Berlin, 2001) 241–72.

Weber, M. M. 1993. *Ernst Rüdin. Eine kritische Biographie* (Munich, 1993).

Weindling, P. J. 1985. 'Weimar Eugenics: the Kaiser Wilhelm Institute for Anthropology, Human Heredity and Eugenics in Social Context', *Annals of Science*, 42 (1985) 303–18.

Weindling, P. J. 1996a. 'Ärzte als Richter: Internationale Reaktionen auf die medizinischen Verbrechen während des Nürnberger Ärzteprozesses im Jahre 1946–47', in C. Wiesemann and A. Frewer (eds), *Medizin und Ethik im Zeichen von Auschwitz* (Erlangen, Jena, 1996) 31–44.

Weindling., P. J. 1996b. 'Human Guinea Pigs and Experimental Ethics: the BMJ's Foreign Correspondent at the Nuremberg Medical Trial', *British Medical Journal*, 313 (1996) 1467–70.

Weindling, P. J. 2000a. *Epidemics and Genocide in Eastern Europe, 1890–1945* (Oxford, 2000).

Weindling, P. J. 2000b. 'From International to Zonal Trials: the Origins of the Nuremberg Medical Trial', *Holocaust Genocide Studies*, 14 (2000) 367–89.

Weindling, P. J. 2000c. '"Tales from Nuremberg": the Kaiser Wilhelm Institute for Anthropology and Allied Medical War Crimes Policy', in D. Kaufmann (ed.), *Geschichte der Kaiser-Wilhelm-Gesellschaft im Nationalsozialismus. Bestandsaufnahme und Perspektiven der Forschung*, 2 vols (Göttingen, 2000) 635–52.

Weindling, P. J. 2001a. 'Die Internationale Wissenschaftskommission für medizinische Kriegsverbrechen', in K. Dörner and A. Ebbinghaus (eds), *Vernichten und Heilen: Der Nürnberger Ärzteprozeß und seine Folgen* (Berlin, 2001) 439–51.

Weindling, P. J. 2001b. 'Gerechtigkeit aus der Perspektive der Medizingeschichte: "Euthanasie" im Nürnberger Ärzteprozeß', in A. Frewer and J. N. Neumann (eds), *Medizingeschichte und Medizinethik 1900–1950* (Göttingen, 2001) 311–33.

Weindling, P. J. 2001c. 'The Origins of Informed Consent: the International Scientific Commission on Medical War Crimes, and the Nuremberg Code', *Bulletin of the History of Medicine*, 75 (2001) 37–71.

Weindling, P. J. 2001d. 'Zur Vorgeschichte des Nürnberger Ärzteprozesses', in K. Dörner and A. Ebbinghaus (eds), *Vernichten und Heilen: Der Nürnberger Ärzteprozeß und seine Folgen* (Berlin, 2001) 26–47.

Weizäcker, V. von. '"Euthanasia" und Menschenversuche', *Psyche*, 1 (1947/48) 68–102.

Wiesemann, C. and A. Frewer (eds) 1996. *Medizin und Ethik im Zeichen von Auschwitz. 50 Jahre Nürnberger Ärzteprozeß* (Erlangen, Jena, 1996).

Wiesing, U. 1997. 'Der "Nürnberger Kodex 1997". Ein Kommentar', *Ethik in der Medizin*, 43 (1997) 335–9.

Wille, S. 1949. 'Grundsätze des Nürnberger Ärzteprozesses', *Neue Juristische Wochenschrift*, 2 (1949) 377.

Winau, R. 1996. 'Medizin und Menschenversuch. Zur Geschichte des "Informed Consent"', in C. Wiesemann and A. Frewer (eds), *Medizin und Ethik im Zeichen von Auschwitz* (Erlangen, Jena, 1996) 13–29.

Winau, R. 2001. 'Der Menschenversuch in der Medizin', in K. Dörner and A. Ebbinghaus (eds), *Vernichten und Heilen: Der Nürnberger Ärzteprozeß und seine Folgen* (Berlin, 2001) 93–109.

'Wir brauchen ein zentrales Strafgericht', *Der Spiegel*, 27 (2001) 147–50.

Wolfe, R. 1998. 'Flaws in the Nuremberg Legacy: an Impediment to International War Crimes Tribunals' Prosecution of Crimes Against Humanity', *Holocaust and Genocide Studies*, 12 (1998) 434–53.

Wunder, M. 1998, 'Bioethik – Eine Philosophie ohne Menschlichkeit', in S. Kolb and H. Seithe (eds), *Medizin und Gewissen: 50 Jahre nach dem Nürnberger Ärzteprozeß* (Frankfurt a.M., 1998) 313–19.

Wunder, M. 2000. 'Der Nürnberger Kodex und seine Folgen', in K. Dörner and A. Ebbinghaus (eds), *Vernichten und Heilen: Der Nürnberger Ärzteprozeß und seine Folgen* (Berlin, 2001) 476–88.

Young, S. N. 1998. 'Risk in Research – From the Nuremberg Code to the Tri-Council Code: Implications for Clinical Trials of Psychotropic Drugs', *Journal of Psychiatry and Neuroscience*, 23 (1998) 149–55.

Zweig, S. 1982. *Die Welt von Gestern. Erinnerungen eines Europäers* (Frankfurt a.M., 1982).

Index

376 *Index*